GPU-Accelerated Computing with Python 3 and CUDA

From low-level kernels to real-world applications in scientific computing and machine learning

Niels Cautaerts | Hossein Ghorbanfekr

<packt>

GPU-Accelerated Computing with Python 3 and CUDA

Portfolio Director: Kunal Chaudhary
Relationship Lead: Srishti Seth
Project Manager: K. Loganathan
Content Engineer: Sujata Tripathi
Technical Editor: Irfa Ansari
Copy Editor: Safis Editing
Proofreader: Sujata Tripathi
Indexer: Pratik Shirodkar
Production Designer: Ajay Patule
Growth Lead: Vinishka Kalra

First published: March 2026

Production reference: 1270326

Published by Packt Publishing Ltd.
Grosvenor House
11 St Paul's Square
Birmingham
B3 1RB, UK.

ISBN 978-1-80324-542-3
www.packtpub.com

To my daughters, Julie and Hannah, who made it nearly impossible to focus on this book yet gave me the strength and motivation to push through.

– Niels

To my son, Suren, who is my hope for the future, and to my nieces, Mahsa and Mahak.

– Hossein

Contributors

About the authors

Dr. Niels Cautaerts is a research software developer and data scientist with a decade of experience pushing the limits of Python for scientific computing. His GPU programming journey began with speeding up the processing of massive electron microscopy datasets. Since then, he has contributed CUDA kernels to open source projects, built GPU-accelerated frameworks for real-time object detection in image streams, and optimized performance across a wide range of applications.

Niels is based in Belgium and holds a master's in materials science from KU Leuven and a Ph.D. in applied physics from the University of Antwerp. He shares his insights through educational content on YouTube and Medium, helping others write more performant Python.

I want to thank all the people who supported me in completing this project, especially my wife, Rani, my parents, and my mother-in-law. This project would never have been possible without sharing the burden with my co-author, Hossein. Thanks to the Packt team for keeping the project on course and to the technical reviewers for their suggestions.

Dr. Hossein Ghorbanfekr is a computational physicist with over a decade of experience in scientific programming, specializing in C/C++ and Python. During his Ph.D., he developed various code leveraging parallel computing and GPU acceleration for atomistic simulations. He has worked as a data scientist and later as a computational scientist, focusing on drug discovery. He is the developer of Pantea, an open source GPU-accelerated framework for developing machine learning interatomic potentials.

Hossein holds a master's in quantum computing from Sharif University of Technology in Iran and a Ph.D. in condensed matter physics from the University of Antwerp in Belgium.

I would like to thank my wife, Simin, for her unconditional support. I sincerely thank my co-author, Niels, for the opportunity and collaboration. My thanks also to the Packt team for their assistance and the technical reviewers for their constructive suggestions.

About the reviewers

Rahul Nayar is a software engineer at Meta Platforms, where he works on large-scale software systems and infrastructure that support modern computing platforms. He has extensive experience in distributed systems, high-performance computing, and machine learning infrastructure, with a strong focus on designing scalable and reliable engineering solutions.

Throughout his career, Rahul has worked on complex technical problems involving performance optimization, large-scale data processing, and systems programming. He brings deep expertise in languages such as C++, Python, and Java, and maintains a strong interest in modern systems development, emerging programming languages, and AI-driven engineering tools. His work focuses on bridging practical engineering challenges with evolving technologies used to build systems at scale.

Rahul is passionate about advancing engineering excellence and enjoys exploring new ideas in software architecture, developer productivity, and the future of intelligent software systems.

I would like to thank my family for their constant encouragement and support throughout this journey. I am especially grateful to my wife for her patience, understanding, and encouragement while I worked on this project. I would also like to thank my father, who authored two books himself and inspired my interest in writing and sharing knowledge. My sincere thanks also go to my mother, my brother, his wife, and their son for their continued support and belief in me.

Anand Raja is a software engineer and technical lead with over a decade of experience in high-performance computing and GPU programming. He specializes in the optimization of large-scale systems, with a deep technical focus on GPU kernel development, parallel programming algorithms, and the ML software stack. Anand has applied his expertise to a wide range of domains, including medical image analysis and image processing, computer vision, self-driving cars, and, most recently, large language models. As a leader, he manages specialized engineering teams dedicated to pushing the boundaries of what is possible in accelerated computing and AI infrastructure.

Raymond Tay is *Head of Engineering* in the aviation domain in Singapore, where he leads large-scale software engineering practices for mission-critical, safety regulated systems. With over two decades of experience in distributed systems, high-performance computing and cloud-native architectures, he specializes in building resilient and scalable platforms in highly regulated environments. He is the author of *Developing an Akka Edge* and *OpenCL Parallel Programming Development Cookbook*, and is an advocate for modern engineering practices, DevSecOps, AIOps and formal approaches to system reliability.

Table of Contents

Chapter 4: Profiling and Debugging CUDA Code 79

Preface

General-purpose GPU computing (GPGPU) has revolutionized scientific and engineering fields, driving advancements in physics, chemistry, machine learning, and beyond. CUDA, the leading GPGPU framework, underpins these breakthroughs—including the AI revolution and the rise of large language models.

Until recently, GPU programming remained in the domain of professional software engineers with deep expertise in C/C++ and GPU hardware. However, NVIDIA's push to integrate low-level CUDA primitives directly into Python, culminating in the 2025 CUDA Python project, is challenging this paradigm. Combined with the RAPIDS ecosystem, which offers GPU-accelerated alternatives to familiar Python libraries, GPU programming is now accessible to data scientists, researchers, and Python developers without requiring them to leave the comfort of Python.

This book is about bridging the gap between low-level GPU programming and high-level Python tools. The first half focuses on CUDA fundamentals using Numba-CUDA, emphasizing performance and profiling. The second half builds on these foundations, exploring high-level libraries in the RAPIDS and JAX ecosystems. The final chapters bring everything together through practical applications across various disciplines, demonstrating both the power and limitations of GPGPU.

Our goal is to make GPU computing accessible to every Python programmer, beyond just using a high-level machine learning framework, empowering you to leverage its potential in your own work.

Who this book is for

This book is for Python developers, data scientists, engineers, and researchers who want to accelerate numerical computations using GPUs, without needing to master C/C++. If you're a domain expert who relies on Python for scientific computing or data-intensive tasks and need finer control than high-level frameworks provide, this book will help you unlock GPU performance and understand the fundamentals of hardware acceleration.

You'll get the most out of this book if the following apply:

- You have experience with Python programming and the scientific Python ecosystem (NumPy, pandas, SciPy, and Matplotlib) and are comfortable running command-line applications

- You have a background in mathematics, physics, or computer science, including familiarity with linear algebra and calculus
- You understand basic computing concepts such as memory, pointers, and arrays

This book bridges the gap between high-level tools and low-level control, empowering you to write efficient, high-performance GPU code, all while staying in Python.

What this book covers

Chapter 1, Why GPU Programming with CUDA in Python 3?, introduces GPGPU and how GPUs achieve impressive computing speed through massive parallelization. The rest of the chapter explores the benefits and limits of parallelization using theory (e.g., Amdahl's law) and practice (profiling).

Chapter 2, Setting Up a GPU Programming Environment Locally and in the Cloud, guides you through the process of setting up a development environment with Pixi for working with CUDA in Python on your local machine (Windows, WSL, or Linux) or in the cloud (Google Colab, Lambda Labs, or an EC2 virtual machine on AWS).

Chapter 3, Writing and Executing CUDA Kernels with Numba-CUDA, covers CUDA kernel development using the CUDA backend to Numba, a Python JIT compiler. All the basic elements of the CUDA programming model are covered, including kernels, kernel launch configurations (grids, blocks, and threads), device functions, host-device data transfers, thread synchronization, and atomics. In addition, Numba-CUDA-specific features, such as the vectorize decorator, are also covered.

Chapter 4, Profiling and Debugging CUDA Code, introduces several profilers to investigate the performance of CUDA code in Python, including Python's built-in timing functionality, Scalene, Nsight Systems for application- and system-level profiling, and Nsight Compute for detailed kernel-level profiling. In addition, debugging techniques such as printing from a CUDA kernel and emulating GPU execution on the CPU are covered.

Chapter 5, Optimizing the Performance of CUDA Code, explores GPU hardware and the CUDA execution model, laying the groundwork for identifying common bottlenecks in CUDA applications. Core principles for performance optimization, including maximizing occupancy, hiding latency through parallelism, and designing efficient memory access patterns, are covered. Kernel profiling is used to demonstrate their impact.

Chapter 6, Enabling Concurrency Using CUDA Streams, shows how CUDA streams can be used with Numba-CUDA to perform data transfers and computation concurrently, thereby improving the performance of some applications. Several pitfalls related to implicit synchronization are demonstrated. Finally, cross-stream synchronization via CUDA events is also demonstrated.

Chapter 7, Scaling to Multiple GPUs, introduces multi-GPU computing and explains the key use cases. First, the principle is demonstrated at a low level by explicitly managing multiple devices with Numba-CUDA. Then, practical multi-GPU workflows in Python are illustrated using Dask-CUDA and JAX.

Chapter 8, Bringing NumPy and SciPy to the GPU with CuPy, shows how to execute high-level NumPy-like and SciPy-like operations on the GPU, using the CuPy library. The API of CuPy is covered, as well as how CuPy interoperates with other libraries, such as Numba-CUDA. Performance tips are covered, as well as some tricks to write GPU-agnostic code.

Chapter 9, Bringing pandas and scikit-learn to the GPU with RAPIDS, introduces the cuDF and cuML libraries from the RAPIDS ecosystem to perform data science on the GPU using familiar pandas and scikit-learn workflows. The chapter covers the essentials of the cuDF and cuML API and works out an example data science regression use case.

Chapter 10, Solving Optimization Problems on the GPU with JAX, introduces JAX as a powerful framework for optimization, highlighting its key features: JIT compilation, automatic differentiation, and vectorization. JAX is demonstrated by solving a linear regression problem, building a neural network from scratch, and modeling an electrical circuit using a physics-informed neural network.

Chapter 11, Solving the Heat Equation on the GPU, is an application-focused chapter that tackles the Laplace heat equation, a fundamental second-order partial differential equation, using the finite differences method. The chapter covers discretization and boundary conditions and progresses from a CPU implementation to a GPU-accelerated version with Numba-CUDA. The chapter concludes with profiling the GPU kernel to pinpoint performance bottlenecks.

Chapter 12, Image Processing and Computer Vision on the GPU, explores the fundamentals of image processing on the GPU, using both Numba-CUDA kernels and high-level libraries such as cuCIM (RAPIDS). A spatial convolution filter is implemented for blurring and edge detection and then profiled. Then, a real-world object detection task is tackled, using several techniques for segmenting and classifying objects in an image. Three classification approaches are compared: shape-based description, template matching, and a convolutional neural network built with JAX.

Chapter 13, Simulating Atomic Interactions on the GPU, introduces the principles of molecular dynamics (MD) simulations and demonstrates how to implement and run them on the GPU. The theory of interatomic potentials and time integration is covered, culminating in a simulation of a monoatomic gas. The chapter concludes with profiling the code to identify bottlenecks and optimization opportunities.

Chapter 14, Implementing Your Own Transformer-Based Language Model, is the final application chapter that walks through the process of creating a language model from scratch using JAX, Flax, and Optax. The transformer architecture and the attention mechanism are explained and implemented, and the model is trained on the IMDb dataset. In the process, the text preprocessing steps, such as tokenization, are also explained.

Chapter 15, Expanding and Deepening Your GPU Programming Knowledge, rounds off the book by exploring and providing references for several advanced low-level topics (such as interfacing CUDA-C with Numba-CUDA), specialized applications (such as graph analytics), other heterogeneous computing paradigms (such as OpenCL), and graphics APIs (such as Vulkan).

To get the most out of this book

You will need an NVIDIA GPU with compute capability 7.5 or later, a recent version of Python, and the CUDA Toolkit, as well as several Python packages. It is recommended to create the development environment using the Pixi package manager, using the `pyproject.toml` and `pixi.lock` files, which can be found in the associated GitHub repository (see the next section). If you don't have access to a CUDA-enabled GPU on your local system, *Chapter 2* explains how to rent one in the cloud and set up the environment there.

Software/hardware covered in the book	**Operating system requirements**
Python 3.12	Windows or Linux if developing locally. Any OS if developing in the cloud.
CUDA Python (Numba-CUDA)	Internet connectivity
RAPIDS (cuDF, cuML, cuCIM)	
JAX, Flax, Optax	
Nsight Systems and Nsight Compute	

Installation instructions are detailed in *Chapter 2* of the book. If any other dependency is required, this is detailed at the start of the chapter.

If you are using the digital version of this book, we advise you to type the code yourself or access the code from the book's GitHub repository (a link is available in the next section). Doing so will help you avoid any potential errors related to the copying and pasting of code.

Download the example code files

The code bundle for the book is hosted on GitHub at `https://github.com/PacktPublishing/GPU-Accelerated-Computing-with-Python-3-and-CUDA`. We also have other code bundles from our rich catalog of books and videos available at `https://github.com/PacktPublishing`. Check them out!

Download the color images

We also provide a PDF file that has color images of the screenshots/diagrams used in this book. You can download it here: `https://packt.link/gbp/9781803245423`.

Conventions used

There are a number of text conventions used throughout this book.

`CodeInText`: Indicates code words in text, database table names, folder names, filenames, file extensions, pathnames, dummy URLs, user input, and Twitter handles. For example: "We can time all these different parts using `time.perf_counter` to estimate how much our code would benefit from parallelization"

A block of code is set as follows:

```
import time
start = time.perf_counter()
# code we want to time here
end = time.perf_counter()
print(end - start)
```

Any command-line input or output is written as follows:

```
python -m cProfile -s cumtime script.py
```

Bold: Indicates a new term, an important word, or words that you see on the screen. For instance, words in menus or dialog boxes appear in the text like this. For example: "However, many problems are **memory-bound** (i.e., the bottleneck is the speed at which cores can get the data they need)"

> **Note**
>
> Warnings or important notes appear like this.

> **Tip**
>
> Tips and tricks appear like this.

Get in touch

Feedback from our readers is always welcome.

General feedback: If you have questions about any aspect of this book or have any general feedback, please email us at `customercare@packt.com` and mention the book's title in the subject of your message.

Errata: Although we have taken every care to ensure the accuracy of our content, mistakes do happen. If you have found a mistake in this book, we would be grateful if you reported this to us. Please visit `http://www.packt.com/submit-errata`, click **Submit Errata**, and fill in the form.

Piracy: If you come across any illegal copies of our works in any form on the internet, we would be grateful if you would provide us with the location address or website name. Please contact us at `copyright@packt.com` with a link to the material.

If you are interested in becoming an author: If there is a topic that you have expertise in and you are interested in either writing or contributing to a book, please visit `http://authors.packt.com/`.

Free benefits with your book

This book comes with free benefits to support your learning. Activate them now for instant access (see the "*How to Unlock*" section for instructions).

Here's a quick overview of what you can instantly unlock with your purchase:

How to Unlock

Scan the QR code (or go to `packtpub.com/unlock`). Search for this book by name, confirm the edition, and then follow the steps on the page.

UNLOCK NOW

Note: Keep your invoice handy. Purchases made directly from Packt don't require one

Share your thoughts

Once you've read *GPU-Accelerated Computing with Python 3 and CUDA*, we'd love to hear your thoughts! Scan the QR code below to go straight to the Amazon review page for this book and share your feedback.

https://packt.link/r/1803245425

Your review is important to us and the tech community and will help us make sure we're delivering excellent quality content.

Part 1

Fundamentals of GPU programming with CUDA in Python 3

This part introduces the core principles of GPU acceleration and how parallelization drives performance, as well as exploring its practical limits through theory and profiling. We will guide you through setting up a CUDA development environment locally or in the cloud, then dive into CUDA kernel development using Numba-CUDA. Finally, we will cover how to profile and debug CUDA code. By the end, you'll have the foundational knowledge to write, execute, profile, and debug CUDA code in Python, which you can use to solve practical problems.

This part of the book includes the following chapters:

- *Chapter 1, Why GPU Programming with CUDA in Python 3?*
- *Chapter 2, Setting Up a GPU Programming Environment Locally and in the Cloud*
- *Chapter 3, Writing and Executing CUDA Kernels with Numba-CUDA*
- *Chapter 4, Profiling and Debugging CUDA Code*

1

Why GPU Programming with CUDA in Python 3?

What do blockchain and **artificial intelligence** (**AI**) have in common?

At a surface level, both technologies have, in recent years, garnered a lot of media attention and investment and formed the basis for many start-ups. But beneath these applications lies a common technological foundation: **general-purpose computing on graphics processing units** (**GPGPUs**) to accelerate massively parallel computations. While the long-term impact of AI and blockchain is yet to be felt, GPGPU has already demonstrated its immense value across a multitude of fields and application areas, despite receiving significantly less public attention.

GPU programming is traditionally taught through low-level programming languages such as C or C++. This book takes a different approach and teaches GPGPU through various libraries available in **Python 3**. This makes the subject more accessible to our target audience: data scientists and researchers who primarily use Python and seek to accelerate computationally intensive code. This book focuses entirely on the **CUDA** platform, which is the most popular GPU programming framework that runs exclusively on NVIDIA hardware.

In this chapter, we will learn what GPGPU and CUDA are and how to recognize scenarios that benefit from GPGPU. We will also learn how to estimate and measure the benefits of accelerating our computations using GPGPU. We will also review the limitations of GPGPU, because unfortunately, it is not a magic bullet that can speed up any computation:

- Understand the benefits, application areas, and limitations of GPU computing
- Calculate the theoretical compute capacity of devices
- Identify which types of problems benefit from massive parallelization, and estimate performance gains with Amdahl's law

- Recognize additional factors, such as data transfers, that influence computing performance
- Use `cProfile` and Scalene to discover bottlenecks in Python code

> Note
>
> **Your purchase includes a free PDF copy + exclusive extras**
>
> Your purchase includes a DRM-free PDF copy of this book, 7-day trial to the Packt+ library (no credit card required), and additional exclusive extras. See the *Free benefits with your book* section in the *Preface* to unlock them instantly and maximize your learning.

Technical requirements

To run the code in this chapter, you will need an installation of Python 3 with the `numpy`, `matplotlib`, `numba`, and `scalene` packages installed. The recommendation is to create a `pixi` environment based on the `pixi.lock` and `pyproject.toml` files in the Github repository associated with this book: `https://github.com/PacktPublishing/GPU-Accelerated-Computing-with-Python-3-and-CUDA`.

Installation instructions can be found in the `README.md` file.

If you've worked with Python for a while, you may not yet be familiar with the Pixi package manager. The reasons we chose Pixi for this book are explained in *Chapter 2*.

What is GPGPU?

A **graphics processing unit** (**GPU**) is a specialized processor originally designed to render images on a computer screen. This requires calculating the color of millions of pixels on the screen and updating it multiple times a second. Calculating the value of each pixel is independent and can therefore be computed in parallel. GPUs were designed to perform millions of these computations in parallel to enable fast rendering of images for applications such as computer games.

A few decades ago, researchers realized they could employ the massive parallelization power of GPUs to dramatically speed up calculations unrelated to graphics. However, writing non-rendering GPU programs used to be extremely difficult and out of reach for most programmers. That was until CUDA was released.

What is CUDA?

CUDA is a platform first released in 2007 by the company **NVIDIA** for making GPGPU more accessible. NVIDIA is the market leader in designing chips for GPUs. CUDA includes a high-level **API**, a programming model, and several libraries for running non-rendering algorithms on NVIDIA GPUs. CUDA unleashed the power of GPGPU in numerous domains by enabling programmers to easily write massively parallel algorithms.

CUDA is the main enabler of GPGPU and, by extension, the AI boom. It is what makes NVIDIA hardware the de facto standard for GPGPU. This unique market position is reflected in NVIDIA's remarkable stock price performance over the past few years:

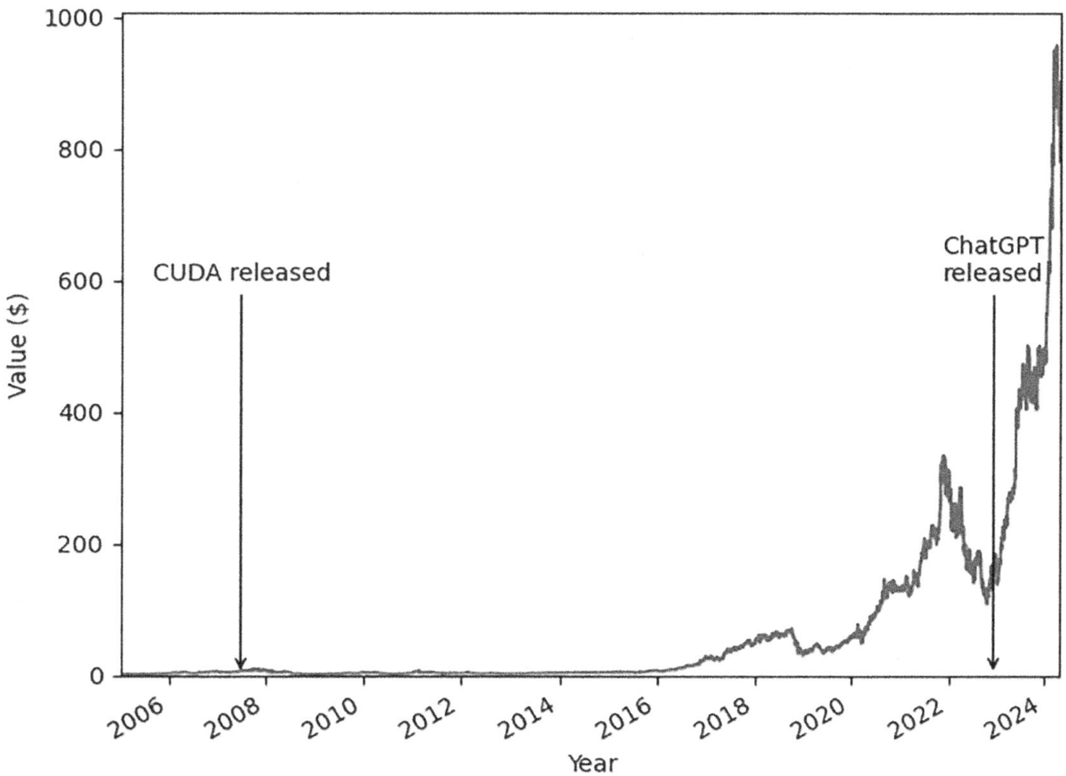

Figure 1.1 – NVIDIA stock price evolution over time (source data: Kaggle)

Originally, CUDA was designed to be used primarily through CUDA C with NVIDIA's **NVCC compiler**. As a result, CUDA programming has traditionally been taught using C or C++. Python libraries seeking to leverage GPU acceleration often had to wrap CUDA C code, which adds complexity.

In recent years, NVIDIA has invested significantly in making CUDA more accessible directly from Python, broadening its appeal to a wider audience of programmers. These efforts are centralized in the **CUDA Python** project (see `https://nvidia.github.io/cuda-python/latest`), a collection of tools and libraries that enable Python developers to write and interact with CUDA code more seamlessly.

In the first half of this book, we will focus on **numba.cuda**, a key component of the CUDA Python ecosystem. Numba is a **just-in-time (JIT)** compiler for Python, and `numba.cuda` is an extension that allows us to write CUDA-like code using Python syntax. This approach eliminates the need to mix multiple programming languages, enabling us to write all our code in familiar Python. Still, `numba.cuda` allows us to write low-level code, which will help you understand what goes on *under the hood*.

In the second half of the book, we will introduce high-level libraries that abstract these primitives and simplify common functionality such as array programming, data manipulation, and machine learning. In the final chapters, we will integrate these concepts and explore real-world applications, including image processing and atomistic simulations. CUDA is the foundation for nearly all the tools discussed throughout this book.

Why GPGPU is attractive

Like a CPU, a GPU contains many **cores**: physical processing units capable of performing arithmetic operations at extremely high speeds. Think of each core as a tiny calculator, executing simple operations rapidly. However, the key difference lies in scale and design: while a modern CPU typically features a few complex cores optimized for fast, sequential execution, a GPU may contain thousands of simpler cores specifically designed for massively parallel execution. When a problem can be divided into many smaller, independent tasks, and those tasks can be distributed across all these GPU cores, dramatic speedups can be achieved compared to traditional CPU execution.

To quantify this difference, we can calculate the theoretical maximum compute speed of a device in **floating-point operations per second (FLOPS)** using the following equation:

$$\text{FLOPS} = (\#\ \text{cores}) \times (\text{clock frequency}) \times (\#\ \text{ops per clock cycle})$$

The **clock frequency** is the internal metronome of the device that indicates how fast it can perform computational work, a bit like a heartbeat. It is expressed in cycles per second, or Hz. The number of clock cycles required for a single operation depends on the type of operation we want to perform (e.g., 32-bit versus 64-bit floating-point numbers) and the architecture of the device; for some operations on some devices, it is possible to perform multiple in a single cycle.

Let's use this equation to compare the theoretical compute capacity for 32-bit floating-point numbers of an Intel Core i9 processor CPU, which has 24 cores, to that of an NVIDIA GeForce RTX

4080 GPU with 9,728 cores; both are consumer-grade hardware. The CPU has a clock frequency of 3.5 GHz, and with the AVX instruction set, each core can perform 16 floating-point operations per clock cycle. By plugging these values into the equation, we can estimate that the CPU has a theoretical compute capacity of a little over 1 **TerraFlop** (**TFLOP**). The GPU has a slightly lower clock frequency of 2,210 MHz, and the cores can only perform 2 operations per cycle. Still, because the GPU has so many more cores than the CPU, the theoretical compute capacity is a whopping 43 TFLOPS!

Despite the GPU's reputation as being an expensive and power-hungry device, it is much more economical and energy efficient than the CPU when measured per TFLOP. At a retail price of around 1,100 USD and a power draw of up to 300 W, the RTX 4080 GPU costs 26 USD and consumes 7 W per TFLOP. The Intel processor retails around 500 USD and draws up to 125 W; the GPU is therefore roughly 20 times cheaper and energy efficient when measured per TFLOP!

When is GPGPU useful?

The calculation of theoretical compute capacity illustrates that the biggest factor in GPU compute power is the massive number of cores. CPUs generally outperform GPUs in terms of clock frequency and number of operations per clock cycle. This means that if we only use a single GPU core, the calculation will be slower than on the CPU. Only code that can make simultaneous use of a large number of cores will benefit from GPGPU.

GPU cores are not interchangeable with CPU cores. Whereas CPU cores operate more or less independently from each other, GPU cores are grouped into larger units called **streaming multiprocessors** (**SMs**). Cores in the same SM do not operate independently and execute instructions in a coordinated manner; we will explore the details in *Chapter 5*. The consequence is that a GPU is best suited for one specific type of parallelism: data parallelism.

Work can be parallelized in two fundamental ways: **task parallelism** and **data parallelism**. Task parallelism involves executing distinct and independent tasks concurrently across different workers (e.g., CPU cores). Data parallelism, on the other hand, divides a single task into identical operations executed simultaneously across multiple data elements, such as applying the same operation to every element in an array.

GPUs are optimized for data parallelism because their architecture allows thousands of **threads** (sequences of instructions) to execute the same instruction in lockstep, maximizing throughput for uniform workloads such as matrix operations or image processing. We will see in *Chapter 3* that the data parallelism model is almost baked into the CUDA programming model.

GPUs struggle with task parallelism and divergent execution paths. When threads within a **warp** (a group of 32 GPU threads) follow different control flows (such as taking different branches in an `if-else` statement), performance degrades significantly due to a phenomenon called **warp divergence**. We will explain warps and warp divergence in more detail in *Chapter 5*.

Note

Task parallelism on the GPU

There are strategies for employing task parallelism on the GPU using techniques such as **warp specialization**: assigning different tasks to different warps. However, this can result in very complex code and is reserved for advanced use cases.

Application areas of GPGPU

In the previous section, we mentioned that the GPU excels at accelerating computations by leveraging data parallelism. It turns out that many problems from diverse fields benefit from this approach. In recent years, deep learning, AI, and blockchain have received significant attention, but other application areas include the following:

- Scientific computation and simulations in fields such as quantum mechanics, fluid dynamics, and astrophysics
- Bioinformatics, analysis of genetic data, and predictions of protein structures (e.g., **AlphaFold**)
- Signal processing: image, video, and audio
- Computer vision and object detection
- Medical imaging and CT reconstruction
- Computational finance
- Operations research

We aim to illuminate some of these application areas through example cases in this book.

Estimating the benefits of parallelization

While writing code on the GPU is certainly easier than it once was, writing CUDA code is still not easy. Converting a straightforward serial implementation of an algorithm into a massively parallel version that runs on the GPU takes development time. Therefore, it is important to be able to estimate up front whether the speedups we can gain at runtime are worth the effort.

A very naive approach to calculate speedup would be to divide the theoretical compute capacity of the GPU by the compute capacity of a single CPU core. In our example from the previous section, we should expect a speedup of *43 TFLOPS / 0.056 TFLOPS ≈ 770×* for 32-bit floating-point operations when translating an algorithm from a serial implementation that runs on a single core of the Intel Core i9 CPU to a parallelized implementation that runs on the RTX 4080 GPU. Impressive! Unfortunately, this is very unrealistic.

Not all work is parallelizable; there will always be some serial operations in any code. The amount of code that cannot be parallelized has a massive impact on the maximum speedup. This can be illustrated with Amdahl's law, which we will now discuss.

Using Amdahl's law for speedup estimation

Suppose we have some code that requires a time, t, to run if we do not use any parallelization. Let's assume our code can be split into two portions: a parallelizable part and a non-parallelizable part. The fraction of code that is parallelizable we will denote as p, which means that $1-p$ is the fraction of non-parallelizable code. Therefore, in the serial implementation, the time taken by the parallelizable part is pt and $(1-p)t$ for the non-parallelizable part.

Now, suppose we add compute resources that speed up the parallelizable part of the code by a factor, s. The time to run the non-parallelizable code is not affected. This means that the total runtime with parallelization t_s becomes the following:

$$t_s = (1-p)t + \frac{pt}{s}$$

The speedup we gain from adding compute resources is as follows:

$$\frac{t}{t_s} = \frac{t}{(1-p)t + \frac{p}{s}t} = \frac{1}{1-p+\frac{p}{s}}$$

This equation is known as **Amdahl's law**. It can give us a much more sobering estimate of the speedups we can expect. *Figure 1.2* shows a plot of expected speedup, t/t_s, versus the speedup factor of the parallel part, s. Note that the x axis has a logarithmic scale. The different lines represent different values of p.

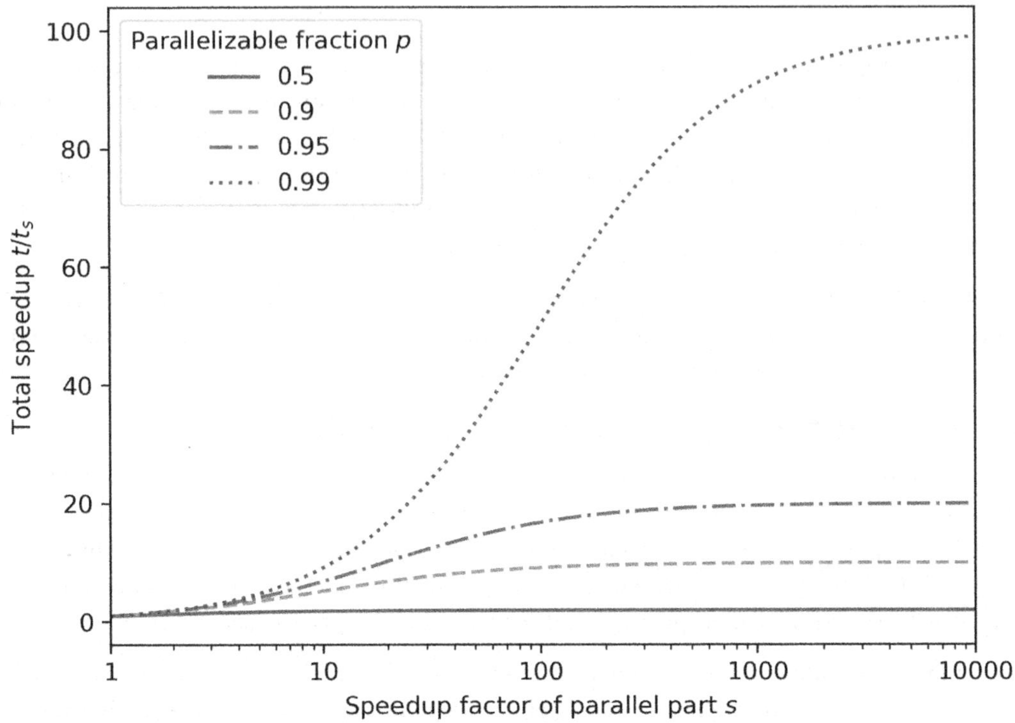

Figure 1.2 – Amdahl's law showing the total speedup versus the speedup of the parallel part for different parallelizable fractions

All curves, no matter what p is, plateau out, which means that adding more workers to speed up the parallel part of the code has diminishing returns. The reason we always reach a plateau is that as s becomes large, the fraction p/s in the denominator becomes small. In the limit as s goes to infinity, the maximum speedup we can reach is $1/(1-p)$. When only 50% of the code is parallelizable ($p=0.5$), the maximum speedup we can ever reach by adding an infinite number of workers is *2*. Even when 99% of our code is parallelizable ($p=0.99$), we eventually reach a plateau near *100*.

If we bring this back to our GPU/CPU example, the most optimistic estimate for s is *770*. We can either draw a vertical line on the plot at *770* or plug $s=770$ into the equation to estimate more realistic speedups if we know p. The takeaway is that in many cases, the most important factor in determining our speedup is the fraction of code that cannot be parallelized, as it sets our speedup ceiling. Depending on this ceiling, we could make a determination on whether implementing a GPU version of the code is worthwhile at all.

How can we estimate *p*? First, we need to have a good understanding of our algorithms so that we know which parts can be parallelized. Second, we need to know the time taken by each part of our algorithm. We can figure this out using code profiling.

Profiling code for generating a Julia set fractal

Let's work through an example. We will calculate an image of a Julia set fractal. Julia sets are sets of complex numbers defined by a recursive relation. When plotted as an image, they take the shape of a beautiful fractal.

To define the Julia set, first, we define the infinite recursive sequence $Z_{n+1} = Z_{n^2} + c$ for complex numbers z_n, z_{n+1}, and c and natural number n. Julia sets are defined as the set of all complex numbers that start the sequence z_0 for which the modulus $|z_n|$ does not diverge to infinity as n goes to infinity. In practice, when any term $|z_n| \geq R$ with R a cut-off radius, we know that the modulus diverges. c is a constant we choose, and it defines how the Julia set looks. We can generate beautiful fractal images by coloring all z in the complex plane based on the number of iterations until the sequence diverges.

Note

For the not-so-mathematically inclined reader

Don't worry if the mathematical details of the Julia set are too complicated; it doesn't really matter. Just think of the Julia set as a map where each point (pixel) is colored based on how quickly a simple mathematical rule causes it to *'escape'* to infinity. Points that escape slowly form the intricate, beautiful patterns of a fractal. We use the Julia set example because it can be easily parallelized and produces nice images.

A Python function that generates an image of a Julia set can be implemented rather naively as follows:

```
import numpy as np
from numpy.typing import NDArray

def calculate_julia(
    z_0: NDArray[np.complex64],
    c: complex,
    max_iter: int,
) -> NDArray[np.int32]:
    julia_set = np.zeros(z_0.shape, dtype=np.int32)
    R = 0.5 + 0.5 * np.sqrt(1 + 4 * abs(c))
```

```
    for i in range(z_0.shape[0]):
        for j in range(z_0.shape[1]):
            z = z_0[i, j]
            for iteration in range(1, max_iter + 1):
                if abs(z) > R:
                    julia_set[i, j] = iteration
                    break
                z = z ** 2 + c
    return julia_set
```

The arguments we supply to the function are the 2D input array of complex numbers, `z_0`, the complex constant, `c`, and the maximum number of times we will repeat the iteration to check whether the number is part of the set.

In the function, first, we allocate a zeroed `julia_set` output image, the size of which is determined by our input array. Then, the cut-off radius, `R`, is calculated from `c` according to a known formula.

In a double loop, we iterate over all elements of `z_0`. In the inner loop, `z` is repeatedly updated using the aforementioned recursive expression, a maximum of `max_iter` times. When `|z| > R`, we know the sequence diverges and `z_0` is not part of the Julia set; thus, we set the corresponding element in the output array to the number of iterations until divergence and break out of the loop. If we do not break out of the loop, then the value of that coordinate in `julia_set` remains `0`, and we assume the number is part of the Julia set after a maximum number of iterations.

Before we can run the calculation, we must first create our 2D `z_0` array as follows:

```
a = np.linspace(-1.7, 1.7, 1200, dtype=np.float32)
b = np.linspace(-1.7, 1.7, 1200, dtype=np.float32)
A, B = np.meshgrid(a, b)
z_0 = A + 1j * B
```

We can then calculate the Julia set for a chosen `c=-0.8+0.156j`, as follows:

```
julia_set = calculate_julia(
    z_0,
    c=-0.8+0.156j,
    max_iter=3000,
)
```

We can visualize julia_set by mapping each value in the array to a color, for example, using the imshow function in matplotlib:

```
import matplotlib.pyplot as plt
fig, ax = plt.subplots(figsize=(6, 6))
im = ax.imshow(julia_set, cmap="magma",
               vmax = 0.25 * np.max(julia_set))
```

We specify vmax to increase the contrast. Then, we can save the image to a file using the following:

```
fig.savefig("path/to/file")
```

The result is this intricate fractal image:

Figure 1.3 – Julia set with c=-0.8+0.156j

Calculating this fractal image takes a bit of time (on this machine, it took about 14.5 seconds). This is because we calculate each pixel sequentially. However, each pixel is independent, so we could potentially calculate all of them in parallel.

Creating our z_0 input array and allocating memory for the julia_set output array are sequential operations, and so are plotting and saving our image to disk. We can time all these different parts using `time.perf_counter` to estimate how much our code would benefit from parallelization. To do this, we can wrap the relevant pieces of code as follows:

```
import time
start = time.perf_counter()
# code we want to time here
end = time.perf_counter()
print(end - start)
```

On the machine where these code examples were run, creating `z_0` takes about 0.005 seconds, and plotting and saving the result takes 0.1 seconds. Calculating the Julia set takes about 13.8 seconds. The time to allocate a zeroed `julia_set` array is negligible. Therefore, if we assume that `calculate_julia` is fully parallelizable and the rest is fully serial, then `p = 13.8/(13.8+0.105) = 99.2%`. That means, according to Amdahl's law, by adding an infinite number of compute resources, we could only reach a speedup of `1/(1-0.992)=125×`. All these numbers will vary depending on the specific hardware on which the examples are run.

Performing more advanced profiling with cProfile and Scalene

In this simple example, we could manually identify the interesting pieces of code to profile. As our applications get more complex, this approach does not scale. Therefore, it is important to be aware of profilers such as **cProfile** and **Scalene**.

`cProfile` is a profiler that is part of the Python standard library. If our Python code is in a script, we can profile the script using the command line as follows:

```
python -m cProfile -s cumtime script.py
```

We use the `-s` flag to sort by `cumtime`, which is the total time spent in the function, including sub-functions. When we profile only the code that calculates the Julia set and exclude the code that plots and saves the result, we get a table that looks something like this (rows are split over two lines to fit on the page):

```
34137406 function calls (34135254 primitive calls) in 21.307
seconds
   Ordered by: cumulative time
   ncalls  tottime  percall  cumtime  percall \
filename:lineno(function)
     96/1    0.000    0.000   21.307   21.307 \
{built-in method builtins.exec}
```

```
        1    0.003    0.003   21.307   21.307 \
cprofile.py:1(<module>)
        1   16.710   16.710   21.168   21.168 \
cprofile.py:5(calculate_julia)
 34040305    4.459    0.000    4.459    0.000 \
{built-in method builtins.abs}
    ...
```

We get a table that shows how often each function was called (`ncalls`), what the total time was spent in each function over all calls (`tottime` and `cumtime`), and how much time was spent per call of each function (`percall`). The difference between `tottime` and `cumtime` is that `tottime` tries to exclude the time spent in sub-functions. For example, `cProfile` measures the built-in `abs` function, which is used inside the `calculate_julia` function. According to `cProfile`, evaluating $|z|$ takes about 4.5 seconds or roughly 20% of the total runtime. The total time of `calculate_julia` is the time taken by `abs` subtracted from the cumulative time.

Notice how running the code with the profiler is substantially slower than running it without the profiler. This is because profiling adds a tiny bit of overhead to each function call, and in this example, there are a lot of small function calls, which makes the overhead very large. With the profiler, this code takes more than 50% more time than without (21 seconds versus 14 seconds), which means that these results are not very reliable in an absolute sense; a manual timing of specific code sections will give more accurate results. Still, `cProfile` can give us quick insight into the bottlenecks that exist in our code. It is convenient and always available in the Python standard library.

> Note
>
> **Using cProfile in Jupyter Notebooks**
>
> When working in a Jupyter notebook, we can use the `%%prun` magic command at the start of a cell to profile that cell with `cProfile`. However, the Jupyter, IPython processes, and interactive backends from `matplotlib` can interfere with the profiler and skew the results. We highly suggest using `cProfile` outside Jupyter notebooks and not profiling `matplotlib` code with it.

`cProfile` is limited to timing function calls, and the results are not always reliable, as our example shows. We want to get more insight into the bottlenecks of our `calculate_julia` function, but this is not possible with `cProfile` unless we split our function into more useful subfunctions.

In this case, a line profiler is more appropriate. With line profilers, individual lines of Python are timed. **Scalene** is a powerful profiler that can do line profiling. In addition, it performs memory profiling, GPU profiling, and measures how much time is spent in Python versus "native" (i.e., compiled) code. It also claims to add a minimal amount of runtime overhead, thereby providing reliable timings. It can also be easily used from Jupyter notebooks. It is a third-party package that can be installed with any Python package manager, such as `pip`, `conda`, or `pixi`.

To use Scalene from a Jupyter notebook, first load the extension:

```
%load_ext scalene
```

Then, we can profile code by adding the following to the top of the cell that needs to be profiled:

```
%%scalene
```

Alternatively, we can put our code in a `.py` script file and run it with `scalene my_script.py`. Note that in both cases, for line profiling to be useful, we need all the relevant code in the same script or Jupyter notebook cell. We will get output that looks something like this:

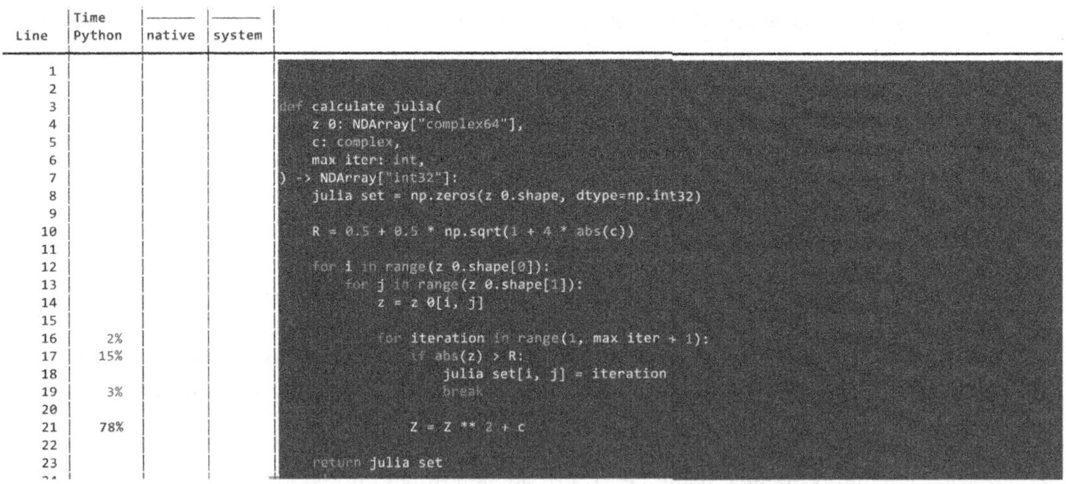

Figure 1.4 – Line profiling results obtained with Scalene

The leftmost column shows the percentage of time spent by the Python interpreter. The results show that almost 80% of the time of all our code is spent on the line that updates `z` in the `calculate_pixel` function. We could not derive from the results of `cProfile`, as this line is not a function. We also see that a good chunk of time is spent on evaluating the `abs` function, which is in line with the `cProfile` results.

Using this type of information, we can identify bottlenecks in our code, which should be the first target for optimization.

Understanding the factors that limit parallelism

In the previous section, we made an important omission about Amdahl's law: the fraction of parallelizable code is not a constant but depends on the size of our inputs. Obviously, if we calculate a smaller image and use fewer iterations, the time to calculate the Julia set decreases, and so does the fraction of parallelizable code. The larger our problem, the larger the fraction of parallelizable code, the more we will benefit from parallelization. Therefore, we don't only need to understand the code; we also have to know what the size of the problem will be.

Secondly, Amdahl's law assumes we can infinitely speed up the parallel part by adding more resources. However, in our Julia set example, it is clear that there is no benefit to adding more workers than there are pixels. The number of tasks is a discrete number, and so is the number of workers. The best we can do is to have one worker per task, in which case the runtime is reduced to the slowest-running task. If some workers get more work than others, some workers will be idle as they wait for busy workers to catch up. This is relevant in our Julia set example, since some pixels converge in just one iteration, while others require the full `max_iter` iterations to complete.

Third, Amdahl's law only applies to **embarrassingly parallel** problems, for which tasks have no interdependencies. The expected speedup of the parallel part is assumed to be linearly related to the compute capacity. This is the case for our Julia set example: each pixel can be calculated independently. However, for other problems, tasks may have interdependencies, in which case they need to wait for each other or communicate with each other. Communication and synchronization add overhead, which reduces the effectiveness of parallelization.

Finally, Amdahl's law assumes the bottleneck in running parallelizable code is the compute capacity. However, many problems are **memory-bound** (i.e., the bottleneck is the speed at which cores can get the data they need). The speed of these data transfers is governed by two key concepts: **latency** and **bandwidth**. Latency refers to the delay between requesting data and receiving it; imagine waiting for a single package to arrive by mail. Bandwidth, on the other hand, is the maximum rate at which data can be transferred, such as the number of packages a delivery truck can carry in an hour. For small amounts of data, latency dominates the total transfer time, while for large amounts of data, bandwidth becomes the limiting factor. If workers are waiting for data, then adding more workers will not speed anything up. Memory bottlenecks are so important to many problems that all modern processors, including both CPUs and GPUs, incorporate multiple layers of cache to optimize **data locality**, keeping frequently accessed data close to the compute units. When we start to optimize code, it is essential to figure out whether our problem is compute-bound or memory-bound.

Despite its limitations, Amdahl's law is a useful rule of thumb that can help us estimate an upper bound on the expected benefit of adding more workers. However, due to the aforementioned reasons, such as memory bottlenecks and synchronization, performance rarely scales linearly with compute capacity. Therefore, the only way to measure the benefits of parallelization is to run the code with different levels of parallelism.

Measuring the benefits of parallelization empirically

Let us measure the effect of adding workers for our Julia set example using `numba`, and illustrate why Amdahl's law is still too optimistic.

As mentioned earlier in the chapter, `numba` is a JIT compiler for Python. In the next few chapters, we will focus on the `numba.cuda` plugin, which allows us to use Numba to write CUDA code. Here, we will compile Python code to machine code for execution on the CPU and parallelize it over CPU cores.

To compile a Python function with `numba`, we use the `njit` **decorator** on the function as follows:

```
from numba import njit, prange
@njit
def calculate_julia(...):
    ...
```

When we invoke the function for the first time, `numba` will figure out the types we pass into the function and compile the function to a fast machine code version specialized to those types. Compiling a function takes a bit of time, especially with complex functions. However, compiled versions of the function are cached, so executing the function a second time will be very fast. Whenever we pass different types into the function, `numba` has to compile another version of the function.

> Note
>
> **njit versus jit**
>
> The `jit` decorator can also be used for compiling a function. The difference with `njit` is that `jit` allows for "partial" compilation. If Numba cannot compile all parts of a function, it will fall back on the Python interpreter for those bits of code. This has a large negative impact on performance. With `njit`, which stands for *no-python JIT*, we disallow this behavior and force Numba to throw an error when it cannot compile the entire function.

numba supports auto-parallelization of loops using prange. When we replace range with prange in a loop, we tell numba that it can distribute different iterations of that loop among multiple workers, in this case, CPU cores. Remember, no GPU is involved at this point. If our CPU has only a single core, there will be no parallelization. To enable parallelization, we must pass the parallel=True argument to the @njit decorator; otherwise, prange behaves identically to range. In our implementation of calculate_julia, only the range of the outer loop was replaced with prange. We could also put prange in the second loop, but profiling showed that this has no effect on performance. Hence, the JITted calculate_julia function looks as follows:

```
@njit(parallel=True)
def calculate_julia_jit(
    z_0: NDArray[np.complex64],
    c: complex,
    max_iter: int,
) -> NDArray[np.int32]:
    julia_set = np.zeros(z_0.shape, dtype=np.int32)
    R = 0.5 + 0.5 * np.sqrt(1 + 4 * abs(c))
    for i in prange(z_0.shape[0]):
        for j in range(z_0.shape[1]):
            z = z_0[i, j]
            for iteration in range(1, max_iter + 1):
                if abs(z) > R:
                    julia_set[i, j] = iteration
                    break
                z = z ** 2 + c
    return julia_set
```

This code was run and timed using one, two, four, and eight threads, using numba.set_num_threads, on a CPU with eight cores. The results are plotted in *Figure 1.5*, which shows execution time, speedup (ratio of execution time with one worker and the execution time with *n* workers), and efficiency (ratio of speedup and the number of workers):

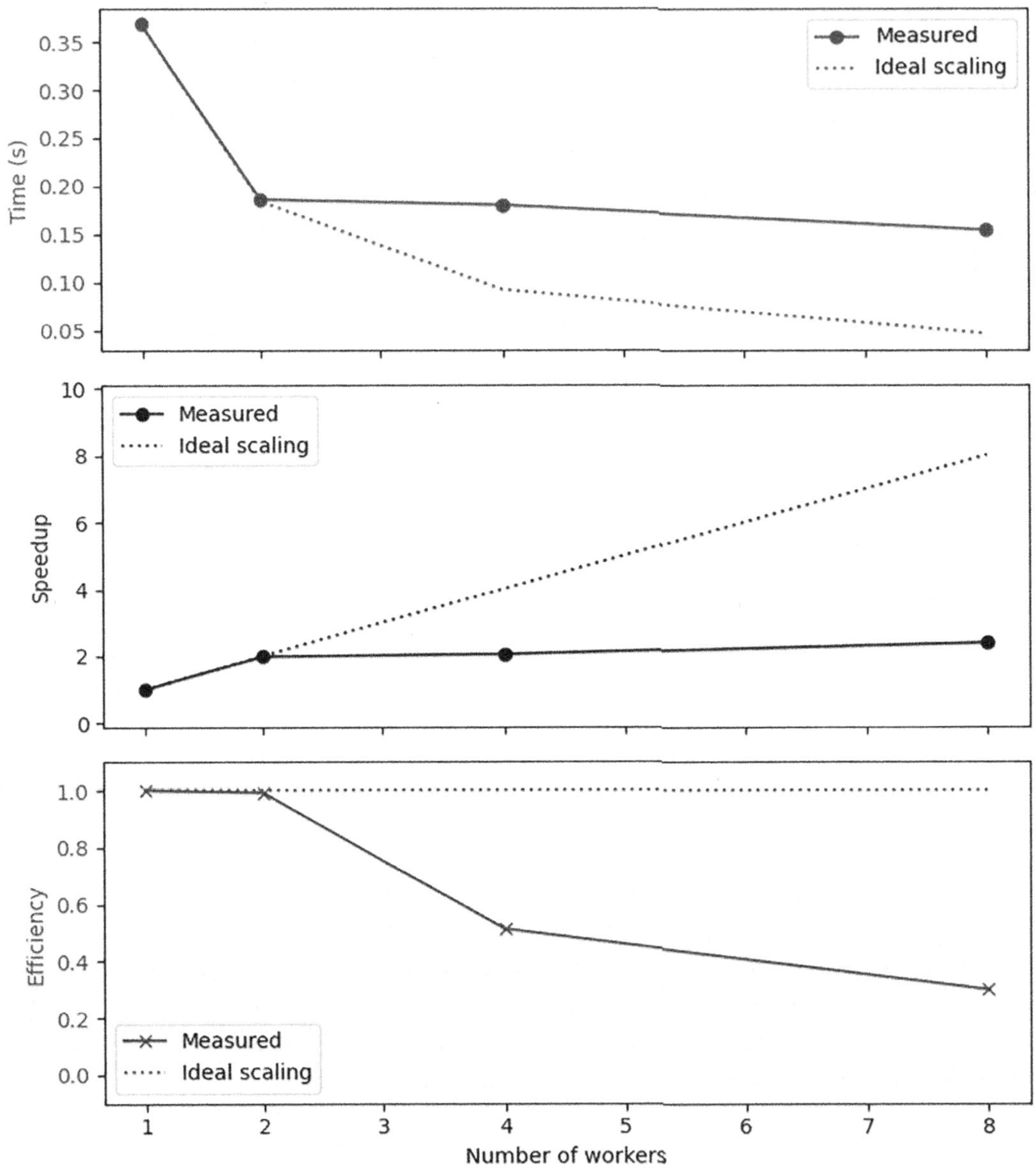

Figure 1.5 – Time, speedup, and efficiency of calculate_julia as a function of the number of workers

The measured times are compared to what would be expected based on ideal scaling (i.e., doubling the number of workers halves the execution time). The results show the diminishing returns of adding workers. Whereas going from one to two cores very closely follows ideal scaling (efficiency is close to one), adding any more workers barely improves the runtime.

These timings only take into consideration the `calculate_julia_jit` function, which we considered to be almost 100% parallelizable. Therefore, the ideal scaling lines should closely reflect what Amdahl's law predicts. Our measurements show that even Amdahl's law is far too optimistic, and many more factors are at play, as mentioned in the previous section.

Note

JIT compilation performance

Compiling the function with `numba.njit` drastically reduced the runtime from around 14 seconds to around 0.35 seconds when using a single CPU thread. This impressive performance gain can be achieved because Numba circumvents the Python interpreter entirely and compiles the code to machine code with near-C performance.

This does not mean that there is no point in using the GPU where we could leverage thousands of threads/cores. However, we cannot simply extrapolate the CPU graph for the GPU, since we cannot directly compare CPU and GPU implementations. CPU and GPU threads are different, the flow of data is different, and the execution models are different.

To illustrate, we ran a GPU implementation of the `calculate_julia` algorithm on an A100 GPU, which has over 6,000 **CUDA cores**. We will learn how to write GPU implementations of algorithms in *Chapter 3*; in this chapter, the goal is only to illustrate a point on performance. Just like in the CPU implementation, we ran it multiple times on the GPU with different numbers of threads, starting with one and going up to about four million. The execution times versus the number of threads are shown in *Figure 1.6* on a log-log graph. For comparison, the CPU execution times, which we measured earlier, are also plotted, in addition to the times that would be expected given ideal scaling. One arrow indicates the number of CUDA cores available on the device; the other arrow points to the number of array elements that need to be calculated, which is equivalent to the number of tasks that can be run in parallel.

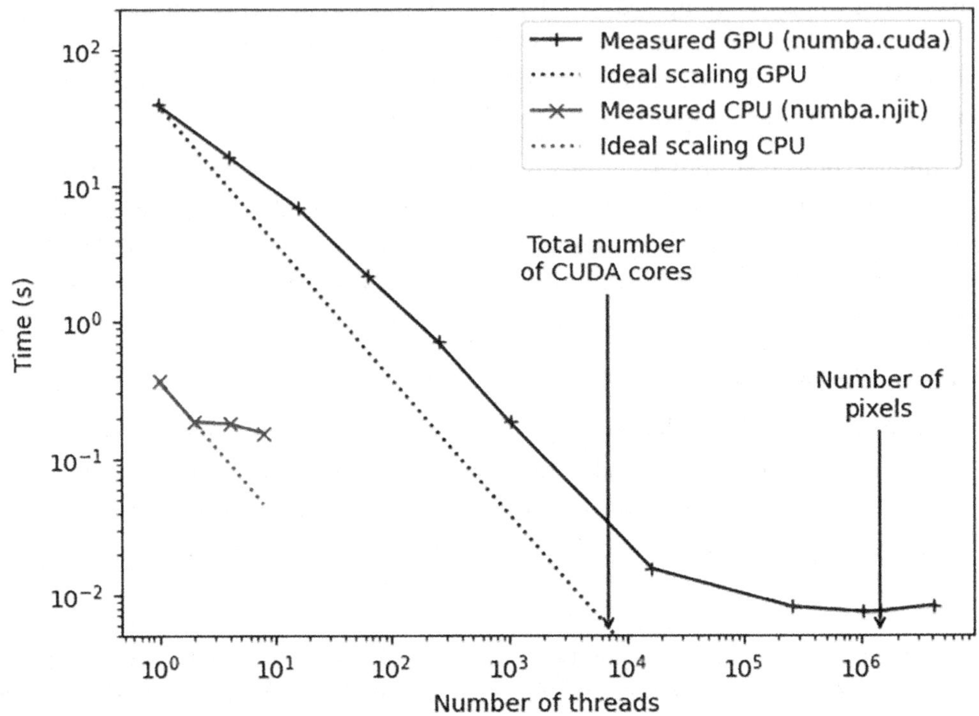

Figure 1.6 – Comparison of execution time between CPU and GPU implementations for different numbers of threads

The figure highlights that a CPU thread cannot be compared to a GPU thread. With a small number of threads, the GPU is heavily underutilized, and the performance is almost 100× worse compared to one CPU thread. Only when we launch about 500 GPU threads is the performance comparable to one CPU thread. Performance peaks when the number of threads is approximately equal to the number of parallelizable tasks (roughly 1.5M). In this case, we achieve a performance that is 20× better than 8 CPU threads and almost 50× better than one CPU thread. This is good, but almost an order of magnitude removed from what we might expect based on the difference in theoretical compute capacity: the A100 GPU has a compute capacity of 19.5 TFLOPS for 32-bit floats, whereas one CPU core has a compute capacity of roughly 0.05 TFLOPS; a difference of almost 400×.

When we run the calculation with more threads than tasks, execution time increases slightly compared to the minimum. While GPU threads incur only a small overhead, launching threads that have nothing to do obviously decreases performance.

Typically, we do not think of the GPU as a collection of cores, but as a single powerful processor that we aim to fully occupy. A rule of thumb and a good starting point to fully occupy the GPU is to launch a thread for each parallelizable task. The GPU is best equipped to schedule these threads efficiently on the available cores.

This analysis omits a lot of important details, since CUDA does not allow us to simply select the number of threads we want to use to execute some code. CUDA kernel execution involves additional concepts like grids and blocks. We will learn all about that in *Chapter 3*.

The main point of this section is to demonstrate that the most reliable way to figure out how much parallelization benefits our code is to measure its effects. Even code that we believe to be "fully parallelizable" may have additional bottlenecks that limit the effectiveness of additional workers.

Summary

In this chapter, we discussed what GPGPU is, what the motivation behind it is, and what the application areas are. We explained that GPU computing is valuable for problems that can be solved with data parallelism, i.e., dividing the problem into small chunks and running the same task on all those chunks. A GPU has a high theoretical compute capacity due to its massive number of cores. If a problem cannot be split up and distributed over multiple cores, the GPU will not speed up the computation.

After considering theoretical compute capacity, we refined our estimates of code speedup using Amdahl's law and showed that the fraction of non-parallelizable code eventually dominates. We illustrated this with an example of calculating a Julia set fractal. We profiled the code and related the results back to Amdahl's law. We also discussed the limitations of Amdahl's law and other factors that limit parallelism. We demonstrated the effect of these factors on the performance of the Julia set example by measuring parallelization efficiency. In the process, we briefly learned about Numba, JIT compilation, and parallelization over CPU cores. We also compared our CPU implementation against a GPU implementation, which showed that we cannot simply compare a CPU thread and a GPU thread.

Even though we have not learned how to program a GPU, we are now well equipped to estimate, measure, and recognize the limitations of using a GPU for speeding up computations. In the next chapter, we will learn how to set up an environment that will allow us to write and execute CUDA code.

Questions

1. If we have a problem that is 90% parallelizable, what is the maximum speedup we can achieve? How many compute resources would be needed to achieve 90% of this limit? How many compute resources are needed to reach 99% of this limit?

2. For the first problem, we only achieve 50% of the theoretical maximum speedup. What could be the reasons?
3. Can we parallelize the third (inner) loop in the Julia set function? Why or why not?
4. How can `numba` JIT compilation speed up Python code by a factor of >100?
5. Can we do line profiling on JIT-compiled functions?
6. Why does the execution time of the GPU code decrease even when there are more threads than CUDA cores? Why is this typically not the case for CPU threads?

Answers

1. The non-parallelizable part of the code is 10% or 0.1. Therefore, according to Amdahl's law, the maximum speedup is 10×. If we want to reach 90% of that, we want to achieve a speedup of 9×. If we plug this into Amdahl's law again and solve for *s*, we need to speed up the parallelizable part 81×, so if we assume linear scaling, we need 81× the amount of compute resources. To reach 99% of the maximum speedup, we want to reach a speedup of 9.9×. This corresponds to *s=891*; in other words, we need 891× the amount of compute resources. In reality, we would need even more resources to account for imperfect scaling.
2. Memory bottlenecks, coordination/synchronization/communication between workers, and workload imbalance between workers.
3. No. The loop serves to sequentially update a single variable. If we distribute this over multiple threads, we will get completely non-deterministic behavior as different threads compete to try to update z.
4. The key is that, while the Numba decorated function *looks* like a Python function, it no longer *is* a Python function. Numba compiles the function to machine code, which is similarly efficient as compiled C and Fortran.
5. No. Because the JITed function is no longer running on the Python interpreter, it is no longer being run line by line, and line profiling becomes meaningless.
6. GPU threads are very lightweight, and the GPU is very good at efficiently scheduling those threads and switching between them. When there is more work to be done than there are threads, we are trying to do the job of the scheduler, because we are instructing our threads to do multiple tasks that could be parallelized. CPU threads are heavyweight, and typically, there is no benefit to adding more threads than the number of cores.

Get this book's PDF version and more

Scan the QR code (or go to `packtpub.com/unlock`). Search for this book by name, confirm the edition, and then follow the steps on the page.

UNLOCK NOW

Note: Keep your invoice handy. Purchases made directly from Packt don't require an invoice.

Get this book's PDF version and more

2

Setting Up a GPU Programming Environment Locally and in the Cloud

Before we can write code for the GPU and run GPU programs, we need to configure our environment. In this chapter, we will learn how to set up a development environment. For readers who own a CUDA-enabled GPU, we will first walk through the setup process on a local machine. For readers who do not own an NVIDIA GPU, we will also walk through setting up a machine in the cloud where GPUs can be rented. We will learn how to install the NVIDIA driver, the CUDA Toolkit, and the Python libraries used throughout the rest of this book.

For local machines, we will discuss only three platforms: Ubuntu-LTS, Windows 10, and **Windows Subsystem for Linux** (**WSL**), all on a machine with a CPU with the AMD64 architecture. For cloud machines, we will only consider Ubuntu Linux with a CPU with the AMD64 architecture.

The learning outcomes for this chapter are as follows:

- Set up a CUDA-Python development environment on a local machine in Ubuntu, Windows 10, or WSL
- Set up a CUDA-Python development environment on a **virtual machine** (**VM**) in the cloud on **Amazon Web Services** (**AWS**) or Lambda Labs
- Use Google Colab to test CUDA code with zero setup
- Run and connect to a JupyterLab environment on a local or remote host

Technical requirements

The only technical requirement for this chapter is that you have a computer with internet access.

To set up a local environment, your machine will need to have an NVIDIA GPU with **compute capability** 7.5 or higher. Most consumer-grade cards for gaming released after 2018 fit this criterion; look up the compute capability of different models on this page: `https://developer.nvidia.com/cuda-gpus`. The compute capability is a version number that determines which CUDA features and instructions the hardware supports; the higher the number, the more recent the GPU and the more features are supported.

To set up an environment in the cloud, you will need a credit card to set up an account. If you will only be experimenting with the free version of Google Colab, you will only need a Google account.

Setting up a local development environment

Follow these instructions if you have your own GPU (compute capability 7.5 or higher; see `https://developer.nvidia.com/cuda-gpus`) and you will develop on your own hardware. If you don't, you can skip this section entirely and go to the *Setting up a remote development environment* section.

To set up a local development environment, we need to take the following steps:

1. Verify that we have the appropriate hardware.
2. Install the **NVIDIA driver**.
3. Install the **CUDA Toolkit**.
4. Install Python and the necessary Python libraries.

The NVIDIA driver is a software abstraction layer that acts as an intermediary between the GPU hardware and the operating system. It allows the operating system to recognize the GPU, manage its resources, and execute commands.

The CUDA Toolkit is NVIDIA's software development platform for GPU-accelerated computing. Depending on the distribution, it includes everything that is needed to develop and run applications that leverage CUDA-enabled GPUs, including compilers, libraries, and APIs, to the driver. A bare-bones CUDA Toolkit, for example, the one we will install from Anaconda.org, may only include the necessary dependencies (runtime libraries) to run and use precompiled CUDA code. Libraries and compilers may be installed separately.

The CUDA Toolkit must be compatible with the driver; each CUDA Toolkit version has a minimum compatible driver version. The NVIDIA driver is backward compatible: newer drivers support older CUDA Toolkit versions, but older drivers do not support newer CUDA Toolkit versions.

The CUDA Toolkit must also be compatible with the compute capability of the device. The compute capability determines the minimum CUDA version; compute capability 7.5 and above requires at least CUDA 12.0.

To install both the CUDA Toolkit and other dependencies (steps 3 and 4), we will use a tool and package manager called Pixi (`https://pixi.sh/latest/`).

> Note
>
> **Why Pixi and not conda or pip?**
>
> In this book, we chose to use Pixi instead of `conda` or `pip` for managing dependencies. Pixi is a new and modern package manager, written in Rust, that implements deterministic dependency management with an automated lock-file management mechanism. This guarantees the reproducibility of the environment. Pixi builds on the `conda` ecosystem and creates `conda`-like environments, which gives us access to a very large number of packages, including non-Python packages. The `conda` ecosystem allows us to install CUDA and all NVIDIA libraries directly and reproducibly in our environment. With `pip`, this is not possible, and the CUDA Toolkit and CUDA tools would need to be installed separately at the system level. Pixi is also faster and more ergonomic than `conda`, and simple to install and uninstall since it is shipped as a standalone binary.

We will go through all the steps for Linux (Ubuntu 24.04 LTS), Windows 10, and WSL. Skip ahead to the section pertaining to your operating system.

Linux (Ubuntu 24.04 LTS)

We need a CUDA-enabled GPU with compute capability 7.5 or higher installed on our machine. To check, open a terminal and run the following:

```
lspci | grep -e "NVIDIA"
```

The output shows the model of the available GPU. Then, check the compute capability of the device on this page: `https://developer.nvidia.com/cuda-gpus`.

Install the driver with the `ubuntu-drivers` shell utility. In a terminal, list the available drivers with the following:

```
sudo ubuntu-drivers list
```

The tool auto-detects the drivers best suited to the device. Install the driver with the following:

```
sudo ubuntu-drivers install
```

Optionally, specify the driver version to install by appending it to the previous command, for example, `nvidia:535`. To work with CUDA 12.3, which we use in this book, the minimum driver version is `525.60.13`, but newer is recommended since the driver is backward compatible with older CUDA versions.

> Note
>
> **Using a different CUDA version**
>
> Each CUDA version has different requirements for the minimum driver version. This is documented in the CUDA release notes of the CUDA version, which can be found at a URL with the following structure: `https://docs.nvidia.com/cuda/archive/x.y.0/cuda-toolkit-release-notes/index.html`, where *x* and *y* should be replaced with the major and minor versions of the CUDA release. When updating the CUDA Toolkit, compatibility with the driver version must be considered.

Check whether the driver was correctly installed by running `nvidia-smi` in the terminal. This should show output that looks something like the following:

```
+-----------------------------------------------------------------------------+
| NVIDIA-SMI 550.54.14           Driver Version: 550.54.14     CUDA Version: 12.4   |
|-------------------------------+----------------------+----------------------+
| GPU  Name           Persistence-M | Bus-Id        Disp.A | Volatile Uncorr. ECC |
| Fan  Temp   Perf    Pwr:Usage/Cap |         Memory-Usage | GPU-Util  Compute M. |
|                                   |                      |               MIG M. |
|===================================+======================+======================|
|   0  NVIDIA A100-PCIE-40GB    Off | 00000000:61:00.0 Off |                    0 |
| N/A   31C    P0       33W /  250W |      0MiB /  40960MiB |      0%      Default |
|                                   |                      |             Disabled |
+-----------------------------------+----------------------+----------------------+
```

Figure 2.1 – The output of a successful nvidia-smi invocation

Now install Pixi by following these instructions: `https://pixi.sh/latest/#installation`. At the time of writing, to install Pixi, you need to run the following single command in a terminal:

```
curl -fsSL https://pixi.sh/install.sh | bash
```

Now we will create our environment containing all the CUDA and Python dependencies. The environment we use throughout this book is specified in the `pixi.lock` and `pyproject.toml` files in the code repository associated with this book: `https://github.com/PacktPublishing/GPU-Accelerated-Computing-with-Python-3-and-CUDA`. To create an identical environment, at least these two files are needed. The easiest way to obtain them is to simply run `git clone` on the entire code repository to clone it to some local directory. For this, `git` needs to be installed on the system; install it with `apt install git`.

From the terminal, navigate to the cloned repository. Install the environment by running this command:

```
pixi install --frozen
```

This will ensure that the same dependencies are installed as those used to create the examples in this book.

Activate the environment with the following:

```
pixi shell
```

Once the environment is active, Python scripts that depend on CUDA can be run by simply using `python <name of script>`.

Most of our examples are provided as Jupyter notebooks. Notebooks can be run by starting JupyterLab. To start JupyterLab, first activate the Pixi environment. Then, from the terminal, run the following:

```
jupyter-lab
```

This should open a browser tab with the Jupyter interface. In the file explorer on the left, the directory from which JupyterLab was launched is shown. In the center, there is an icon to create a new notebook with the Python 3 kernel, which corresponds to the active Pixi environment. When opening an existing notebook file, the `Python 3` kernel will need to be selected.

Debugging the driver

Installing NVIDIA drivers on Linux has a reputation for being tricky. If `nvidia-smi` does not show the expected output, investigate using the following steps.

First, check whether the NVIDIA kernel module is correctly installed by running the following command:

```
modinfo nvidia
```

If the output reports the expected driver version, the driver should be correctly installed. If the output reports `modinfo: ERROR`, the driver needs to be reinstalled.

Second, check whether the module is loaded using the following command:

```
lsmod | grep nvidia
```

If there is no relevant output, try to run the following command:

```
sudo modprobe nvidia
```

Finally, check whether something is going wrong with loading the driver at boot time with the following command:

```
dmesg | grep nvidia
```

Windows 10

> Note
>
> **Warning**
>
> We cannot guarantee that all of the code provided in the accompanying GitHub repository will run without modification on Windows, as the authors have always developed on Linux. If your operating system is Windows, we highly recommend setting up your development environment on WSL as described in the next section.

The machine needs a CUDA-enabled GPU with a compute capability of at least 7.5 or higher. To check, open the Windows Control Panel using the search button on the bottom left of the taskbar, next to the Windows icon.

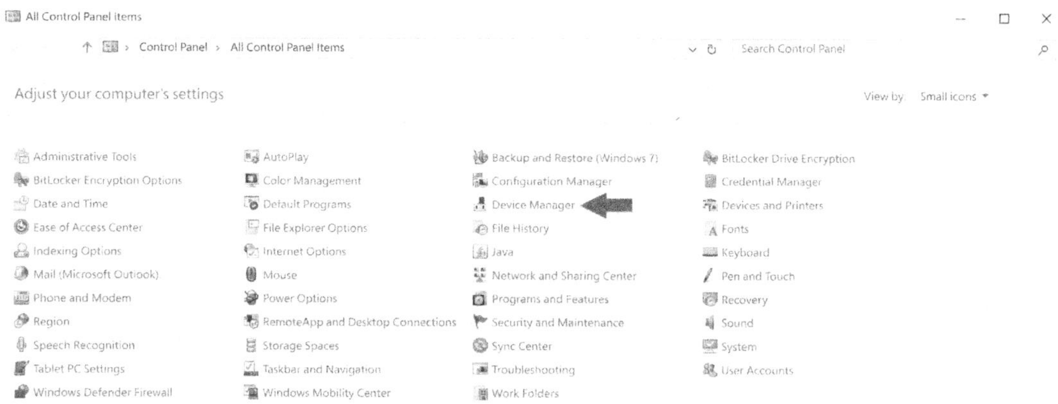

Figure 2.2 – Device Manager in the Windows control panel

Click on **Device Manager** and then on the **Display adapters** dropdown. Here, there should be an entry for an NVIDIA GPU, and its properties can be checked by double-clicking on the entry. Check the compute capability by looking up the GPU model on this page: `https://developer.nvidia.com/cuda-gpus`.

Once the availability of appropriate hardware has been verified, it's time to install the NVIDIA driver. Visit `https://www.nvidia.com/en-us/drivers/` and find the latest driver that is compatible with the device; the site provides a handy form to make an appropriate selection. Download the driver and follow the wizard to install it. Since we are working with CUDA 12.3 in this book, the minimum driver version is `527.41`, but a newer version is recommended.

To verify that the driver works properly, run the `nvidia-smi` program, which provides information about the GPU in a Command Prompt window. By default, `nvidia-smi` may not exist on the system path. If running `nvidia-smi` does not work in a fresh Command Prompt window, the binary should exist at `C:\Program Files\NVIDIA Corporation\NVSMI\nvidia-smi.exe`, and pasting this entire path into a PowerShell or Command Prompt window should fix the issue.

Now install Pixi by following the instructions here: `https://pixi.sh/latest/#installation`. At the time of writing, installing Pixi involves running the following single command in a PowerShell window:

```
powershell -ExecutionPolicy ByPass `
-c "irm -useb https://pixi.sh/install.ps1 | iex"
```

Now we will create our environment containing all the CUDA, NVIDIA, and Python dependencies. The environment we use throughout this book is specified in the `pixi.lock` and `pyproject.toml` files in the code repository associated with this book: `https://github.com/PacktPublishing/GPU-Computing-with-Python-3-and-CUDA-`. To create an identical environment, these two files need to be available. The easiest way to obtain them is to simply run `git clone` on the entire repository to clone it to some local folder. For this, `git` needs to be installed on the system; see `https://git-scm.com/downloads`.

With PowerShell or Command Prompt, navigate to the cloned repository. Install the environment by running this command:

```
pixi install --frozen
```

This will ensure that the same dependencies are installed as those used to create the examples in this book.

Activate the environment by using PowerShell or Command Prompt to run the following:

```
pixi shell
```

Once the environment is active, Python scripts that depend on CUDA can be run simply by using `python <name of script>`.

Most of our examples are provided as Jupyter notebooks. You can run the notebooks by starting JupyterLab. To start JupyterLab, first activate the Pixi environment. Then, run the following command:

```
jupyter-lab
```

This should open a browser tab with the Jupyter interface. In the file explorer on the left, the folder from which JupyterLab was launched is shown. In the center, there is an icon to create a new notebook with the Python 3 kernel, which corresponds to the active Pixi environment. When opening an existing notebook file, the `Python 3` kernel will need to be selected.

WSL

In general, setting up a working development environment on Windows can be more challenging than on Linux, mostly because Windows lacks a good terminal. In addition, most production code eventually will have to run on a Linux machine. Therefore, it is often preferable to also develop in a Linux environment.

WSL provides a Linux environment on Windows, without having to replace the Windows host operating system with desktop Linux. WSL is a lightweight Linux VM that is tightly integrated with the host Windows environment, and therefore, it offers the best of both worlds.

To do CUDA programming in WSL, WSL 2 and an appropriate Windows NVIDIA driver are needed. First, follow the instructions for installing the NVIDIA driver on Windows as described in the previous section.

To install WSL, follow the official instructions provided on Microsoft's website: `https://learn.microsoft.com/en-us/windows/wsl/install`. Then, install a Linux distribution. To install Ubuntu 24.04 LTS, run the following in PowerShell:

```
wsl --install -d Ubuntu-24.04
```

Ubuntu can be opened by searching for it in the Windows Start menu. A terminal should open, which is the interface to the Ubuntu VM. If the NVIDIA driver on the Windows host machine was correctly installed, the GPU should be accessible from inside WSL. The environment can now be installed as described in the installation steps in the *Linux (Ubuntu 24.04 LTS)* section, except for one modification: **do not install the NVIDIA driver for Linux**. Doing so may make the GPU inaccessible from WSL. For more information, read the official documentation from NVIDIA: `https://docs.nvidia.com/cuda/wsl-user-guide/index.html`.

Setting up a remote development environment

GPUs are expensive, especially models that need to perform serious number crunching. Consumer-grade gaming GPUs in the upper price segment are quite powerful, but pale in comparison to data center-grade GPUs that cost one or two orders of magnitude more. However, we can get access to the most powerful GPUs by renting them in the cloud. This is not cheap, but it can be far more affordable than buying, maintaining, and monitoring the hardware, since in the cloud, we only pay for the time we use the device and don't have to worry about maintenance.

This section will cover two approaches for using a GPU in the cloud: with managed notebook services and with cloud VMs. The managed notebook services will be illustrated with Google Colab. VMs will be demonstrated on Lambda Labs and AWS. These services are some options among many; their inclusion in this book does not constitute an endorsement or advertisement.

Google Colab

Google Colab is a service that offers zero-setup Python and R **notebooks**. The service can be used to run notebooks on a machine with an NVIDIA GPU.

To get access, log in at `https://colab.research.google.com/` with a Google account. The landing page looks like this:

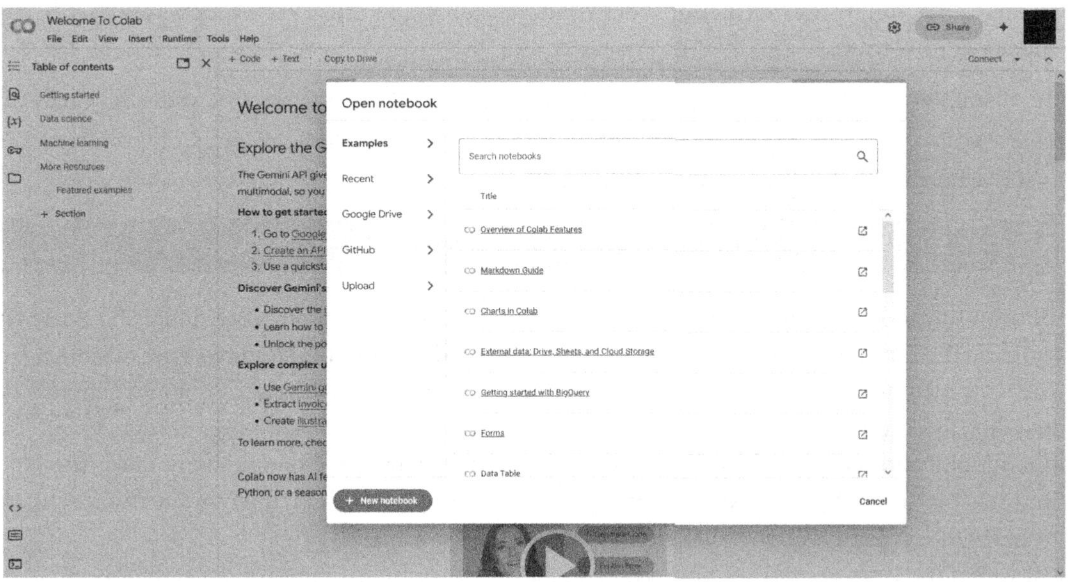

Figure 2.3 – Google Colab welcome screen

Test whether one of the examples/tutorials can be opened, for example, the introduction to cuDF:

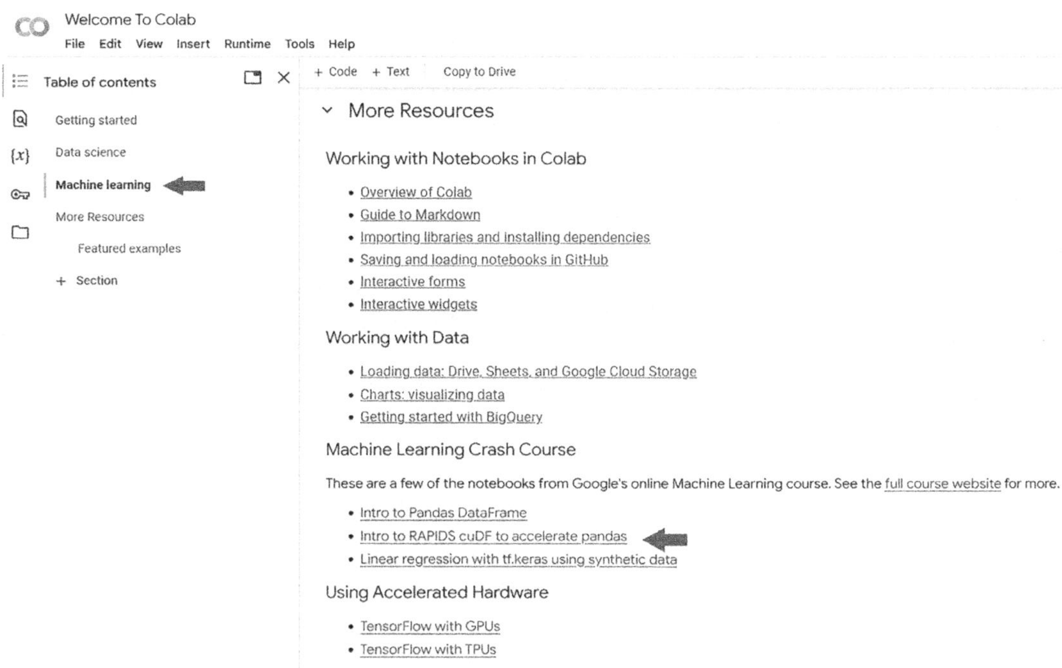

Figure 2.4 – Navigating to the Intro to RAPIDS cuDF to accelerate pandas tutorial in Google Colab

This will open the example notebook, which should look and feel familiar to readers used to Jupyter notebooks. In the top right, change the runtime:

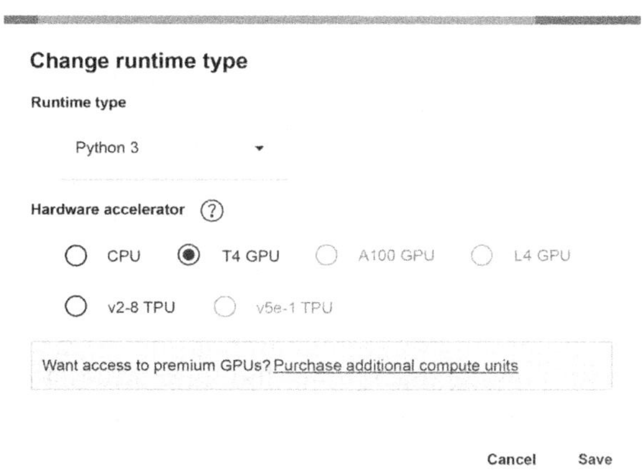

Figure 2.5 – Selecting a runtime and hardware accelerator

Depending on which combination of runtime and hardware accelerator is chosen, the session will be connected to a different type of VM in the background that handles the computations.

Selecting Python and T4 GPU will connect the session to a VM with an NVIDIA T4 GPU that has most of the packages that are needed throughout this book installed.

This is pretty much all there is in terms of setup. Notebooks can be created and/or uploaded, then run by pressing *Shift* + *Enter* over all the cells. Most of the code in this book is provided in a separate repository as Jupyter notebooks.

Google Colab also has access to the files on the Google Drive of the logged-in user. If there is a missing package, try to install it by running shell commands in a notebook cell, as follows:

```
!pip install <name of package>
```

Google Colab is an easy and free tool to start experimenting with CUDA and deep learning in Python.

However, there are also some major downsides. The free tier only provides access to the cheaper NVIDIA T4 GPU for 12 hours. The session will be terminated if it is inactive for too long. Except for the notebooks themselves, which are persisted on Google Drive, no data is persisted between sessions since sessions always connect to a random VM. Any additional packages that are installed, or any results that are saved to disk, will be gone when the session disconnects.

Additionally, the terminal of the VM is not accessible, so all commands must run through the notebook interface. This can make some operations feel very hacky. For the local setups, we created fully reproducible environments with Pixi. This can be very difficult to do in Google Colab. Instead, if a package is missing, we recommend trying to use `pip` to install it, as mentioned before. This will not work for command-line utilities such as Nsight profilers, which we will use later in this book. This approach may also result in unforeseeable issues due to package conflicts, because the environment that will be created will not be identical to the one used in this book.

Google Colab also provides a paid tier. This gives users a wider range of GPUs to choose from, the option to persist data, access to the VM terminal, and increased session timeout. However, renting a bare-bones VM and setting it up from scratch is usually the cheaper and more flexible option. Let's have a look at how to do this, first on Lambda Labs.

Lambda Labs

Lambda Labs is a small cloud provider that specifically targets AI development. They make it easy to rent GPU instances at reasonable prices, with some of the best GPUs available on the market. The entire setup takes less than an hour.

To make an account, visit `https://lambdalabs.com/`, click the **Create Account** button, and follow the process. Once signed in, add a payment method (e.g., a credit card) and billing information in the settings:

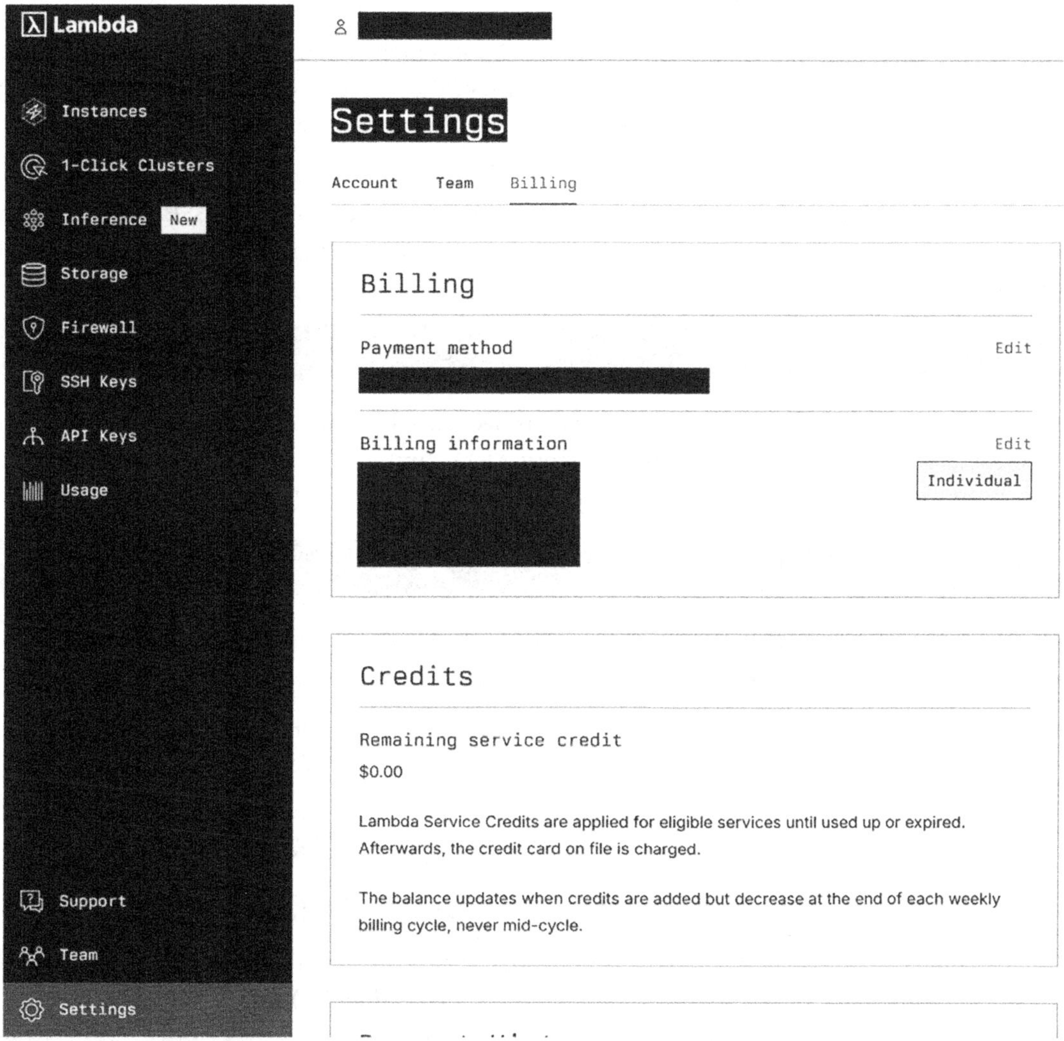

Figure 2.6 – Add billing information and a payment method in Lambda Labs

It is also best practice to set up **multi-factor authentication** (**MFA**) to secure the account.

Then, set up an instance. Go to **Instances** and click on **Launch instance**. Go through the form for selecting an instance type (type of GPU, number of CPU cores, amount of RAM, and amount of storage) with an associated price. For this demo, an instance was chosen with an A100 GPU, 30 CPU cores, 214 GB of RAM, and 550 GB of SSD storage for 1.24 dollars per hour. Pick a region, ideally one that is closest to you geographically, to minimize latency.

Then, select a filesystem or create one. This is the volume on which data can be persisted across sessions, so that data can be reused in another VM at a later point. Think of a volume like an external cloud hard drive. Note that volumes incur monthly charges for the data they store: 0.20 US dollars per GB per month at the time of writing. A VM can also be created without mounting a persisted filesystem, but then no data will be persisted.

Finally, to get remote access to the VM, provide an SSH public key. Create an SSH key pair if you do not already have one. On Linux, Mac, or WSL, open a terminal. On Windows, open PowerShell or Command Prompt. Then, run the following:

```
ssh-keygen
```

Follow and respond to the remaining questions as needed. A key pair, in the form of two files, will be created in the `<user_home>/.ssh>` directory. On Linux and Mac, fetch the public key by running the following in a terminal and copying the output to the clipboard:

```
cat ~/.ssh/id_rsa.pub
```

On Windows, fetch the public key by opening the `C:\Users\<user_name>\.ssh\id_rsa.pub` file with a program such as Notepad and copying the entire contents.

After clicking **OK**, the instance will boot. This can take a few minutes. Once it is running, the following information will be displayed in the instances table:

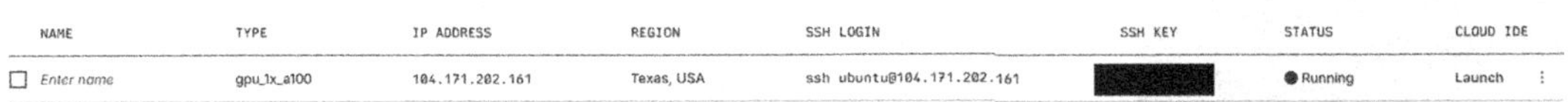

Figure 2.7 – A running instance in the Lambda UI

The machine can be accessed through SSH or JupyterLab. To access the machine via SSH, in the terminal (Linux/Mac), or Command Prompt or PowerShell (Windows), run the following:

```
ssh ubuntu@<ip address of instance>
```

If a valid SSH key was provided in the setup, the terminal should now be connected to the VM. The setup of the NVIDIA driver is already done, which can be confirmed by running `nvidia-smi`:

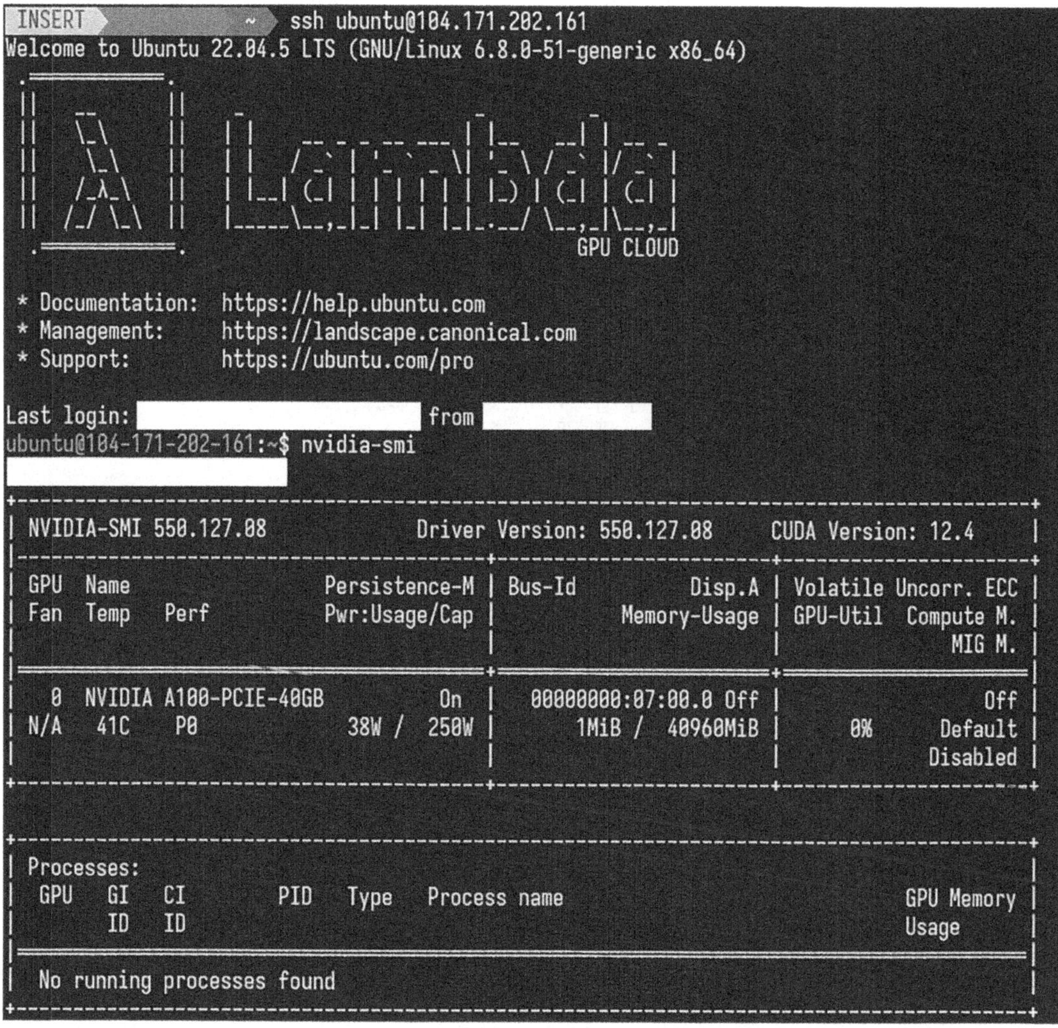

Figure 2.8 – SSH access to the Lambda instance

This SSH connection can be used to do remote development with an editor or **integrated development environment (IDE)** of choice. PyCharm and VS Code support this functionality.

To get access to the JupyterLab interface, simply click on **Launch** under **Cloud IDE**. This will open a separate tab with JupyterLab running on the VM:

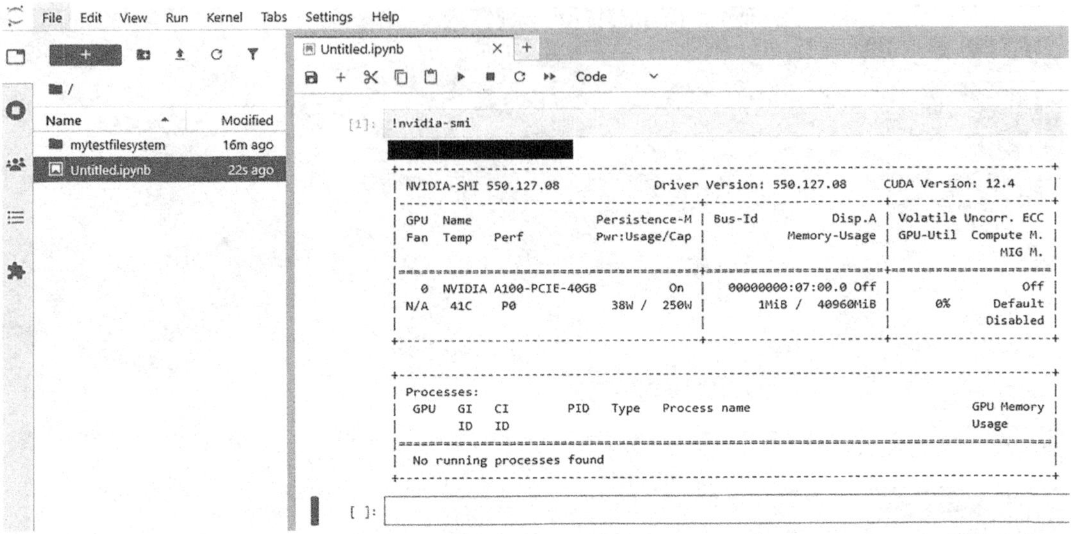

Figure 2.9 – Jupyter Lab interface to the Lambda instance

Here, notebooks and files can be created or uploaded as expected. If a filesystem was created during the setup step, there will be an extra folder in the file explorer, in this example, `mytestfilesystem`. Only what is saved in this folder will be persisted across sessions; everything else will be gone when the instance is terminated.

After creating a notebook, the default Python 3 kernel will be active. CUDA and most libraries that are needed are installed by default. Some libraries used in this book, such as `cupy`, may not be installed.

There are two options for configuring the environment.

The first option is to connect with SSH (or open the terminal in the JupyterLab interface) and run `pip install` to install missing dependencies. This is simple, but the downside is that there is no guarantee that the environment will work the same way as the one used to make this book. In addition, none of the dependencies will persist after terminating the instance.

The second, and preferred, option is to create a custom environment with all dependencies using Pixi. To ensure this environment has persisted, create it inside the mounted folder. To set up the environment, follow the same instructions as those for a local Linux machine, which can be found in the *Linux (Ubuntu 24.04 LTS)* section in this chapter.

To make this environment visible to Jupyter as a kernel, inside the folder containing the `pyproject.toml` and `pixi.lock` files, run the following:

```
$ pixi shell
$ python -m ipykernel install --user \
  --display-name "Python 3 (python_cuda)"
```

Refresh the JupyterLab page, and now the new kernel should be visible. This last step will have to be repeated if the session is terminated and later resumed.

It is very important to terminate instances when they are no longer used. A GPU instance of 1.5 dollars per hour costs over *1,000 dollars per month* to keep running at all times. After terminating an instance, it will disappear from the overview, and it will no longer be billed to the user. To resume work, simply follow the same steps for creating a new instance, but mount the existing filesystem with the persisted data. However, instances must always be chosen in the same region to be able to mount the filesystem. The persisted data will be stored until the filesystem is deleted in the **Filesystems** tab. When the filesystem is not mounted to a VM, it will show up in the UI as follows:

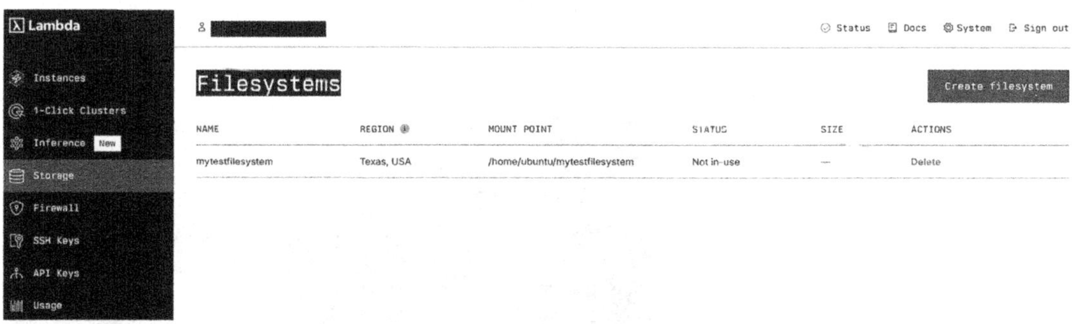

Figure 2.10 – The unmounted filesystem

Delete the persisted data if it is no longer used, since keeping it active will incur a monthly fee for storage.

In short, Lambda Labs provides a very convenient service to get quick, frictionless access to top GPUs for a reasonable price. A cloud VM provides full flexibility on what can be installed and run. While it can be described as cheap, be mindful that *cheap* is a relative term; forgetting to turn off instances will be very costly. Creating and setting up new instances each time can be a bit more cumbersome than owning hardware. Finally, Lambda is a small company that runs its own data centers; the availability of instances can be limited as demand often outstrips supply.

AWS EC2

AWS is the market leader in providing cloud services. Compared to other cloud providers, AWS is not cheap, but most professionals will have to interact with AWS at some point in their careers. Therefore, we will also walk through the process of creating a GPU VM on AWS.

The process is quite a bit more convoluted than getting an instance on Lambda Labs. The AWS UI is notorious for being complicated and unfriendly to users. The advantage is that AWS is a much bigger cloud provider, with near-limitless availability and flexibility. **Elastic Compute Cloud (EC2)** is the service inside AWS in which VMs are provisioned. Therefore, these VMs are often called EC2 machines.

The method described in this section is best suited for when an active or corporate AWS account is available. It is much more difficult to set up the environment on a fresh AWS account because AWS does not give fresh accounts the ability to launch EC2 machines with a GPU.

To get access to the services of AWS, first create an account. Visit `https://aws.amazon.com/` and click on the **Sign In to the Console** button. This opens the following page:

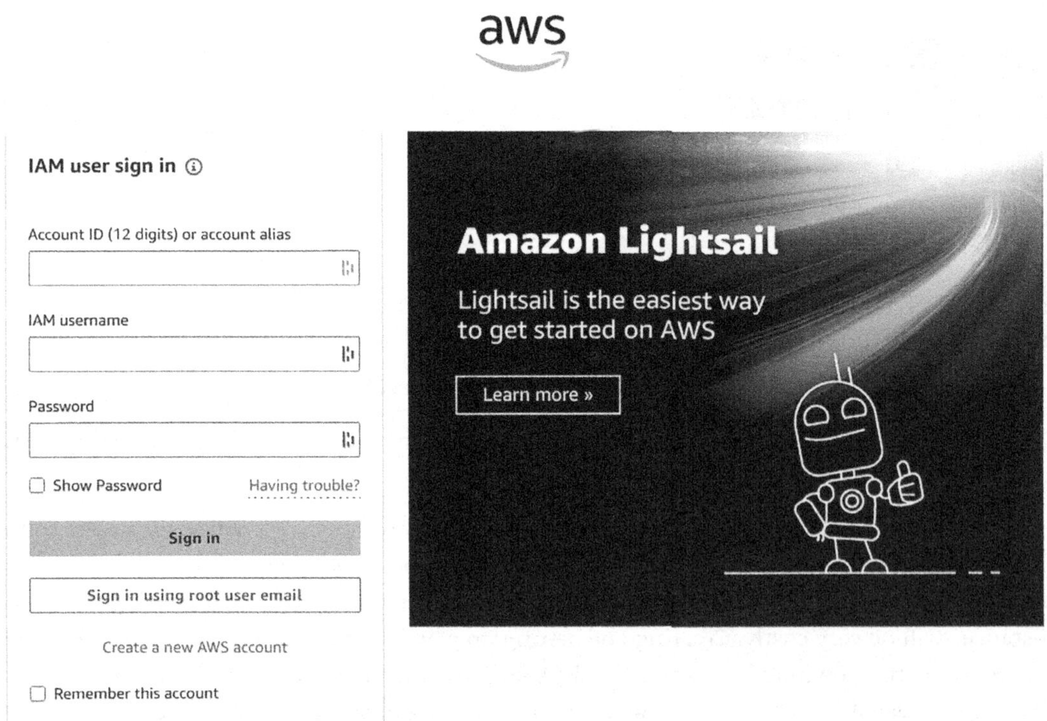

Figure 2.11 – AWS login page

Click on **Create a new AWS account**. Follow the instructions through the signup process. An email address must be provided and validated. Additionally, personal contact details and a credit card must be provided. At the end of the signup process, there is a button that takes us to the console, which is the entry point to all AWS services:

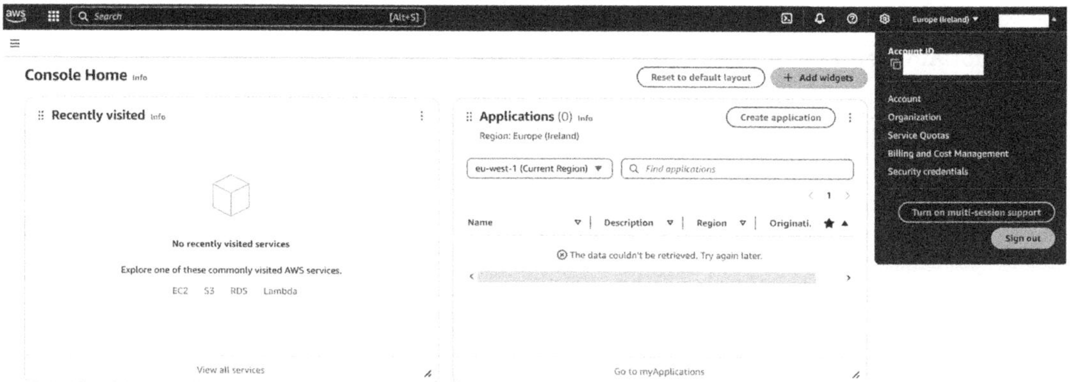

Figure 2.12 – AWS console

For security, it's best to set up MFA. In the search bar, search for `IAM`. In the IAM service, click on the **Add MFA** button and follow the instructions:

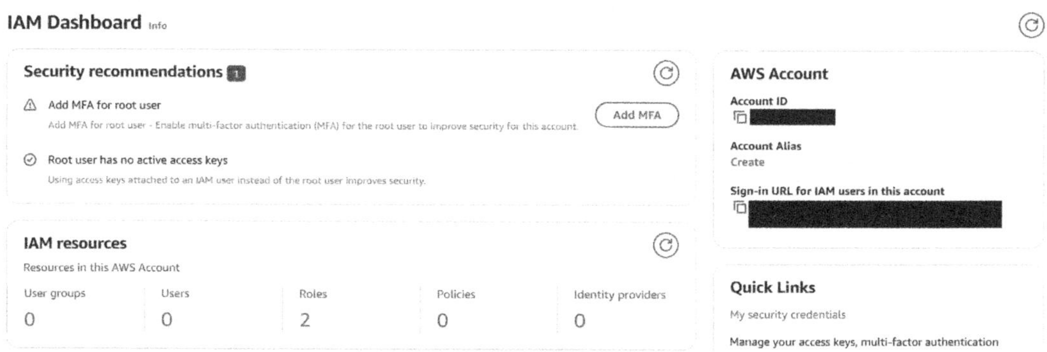

Figure 2.13 – AWS IAM

Optionally, inside IAM, create an IAM user for logging in to the AWS console. Since this account is for personal use, this is not strictly necessary; it is always possible to log in with the root email and password.

In a fresh AWS account, GPU instances cannot be used immediately; first, a manual quota increase request must be made. In the search bar, search for `Service quotas`. Then, go to the quotas for **Amazon Elastic Compute Cloud (Amazon EC2)**. Then, search for the quota related to G and VT instances, and click on **Running On-Demand G and VT instances**:

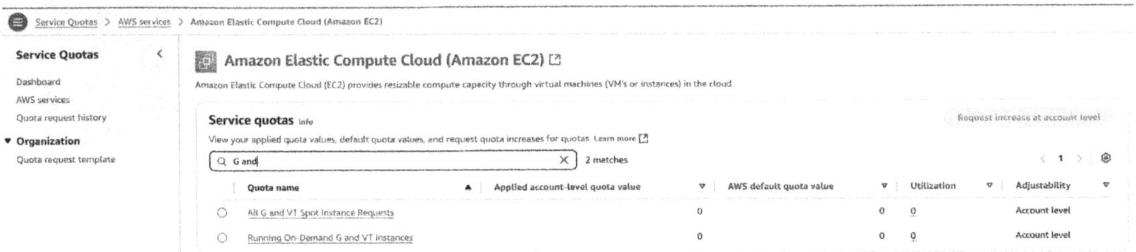

Figure 2.14 – AWS service quota

Then, click to request a quota increase and set it to 1. Wait until AWS reviews the case. A request made on an active AWS account will likely be approved. However, on a fresh AWS account, the request may be denied, and getting this reversed requires convincing AWS support to reverse the decision.

Once the quota increase has been granted, a VM can be provisioned. In the console search bar, search for EC2. In the top-right corner, select the AWS Region that is closest geographically; this is the Region where the VM will be hosted. Once inside EC2, click on **Launch instance**. On the subsequent page, give the VM a name and select **Ubuntu** as the operating system:

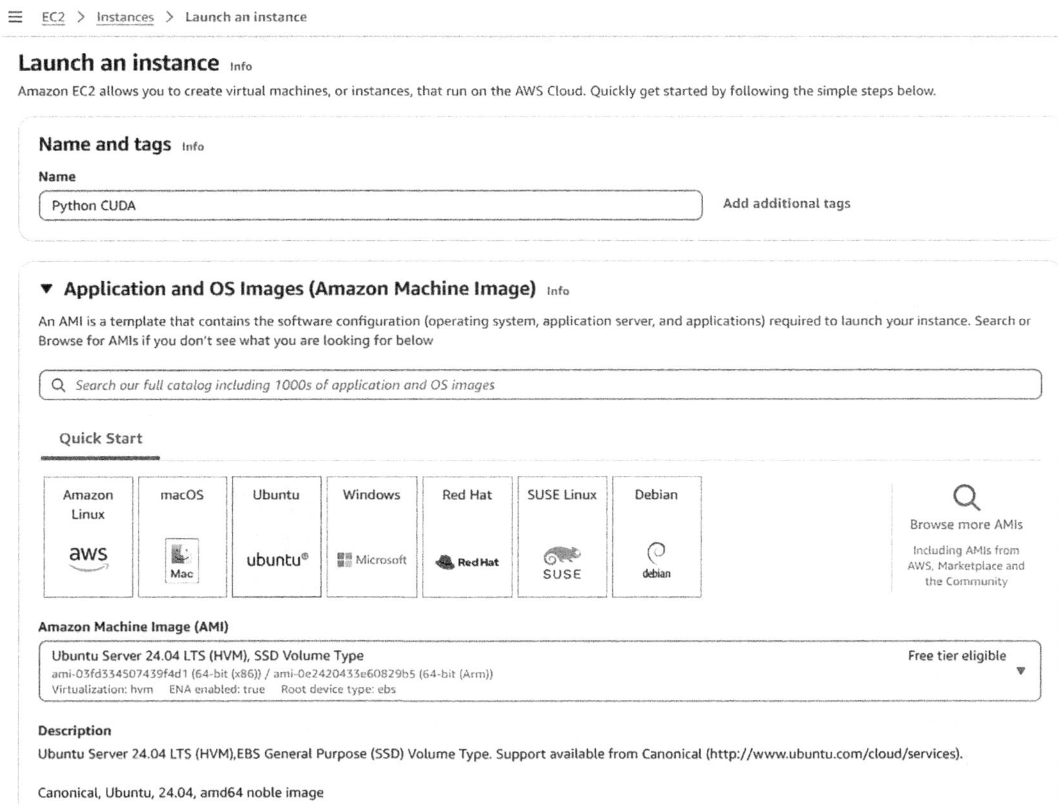

Figure 2.15 – Selecting a name and operating system for the EC2 machine

For the instance type, search for instances that start with `g4ad`. These instances provide access to the less-powerful NVIDIA T4 GPUs and are quite affordable, starting at around 0.5 dollars per hour. A `g4ad.xlarge` instance should be more than sufficient to work through the examples in this book:

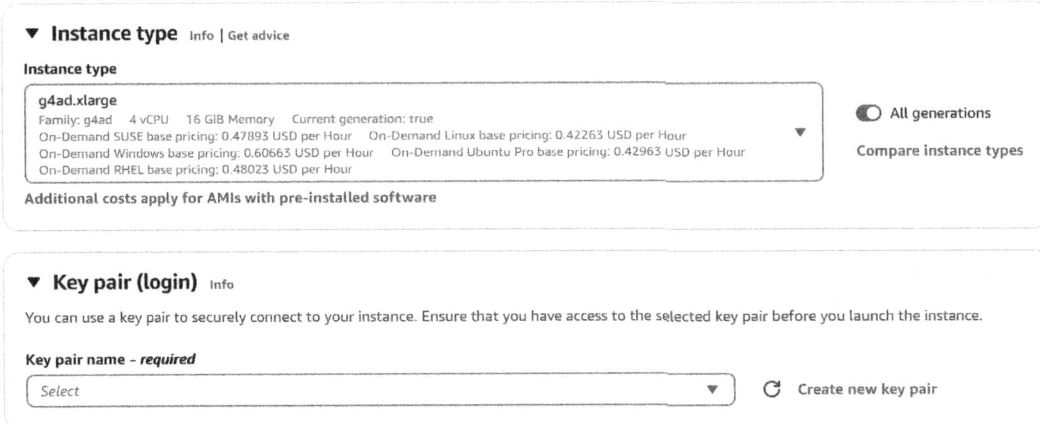

Figure 2.16 – Selecting an instance type and access key for the EC2 machine

Then, create a new key pair. This will prompt a download of the key. Keep this file safe, as it will be used to SSH into the VM!

For the other settings, the defaults should be fine. Launch the instance with the big **Launch instance** button on the right.

After a while, the instance should be in the **Running** state, and it will accept SSH connections. To demonstrate how the interface should look, a t2.micro instance (which does not have a GPU) was launched:

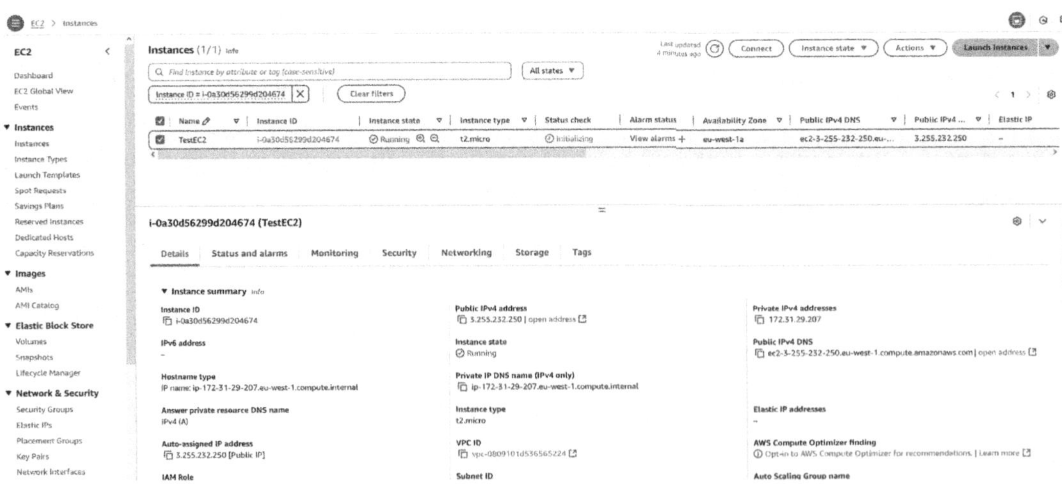

Figure 2.17 – Overview of running EC2 instances

To connect to the VM, run the following in a terminal:

```
ssh -i <path to downloaded .pem key file> \
ubuntu@<public IP v4 address>
```

If this is successful, the terminal should show the following:

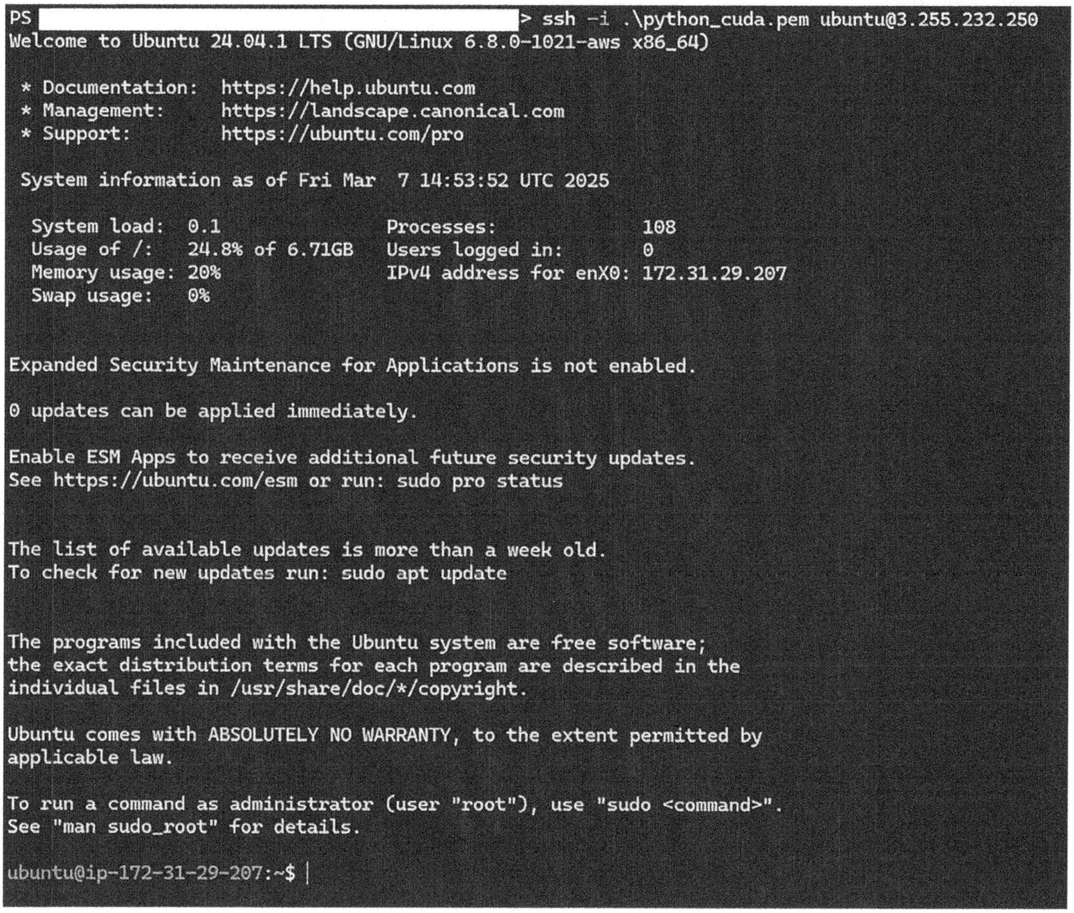

Figure 2.18 – Connecting to the remote EC2 machine with SSH

From here, follow all the same instructions as setting up an environment on a local Linux machine, as described earlier in the chapter. The NVIDIA driver will probably already be installed, so only Pixi and the CUDA and Python dependencies must be installed.

By default, the only traffic allowed to the machine is SSH on port 22. To run and access services on the VM, such as TensorBoard, JupyterLab, or Code Server, use **port forwarding**.

For example, to run JupyterLab on the VM, first SSH to the VM, then run the following:

```
pixi shell
jupyter lab --no-browser
```

In the output, there will be a browser link that is accessible on the remote host. In another terminal window on your local machine, run the following:

```
ssh -i <path to key file> -N -L 8888:localhost:8888 \
ubuntu@<public IP v4 address>
```

This will produce no output but bind port 8888 of the local machine to the remote machine. Click on the link in the output of the first terminal where JupyterLab was started. This should open JupyterLab in the browser of the local machine. A similar process can be followed for other services.

Be sure to stop the instance from the AWS console when it is no longer used. When the instance is turned off, no charges will be incurred. However, AWS charges for the storage volume (EBS) that is attached to the machine, which persists even when the VM is off. To stop all costs, the EC2 instance must be terminated by clicking on **Terminate**. By default, the EBS volume is also deleted when the EC2 instance is deleted.

Unlike the Lambda Labs VMs, stopped EC2 instances remain in the overview and can be switched back on at any time. Moving a storage volume to another EC2 instance is possible but not entirely trivial.

Summary

In this chapter, we demonstrated how to set up a development environment to do CUDA programming with Python, which will be required to follow along with the rest of this book. We explained how to configure a local environment on Linux, Windows, and inside WSL, which is applicable when an NVIDIA GPU is available. Data center-grade GPUs can be rented at a fraction of the cost using cloud VMs or services such as Google Colab. However, always remember to turn off VMs when they are no longer in use!

To easily install all the CUDA and Python libraries, we introduced the Pixi package manager, which creates reproducible environments and installs packages from the conda ecosystem.

Now that we have a working environment with which we can run scripts and notebooks, it's time to get our hands dirty. In the next chapter, we will introduce the basics of CUDA programming using `numba.cuda`.

Questions

1. Why do we use Pixi instead of other package managers, such as `pip` or `conda`?
2. Why can't we install the NVIDIA driver with Pixi?
3. Will the notebook created on the Lambda VM be persisted?
4. What problems might arise if we try to use `pip` to install the necessary packages?
5. Why do we launch JupyterLab on the AWS VM but not on the Lambda VM?
6. Why can we not access JupyterLab at `<public IP v3 address>:8888` on the AWS VM?

Answers

1. Pixi is a modern package manager that follows deterministic dependency management practices. It builds on the `conda` ecosystem. We can use it to install both the CUDA dependencies and Python packages in a fully reproducible way for multiple operating systems. This is much more complicated to do with any other package manager.
2. The NVIDIA driver is a low-level system dependency that is not distributed via `conda` channels.
3. No, it is not saved in the `mytestfilesystem` folder, so it will not be stored in my persisted volume.
4. We may get conflicts between packages and unexpected behavior due to a non-deterministic installation process. `pip` and `conda` packages should not be mixed unless necessary.
5. On the Lambda VM, it is already running by default for convenience.
6. Because the firewall rules on the EC2 machine prohibit all traffic on ports that are not 22.

Get this book's PDF version and more

Scan the QR code (or go to `packtpub.com/unlock`). Search for this book by name, confirm the edition, and then follow the steps on the page.

3

Writing and Executing CUDA Kernels with Numba-CUDA

Now that we have set up an appropriate environment, we are ready to start programming with CUDA in Python. Specifically, we will use `numba.cuda`, a key component of CUDA Python, to write CUDA kernels.

A CUDA kernel is a special function that executes in parallel on the GPU. Numba-CUDA compiles a restricted subset of Python code into CUDA kernels. It is a plugin for the Numba JIT compiler, which was introduced in *Chapter 1*. As our main working example, we will revisit the Julia set from *Chapter 1* and reimplement it to run on the GPU. Along the way, we will get an appreciation for the challenges of parallel programming compared to synchronous programming.

The learning outcomes for this chapter are as follows:

- Understand the CUDA programming model, including grids, blocks, and threads
- Translate a CPU implementation of an algorithm into a robust CUDA kernel with `numba.cuda`
- Allocate memory and manage data transfers between the host and device
- Make kernels modular with device functions
- Query the GPU device information
- Understand the features and limitations of `numba.cuda` kernels
- Simplify kernel creation and invocation for specific problems with `vectorize` and `reduce`

Technical requirements

To run the code in this chapter, an installation of the CUDA Toolkit and Python 3 is needed, including a number of Python packages, as described in *Chapter 2*. It is recommended to create a `pixi` environment based on the `pixi.lock` file in the GitHub repository associated with this book: `https://github.com/PacktPublishing/GPU-Accelerated-Computing-with-Python-3-and-CUDA`.

The details are explained in the `README.md` file.

Writing and executing a CUDA kernel

In this section, we will write and execute a **CUDA kernel** to calculate an image of the Julia set fractal from *Chapter 1*. CUDA kernels are at the heart of GPU programming. However, kernels behave very differently from synchronous programs, and writing them requires a perspective shift. To start, let's first go over the basics of the **CUDA programming model**.

The CUDA programming model

GPUs speed up calculations through **massive parallelism**, where a large task is divided into smaller subtasks. These subtasks are distributed across hundreds or thousands of GPU cores and executed simultaneously.

In the CUDA programming model, the parallel execution of a task is organized using a **grid** and a CUDA kernel.

The grid represents the entire workload, logically divided into smaller units of execution. It consists of thousands of **threads**, where each thread acts as an independent worker responsible for a subtask. Logically, all threads can run concurrently. Grids can be one-, two-, or three-dimensional, which can be convenient for a number of problems.

The grid is structured hierarchically: threads are grouped into **blocks**, and blocks collectively form the grid. All blocks within a grid have the same shape and size. The underlying reasons for this hierarchical structure are related to hardware details; these are discussed in *Chapter 5*. Blocks must match the dimensionality of the grid.

The **kernel execution configuration** defines how many threads are assigned to each block and how many blocks compose the grid. This configuration determines the total number of threads launched for the task. If the grid is 2D, the kernel execution configuration must specify the width (size in the x direction) and height (size in the y direction) of both the blocks and the grid. In the case of a 3D grid, the depth (size in the z direction) must also be specified for both.

The CUDA kernel is the function containing the logic executed by each thread. When the kernel is launched over the grid, every thread runs the same kernel code. The logic within the kernel dictates the specific actions each thread performs, allowing the GPU to perform the entire workload in parallel.

Before a CUDA kernel can be executed on the GPU, the necessary data must be transferred from the **host** (the CPU and its memory) to the **device** (the GPU and its memory). The host is responsible for launching kernels, managing data transfers, and allocating memory in device memory. The device performs the actual computation. After computation, the host can request to transfer the results back to host memory. Under most circumstances, the device cannot directly access data in host memory, and the host cannot directly access data in device memory.

Let's revisit the Julia set fractal example and see how these concepts work in practice.

Writing a CUDA kernel to compute the Julia set fractal

Recall from *Chapter 1* that the Julia set is the set of complex numbers z_0 for which the recursive relation $Z_{n+1} = Z_{n^2} + c$ converges. The constant c is a complex number that can be chosen arbitrarily; it determines the shape of the fractal. An intricate fractal image emerges when each pixel is colored based on the number of iterations that are required until the corresponding complex number diverges. The mathematical details are not that important; in essence, a complex function is applied over a 2D grid to generate an image.

In *Chapter 1*, we calculated the value of each pixel sequentially using two nested `for` loops; one for the y coordinate and one for the x coordinate of the pixel, corresponding to the imaginary and real components of z_0, respectively. The value of each pixel is calculated using the following logic:

```
pixel_value = 0
for iteration in range(1, max_iter + 1):
    if abs(z) > R:
        pixel_value = iteration
        break

    z = z ** 2 + c
```

By default, z is assumed to be part of the Julia set, and the pixel value is `0`. The recursive relation is then applied repeatedly to update z. If the magnitude of z exceeds the "escape radius," `R`, this means the sequence diverges, so z is not part of the Julia set, and the pixel value is set to the number of iterations. If a maximum number of iterations is reached, the default is assumed: z is part of the Julia set.

All pixels could be calculated independently of each other, and therefore in parallel. This is an example of an **embarrassingly parallel** problem; these types of problems are well suited for acceleration on the GPU. Instead of calculating each pixel value sequentially, each pixel value could be calculated by an independent GPU thread.

In this approach, we would need a grid with a number of threads equal to the total number of pixels in the output image. Because the desired output image is two-dimensional, a two-dimensional grid is a natural choice.

Next, we need a CUDA kernel. Since a kernel is the logic that is executed by each thread in the grid, the kernel should implement the pixel value calculation logic as described previously. To create a CUDA kernel with `numba.cuda`, a Python function must be decorated with `cuda.jit`, as follows:

```
from numba import cuda

@cuda.jit
def my_cuda_kernel():
    ...
```

Unlike a regular function, a CUDA kernel cannot return anything, nor can new arrays be created inside a kernel. Therefore, our Julia set kernel needs to be passed an input array, `z_0`, and an empty output array to store results in:

```
@cuda.jit
def julia_kernel(
    z_0: NDArray[np.complex64],
    julia_set: NDArray[np.int32],
    c: complex,
    R: float,
    max_iter: int,
) -> None:
    ...
```

Note

The NDArray type

The arrays passed into our kernel are annotated with the `NDArray[dtype]` type, which is a standard interface provided by `numpy.typing`. These type hints mainly serve for readability; they are not used by Numba.

We still need a way to tell threads which element of `julia_set` they are responsible for. Fortunately, each thread can access information about its position in the grid at runtime. The thread's position in the grid can then be mapped to positions of relevant data elements.

Inside a kernel, the global position of a thread in a 2D grid can be calculated as follows:

```
x = cuda.threadIdx.x + cuda.blockIdx.x * cuda.blockDim.x
y = cuda.threadIdx.y + cuda.blockIdx.y * cuda.blockDim.y
```

The `threadIdx`, `blockIdx`, and `blockDim` special variables only have a value inside a running kernel. `blockDim` contains the shape of the blocks, `blockIdx` contains the position of the block with the running thread, and `threadIdx` contains the position of the running thread relative to its block. To illustrate these variables, consider the 1D grid containing 3 blocks of 3 threads shown in *Figure 3.1*:

blockIdx.x	0			1			2		
treadIdx.x	0	1	2	0	1	2	0	1	2
x	0	1	2	3	4	5	6	7	8

Figure 3.1 – A one-dimensional CUDA grid with three blocks of three threads

In this grid, `blockDim.x` would be equal to 3. Each block has an ID, `blockIdx.x`, shown in the top row. Each thread in each block has an ID relative to the block, `threadIdx.x`, shown in the second row. Finally, the global thread ID in the grid, `x`, is shown in the last row. It's easy to verify that the preceding equation for `x` correctly relates all these quantities.

For 2D and 3D grids, all these quantities also have `y` and `z` attributes, which contain the index or shape in the corresponding dimension.

Because calculating global thread IDs is a very common and tedious calculation, `numba.cuda` provides a more convenient `cuda.grid(d)` function, where `d` is the number of grid dimensions. The function returns the global thread ID as a tuple. Hence, the following is an equivalent way to get the global position of a thread in a 2D grid:

```
x, y = cuda.grid(2)
```

Now, we can put everything together in the following functioning kernel:

```
@cuda.jit
def julia_kernel(
```

```
    z_0: NDArray[np.complex64],
    julia_set: NDArray["int32"],
    c: complex,
    R: float,
    max_iter: int,
) -> None:
    x, y = cuda.grid(2)

    z = z_0[y, x]

    for iteration in range(1, max_iter + 1):
        if abs(z) > R:
            julia_set[y, x] = iteration
            return

        z = z ** 2 + c

    julia_set[y, x] = 0
```

When this kernel is launched, each thread stores its own position in the grid in local variables, `x` and `y`. Local variables are stored in **registers**, which are private memory locations for each thread. The `x` and `y` coordinates are used to load an element from the `z_0` input array into a local variable, `z`. Then, the kernel performs the desired pixel value calculation, updating `z` in a loop as discussed earlier. If the divergence criterion is met, the corresponding element in the `julia_set` output array is set to the number of iterations, and the thread is terminated with `return`. If no `return` is encountered in the `for` loop, the corresponding element in the `julia_set` array is set to `0`.

This kernel is functional, but does not yet follow the best practices. We will have a look at how to make this kernel more robust later in this chapter.

First, we will learn how to execute kernels.

Executing the kernel

A CUDA kernel can be invoked and run on the GPU as follows:

```
kernel[blocks_in_grid, threads_in_block](arguments)
```

The values between the square brackets constitute the kernel launch configuration. `blocks_in_grid` represents the number of blocks in the grid. `threads_in_block` represents the number of threads in a block. If the grid is 1D, these values are both integers; if the grid is 2D or 3D, these values must be tuples that represent the number of blocks/threads per dimension.

Before the kernel can be launched, the `z_0` and `julia_set` arguments must be initialized. `z_0` can be prepared on the host with `numpy`, as in *Chapter 1*:

```
a = np.linspace(-1.7, 1.7, 1200, dtype=np.float32)
b = np.linspace(-1.7, 1.7, 1200, dtype=np.float32)
A, B = np.meshgrid(a, b)
z_0 = A + 1j * B
```

Since a CUDA kernel can only operate on arrays that reside in the memory of the GPU, this data must be copied to the device as follows:

```
z_0_dev = cuda.to_device(z_0)
```

For the `julia_set` array, only an uninitialized buffer of device memory is needed, since the kernel overwrites all elements in the array. Therefore, since the output shape is the same as the input array and the data type is known, it can be allocated directly on the device as follows:

```
julia_set_dev = cuda.device_array(z_0_dev.shape, dtype=np.int32)
```

Directly allocating memory is more efficient, since no data needs to be transferred over the PCIe connection between the host and the device. However, these arrays are uninitialized (similar to `np.empty`) and may contain garbage data, so the data must be overwritten before use.

These device arrays can be passed into the kernel invocation. The other arguments are simple scalar parameters; they can be passed directly without explicit copying.

The final step is determining the kernel launch configuration parameters based on the problem size. Let us choose a block size of 16 by 16 threads:

```
threads_in_block = (16, 16)
```

The grid must be of the same shape as the input and output arrays, since the kernel mandates a one-to-one mapping between thread and data elements. Therefore, the number of blocks in the grid is calculated as follows:

```
blocks_in_grid = (
    z_0.shape[1] // threads_in_block[0],
    z_0.shape[0] // threads_in_block[1],
)
```

Note

Dimension ordering

The CUDA grid orders dimensions in the *x*, *y*, *z* order. In this example, the *x* coordinate is mapped to the columns (dimension 1 in the arrays) and the *y* coordinate is mapped to the rows (dimension 0 in the arrays).

The `julia_kernel` can now be invoked as follows:

```
c = -0.8+0.156j
R = 0.5 + 0.5 * np.sqrt(1 + 4 * abs(c))

julia_kernel[blocks_in_grid, threads_in_block](
    z_0_dev,
    julia_set_dev,
    c, R, 3000,
)
```

Recall that the value of `c` can be chosen arbitrarily; this value was chosen because it is known to generate a nice image. `R`, the escape radius, is calculated based on `c` as shown. It is calculated outside the kernel since it only needs to be computed once; if calculated inside the kernel, it would be computed independently by each thread.

To visualize the result, the data must be copied back to the host as follows:

```
julia_set = julia_set_dev.copy_to_host()
```

By plotting the result, we again get the same familiar fractal from *Chapter 1*, but this time, calculated on the GPU. Congratulations, you have written and executed your first CUDA kernel!

Figure 3.2 – Julia set (c=-0.8+0.156i) image of size 1200 by 1200 pixels calculated on the GPU

To summarize, to convert a CPU implementation to a CUDA implementation, the part of the logic that can be parallelized must be identified and isolated. This is the starting point for the kernel. The grid dimension is determined by the problem size. Indices of threads can be accessed inside the kernel at runtime and can be mapped to array indices. In some cases, such as the Julia set example, there is an obvious one-to-one mapping between data elements (e.g., pixels) and threads, which makes a GPU implementation straightforward. For other algorithms (e.g., sorting algorithms), creating an efficient GPU implementation can be highly non-trivial as it requires some degree of thread cooperation.

> Note
>
> **Mapping thread coordinates to data elements**
>
> In this example, the *x* coordinate of the thread in the grid was mapped to dimension 1 of the arrays, and the *y* coordinate was mapped to dimension 0. It is possible to reverse the order and map the *x* coordinate to dimension 0 instead; logically, this is identical. However, for performance, the choice of mapping is not arbitrary. We will revisit this topic in *Chapter 5*.

In the next section, let's look at how we can make our CUDA kernels more robust in dealing with situations where there is a mismatch between the grid and data arrays.

Dealing with a mismatched grid and problem size

In the Julia set example, an image of 1,200 by 1,200 pixels was generated, which required a grid that perfectly matched the output image. Unfortunately, this strategy does not always work. It is possible that the computational grid needs to be either smaller or larger than the output image. The current implementation cannot deal with either of these situations.

A grid that is (slightly) larger than the problem is very common, and therefore a scenario that must be dealt with in most kernels. Threads that do not map to valid data elements will attempt to access invalid data and crash the program.

The reason grids must sometimes be larger than the problem is that they must be constructed from an integer number of blocks, and blocks have multiple constraints on their size:

- Blocks can *at most* contain a total of 1,024 threads.
- Blocks should contain a multiple of 32 threads, for performance reasons, which will be explained in *Chapter 5*.
- Blocks can contain a minimum of one thread, but this will result in wasted hardware resources. The device can only process a limited number of blocks simultaneously, so a block size of 128 threads or more is often recommended.

> Note
>
> **Deciding the block shape**
>
> Depending on the problem, the block shape can have a big impact on performance. In practice, the only real way to find the best launch block shape is through experimentation and profiling. No universal optimal configuration exists, but blocks with a total of 128 to 256 threads are often used as a starting point. The selection of 2D or 3D block dimensions is typically informed by considerations such as memory layout, memory transactions, and the CUDA execution model. Details on these advanced topics will be discussed in *Chapter 5*.

In the Julia set example, a block size of 16 by 16 threads was chosen. This fits all criteria: the block has a total of 256 threads, which is a multiple of 32 between 128 and 1,024. Conveniently, 1,200 is divisible by 16, so an integer number of blocks perfectly matches the problem size.

If, however, the desired output image is 1,193 by 1,193 (a prime number), there is no way to create a grid that matches the size of the image unless blocks with 1 thread are used. So, the kernel must be adapted to deal with a grid that is larger than the output image.

Fortunately, this is a very easy fix: at the start of the kernel, each thread should check whether the indices it maps to are out of bounds. If so, the thread should exit with an early `return`. In the Julia set kernel, this can be achieved as follows:

```
...
x, y = cuda.grid(2)
if x >= julia_set.shape[1] or y >= julia_set.shape[0]:
    return
... # continue kernel here
```

Only threads that map to valid data are able to continue. Even though bounds checks carry a very small performance penalty, it is best practice to always include them at the start of kernels.

Note

Examples in this book

There are example kernels in this book that don't have bounds checks in the interest of conserving page space and kernel simplicity. For real kernels, always implement bounds checks.

This change in the kernel also requires a change in the way the number of blocks in the grid is calculated. Ideally, the grid is sized such that the number of threads doing nothing is minimized. There should not be entire blocks of threads with no work to do. To guarantee this condition, the block size in each dimension can be calculated as follows:

```
blocks_in_grid = (
    (
        (z_0.shape[1] + threads_in_block[0] - 1)
        // threads_in_block[0]
    ),
    (
        (z_0.shape[0] + threads_in_block[1] - 1)
        // threads_in_block[1]
    ),
)
```

When `z_0.shape[1]` is divisible by `threads_in_block[0]`, then the expression is the same as `z_0.shape[1] // threads_in_block[0]`. As soon as there is a remainder larger than `0`, the extra `threads_in_block[0] - 1` terms ensure that one extra block is added to the grid.

The grid can also be smaller than the problem. In the Julia set kernel, this would mean there are data elements with no corresponding thread, meaning garbage data is left in the output.

Firstly, there is a hardware limit to the number of blocks that can be in the grid, and therefore the size of the grid. If the problem is larger than this limit, the kernel cannot handle it.

The maximum number of blocks in the grid can be found by querying the **device attributes** by using the `numba.cuda.get_current_device()` method:

```
from numba import cuda

device = cuda.get_current_device()
```

This returns an object that has many attributes with information about the device, as in this example:

```
print("Max Grid Dim X:", device.MAX_GRID_DIM_X)
print("Max Grid Dim Y:", device.MAX_GRID_DIM_Y)
print("Max Grid Dim Z:", device.MAX_GRID_DIM_Z)
```

On the A100 GPU used to run these examples, this prints the following:

```
Max Grid Dim X: 2147483647
Max Grid Dim Y: 65535
Max Grid Dim Z: 65535
```

So, in a 1-dimensional problem, there can be at most 2,147,483,647 (2^{31} - 1) blocks, each with at most 1,024 threads. Luckily, problems this large are rare. The upper size limit of the grid should not be a major consideration, except on older devices where the limit may be smaller.

A grid that is smaller than the problem may also be chosen deliberately for valid performance reasons. In this case, the **grid stride loop** pattern is recommended, which generalizes the kernel to any grid and problem size. The principle is illustrated in *Figure 3.3* for a one-dimensional problem. The problem has 10 elements, while the grid has only 4 threads:

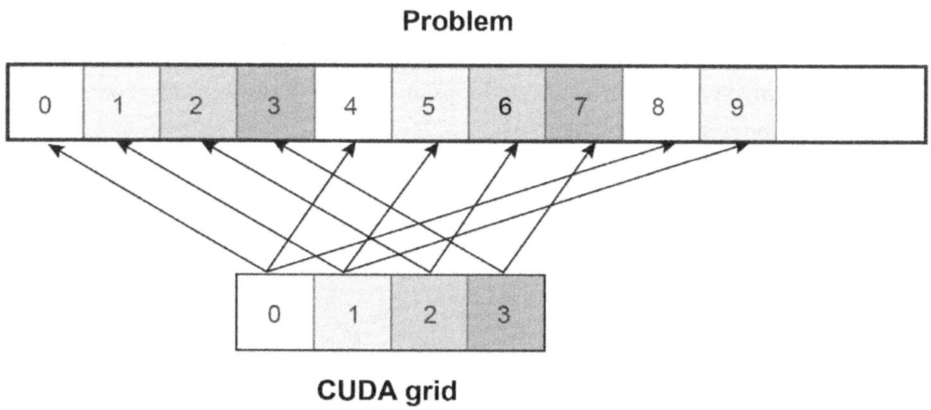

Figure 3.3 – Illustration of the striding technique when the grid is smaller than the problem

Conceptually, the grid is tiled over the problem. The key idea is that each thread becomes responsible for more than one element. This is done by introducing a loop in the kernel as follows:

```
x = cuda.grid(1)
grid_size = cuda.gridsize(1)

for index in range(x, n, grid_size):
    # read/write data using `index`
```

The special `cuda.gridsize` function is a shorthand for returning the total number of threads in the grid. It can also be calculated as follows:

```
grid_size = cuda.gridDim.x * cuda.blockDim.x
```

By passing `grid_size` as the stride to `range`, each thread loops over elements spaced by `grid_size` starting from the global thread index until the end of the array, as indicated in *Figure 3.3*.

The grid stride loop pattern also eliminates the need for additional bounds checking. In the dummy example of *Figure 3.3*, thread *0* sees `range(0, 10, 4)`, which corresponds to elements *0*, *4*, and *8*. Thread *3* sees `range(3, 10, 4)`, which corresponds to elements *3* and *7*. The pattern still works for grids larger than the problem: in-bounds threads will loop over a single element, and out-of-bounds threads will loop over no elements. The following blog post by NVIDIA gives additional details on the pattern: `https://developer.nvidia.com/blog/cuda-pro-tip-write-flexible-kernels-grid-stride-loops`.

In 2D and 3D problems, two and three nested loops are required, respectively. For example, in the Julia set kernel, this looks something like this:

```
start_x, start_y = cuda.grid(2)
stride_x, stride_y = cuda.gridsize(2)

for y in range(start_y, z_0.shape[0], stride_y):
    for x in range(start_x, z_0.shape[1], stride_x):
        z = z_0[y, x]
        for iteration in range(1, max_iter + 1):
            if abs(z) > R:
                julia_set[y, x] = iteration
                break

            z = z ** 2 + c
```

Now, we are familiar with some of the patterns for generalizing a kernel to different grid sizes. Next, let's have a look at making kernels more readable and modular.

Making kernels modular with device functions

Long and complex kernels are often difficult to read, reason about, and maintain. To improve modularity, parts of the kernel logic can be factored out using **device functions**. By breaking code into smaller components, both readability and code reuse are enhanced, as device functions may be shared across multiple kernels.

Let's illustrate device functions by using the Julia set kernel. The logic for calculating the next iteration of z could be calculated with the following small function:

```
@cuda.jit(device=True, inline=True)
def update_z(z: complex, c: complex) -> complex:
    return z ** 2 + c
```

By passing `device=True` to the `cuda.jit` decorator, the function is converted to a device function instead of a kernel. `inline=True` will ensure that when the kernel compiles, the device function logic is directly inserted into the kernel, which avoids the overhead of a function call. This device function can be called in the kernel as follows:

```
z = update_z(z, c)
```

Device functions can only be called from the device, which means from a kernel or from another device function. A device function can be recursive, i.e. it can call itself.

Device functions support all the same language features as kernels. For example, information about the grid and the threads can be queried. They are also subject to many of the same limitations; for example, no new arrays can be allocated. Unlike kernels, device functions can return values.

In summary, device functions can be used to make our GPU code more modular and readable.

So far in this chapter, we have only dealt with simple embarrassingly parallel problems. There are other types of problems in which threads are required to cooperate. This can introduce all kinds of problems related to **race conditions**. In the next section, we'll cover ways to guard against these problems.

Avoiding race conditions in CUDA kernels

In the CUDA programming model, all threads are assumed to potentially execute concurrently, with no predictable scheduling order. As a result, when multiple threads attempt to write different values to the same memory location, the final value becomes non-deterministic. Even simple operations, such as incrementing a shared value, are unsafe because it requires a *read-modify-write* sequence, which can lead to inconsistencies if threads access outdated values.

Race conditions may also arise when threads depend on data computed by other threads, as there is no guarantee that computations will complete in a specific order on different threads. While embarrassingly parallel problems avoid these issues, many algorithms require shared data access, making careful kernel design necessary to prevent race conditions. The following sections introduce the two primary mechanisms for managing thread cooperation: thread synchronization and atomic operations.

How to use thread synchronization

Thread synchronization is used when threads must wait for data computed by other threads in the same block. For example, it is often used when threads cooperate to populate an intermediate array, which is then used in further computation. Another application is in **reduction** kernels, as will be illustrated with an example. Without synchronization, faster threads may proceed with incomplete or outdated data, leading to non-deterministic results.

Thread synchronization acts as a **block-level barrier**: all threads in the block pause at the synchronization point until every thread in the block reaches it. This ensures that all threads complete a phase of computation before any proceed further.

Practically, thread synchronization is performed using the `cuda.syncthreads` function inside a kernel. Consider the following example kernel that calculates the blockwise sum of array elements, an example of a reduction kernel:

```
@cuda.jit
def block_add(arr: NDArray) -> None:
    idx = cuda.grid(1)
    tid = cuda.threadIdx.x
    block_size = cuda.blockDim.x

    stride = block_size // 2
    while stride > 0:
        cuda.syncthreads()

        if tid < stride:
            arr[idx] += arr[idx + stride]

        stride = stride // 2
```

Figure 3.4 illustrates how this kernel works for a very small grid of one block with eight threads:

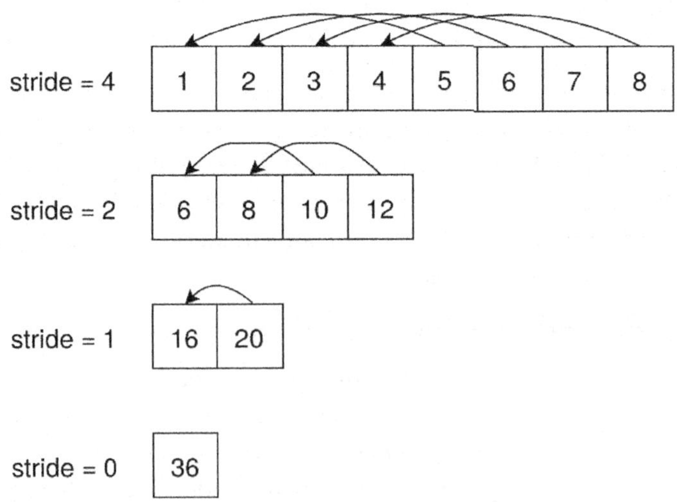

Figure 3.4 – Illustration of the block_add kernel

The algorithm works by iteratively halving the stride between elements. In each step, threads add the element at a distance of the current stride to their own element. The stride is halved after each step, and synchronization ensures that all threads complete their additions before the next iteration. After the final step, the sum of all elements in the block is stored in the first element.

The kernel is executed for this small grid as follows:

```
input_array = np.arange(1.0, 9.0, dtype=np.float32)
input_dev = cuda.to_device(input_array)
block_add[1, 8](input_dev)
output = input_dev.copy_to_host()
```

Note

Kernel generalizability

This kernel will only work for blocks that have a number of threads that is a power of 2, and when all threads map to valid data. Additional bounds checks are necessary to generalize the kernel.

This approach is very efficient. Instead of summing elements sequentially, which would require as many steps as there are elements, this method completes the reduction in logarithmic time relative to the block size. For example, a block of eight threads sums all elements in just three steps. This efficiency becomes more significant as the block size increases.

Thread synchronization is crucial in this algorithm. After each stride, all threads must wait at a synchronization barrier to ensure that every thread has completed its addition before the next iteration begins. Without this synchronization, race conditions could occur, leading to non-determinism and potentially incorrect results.

Thread synchronization carries a performance penalty, since fast threads will be forced to idle waiting for slower threads. For some algorithms, such as parallel reduction, there is no alternative, but they should only be used when required.

Using atomics

Atomics are CUDA's way to safely allow multiple threads to update the same piece of shared data. Consider the following kernel for calculating the largest value of an input array:

```
@cuda.jit
def maximum_kernel(array: NDArray, result: NDArray) -> None:
    idx = cuda.grid(1)
```

```
    if idx >= array.shape[0]:
        return

    cuda.atomic.max(result, 0, array[idx])
```

The kernel requires an input array and an output array with (at least) one element. The last line in this kernel is equivalent to a thread-safe implementation of `result[0] = max(result[0], array[idx])`. All threads that map to valid data verify whether element `0` in the `result` array is larger than their own element. This way, the thread that has the maximum value wins over the other threads.

The kernel is executed as follows:

```
arr = np.random.randint(1, 100, size=1000)
arr_dev = cuda.to_device(arr)
result = np.zeros(1)
result_dev = cuda.to_device(result)
maximum_kernel[5, 200](arr_dev, result_dev)
result = result_dev.copy_to_host()
```

The result can be verified as follows:

```
assert result[0] == arr.max()
```

Notice that, unlike thread synchronization, atomics work across the entire grid. However, this also means they carry a much bigger performance penalty. Whenever possible, prefer thread synchronization.

Note

Why use single-element arrays?

Recall that CUDA kernels cannot return values directly. Instead, results must be written to memory passed into the kernel. While scalar values (e.g., `float` or `int`) are passed by value and cannot be modified inside the kernel, arrays are passed by reference. A single-element array acts as a reference to a memory location, allowing the kernel to persist and return a single result.

Now, all the basic tools have been discussed to write CUDA kernels for any problem. The next section goes over the supported Python language features in Numba-CUDA kernels.

Language features that can be used in Numba-CUDA kernels

To understand the rationale behind the supported language features, it is instructive to first look at how `numba` creates CUDA kernels in the first place.

The CUDA kernels written using Numba appear as standard Python functions, but their execution follows a fundamentally different process. When a function is decorated with `@cuda.jit`, it is transformed into a `CUDADispatcher` object, which serves as the bridge between Python and the GPU-executable code. Upon invocation, the dispatcher inspects the types of the input arguments. If this is the first time the kernel is called with a specific combination of argument types, Numba-CUDA initiates a compilation pipeline to translate the Python function into GPU-executable code. The compilation process can be visualized as a multi-stage transformation, illustrated in *Figure 3.5*:

Figure 3.5 – A simplified diagram of the compilation process from Python function to GPU executable code

The Python function is first converted into LLVM **intermediate representation** (**IR**), a hardware-agnostic, low-level representation akin to assembly language. LLVM, a widely used compiler infrastructure, supports multiple programming languages (e.g., Julia and Rust) and provides backends for various platforms. Its IR enables cross-platform code generation.

Next, the LLVM IR is translated into **PTX assembly**, an IR understood by NVIDIA's **CUDA driver API**. PTX is not directly executable; instead, the driver further compiles it into **CUBIN**, the low-level machine code tailored to a specific GPU architecture. While CUBIN is not human-readable, PTX can be inspected for optimization purposes; this is a topic that is explored further in *Chapter 5*.

To optimize performance, Numba-CUDA caches the compiled representations (LLVM IR, PTX, and CUBIN). Subsequent calls to the kernel with the same input argument types reuse the cached version, avoiding recompilation. However, if the kernel is invoked with new argument types, the compilation process repeats. The combination of input argument types is uniquely identified by a **signature**, which maps compiled kernels to their corresponding input types. This compilation pipeline explains why Numba-CUDA kernels support only a limited subset of Python's features: the code is statically compiled to LLVM IR, which requires explicit types and excludes dynamic Python behaviors, while CUDA itself imposes additional constraints, such as the absence of recursion and limited object-oriented features.

With this understanding, we can now examine the specific language features supported by Numba-CUDA.

Types that can be used in a kernel

CUDA kernels are limited to types that can be efficiently represented on the GPU. Arbitrary Python objects cannot be passed to or created inside a kernel. Numerical fixed-size primitives such as `int32`, `float32`, `bool`, and `complex64` are supported and can be passed as arguments or created within the kernel. These values are usually stored in thread-local registers.

Fixed-size collections such as tuples and named tuples are also supported, as their memory layout is known at compile time. They are useful for grouping related arguments.

Dynamic collections such as lists, dictionaries, and strings are not supported, nor are custom Python classes. CUDA is designed for numerical array processing, where threads operate on individual elements in parallel.

Language constructs that can be used in a kernel

Numba-CUDA supports the most common Python syntax for basic control flow: `if` statements, `for` loops, `while` loops, and so on. At the time of writing, Numba-CUDA does not support `try-except`, the `with` statement, list comprehension syntax, the walrus operator, or generators with the `yield` statement.

Functions that can be called from a kernel

Numba-CUDA supports most of the common built-in Python functions, including `abs`, `len`, `zip`, `min`, `max`, and `range`, as well as functions from the `math` module. Even `print` is supported, which can be useful for debugging.

> Note
>
> **Be careful with printing from the kernel**
>
> If care is not taken, each thread in the grid will attempt to call `print`. In a grid with thousands of threads, this overwhelms the output. Always restrict printing to a subset of threads, such as only thread `0`.

Custom functions can be called inside a kernel, provided they are defined as device functions. Device functions are subject to the same limitations as CUDA kernels, including restrictions on dynamic Python features. They must be decorated with `@cuda.jit(device=True)` to indicate that they are intended for GPU execution.

Numba-CUDA does not support calling other CUDA kernels from within a kernel, a feature known as **dynamic parallelism**. While dynamic parallelism is available in CUDA C/C++, it is not supported in `numba.cuda`. This limitation means that complex algorithms requiring nested kernel launches must be restructured or implemented in another language.

The limited set of available Python features in CUDA kernels often results in code that appears primitive. Beyond basic math functions, most operations must be implemented manually using low-level constructs, which can make complex kernels verbose and hard to read. This issue can be mitigated by using device functions to modularize code or by leveraging higher-level primitives where available. The latter will be explored in the next section.

Alternative methods for kernel definition and invocation

Writing and executing CUDA kernels often involves a significant amount of boilerplate code. A grid must be defined, threads must be mapped to array elements, and data must be explicitly copied between the host and device. While this may seem cumbersome for simple operations, such as mapping a function to array elements and executing it in parallel on the GPU, this level of control is necessary for solving more complex problems and achieving maximum performance.

For common problem types where kernel-launch steps follow a predictable pattern, Numba provides shortcuts to abstract away some of this complexity. These tools use the same underlying kernel execution model, but reduce the burden of writing repetitive boilerplate code. This can improve prototyping productivity and reduce debugging time. However, the trade-off is a potential loss of fine-grained control over aspects such as the computational grid, which may impact performance in some cases.

Defining kernels with vectorize

One problem type that comes up often is mapping a function to all elements in an array. A CUDA kernel for such a problem typically has a one-to-one mapping between threads in the grid and output array elements. The Julia set kernel is an example of this type of problem.

For these types of problems, where a **user-defined function** or **ufunc** needs to be applied to all elements in an array, `numba` provides the `vectorize` decorator. The `vectorize` decorator can be used to generate code for the CPU, but also for the GPU by passing the `target="cuda"` argument. The following is the Julia set kernel rewritten using `vectorize`:

```
from numba import vectorize

@vectorize(
    'int32(complex64, complex64, float32, int32)',
```

```
    target='cuda'
)
def calc_julia_set(
    z: complex,
    c: complex,
    R: float,
    max_iter: int,
) -> int:
    for iteration in range(1, max_iter + 1):
        if abs(z) > R:
            return iteration
        z = z ** 2 + c
    return 0
```

Aside from the decorator itself, the code looks more straightforward than the original kernel. In addition, Numba-CUDA automatically deals with the compute grid. Instead of passing an output array and writing results to it, the value return syntax is required.

In the decorator, the types for which Numba should compile the kernel must be specified using a signature. The signature first states the type of the return value (`int32`) and then the types of all inputs in parentheses. These must be types that correspond to individual elements (i.e., they must not be arrays).

> Note
>
> **Type hints versus signature**
>
> The type hints in the function declaration are there only for readability. They are not used or understood by Numba. Numba only understands very specific types such as `int32` and `float32` provided in the signature.

To use `ufunc`, it must be passed a 2D array, `Z`, constructed in the same way as `z_0` before, with the regular kernel.

Then, `ufunc` can be called like a normal function:

```
result = calc_julia_set(Z, c, R, 3000)
```

We can verify that `result` is an array containing the expected Julia set data.

Note

NumPy array or device array as input

Both NumPy arrays and device arrays can be passed into vectorized functions and kernels. When NumPy arrays are passed, the device transfers happen automatically, and the result is also automatically transferred back to the host. Passing a device array will also return a device array. Explicitly transferring data and using device functions is generally preferred.

The `vectorize` approach significantly reduces complexity when calculating the Julia set on the GPU. It eliminates the need to manually define a CUDA grid or handle indexing within the kernel, as these details are managed automatically.

However, this convenience comes with trade-offs. The loss of control over the CUDA grid structure can negatively impact performance and memory usage. For example, the grid configuration can have a substantial effect on performance, as will be discussed in *Chapter 5*. While `vectorize` relies on Numba's default grid settings, these may not always be optimal. Performance measurements on a machine with an A100 GPU show that the original `julia_kernel` implementation runs in about 7 ms, while the vectorized version takes 15 ms.

In summary, `vectorize` simplifies kernels where each thread processes a single data element, such as in the Julia set calculation. However, not all types of work are suitable for this approach. In the next section, we will explore another specialized class of problems known as **reduction**.

Defining reduction kernels

As discussed earlier, reduction involves combining many elements into a single value using a binary operation, such as calculating the maximum, minimum, sum, or average of an array. Writing an efficient, parallelized CUDA kernel for reduction can be surprisingly complex due to the need for careful thread synchronization.

Fortunately, `numba.cuda` provides a convenient `reduce` decorator that automatically generates a reduction kernel based on a user-defined binary operation. This decorator works similarly to Python's `functools.reduce`: it defines a function that takes two values and returns one. The decorator ensures that this operation is applied across all elements of the input array, returning a single result. For example, calculating the maximum of an array can be done as follows:

```
@cuda.reduce
def maximum(a, b):
    return max(a, b)
```

```
a = np.array([1, 4, 2, 9, 3])
a_dev = cuda.to_device(a)
maximum(a_dev)  # returns 9
```

This approach achieves in a few lines what would otherwise require tens to hundreds of lines of code to implement an equally efficient reduction using a bare `@cuda.jit` kernel. The `reduce` decorator handles grid configuration, thread synchronization, and memory management automatically, significantly simplifying the process.

Summary

In this chapter, we learned about the concepts behind the CUDA programming model. We learned what a kernel is and how it can be launched on a grid of threads. The grid is composed of blocks, which are, in turn, composed of threads. We applied these concepts to write a GPU implementation for calculating a Julia set.

We then saw some patterns for writing more robust kernels that are flexible to the size of the grid, and applied them to our Julia set kernel. We looked at ways to make kernels more modular with device functions. We touched upon techniques for thread coordination for problems that are not embarrassingly parallel: atomics and thread synchronization. We looked at how `numba.cuda` turns Python functions into CUDA kernels, and went over the language features that `numba.cuda` supports in kernels. Finally, we looked at specific types of problems that we can solve with less code using `vectorize` and `reduce`.

Writing correct and performant CUDA kernels is not easy. Therefore, in the next chapter, we will look at profiling and debugging GPU code.

Questions

1. In a 1D grid, what will be the values of the `y` and `z` indices of threads and blocks? What about the dimensions?
2. When the grid is smaller than the problem, why do we use strides instead of assigning multiple consecutive elements to the same thread?
3. Explain how the `block_add` kernel performs a reduction operation. Why is thread synchronization necessary in this kernel, and what would happen if it were omitted?
4. When might you want to use dynamic parallelism? Since you can't do this with `numba`, what would be another way to achieve the same?

Answers

1. If you were to call `cuda.grid(3)` when dealing with a 1D grid, you will still get a `y` and `z` index for a thread. However, they will be `0`. Dimensions will be `1`.
2. If you give the consecutive element approach a try, you will quickly realize that it is much more complicated to implement to deal with all the edge cases. Striding is a very natural approach that works for any problem size. Additionally, it results in more efficient memory access patterns, which is something we will discuss further in *Chapter 5*.
3. The `block_add` kernel performs a reduction by iteratively halving the stride between elements and having threads add pairs of elements. Thread synchronization (`cuda.syncthreads()`) is necessary to ensure that all threads complete their additions at each stride before moving to the next step. Without synchronization, faster threads might proceed with outdated data, leading to race conditions and incorrect results.
4. Dynamic parallelism is useful for problems where we don't know ahead of time what the required parallelism will be. Often these are recursive problems, such as when you want to call the kernel from itself using a different grid size. This comes up in problems such as sorting, graph algorithms, reductions, and many more. The alternative way to get the same result is to launch the kernel multiple times with different configurations (i.e., use the result from one launch to launch the next). These types of algorithms are complex to design and implement.

4

Profiling and Debugging CUDA Code

Developing efficient CUDA applications involves much more than simply running code on a GPU. It requires identifying performance bottlenecks, analyzing kernel execution behavior, and optimizing data access patterns. This chapter particularly focuses on the tools and techniques for profiling and debugging CUDA programs to detect such bottlenecks. Once these are identified, we can apply targeted optimizations to improve performance.

We'll begin by discussing why profiling and debugging are important and why this is challenging on the GPU. Then, we'll demonstrate basic profiling tools available in Python and Linux environments. Next, we'll explore NVIDIA's dedicated tools, **Nsight Systems** and **Nsight Compute**, which enable detailed tracing and performance analysis of CUDA code at both the system and kernel levels. Finally, we'll cover simple but still useful debugging utilities for Numba-CUDA kernels.

By the end of this chapter, you will have learned about the following:

- The basics and challenges of GPU profiling
- Knowing key aspects in identifying bottlenecks in CUDA applications
- Using basic profilers to measure execution time and GPU resource utilization
- Profiling the GPU execution timeline using Nsight Systems
- Utilizing Nsight Compute to obtain in-depth and kernel-level performance metrics
- Debugging and inspecting Numba-CUDA kernels in Python

Technical requirements

To be able to run the provided example codes in this chapter, you will need a system equipped with an NVIDIA GPU. We use **Pixi** as a dependency management tool that installs all required packages, including the Numba-CUDA library. To set up the environment, simply run `pixi install` in the root directory of the book's GitHub repository. This will ensure that all dependencies are installed. Once the installation is complete, you can activate the environment using `pixi shell`.

To use JupyterLab, run the following command:

```
pixi run jupyter-lab
```

You will also need to install NVIDIA Nsight Systems separately to enable profiling and visualization of the CUDA stream timeline. You can always get the latest version from NVIDIA's official Developer site (`https://developer.nvidia.com/tools-downloads`) available for different platforms such as Linux, Windows, and macOS. To obtain NVIDIA Nsight Compute metrics, we rely only on the CLI outputs. However, Nsight Compute can also be similarly installed with a graphical interface for more detailed analysis and visualization.

The chapter's code is available on GitHub and can be accessed via this link: `https://github.com/PacktPublishing/GPU-Accelerated-Computing-with-Python-3-and-CUDA`. We recommend cloning the repository and following the instructions in the `README` file to get started on building the environment.

Why profiling and debugging matter

GPUs are massive parallel processors capable of executing tens of thousands of lightweight threads simultaneously. However, achieving peak performance is challenging and requires a deep understanding of how the GPU schedules threads, manages memory, and communicates with the CPU. Even small suboptimal memory access patterns or excessive synchronization can result in noticeable slowdowns that waste computational resources and energy.

This is where **profiling** becomes essential. Profiling reveals what our code is actually doing on the GPU rather than what we think it is doing. Particularly, it provides **quantitative** insights into performance behavior such as which kernels dominate execution time, how efficiently GPU resources are utilized, where memory bottlenecks occur, and how data transfers overlap with computation. Optimization efforts without profiling are often reduced to guesswork, as we may spend hours rewriting code that is already efficient, while the true bottlenecks remain hidden. Equally important is **debugging**, which helps ensure that kernels produce correct results and behave reliably under parallel execution because of issues such as synchronization, data hazard, and race conditioning. Debugging allows tracing kernel execution, inspecting thread states, and catching issues such as out-of-bounds memory accesses or race conditions that would otherwise be extremely difficult to reproduce.

In this chapter, we will learn how to base our optimization efforts on profiling measurements rather than relying on intuition alone. This is a recommended and systematic approach to performance tuning. We will begin with simple profiling and explore low-level profiling techniques while working through several examples to identify performance bottlenecks. GPU-specific optimization techniques will be covered in *Chapter 5*.

Challenges in GPU profiling and debugging

Profiling and debugging GPU applications pose challenges compared to CPU programs, as thousands of concurrent threads executing introduce new layers of complexity in understanding, controlling, and diagnosing program behavior. We will highlight a few of these challenges encountered in GPU profiling, such as asynchronous execution of threads, the heterogeneous nature of CUDA code, and the differences between GPU and CPU timing.

Asynchronous execution and concurrency

One of the core challenges in CUDA development arises from the **asynchronous execution** of GPU operations. When a kernel is launched from the host (CPU), control is almost immediately returned to the host thread, even while the GPU is still executing the kernel. However, this asynchronous execution also makes debugging and reasoning about program behavior difficult. For instance, a kernel that fails on the GPU might not immediately trigger an error on the host, leading to confusing or delayed crashes. Errors such as invalid memory accesses may not manifest until later synchronization points, obscuring the true source of the problem. As an example, later in this chapter, we will demonstrate that the Numba-CUDA simulator can detect out-of-range memory access errors.

Device versus host code separation

CUDA programs are inherently **heterogeneous**, combining two distinct types of code: **host** code, which runs on the CPU, and **device** code, which executes on the GPU. These two environments have separate memory spaces, execution models, and debugging mechanisms. A bug might appear to originate in one but actually be caused by the other. For example, incorrect memory access or improper synchronization between host and device operations can cause data inconsistencies, where the GPU operates on stale or incomplete data. Debugging across this boundary is often hard because standard CPU debuggers cannot directly inspect GPU thread states or device memory. We will discuss NVIDIA profiling tools, which are needed to step through device code, inspect kernel variables, and correlate GPU execution back to the host control flow.

CPU time versus GPU time

Another subtle challenge is understanding the difference between CPU time and GPU time. When profiling CPU programs, timing is relatively straightforward. In CUDA, however, the CPU and GPU execute independently and often concurrently. This means that the CPU's perception of elapsed time does not necessarily represent the actual time the GPU spent executing a kernel. For example, the CPU might launch multiple kernels in quick succession, while the GPU queues and executes them later. As a result, a simple wall-clock timer on the host can sometimes misrepresent the true performance characteristics of the GPU portion of the code. To accurately measure GPU execution time, we must rely on **CUDA events** or timeline profiling, which records timestamps directly on the device.

> Note
>
> While the CPU executes instructions and the runtime generally reflects program activity, modern CPUs employ advanced techniques such as out-of-order execution, speculative execution, and instruction-level parallelism to increase efficiency, allowing them to execute instructions more flexibly and effectively than a strictly sequential model would suggest.

Key performance aspects in profiling CUDA applications

In what follows, we briefly discuss the most common performance bottlenecks that we may encounter when profiling GPU applications.

Memory transfer between host and device

One of the most common performance limitations in GPU applications comes from data movement between the host and the GPU device, for example, via PCIe. Transferring data from the host to GPU memory is generally an expensive operation in terms of time, and inefficient transfers can quickly dominate kernel execution time. Tools such as NVIDIA Nsight Systems provide detailed timing and bandwidth metrics for host-device transfers, helping us identify where host-device data transfer is slowing down the application.

It is also important to consider the type of **host memory** used. Transfers from **pageable** memory (regular system memory) are slower than transfers from **page-locked (pinned)** memory, which allows the GPU to perform **direct memory access** (**DMA**) without additional overhead. When using pinned memory, the memory is locked in physical RAM and cannot be moved or swapped out by the operating system. This allows the GPU's DMA engine to transfer data directly between host memory and device memory. In contrast, when data is stored in pageable memory, the operating system may move those pages in physical memory. Therefore, the CUDA runtime must first allocate a temporary pinned buffer, copy the data from pageable memory into this pinned buffer, and then perform the transfer to the GPU. This additional staging step increases latency and reduces effective bandwidth compared to direct transfer from pinned memory. For this reason, using pinned memory can improve data transfer between the host and device. More details about using pinned memory in CUDA streams will be available in *Chapter 6*.

Memory- versus compute-bound kernels

A CUDA kernel is said to be **memory-bound** when its performance is limited primarily by the rate at which data can be moved between GPU memory rather than by the number of arithmetic operations the GPU can execute per unit time. This means that if threads spend most of their time waiting for data, adding more computation will not improve performance. For example, a simple vector addition (`C = A + B`) performs one floating-point operation per two memory loads and one store. Such operations saturate memory bandwidth long before utilizing the computing capacity. In contrast, a **compute-bound** kernel performs a large number of arithmetic operations per memory access. In this case, the performance is limited by the GPU's arithmetic pipeline efficiency and instruction scheduling rather than memory bandwidth.

The **roofline performance model** helps visually distinguish between the memory-bound and compute-bound kernels by plotting the achieved *performance*, typically measured in **Giga** or **Terra floating-point operations per second** (**GFLOPS** or **TFLOPS**), against its *operational intensity*, which represents how many arithmetic operations are performed for each byte of data read from or written to memory (FLOPS/byte). This plot includes additional lines that represent the hardware's maximum memory bandwidth and peak computational performance, making it easier to see which of these limits constrains.

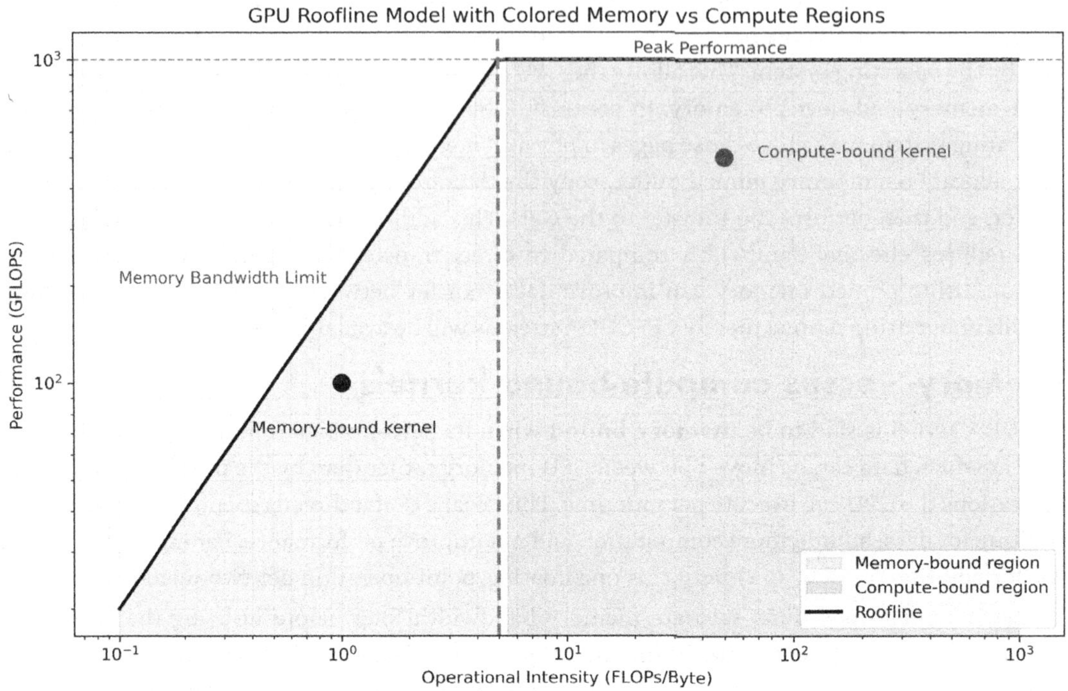

Figure 4.1 – GPU roofline model illustration

The preceding figure illustrates an example roofline model with two colored regions of memory-bound (blue-shaded) and compute-bound (red-shaded). We can easily determine for each kernel whether our optimization efforts should be focused on improving memory access or increasing computational efficiency. NVIDIA profiling tools can collect desired performance and memory metrics. These tools also allow generating a roofline analysis for any given GPU kernel.

A kernel's position on the roofline can be influenced by several factors, as follows:

- **Memory access patterns**: GPUs fetch data in wide, aligned chunks shared among threads in a **warp** (typically 32 threads). When threads access contiguous memory, requests are **coalesced** into a single transaction, maximizing bandwidth; scattered or irregular accesses are non-coalesced, wasting bandwidth and potentially making a kernel memory-bound.

- **Warp-level divergence**: This occurs when threads in a warp follow different branches in a conditional statement (`if` and `else`), forcing serialized execution and underutilizing compute resources, which can make a kernel compute-bound.
- **Occupancy**: This is the ratio of active warps to the hardware limit, which affects the GPU's ability to hide memory latency and fully utilize arithmetic units. Low occupancy or excessive per-thread resource use can reduce both memory and compute efficiency.

Profiling helps us pinpoint whether a kernel is memory-bound or compute-bound. These factors explain why some kernels are limited by memory bandwidth, while others are constrained by computational throughput.

In the next section, we will discuss how to use basic profiling tools available in Python and Linux environments.

Basic GPU profiling tools

Before discussing NVIDIA profilers, we make use of lightweight tools that can help us to get a quick sense of GPU utilization, execution time, and resource usage. We have already seen Python's built-in timing modules and the Scalene package in *Chapter 1*. These tools are useful during early development or smaller-scale experiments, where diving into the hundreds of metrics provided by a full GPU profiler is an overkill.

Next, we'll discuss a few categories of basic GPU profiling tools available to Python developers and Linux users.

Time profiling using the time and timeit modules

At the most fundamental level, timing our code is the simplest form of profiling. Python's built-in `time` and `timeit` modules are widely used for this purpose. The `time` module provides a straightforward way to measure elapsed wall-clock time between two points in the code. This is extremely useful for quick benchmarks and comparisons between different kernel implementations, as in this example:

```
import time
start = time.perf_counter()
my_gpu_function()
end = time.perf_counter()
print(f"Elapsed time: {end - start:.6f} seconds")
```

However, when timing CUDA code, we must be careful that GPU operations are asynchronous by default. That means the host (CPU) may continue executing before the GPU finishes its work, which affects the reported elapsed time when timing a CUDA kernel. To obtain a realistic measurement, we must synchronize the device before stopping the timer:

```
import numba.cuda as cuda
start = time.time()
my_gpu_kernel[blocks, threads](data)
cuda.synchronize()
end = time.time()
```

Without synchronization, the measured time may drastically underreport the true GPU execution time. This measurement not only captures the GPU execution time, but it also includes the kernel launch overhead on the host, operating system scheduling, and Python overhead.

The `timeit` module provides a more systematic way to measure short snippets of code by executing them repeatedly and reporting average execution times. This helps smooth out timing noise and provides a more stable estimate of performance. Although designed for CPU timing, it can also be used for GPU code with proper synchronization.

Jupyter has built-in magic commands, `%timeit` and `%%timeit`, which support a single line of code or a whole cell.

For example, we can write the following command in a Jupyter notebook cell:

```
%timeit my_gpu_function()
```

In this case, `my_gpu_function()` includes both the kernel launch and synchronization. `%timeit` will correctly capture the total time the GPU takes to finish the work.

The second form is as follows:

```
%%timeit
my_gpu_kernel[blocks, threads](data)
cuda.synchronize()
```

This is used when we want to measure several lines of code, such as launching a CUDA kernel and then explicitly waiting for it to complete. Adding `cuda.synchronize()` ensures that the timing includes the real GPU computation. Note that `%time` and `%timeit` only measure wall-clock time, and therefore, they don't distinguish between CPU and GPU activity.

Python profiler: Scalene

Scalene is a modern, line-by-line Python profiler that offers more metrics than simple timing. Scalene distinguishes CPU time, GPU time, and memory usage, making it particularly valuable for hybrid CPU/GPU workflows often seen in data science or machine learning.

Here's an example of how to use it:

```
scalene python my_script.py
```

Here's another example:

```
python -m scalene python my_script.py
```

Scalene then produces an annotated report showing how much time each line of the code spent executing on the CPU and GPU. This helps identify whether performance issues originate from inefficient CPU preprocessing, GPU kernel launches, or data transfer overheads:

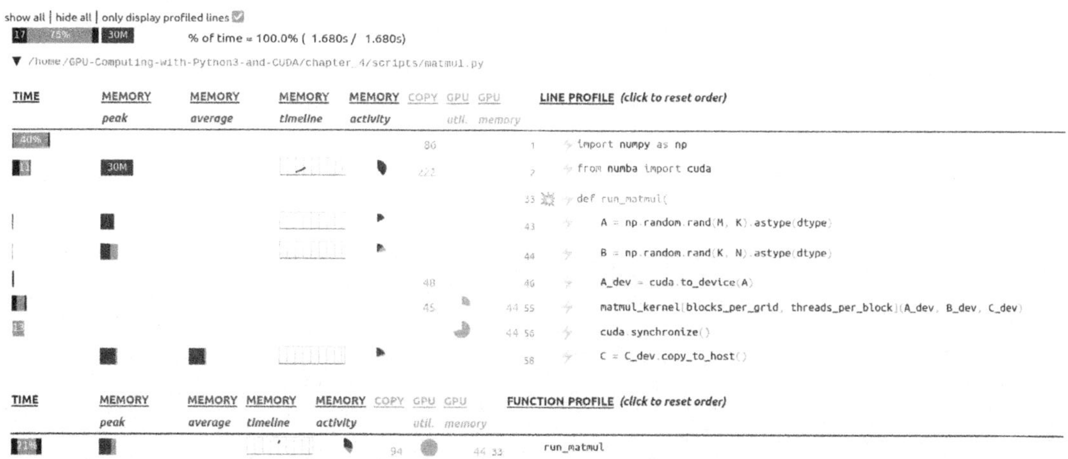

Figure 4.2 – An example of a Scalene profiling report

The preceding figure shows the Scalene profiler report for a Python script (`matmul.py`) that performs GPU-accelerated matrix multiplication using Numba-CUDA. The visualization highlights CPU, memory, and GPU utilization across different lines of code. Most of the reported execution time appears under `cuda.synchronize()`, which is expected because CUDA kernel launches are asynchronous, and Scalene attributes the kernel's actual runtime to the synchronization call that waits for GPU completion. This makes Scalene useful for analyzing Python overhead and memory behavior, but not for detailed GPU kernel performance diagnostics.

The `@profile` decorator is a convenient way to limit profiling to specific functions.

Here is an example:

```
@profile
def a_gpu_function():
    ...
```

Scalene focuses on high-level Python profiling; it cannot provide precise line-by-line profiling inside CUDA JIT-compiled kernels, since this is not possible for the Python interpreter. Also, it doesn't provide deep kernel-level metrics such as occupancy, instruction throughput, or memory coalescing. For low-level CUDA optimization, NVIDIA's Nsight tools are required. Nonetheless, Scalene is an excellent first diagnostic tool to determine whether performance issues are due to Python overhead or GPU execution.

Linux-specific GPU monitoring tool: nvtop

When running CUDA applications on a Linux system, monitoring GPU resource usage in real time is quite useful. Tools such as `nvtop` (NVIDIA `top`) provide system-wide insights, such as the Linux `top` command, but tailored for NVIDIA GPUs. `nvtop` is an interactive terminal-based monitor that displays GPU utilization, memory usage, temperature, power draw, and active processes. It provides a live, visual overview of GPU performance, including GPU usage (%) per process, GPU memory allocation, temperature and power metrics, and real-time graphs for activity:

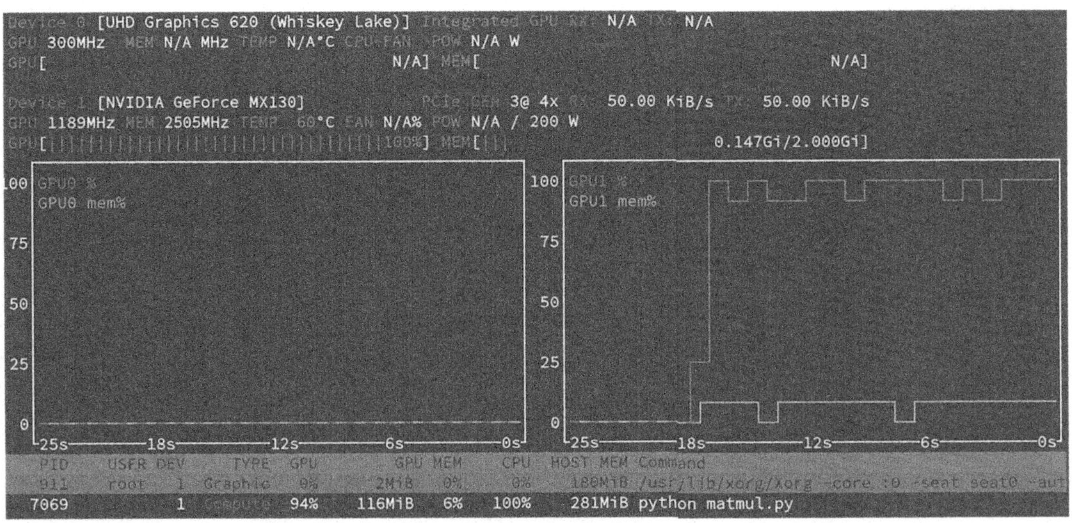

Figure 4.3 – Monitoring GPUs activity using nvtop

The preceding figure shows `nvtop` real-time GPU activity on a system with both an Intel integrated GPU and an NVIDIA GPU. The Intel GPU is mostly idle, handling basic graphical tasks, while the NVIDIA GPU is fully utilized, running at around 100% load with moderate memory use, indicating that it's actively performing computation for a Python process (`matmul.py`). This GPU monitoring tool is particularly useful when running multiple CUDA applications simultaneously or sharing GPUs in a multi-user environment. Similar tools for monitoring GPUs are `nvitop` and `gpustat`. These basic tools form the first layer of performance insight for CUDA applications. They help us understand overall timing, utilization, and high-level bottlenecks before moving on to deeper profiling.

In the next section, we will introduce Nsight Systems and Nsight Compute, which can dissect performance at the kernel and instruction levels.

NVIDIA Nsight profiling tools

NVIDIA Nsight provides a suite of specialized profiling tools designed to help understand and optimize the performance of CUDA and GPU-accelerated applications. Here, we will focus on Nsight Systems and Nsight Compute for performance analysis. Nsight Systems offers a high-level timeline-based view of application execution as it visualizes how CPU threads, CUDA kernels, and memory transfers interact over time. It helps identify performance bottlenecks such as synchronization delays, data transfer overheads, and suboptimal kernel launch patterns. This makes Nvidia Systems ideal for analyzing application flow, concurrency, and overall GPU utilization. Nsight Compute focuses on low-level kernel performance analysis. It provides detailed metrics on GPU hardware utilization, such as memory bandwidth, occupancy, instruction throughput, and cache efficiency, allowing us to pinpoint and optimize performance issues within individual kernels.

> Note
>
> **Legacy NVIDIA profiler for old GPUs**
>
> Before the introduction of the Nsight tool suite, `nvprof` (a CLI tool) and `nvvp` (**NVIDIA Visual Profiler**) were the primary tools for profiling and optimizing CUDA applications. They provided a basic timeline and metrics. However, starting with CUDA 11, both tools were deprecated and replaced by Nsight Systems for system-wide timeline analysis and Nsight Compute for detailed, kernel-level performance profiling.

In the next section, we will discuss GPU timeline profiling using Nsight Systems. After that, we will focus on *sections* and *low-level metrics* profiling provided in Nsight Compute.

Profiling GPU timeline with Nsight Systems

NVIDIA Nsight Systems provides a timeline-based view of a CUDA application's behavior across GPU activities (kernels, memory copies, etc.), CUDA API calls, CPU threads, and more. It offers both a GUI and a CLI, with the CLI generating a report that can later be loaded and analyzed in the GUI.

We can profile any Python script using the `nsys` command, a CLI for Nsight System, as follows:

```
nsys profile -o profiling-report python my_script.py
```

This generates a `profiling-report.nsys-rep` file, which can then be visualized using `nsys-ui`, the Nsight System GUI:

```
nsys-ui report.nsys-rep
```

The next two sections present profiling examples of vector addition and matrix multiplication to illustrate how NVIDIA Nsight Systems performs application profiling.

Vector addition example

Let us profile a Numba-CUDA code that adds two vectors to identify the bottleneck. The kernel to add two vectors can be expressed as follows:

```
from numba import cuda

@cuda.jit
def vecadd_kernel(x, y, out):
    idx = cuda.grid(1)
    if idx< len(x):
        out[idx] = x[idx] + y[idx]
```

The Nsight Systems profiling of this example, with two input vectors each with a size of 1,000,000 and `float32` precision, shows that most of the time is spent on data transfers between the host and device, as shown in the following profiling result:

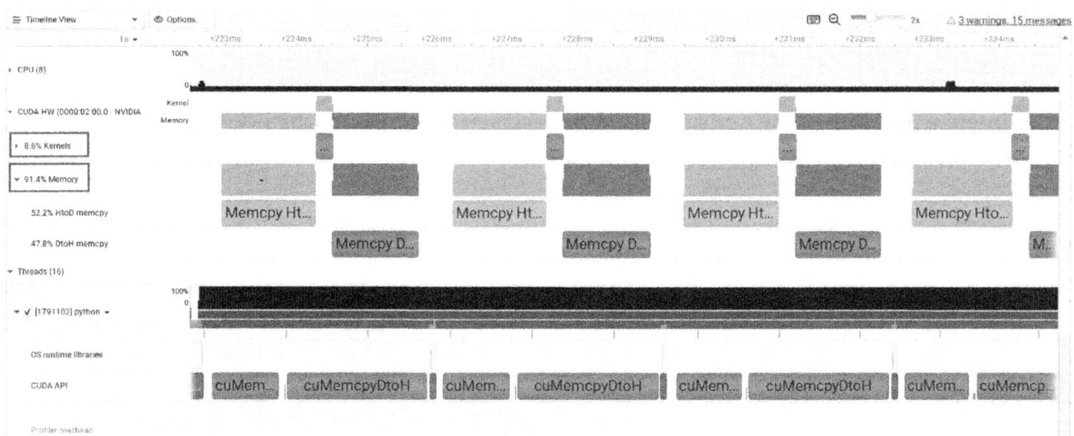

Figure 4.4 – GPU timeline profiling of the vector addition example

The timeline shows that 91.4% of the GPU activity is in the **Memory** track, compared to only 8.6% in **Kernels**. For a tiny compute workload such as vector addition, this is expected; the kernel work itself is trivial. The repeated **Memcpy HtoD** (green) and **Memcpy DtoH** (red) blocks dominate the runtime. This indicates that the bottleneck is host/device data transfer (PCIe-bound). Therefore, the optimization focus should be on data movement. To improve the statistics, our script repeats the data transfer and kernel execution 1,000 times. Each blue block labeled `vecadd_kernel` launches. The kernel execution is almost negligible relative to the data transfers.

Profiling reveals that vector addition does not provide enough work to saturate the GPU due to the low kernel activity. The transfers and kernels happen sequentially, and there is no overlap between *memcpy* and *kernels*. This can be improved by using multiple streams, a topic we will elaborate on in *Chapter 6*. Finally, the CPU is idle while the GPU is working as the CPU thread (Python) is mostly waiting on synchronous CUDA API calls.

Matrix multiplication example

Next, we profile an example of matrix multiplication. The following kernel is a naïve implementation of matrix multiplication:

```
from numba import cuda

@cuda.jit
def matmul_kernel(A, B, C):
    row, col = cuda.grid(2)
    ifrow< C.shape[0] andcol< C.shape[1]:
        tmp = 0.0
        for k in range(A.shape[1]):
```

```
            tmp += A[row, k] * B[k, col]
        C[row, col] = tmp
```

The timeline profiling of the multiplication between two matrices of the `(1024, 1024)` shape and `float64` precision is shown in the following figure:

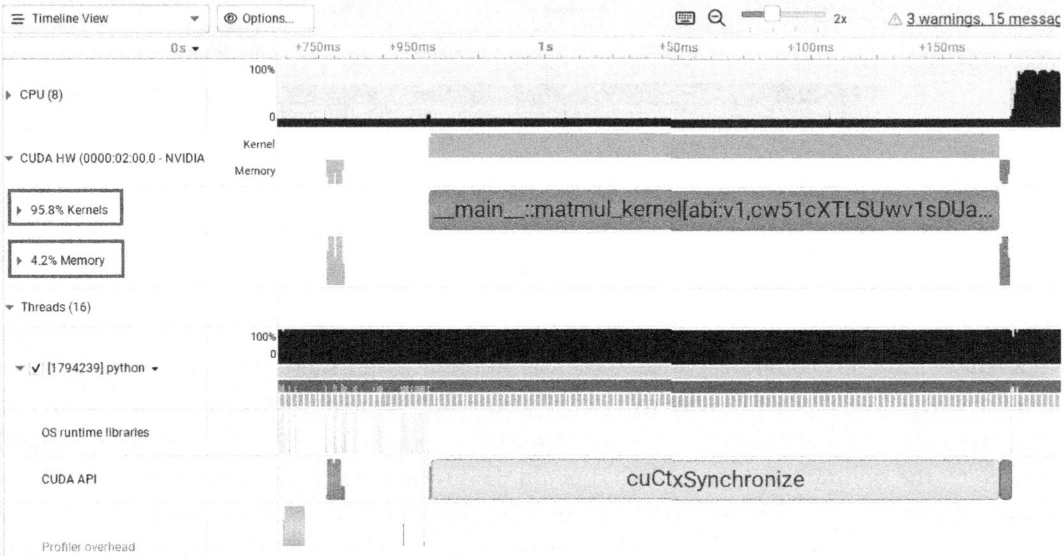

Figure 4.5 – GPU timeline profiling of the matrix multiplication example

A quick interpretation of the visualized results shows an increased kernel utilization compared to the previous vector addition example, since 95.8% of GPU time is spent in kernels and only 4.2% in data transfer between the host and the device. The long blue labeled block represents the matrix multiply kernel running continuously on the GPU. It keeps the GPU busy almost the entire time. This implies higher GPU utilization and not much Python overhead during the computation. The few green and red bars before and after the kernel are `Memcpy HtoD` (input matrices A and B) and `Memcpy DtoH` (output matrix C). The timeline under the Python thread shows it waiting while the GPU is running. This happens because of a blocking synchronization call. This is normal when we wait for kernel results with `cuda.synchronize()` or when copying data back to the host.

It must be noted that these results only show that most of the GPU's time is spent on the kernel execution rather than data transfer. However, it doesn't provide information on why this is the case or how efficiently this kernel runs under the hood. In the next section, we will use Nsight Compute to perform in-depth profiling of kernels and data movement.

Profiling sections with Nsight Compute

The output of profiling GPU kernels using **Nsight Compute Utility** (**NCU**) is divided into *sections*, where each is dedicated to a specific aspect of GPU performance, which helps identify possible bottlenecks. Note that sections give a **structured** view of GPU performance in terms of broad areas (memory, compute, occupancy, etc.).

The following table shows some commonly used profiling sections:

Section name	Description
`ComputeWorkloadAnalysis`	Detailed compute statistics: instruction counts, FLOPs, pipelines, and efficiency
`MemoryWorkloadAnalysis`	Memory access patterns: DRAM/L2/L1, bandwidths, and cache hits/misses
`Occupancy`	How many warps/threads/SMs are active, resource usage vs. capacity
`LaunchStats`	Kernel launch configuration, number of threads/blocks, grid size, and so on
`InstructionStats`	Instruction-level breakdown: types, counts, and classification
`SchedulerStats`	How the SM schedulers issued instructions, possibly idle/busy cycles from scheduling
`SourceCounters`	Correlates source code lines with metrics, stalls, branch efficiency, and so on
`WarpStateStats`	What each warp was doing (active, idle, or stalled), warp occupancy, and efficiency

As a showcase, we will use some of these sections for the matrix multiplication example to drill into possible compute, memory, or scheduling issues. Similar to Nsight Systems, `ncu` is the command-line interface for Nsight Compute, and a complete list of sections can be retrieved via the following:

```
ncu --list-sections
```

We begin by profiling the `ComputeWorkloadAnalysis` section using the following command:

```
ncu --section "ComputeWorkloadAnalysis" python matmul.py
```

This reports a table of relevant metrics and corresponding measured values:

```
Section: Compute Workload Analysis
------------------- ----------- ------------
Metric Name         Metric Unit Metric Value
------------------- ----------- ------------
Executed Ipc Active   inst/cycle        1.15
Executed Ipc Elapsed  inst/cycle        1.15
Issue Slots Busy               %       28.87
Issued Ipc Active     inst/cycle        1.15
SM Busy                        %       30.49
------------------- ----------- ------------
```

The profiling results on our naive implementation show that the GPU is not heavily utilized. Only about 30% of the SM capacity is active, and `Issue Slot` utilization (the percentage of time at least one warp is executing on an SM) is around 30%. This means that there is likely insufficient parallel work and/or the GPU is stalled and waiting for resources.

We can further profile this kernel using the `Occupancy` section, which gives us the following output:

```
Section: Occupancy
------------------------------- ----------- ------------
Metric Name                     Metric Unit Metric Value
------------------------------- ----------- ------------
Block Limit SM                        block           32
Block Limit Registers                 block            8
Block Limit Shared Mem                block           32
Block Limit Warps                     block            8
Theoretical Active Warps per SM        warp           64
Theoretical Occupancy                     %          100
Achieved Occupancy                        %        93.01
Achieved Active Warps Per SM           warp        59.53
------------------------------- ----------- ------------
```

The `Occupancy` profiling results indicate that the kernel achieves high occupancy (93%), with approximately 60% active warps per SM out of a theoretical maximum of 64%. This suggests that sufficient parallelism exists to hide latency.

We profile the memory workload next using the following command:

```
ncu --section "MemoryWorkloadAnalysis" python matmul.py
```

Here is the output:

```
Section: Memory Workload Analysis
-------------------------- ----------- ------------
Metric Name                Metric Unit Metric Value
-------------------------- ----------- ------------
Memory Throughput          Gbyte/second        1.34
Mem Busy                             %        99.66
Max Bandwidth                        %        12.77
L1/TEX Hit Rate                      %        94.20
L2 Compression Success Rate          %            0
L2 Compression Ratio                              0
L2 Hit Rate                          %        98.15
Mem Pipes Busy                       %         5.87
-------------------------- ----------- ------------
```

The memory analysis shows very low global memory bandwidth usage (1.34 GB/s, ~13% of peak). Both L1 and L2 caches exhibit very high hit rates (94% and 98%, respectively), suggesting efficient memory locality, and this explains the low global memory bandwidth usage. A large `Mem Busy` (the percentage of time memory is busy handling load/store requests) value (94%) suggests that the kernel is likely memory-bound. One possible reason is that threads within a warp are accessing memory non-sequentially, known as **uncoalesced memory access**. This access pattern increases the number of memory transactions required to serve the warp, which leads to inefficient use of memory bandwidth and higher memory subsystem utilization. In the next section, we will explore how to profile the efficiency of a kernel's memory access.

Profiling low-level metrics with Nsight Compute

Nsight Compute also allows low-level metrics measurement to quantify GPU performance at a granular level. This tool can collect detailed hardware performance counters directly from the SM, memory subsystems, schedulers, and execution pipelines. While the summary sections, such as *Compute* and *Memory Workload Analysis*, give us direction, these individual metrics provide the proof and exact behavior, for example, on how efficiently the GPU loads and stores data, whether accesses are coalesced, and how much bandwidth is achieved. Nsight Compute contains a vast set of low-level hardware performance metrics that expose how resources are being utilized.

Broadly speaking, we can organize them by hardware domain as follows:

- **SM instruction metrics**: These metrics help analyze instruction mix, issue rate, and pipeline utilization as they measure instruction throughput and pipeline utilization within each streaming multiprocessor.
- **Global memory metrics**: These capture global memory accesses and efficiency at the device memory level. These are key for measuring global memory throughput, coalescing efficiency, and memory bandwidth utilization.
- **Shared memory metrics**: These metrics allow us to measure shared memory bandwidth and bank conflict behavior.
- **Branching and divergence metrics**: These metrics help diagnose warp divergence, branch imbalance, and inefficient control flow as they measure control flow and highlight how warps behave at branches.
- **Occupancy and scheduler metrics**: These metrics reveal occupancy limits and instruction-level parallelism for understanding how well hardware resources are utilized.

The list of available metrics in Nsight Compute is extensive. As a rule of thumb, if we want to measure computation efficiency, then we should focus on SM instruction metrics. It's important to learn how to measure the desired metrics for the performance question at hand. The next chapter will explain how to interpret and use these metrics to drive concrete kernel optimizations.

For the matrix multiplication example, we will profile how efficiently each global memory load uses the full memory sector via the

`smsp__sass_average_data_bytes_per_sector_mem_global_op_ld.pct`

metric, as follows:

```
ncu --metrics smsp__sass_average_data_bytes_per_sector_mem_global_op_ld.pct
python matmul.py
```

Nsight Compute metric names generally follow this structure:

```
<unit>__<metric_expression>.<aggregation or unit>
```

Breaking down the name, `smsp__` refers to SM sub-partition (metrics gathered per SM sub-partition), `sass_average_data_bytes_per_sector_mem_global_op_ld` refers to average bytes of data loaded per memory sector (hardware unit) for global-memory load (`_ld`) operations, and `.pct` expresses as a percentage.

Here's what the output would look like:

```
Section: Command line profiler metrics
-------------------------------------------------------- ---------- -----------
Metric Name                                              Metric Unit Metric Value
-------------------------------------------------------- ---------- -----------
smsp__sass_average_data_bytes_per_sector_mem_global_op_ld.pct         %        26.47
-------------------------------------------------------- ---------- -----------
```

In practice, this metric indicates on each load operation from global memory, how many bytes we fetch per sector, a fixed-size portion of a memory transaction that the GPU can fetch or write independently, versus how many bytes we could have fetched. If the value is low, it means our loads are under-utilizing the memory sector width; we might be doing strided, uncoalesced, or partial loads, which cause the hardware to fetch a full sector, but only a fraction of it is used by our threads. If the value is high (close to 100%), we're using the memory bandwidth well, as each sector fetch is used fully by our threads.

This profiling result specifically shows 26% global memory load efficiency for the matrix multiplication example. It is mainly due to the inefficient memory access of the A matrix when performing the dot product. Changing the A matrix data arrangement to *column major* `order="F"` (Fortran) increases the load efficiency value to 90%. In contrast, our vector addition example gives the load efficiency of 100%. This is expected because of the coalesced memory access in `vecadd_kernel`. More about memory access patterns and optimization techniques will be discussed in *Chapter 5*.

Store operations also contribute to global memory utilization. Different metrics can be used to have further insight into memory access efficiency and total sector counts.

We can combine different metrics using the following command:

```
ncu --metrics \
  smsp__sass_average_data_bytes_per_sector_mem_global_op_st.pct,\
  smsp__sass_average_data_bytes_per_sector_mem_global_op_ld.pct,\
  l1tex__t_sectors_pipe_lsu_mem_global_op_ld.sum,\
  l1tex__t_sectors_pipe_lsu_mem_global_op_st.sum \
  python matmul.py
```

Here's what the output would look like:

```
Section: Command line profiler metrics
---------------------------------------------------------- ----------- ------------
Metric Name                                                Metric Unit Metric Value
---------------------------------------------------------- ----------- ------------
smsp__sass_average_data_bytes_per_sector_mem_global_op_ld.pct        %        26.47
smsp__sass_average_data_bytes_per_sector_mem_global_op_st.pct        %           50
l1tex__t_sectors_pipe_lsu_mem_global_op_ld.sum                  sector    570425223
l1tex__t_sectors_pipe_lsu_mem_global_op_st.sum                  sector       524288
---------------------------------------------------------- ----------- ------------
```

These metrics together show how much global memory traffic the `matmul_kernel` kernel generates and how efficiently that traffic is used.

`smsp__sass_average_data_bytes_per_sector_mem_global_op_st.pct` indicates the same idea but for global stores (`_st`). It reveals how effectively stored transactions pack useful data. `l1tex__t_sectors_pipe_lsu_mem_global_op_ld.sum` metric counts (`.sum`) how many memory sectors were fetched from global memory to serve *load* instructions. A large number means the kernel is doing a lot of global reads or reading inefficiently.

`l1tex__t_sectors_pipe_lsu_mem_global_op_st.sum` similarly counts how many memory sectors were written back for *store* operations. This is useful for understanding global *write* traffic. These results show that this kernel performs a very large number of global memory loads, and only about 26% of each loaded memory sector is used. This is a sign of poor coalescing and little data reuse. Stores are somewhat better (50% efficiency), but the overall issue is too many inefficient accesses. Shared memory tiling and improved access patterns should significantly increase efficiency and performance.

All these profiling tools that we have used let us conclude that our basic implementation for the matrix multiplication is memory-bound due to uncoalesced loads with very low reuse (many load sectors but low utilization). As a result, most GPU cycles are spent waiting on memory, and memory is heavily wasted due to poor access patterns.

In the next section, we focus on basic utilities to debug kernels at runtime and how to inspect JIT compilation in Numba-CUDA.

Debugging Numba-CUDA kernels

Debugging CUDA kernels can be challenging, especially for Python users, because traditional debugging tools such as breakpoints, variable inspection, or step-by-step execution are not directly available within GPU code. Nevertheless, Numba-CUDA provides several features that enable basic debugging and inspection of GPU kernels, such as `print` statements, a CUDA simulator, and JIT compilation. The following sections will discuss each of these in detail.

> Note
>
> Standard CUDA provides debugging tools such as **CUDA-GDB** and **Compute Sanitizer**, which can inspect CUDA applications at runtime. However, we avoid these tools in this book because our target audience consists of Python users who are assumed to have limited experience with the CUDA C workflow.

Using the print statement

Numba provides the ability to inspect variable values inside CUDA kernels using the built-in `print` statement. We can use this to display variable values and program flow during execution. This can be useful for debugging CUDA kernels, especially when verifying intermediate computations or checking the behavior of specific threads and blocks.

The following is an example demonstrating how to use `print()` in the matrix multiplication kernel:

```
from numba import cuda, float64

@cuda.jit
def matmul_kernel(A, B, C):
    row, col = cuda.grid(2)
    ifrow< C.shape[0] andcol< C.shape[1]:
        tmp = 0.0
        for k in range(A.shape[1]):
            tmp += A[row, k] * B[k, col]

        # Print the computed value
        if row == 0 and col == 1:
            print("C[", row, ", ", col, "] =", tmp)

        C[row, col] = tmp
```

When this kernel is executed, the output might look like this:

```
C[ 0 ,  1 ] = 256.856027
```

This confirms that the computation for the `C[0, 1]` element was performed as expected. Using such conditional `print` statements helps us isolate the behavior of individual threads and validate our algorithm.

It's important to know that the `print()` output is serialized and may appear in a non-deterministic order if multiple threads print simultaneously. Also, formatted string literals (**f-strings**) are not supported within CUDA JIT-compiled functions. We must use simple string concatenation or comma-separated values instead.

Emulating GPU code on the CPU

Numba supports a convenient way to emulate CUDA code on the CPU, which can be very useful for debugging and testing purposes. When this mode is active, CUDA kernels decorated with `@cuda.jit` are executed on the CPU, but they behave as if they were running on a GPU. The simulation mode is much slower than actual GPU execution, but it allows us to use standard Python debugging tools, perform detailed inspections, and catch common issues that might otherwise go unnoticed when running directly on GPU hardware. To enable CUDA simulation mode, set the environment variable before importing Numba's CUDA module:

```
import os
os.environ["NUMBA_ENABLE_CUDASIM"] = "1"

from numba import cuda
```

The following example shows how CUDA simulation can help us detect out-of-bounds memory accesses inside a kernel. Normally, such errors fail silently on the GPU, making debugging difficult. However, in simulation mode, the CPU emulator raises Python exceptions such as `IndexError`, helping identify the problematic code section:

```
@cuda.jit
def matmul_kernel(A, B, C):
    row, col = cuda.grid(2)
    ifrow< C.shape[0] andcol< C.shape[1]:
        tmp = 0.0
        for k in range(A.shape[1]):
            tmp += A[row, k] * B[k, col]

        if row == 0 and col == 1:
            A[A.shape[0] + 1, 0]  # Intentional out-of-range access

        C[row, col] = tmp
```

When this kernel runs on a GPU, it may complete without raising any visible error. However, when executed with the CUDA simulator enabled, it produces an error such as the following:

```
IndexError: index 1025 is out of bounds for axis 0 with size 1024
```

This is quite useful for debugging GPU code, as we can even detect errors through raised Python exceptions (e.g., `IndexError`, `ZeroDivisionError`, etc.) that would otherwise be hidden on the GPU.

Inspecting JIT compilation

Last but not least, Numba provides several tools to inspect and analyze CUDA kernels after they have been JIT compiled. These inspection utilities help us understand kernel performance characteristics, such as register usage, shared memory allocation, and even the generated **Parallel Thread Execution** (**PTX**) assembly code, all of which can be important for optimizing performance.

Checking resource usage

Each CUDA kernel compiled with `@cuda.jit` exposes methods that allow querying its resource requirements. For example, we can check the amount of shared memory per block that a kernel uses, as follows:

```
matmul_kernel.get_shared_mem_per_block().values()[0]
```

Here is what the output would look like:

```
0
```

This indicates that the kernel does not allocate any shared memory. If your kernel explicitly uses `cuda.shared.array()`, this value will reflect the corresponding allocation in bytes.

We can also inspect the number of registers used per thread, which can be a factor in determining kernel occupancy (i.e., how many threads can run concurrently on a GPU multiprocessor):

```
matmul_kernel.get_regs_per_thread().values()
```

Here is what the output would look like:

```
32
```

A higher number of registers per thread can limit the number of concurrently active threads per block, potentially affecting performance. This makes register usage analysis a valuable step during kernel tuning. Note that these values can vary depending on the GPU architecture where the JIT-compiled function is executed after its first invocation.

Getting the generated PTX code

For a deeper look into how Numba's CUDA JIT compiler translates our Python code into GPU instructions, we can retrieve the PTX assembly representation of our kernel.

To print the PTX code for the first compiled kernel signature, use the following:

```
print(list(matmul_kernel.inspect_asm().values())[0])
```

Here is the example output (truncated):

```
//
// Generated by NVIDIA NVVM Compiler
//
// Compiler Build ID: CL-33567101
// Cuda compilation tools, release 12.3, V12.3.107
// Based on NVVM 7.0.1
//

.version 8.3
.target sm_50
.address_size 64
...
cvta.to.global.u64      %rd1, %rd40;
mov.u32         %r1, %tid.x;
cvt.s64.s32     %rd41, %r1;
mov.u32         %r2, %ntid.x;
mov.u32         %r3, %ctaid.x;
mul.wide.s32    %rd42, %r2, %r3;
add.s64         %rd2, %rd42, %rd41;
mov.u32         %r4, %tid.y;
cvt.s64.s32     %rd43, %r4;
```

The PTX code provides a low-level view of the compiled kernel, including register assignments, instruction flow, and memory access patterns, which can be useful. For example, verifying that specific optimizations (e.g., loop unrolling, inlining, etc.) have taken effect, comparing performance across architectures or compiler versions, and gaining insights into potential inefficient variable casting in generated code—these inspections offer a transparent view into the

GPU compilation process, which enables us to perform more informed optimization and debugging of CUDA kernels written in Python.

Summary

In this chapter, we began by emphasizing the importance of profiling and debugging in GPU computing. We discussed key challenges in GPU profiling, such as asynchronous execution, discrepancies between CPU and GPU timing, and the separation between host and device operations. Additionally, common CUDA performance bottlenecks were outlined.

We then introduced lightweight profiling tools, starting with Python's `time` and `timeit` modules and the *Scalene* line profiler, followed by `nvtop`, a Linux utility for real-time GPU monitoring. Next, we examined NVIDIA's dedicated profiling tools, beginning with **Nsight Systems** for timeline-based profiling and moving to **Nsight Compute** for detailed kernel-level analysis and access to low-level performance metrics.

Finally, we explored debugging in Numba, demonstrating how to inspect JIT-compiled functions for details such as local and shared memory usage. We also showed how to use the Numba CUDA simulator to detect issues such as out-of-range memory access during kernel execution and how to extract PTX code to gain low-level insights into the compiled kernels.

Now that we understand how to profile GPU code and measure the relevant performance metrics, we are ready to explore optimization techniques in the next chapter.

Questions

1. Profile the GPU activity timeline on your GPU machine for the vector addition example. Do you observe any differences between kernel execution and memory access utilization? If yes, why?
2. Profile the global memory load efficiency for the vector addition example. How does it differ from the matrix multiplication example?
3. Why does changing the memory order of the 2D device array to `"F"` (Fortran order) improve global memory load efficiency?

Answers

1. Depending on your GPU, the exact values may vary, but for the vector addition problem, the dominant portion of the timeline is spent on data transfer between host and device, making it the main performance bottleneck.

2. Because the simple vector addition kernel accesses memory in a contiguous, coalesced pattern, its global memory load efficiency is relatively high. In contrast, more complex kernels, such as matrix multiplication, may have less obvious coalescing.
3. Using Fortran ("`F`") order stores the 2D array in column-major order, aligning memory access across threads for coalescing, which improves global memory load efficiency.

Part 2

Performance Optimization and Advanced CUDA Topics

This part dives into advanced CUDA techniques for maximizing performance. We'll explore GPU hardware and the CUDA execution model to identify and address bottlenecks through kernel profiling. After that, we'll cover CUDA streams for concurrent data transfers and computation. Finally, we'll scale up to multi-GPU workflows. By the end, you'll have the tools to optimize and scale CUDA applications effectively.

This part of the book includes the following chapters:

5

Optimizing the Performance of CUDA Code

With CUDA kernel development and profiling covered, it's time to learn how to optimize CUDA code for maximum performance.

This chapter breaks down how GPU hardware executes kernels and what drives performance. The memory hierarchy, instruction scheduling, and thread execution model are dissected to show their role in code efficiency. Understanding these mechanics allows us to target bottlenecks and use hardware more effectively. The discussion also covers actionable techniques, such as better memory access patterns, warp-level programming, and loop unrolling, to push CUDA applications to the limit.

The learning outcomes of this chapter are as follows:

- Describe GPU hardware architecture and the key factors in performance
- Analyze how kernels are scheduled and executed on GPU hardware
- Understand PTX assembly to interpret low-level kernel behavior
- Maximize occupancy and instruction-level parallelism with CUDA tools and techniques
- Optimize global and shared memory access patterns for low latency and high throughput
- Apply warp-level programming and CUDA intrinsics for efficient data exchange and control

How a GPU executes kernels

In this section, we'll look at how a GPU runs a kernel. Understanding what happens under the hood is the first step to making kernels run faster.

A basic overview of GPU hardware

To better understand what happens when a kernel runs on the device, and to get familiar with the key terms, this section will go over the high-level **hardware architecture**. *Figure 5.1* shows a diagram of the most important components in a GPU:

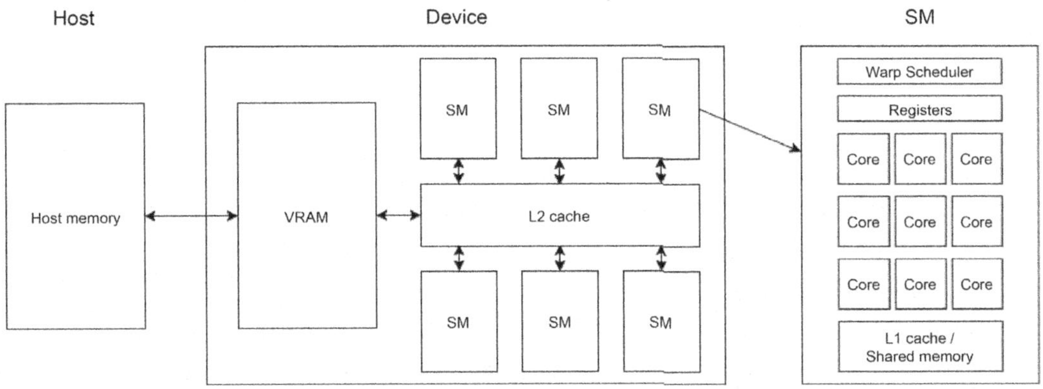

Figure 5.1 – A diagram showing the hardware architecture of a GPU

The core computational units of a GPU are the **streaming multiprocessors** (**SMs**). Each SM contains multiple **arithmetic logic units** (**ALUs**), also referred to as **CUDA cores**, which perform basic arithmetic operations (addition, subtraction, multiplication, ...) for kernel threads. The term "CUDA core" specifically denotes ALUs handling **32-bit floating-point** (**F32**) and **32-bit integer** (**I32**) operations. Some CUDA cores are dedicated to F32, while others support both F32 and I32. Some GPU models include additional ALUs, such as **FP64 units** for double-precision floats and integers, and **tensor cores** optimized for matrix multiplication operations.

Note

Single precision vs double precision

Single-precision (32-bit) numbers are generally recommended for GPU computing whenever possible. Most consumer-grade GPUs prioritize F32 units, making double-precision operations significantly more resource-intensive. These operations often require multiple cores and additional registers to emulate 64-bit behavior, potentially degrading performance by an order of magnitude. Data center GPUs, however, typically feature sufficient FP64 units, enabling efficient double-precision computations. For specific details, consult the product data sheet for the GPU model.

SMs also include hardware for temporarily storing data used or produced by compute units.

The first storage type within SMs is the **register file**, which holds thread-local state. Registers provide the lowest latency memory accessible to compute units; data access is possible within a single clock cycle. All compute operations require data to be loaded into registers, and results must be stored back into registers. To process data, it must first reside in registers; to retain computed results, they must be copied from registers to other memory types.

The second storage type is the **L1 cache**, which offers slower access than registers but remains extremely fast, with latencies measured in a few clock cycles. The L1 cache stores data that can be shared among all threads active on the SM.

The hardware allocated for the L1 cache can also serve as **shared memory**, which is explicitly managed from a CUDA kernel. Shared memory usage is discussed later in this chapter.

Each SM includes one or more **warp schedulers**, responsible for launching and tracking thread execution. The concept of a warp was already mentioned in *Chapter 3* and will be discussed in detail in the next section.

Finally, SMs contain **load/store units** for fetching data from high-latency memory (e.g., VRAM) and **special function units** (**SFUs**) for hardware-accelerated operations such as sine, cosine, and square root calculations. These are not shown in the SM diagram of *Figure 5.1.*

A device contains multiple SMs, and these can all access a second layer of cache, **L2 cache**, as well as the on-board DRAM memory, often called **VRAM** for video RAM. Data transfers from the host to the device involve copying from host RAM to VRAM.

While this architecture is consistent across CUDA-enabled GPUs, the number of SMs, ALUs, and other components per SM, as well as cache, register, and DRAM sizes and bandwidths, vary by model. This information is available in product datasheets, NVIDIA's official documentation, and occasionally on Wikipedia. Some details can be queried directly from the device.

To convey a sense of the magnitudes, the table in *Figure 5.2* compares the core counts, memory sizes, and cache capacities of an RTX 3080 (consumer-grade) and an A100 (data center) GPU:

	RTX 3080	A100
SM count	68	108
CUDA cores per SM	128	64
Total CUDA cores	8704	6912
FP64 per SM	2	32
Tensor cores per SM	4	4
VRAM size	10 GB	40 GB
L2 cache size	5 MB	41 MB
L1 cache size per SM	128 KB	192 KB
Base clock frequency	1440 MHz	1095 MHz

Figure 5.2 – Comparison of the number of cores and the sizes of memory and caches in the RTX 3080 and A100 GPU models

The A100 excels in double-precision calculations as it has 16 times the number of FP64 units per SM, while the RTX 3080 theoretically outperforms the A100 in single-precision floating-point operations due to its higher CUDA core count and clock frequency. However, real-world performance depends on both computational speed and data access latency. Data center GPUs have larger VRAM, L2, and L1 caches, which reduce latency, often making them the better performer in latency-bound problems.

Memory and cache latency and bandwidth are revisited later. Now that a conceptual understanding of the hardware has been established, the next step is to examine how CUDA kernels execute on this architecture.

How a kernel is scheduled

Recall that when executing a kernel, a grid configuration must be specified. The grid consists of blocks, which in turn consist of threads. Grids and blocks can be 1D, 2D, or 3D.

At the hardware level, thread blocks are queued and distributed across SMs based on availability. All threads within a single block execute on the same SM. The SM further divides the block into collections of **32 threads**, called **warps**. Warp schedulers on each SM allocate warps to available hardware resources: cores, registers, and shared memory.

Unlike CPU threads, which are more or less independent, GPU threads within a warp follow the **single instruction, multiple thread** (**SIMT**) model. This means that, when executing the same control flow path, threads execute **in lockstep**, with each thread in a warp using one CUDA core per floating-point operation. Threads can diverge due to conditional branches, in which case subsets of the warp execute sequentially. There is no static thread-to-core mapping; cores are dynamically shared across all warps. The warp scheduler is responsible for filling instruction pipelines to keep the cores busy.

The SM splits blocks into warps deterministically. In a 1D block, the first 32 threads form the first warp, the next 32 the second, and so on. If the block size is not a multiple of 32, the remaining threads are padded with inactive threads to complete the final warp. Since the smallest execution unit is always a warp, blocks should contain a multiple of 32 threads for efficiency.

For 2D and 3D blocks, warps are formed based on the linear thread ID, calculated as follows:

```
linear_id = threadIdx.x + \
            threadIdx.y * blockDim.x  + \
            threadIdx.z * blockDim.x * blockDim.y
```

Threads with linear IDs 0–31 form the first warp, 32–63 the second, and so on. From a hardware perspective, thread blocks are treated as 1D collections of warps.

Note

Deterministic warps

While warp formation is deterministic, execution order is not. Warp 0 is not guaranteed to complete before warp 1. When warps stall (e.g., during memory fetches), the scheduler switches to other warps. Logically, all threads should be assumed to run in parallel, even if physical simultaneity is impossible. Within warps, lockstep execution is expected, but thread synchronicity is not guaranteed.

Kernel execution involves both thread scheduling and data access. The next section addresses how threads interact with the memory hierarchy.

The memory hierarchy and how data travels

The primary objective of GPU computing is to perform rapid data transformations. Input data is processed by a kernel to produce output; both input and output are typically arrays. For this to occur on the GPU, input data must be loaded to the CUDA cores, and results must be stored elsewhere. Efficient data loading and storing is critical to performance, as memory access often becomes the dominant performance bottleneck: many programs are **memory-bound** rather than **compute-bound**. This section discusses data movement and GPU memory types, which are essential for identifying bottlenecks and optimization.

The GPU memory hierarchy, with an order of magnitude estimate for latency and capacity, is shown in *Figure 5.3*. At the top is memory with the lowest latency, but also low capacity. At the bottom is memory with high capacity but also high latency:

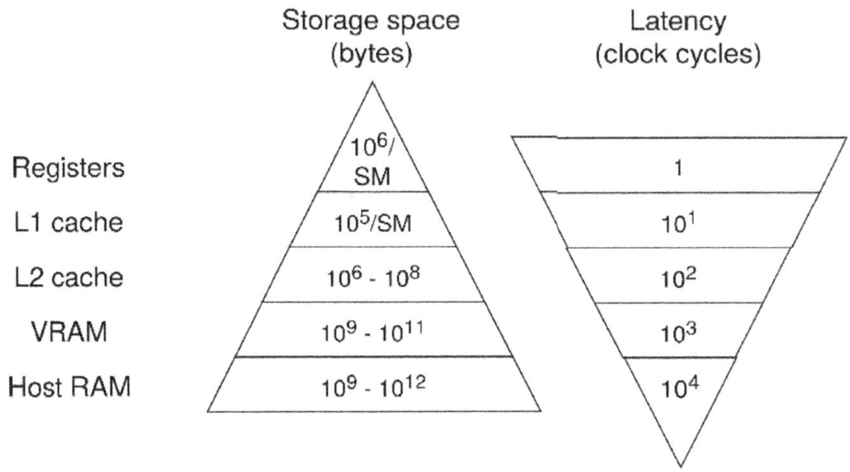

Figure 5.3 – The memory hierarchy, with the fastest but lowest capacity memory at the top and the slowest but highest capacity memory at the bottom

Since registers cannot store all problem data, most data resides in higher-latency memory and is loaded as needed. Threads perform arithmetic operations only on register-resident data, which must be loaded from **global memory** or **shared memory**.

Global memory, residing in VRAM, is the primary memory interface for kernels. Host-device transfers involve moving data to/from global memory. While all threads can access global memory, its high latency often necessitates optimization. Cache utilization (L1/L2) can reduce effective latency, and **coalesced memory access patterns** (discussed further in this chapter) maximize throughput.

Note

Different loading operations

There are multiple types of load and store operations that differ in how and whether data is cached. Selecting non-default load operations is an advanced topic addressed in *Chapter 15*.

Shared memory resides on the same hardware as the L1 cache but is **user-programmable**, acting as a low-latency scratchpad for threads within a block. It is explicitly allocated and managed in kernels and is ideal for storing reused data. However, shared memory is block-scoped, and the data typically originates from global memory.

While L1 cache and shared memory share the same physical hardware, the partitioning is configurable during kernel launch. The default can be modified in the global device settings.

Other types of memory exist for specific use cases, but all of them live on VRAM. For example, **local memory** is thread-private VRAM spillover for large data (e.g., thread-local arrays) when registers are exhausted. This has the same latency characteristics as global memory. There is also **constant memory**, a read-only VRAM region for constants. This data is cached and broadcast to SMs for low-latency access. These memory types will be featured in upcoming application chapters.

> Note
>
> **Latency vs bandwidth**
>
> While latency is critical, bandwidth often dominates performance on large data transfers. PCIe (e.g., Gen 6.0 x16) limits host-device bandwidth (~120 GB/s), whereas global memory-to-GPU bandwidth ranges from 700–3000 GB/s. Efficient host-device transfers are thus vital for performance.

With this understanding of GPU memory hierarchy and data flows, the next step is analyzing performance bottlenecks and mitigation strategies.

Maximizing occupancy

Occupancy measures how effectively SMs are utilized, defined as the ratio of active warps to the maximum possible warps per SM. The maximum number of warps that may be active depends on the GPU architecture and can be found in *Table 28* on this page of the official CUDA programming guide:

`https://docs.nvidia.com/cuda/cuda-c-programming-guide/index.html#features-and-technical-specifications`.

For example, the RTX 3080 with the Ampere architecture and compute capability 8.6 supports a maximum of 48 warps or 1,536 active threads per multiprocessor, or 3,264 warps and 104,448 threads for the entire device with 68 SMs. Notice that the maximum number of threads is an order of magnitude greater than there are CUDA cores on the device. The reason for having more active threads than cores is to **hide latency**.

GPUs perform **latency hiding** by maximizing **throughput**. Let's break that down. A single arithmetic instruction can take anywhere from a few to tens of clock cycles to complete. This means that after a warp sends out an arithmetic instruction, it stalls and waits. Luckily, the CUDA cores do not have to idle, because the warp scheduler can switch to another warp. Switching warps is very fast, typically less than 2 clock cycles. If there are enough active warps that the scheduler can cycle between, the cores can be fully utilized (i.e., they perform an operation every clock cycle). The time to execute a single warp is slow due to instruction latency. However, the GPU ensures it has work to do every clock cycle by executing multiple warps concurrently.

The minimal number of threads required to hide all latency can be calculated as follows: `# cores × latency of instruction`. If there is one core and an operation that has 5 cycles of latency, at least 5 active threads must always be in the queue to ensure that the core has something to do every clock cycle. In case there are multiple cores, the queue must be multiplied by the number of cores. For example, one SM on the RTX 3080 requires 128 cores × 5 cycles/op = 640 active threads or 20 active warps for basic F32 arithmetic instructions. To keep the entire device busy, these values need to be multiplied by 68, so 43,520 active threads or 1,360 warps for the entire device. The device supports more than twice as many warps, but many operations require more cycles per operation, so more active threads are needed to hide all latency. It is good to aim for maximum occupancy. However, if instruction latency is sufficiently hidden, higher occupancy will not improve performance.

A theoretical occupancy can be calculated based on the kernel launch configuration. Alternatively, a desired occupancy can be used to decide on a good kernel launch configuration. To do so, another limiting factor becomes important: the maximum number of blocks that can be resident on an SM. For the RTX 3080, this limit is 16 (see the previously mentioned table in the CUDA guide for reference). If a block size of 32 threads (1 warp) is used, only 16 × 32 = 512 threads can be scheduled on the SM, so the maximum theoretical occupancy is 512 / 1,536 = 33.3%. For this device, a block of 1,536 / 16 = 96 threads is the smallest block required to achieve 100% occupancy. To fully occupy the device, a grid of at least 104,448 / 96 = 1,088 blocks is required.

To maximize theoretical occupancy, the block size should be a divisor of the maximum number of threads per SM. For example, if a block size of 1,024 threads is chosen (the maximum size), only one block can be active per SM at any one time, and the maximum theoretical occupancy with this grid is 1,024 / 1,536 = 66.6%.

There are additional constraints to occupancy that have not yet been taken into consideration in this discussion: registers and shared memory requirements. The number of registers and the amount of shared memory are limited on each SM, but blocks require a fixed amount of these resources depending on the kernel. Blocks can only be scheduled on the SM when enough of these resources are available.

Note

SM limits do not limit grid size

This section is only concerned with the number of blocks and threads that are resident on the streaming multiprocessors. A grid can be much larger, with excess blocks queued for execution on an SM. Once assigned to an SM, the block is divided into warps, which are scheduled by the warp scheduler.

To illustrate, let's measure occupancy and performance on a dummy kernel and experiment with different launch configurations. Consider the following kernel, which calculates the sine of the input array using the first 10 terms of the Taylor series expansion for the sine function:

```
@cuda.jit
def sine_series(
    x: NDArray,
    y: NDArray, # output
) -> None:
    t_id = cuda.grid(1)
    if t_id >= x.size:
        return

    x_i = x[t_id]

    value = x_i
    x_squared = x_i * x_i
    numerator = x_i * x_squared
    sign = -1
    exponent = 3
    denominator = 6  # =3!

    for _ in range(10):
        value += sign * numerator / denominator
        numerator *= x_squared
        exponent += 2
        denominator *= (exponent - 1) * exponent
        sign *= -1

    y[t_id] = value
```

The details of the math in the kernel are not important; verifying that the kernel indeed produces the same output as `sin(x)` is left as an exercise. The focus is on occupancy and performance.

In the grid, each thread handles one `sin(x)` function evaluation. The kernel is tested for three different problem sizes:

- Half the device's total thread capacity (52,224 for the RTX 3080)
- Equal to the device's total thread capacity (104,448 for the RTX 3080)
- Double the device's total thread capacity (208,896 for the RTX 3080)

For each of these problem sizes, the kernel is run with different block sizes. The block sizes are all multiples of 32.

The kernel is profiled, and the occupancy is measured for these different configurations using `Nsight Compute` (see *Chapter 4*):

```
ncu --section Occupancy --csv --log-file results.csv python occupancy_script.py
```

This outputs a `csv` file containing information about occupancy. For all the details on the implementation, see the GitHub repository associated with this book.

Figure 5.4 shows all the results. On the *x* axis is the number of threads in a block; on the *y* axis, the warp occupancy. There are four different curves: one for each problem size, and one containing the theoretical maximum occupancy. The theoretical maximum occupancy does not take into consideration the problem size, only the number of threads per block. These block sizes could achieve 100% occupancy if no other constraints (e.g., registers, shared memory) are violated. Vertical dotted lines are drawn where the block size is a divisor of the maximum number of threads per SM.

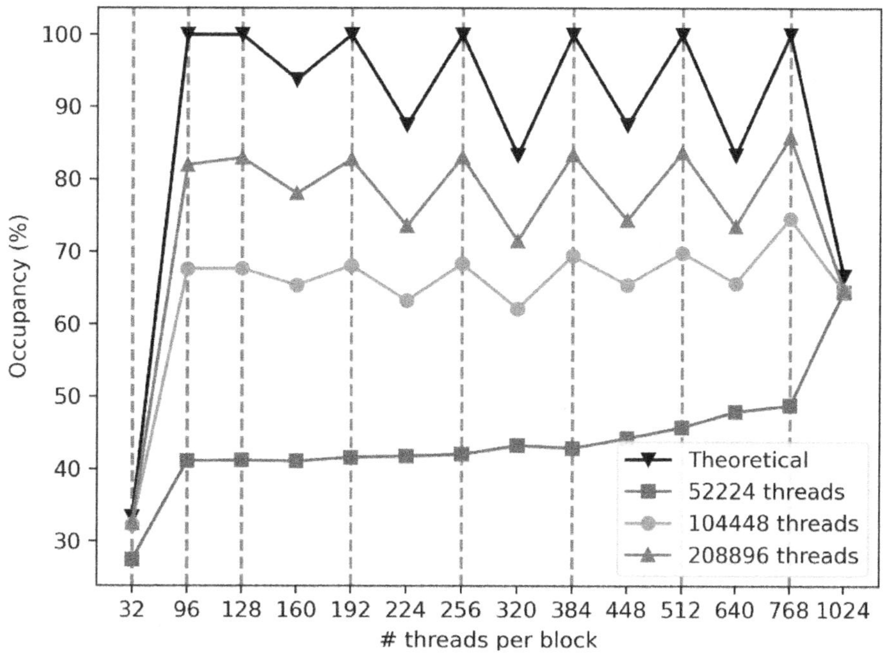

Figure 5.4 – Occupancy for the sine kernel for different grid configurations

As expected, the theoretical occupancy is 100% only where the block size divides the maximum number of threads per SM. In any other scenario, the maximum number of blocks is smaller than the SM capacity. The values for block sizes of 32 and 1,024 threads correspond to the values previously calculated by hand.

However, measured occupancies are consistently lower than theoretical limits. For problem sizes large enough to fully occupy the GPU, the trend follows the theoretical curve. When the problem size is too small to saturate the GPU, the grid configuration has a minimal effect on measured occupancy because all SMs retain unused capacity. Measured occupancy improves as problem size increases, since larger problem sizes reduce the relative overhead of block scheduling and load balancing across SMs.

To correlate occupancy with performance, *Figure 5.5* shows the average runtime per output element (kernel runtime divided by problem size) for all configurations. Kernels were executed 100,000 times to ensure statistical significance, with error bars showing one standard deviation across runs.

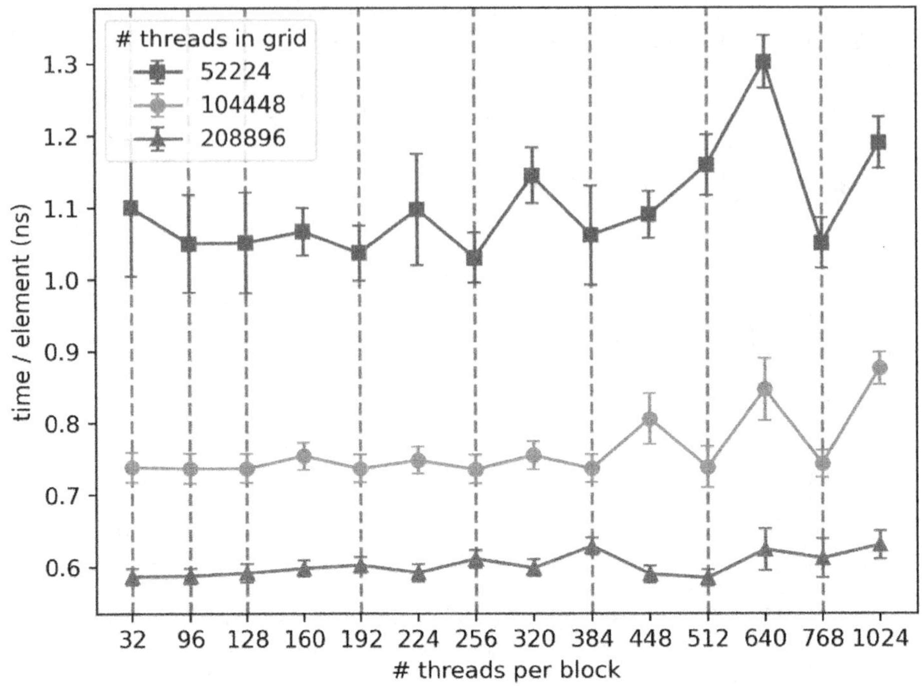

Figure 5.5 – Normalized runtime for the sine kernel for different grid configurations

As the problem size increases, computational efficiency improves: less time is required per output element. This reflects better utilization of the GPU's resources, as fixed overheads (e.g., kernel launch, memory transfers) are amortized over more work, and the device's compute units are kept busier.

For smaller problem sizes, block size has little effect on measured occupancy, but the best performance aligns with configurations that achieve 100% theoretical occupancy. This likely stems from more balanced workload distribution across SMs, minimizing idle time, and maximizing active warps.

As the problem size grows, however, the link between occupancy and performance weakens. This suggests occupancy remains sufficiently high to hide latency, and other bottlenecks, such as the device's compute capacity, dominate. In this kernel, performance becomes limited by the GPU's ability to execute arithmetic operations, not by its ability to schedule warps.

Let's also verify that occupancy is not limited by resource utilization, such as the availability of registers. The maximum number of registers that are available on the multiprocessor can be queried as follows:

```
dev = cuda.get_current_device()
print(dev.MAX_REGISTERS_PER_MULTIPROCESSOR)
```

There are 65,536 registers on each SM of the RTX 3080.

The maximum amount of shared memory per SM is specified in the CUDA documentation. For compute capability 8.6, this is 100 KB.

The number of registers required per thread is kernel-dependent. It can be queried from a compiled kernel as follows:

```
sine_series.get_regs_per_thread()
```

If the kernel has been run at least once (and therefore compiled) for arrays with `dtype` `float32`, the output is as follows:

```
{(Array(float32, 1, 'C', False, aligned=True),
  Array(float32, 1, 'C', False, aligned=True)): 36}
```

This means the SM could support 65,536 / 36 = 1,820 threads, which is more than the maximum of 1,536. Therefore, registers do not limit occupancy for this kernel.

> Note
>
> **Register spilling**
>
> A single thread can use a maximum of 255 registers. If a thread requires more, this data spills over into local memory. This is disastrous for performance, since accessing local memory is hundreds of times slower than accessing registers. Keep this in mind when defining complex kernels.

The amount of shared memory required per block can be queried in a similar way:

```
sine_series.get_shared_mem_per_block()
```

Since no shared memory is used in the kernel definition, the result is 0. How to use shared memory will be explained later in this chapter.

Note

Dispatchers are not strictly kernels

Numba-CUDA kernels are actually `CUDADispatcher` objects, which store multiple compiled versions of the kernel, specialized to different input data types. When running the kernel with unseen input types, the kernel is compiled for those types, and the result is cached in the dispatcher. Different compiled versions of the kernel may have different resource requirements.

To summarize, occupancy measures the ratio of active warps per SM to the maximum supported warps per SM, indicating how effectively GPU resources are utilized. High occupancy helps hide latency, ensuring the GPU remains active every clock cycle by interleaving warps. Maximum occupancy depends on kernel resource requirements, hardware limits, and launch configuration. Launch configuration is the only easily configurable parameter, and for some problems, it can have a measurable impact on performance. Experimentation with different launch configurations, using both timing and profiling, is essential to identify optimal settings for a given kernel and problem size. While occupancy is an important metric, it is not the sole determinant of performance; many other metrics are considered throughout this chapter.

Improving performance by inspecting PTX assembly code

As discussed in *Chapter 3*, Numba-CUDA compiles kernels to a lower-level representation that details low-level instructions for the device. The lowest-level human-readable representation is **PTX assembly**. While assembly code is much more difficult to read compared to the CUDA kernel in a high-level language, it is a more transparent representation of the work that will be performed. Often, many heuristics are used to explain how a change to a kernel impacts performance. However, the most reliable method for understanding what the kernel is doing is by inspecting the assembly code.

This section aims to give a bird's-eye view of PTX assembly, such that you come to understand the syntax. The goal is to be able to read PTX, detect anomalies, and discover clues for how to improve a kernel.

Let's have a look at the assembly representation of the sine kernel from the previous section. The PTX representation of the kernel can be accessed through the `inspect_asm` method. The method returns a dictionary that maps signatures to compilation results. To print the PTX representation for the first signature, run the following:

```
print(list(sine_series.inspect_asm().values())[0])
```

At the top is a header and the definition of some global variables; this is not relevant for the purpose of this section. A bit further down is the kernel definition, which resembles a function:

```
.visible .entry _ZN6cudapy8__main__11sine_series...(
    .param .u64 _ZN6cudapy8__main__11sine_series..._param_0,
    ...
)
```

This kernel takes 14 parameters with a type of 64-bit unsigned integers. These parameters typically include **pointers** that point to where the array data lives in global memory, as well as information on array dimensions and strides.

At the start of the kernel, registers that will be used for computation are declared:

```
    .reg .pred  %p<2>;
    .reg .f32   %f<14>;
    ...
```

The second term on each line represents the data type that will be stored in the register: `.f32` means 32-bit float and `.b64` means 64-bit integer. The number between <> represents how many registers of this type will be used. In this case, there will be 14 `f32` registers with names `%f0` to `%f14`.

Note

Actual register usage varies

Notice that there are more registers declared in the PTX than are actually used by the kernel (36, as discussed previously). In the next stage of compilation (to SASS), the compiler optimizes further by reusing registers.

After register declarations, follow the instructions to perform calculations or load data. These follow syntax like the following:

```
<instruction> <destination> <inputs>
```

Some instructions are self-explanatory – here's an example:

```
mul.f32     %f2, %f1, %f1;
```

This multiplies the 32-bit float in register %f1 by itself, and stores the result in register %f2. Similarly, there is add for addition and div for division.

Loading data from global memory is performed as follows:

```
ld.global.f32   %f1, [%rd15];
```

This loads a 32-bit float into register %f1, where the data is fetched at a location defined by the address stored in %rd15. This instruction likely corresponds to the line x_i = x[t_id], where the x value corresponding to the thread is loaded.

The store operation looks as follows:

```
st.global.f32   [%rd19], %f13;
```

Here, the f32 value stored in register %f13 is copied to global memory at the location specified by the address stored in register %rd19.

Other instructions in the PTX assembly code are as follows:

- shl and shr for left and right bit-shifting values in registers
- cvta for converting integers to pointers
- mov for copying values from one register to another

Associating these instructions with lines of code in the original kernel is not always straightforward.

However, the kernel also contains a lot of these instructions:

```
cvt.f64.f32     %fd5, %f4;
```

This converts the 32-bit float stored in %f4 into a 64-bit float that is stored in %fd5. Given that inputs and outputs are single precision, there should be no reason for conversions to double precision.

The reason this happens is that numerical constants in the kernel have an ambiguous type. By default, Numba assumes these are double precision. Therefore, inputs are upcast to double precision when they are arithmetically combined with the constants. At the end, the results are downcast again to store the output. This is very wasteful, and therefore, the kernel can be improved by explicitly making the constants in the kernel 32-bit floats as follows:

```
from numba import float32

@cuda.jit
def sine_series_explicit(
    x: NDArray,
    y: NDArray,
) -> None:
    t_id = cuda.grid(1)
    if t_id >= x.size:
        return

    x_i = x[t_id]

    value = x_i
    x_squared = x_i * x_i
    numerator = x_i * x_squared
    sign = float32(-1)
    exponent = float32(3)
    denominator = float32(6)

    for _ in range(10):
        value += sign * numerator / denominator
        numerator *= x_squared
        exponent += float32(2)
        denominator *= (exponent - float32(1)) * exponent
        sign *= float32(-1)

    y[t_id] = value
```

On an array of 25 million elements, the original kernel takes 11 ms, while the improved kernel takes only 370 µs on the RTX 3080. This is 30× faster, which is impressive for a very simple change!

The PTX assembly of this improved kernel has no conversions from 32-bit to 64-bit and far fewer total instructions. The new kernel also uses fewer registers; no more `f64` registers are allocated at the top.

One key takeaway from this section is that being explicit about types in CUDA kernels can drastically improve performance. The second takeaway is that understanding assembly code is important, since this casting issue could only be discovered in this way.

Maximizing the use of instruction-level parallelism with loop unrolling

The occupancy discussion established that many active warps are needed to hide instruction latency and maintain device utilization. However, instruction execution is not strictly sequential. When the compiler detects independent instructions within a thread, they can be initiated in parallel, enabling **instruction-level parallelism** (**ILP**). Warp stalls only occur if an instruction depends on unresolved data from a prior instruction.

For specific problems where instruction independence is known but not recognized by the compiler, ILP can be exploited manually. Consider the following kernel:

```
@cuda.jit
def add_arrays(
    x: NDArray,
    y: NDArray,
    z: NDArray,
) -> None:
    t_id = cuda.grid(1)
    start = t_id * 1024
    for i in range(1024):
        z[start+i] = x[start+i] + y[start+i]
```

This kernel performs an element-wise addition of arrays `x` and `y`, storing results in `z`. Instead of assigning one thread per element, each thread processes 1,024 elements sequentially, reducing the required grid size by a factor of 1,024.

In the loop, each iteration depends on the loop index `i`, but the operations within an iteration (loading `x[start+i]`, loading `y[start+i]`, and storing to `z[start+i]`) do not depend on prior iterations. If the compiler does not recognize this independence, it may force sequential execution.

Since iterations are actually independent, the kernel can be rewritten to expose this parallelism:

```
@cuda.jit
def add_arrays_unrolled(
    x: NDArray,
```

```
        y: NDArray,
        z: NDArray,
    ) -> None:
        t_id = cuda.grid(1)
        start = t_id * 1024
        for i in range(0, 1024, 4):
            z[start+i] = x[start+i] + y[start+i]
            z[start+i+1] = x[start+i+1] + y[start+i+1]
            z[start+i+2] = x[start+i+2] + y[start+i+2]
            z[start+i+3] = x[start+i+3] + y[start+i+3]
```

By reducing the loop to one-quarter of the iterations and explicitly repeating the loop body four times per iteration, the independence of operations is exposed. This unrolled version clarifies to the compiler that instructions within the loop body are independent, which should increase ILP per warp and improve performance.

But does this actually yield performance gains? When tested on arrays of roughly 130M elements using a grid of 500 blocks × 256 threads, both the original and unrolled kernels ran in ~65 ms. Despite the optimization attempt, no performance improvement was observed.

The explanation, as always, lies in the assembly.

Inspecting the assembly for `add_arrays` reveals a section beginning with the target label `$L__BB0_1`, which marks the loop entry point. At its end, the following instruction indicates a conditional branch back to the label if the boolean register `%p8` is `true`:

```
@%p8 bra    $L__BB0_1;
```

This confirms the section as the loop body.

The assembly loop body is longer than expected for a simple addition, containing multiple `ld` (load) and `st` (store) operations. This suggests that the compiler already applied loop unrolling automatically. As a result, the manually unrolled version produces assembly nearly identical to the original, explaining the lack of performance difference.

For simple loops with static bounds, compilers often handle unrolling effectively. But how can the effectiveness of unrolling be measured without parsing assembly? Profiling provides the answer.

Using ncu, kernel behavior before and after manual unrolling can be compared by examining two key metrics:

- **Instructions per cycle**: This is critical for compute-bound problems. Profile with `ncu --section ComputeWorkloadAnalysis`.
- **Memory throughput**: This is essential for memory-bound problems. Profile with `ncu --section MemoryWorkloadAnalysis`.

When comparing these metrics for the original and unrolled kernels, no meaningful difference was observed. This confirms that the compiler had already applied unrolling automatically.

The absolute values of these metrics reveal very poor resource utilization. On the compute side, only 0.02 instructions per cycle are executed, indicating the device spends most of its time idling. This is because the kernel is dominated by global memory loads and stores, with minimal time spent on the one addition operation. As a result, the kernel is memory-bound, but the low thread count fails to hide memory access latency.

Memory throughput further confirms this inefficiency: achieving just 180 GB/s—only ~25% of the device's 760 GB/s capability. The issue is clear: ILP cannot compensate for an insufficient number of threads. Since each thread processes 1,024 elements sequentially, most threads spend their time waiting on data.

To illustrate this, let's compare the metrics to a simplified kernel where each thread handles only a single element of x and y:

```
@cuda.jit
def add_arrays_simple(
    x: NDArray,
    y: NDArray,
    z: NDArray,
) -> None:
    t_id = cuda.grid(1)
    z[t_id] = x[t_id] + y[t_id]
```

With this approach, the kernel must be launched with 1,024× more blocks for the same problem size. Profiling reveals that compute efficiency remains similar, but memory bandwidth utilization jumps to 94%. Performance improves dramatically: from 65 ms to ~2 ms, a 30× speedup. In this simplified kernel, memory requests are fully parallelized, nearly saturating the available bandwidth.

The key lesson: on GPUs, distributing work across more threads is generally superior to packing more work into fewer threads and relying on ILP. This contrasts with CPUs, where thread scheduling overhead can degrade performance. Conventional CPU wisdom does not always apply to GPUs.

Loop unrolling remains useful only when work cannot be distributed further across threads, or in complex kernels where the compiler may miss optimization opportunities. For simple kernels, compilers often handle unrolling automatically. For example, revisiting the sine-series kernel's PTX assembly shows the 10-iteration loop was fully unrolled, with many variables (e.g., exponents, denominators) precomputed at compile time and embedded directly in the code.

When in doubt about kernel performance: inspect the assembly, check profiling metrics, and only then experiment with manual unrolling.

Note

Excessive unrolling

Over-aggressive unrolling can backfire by increasing the number of required registers, reducing occupancy, and hurting performance.

Avoiding warp divergence

In *Chapter 3*, threads were assumed to run independently, and the importance of the warp was not considered. However, warp-level behavior significantly impacts performance.

While all threads in a warp execute in lock-step, they can follow independent paths. This is only possible if all threads follow all paths, but only execute relevant instructions. When kernels contain extensive control flow, threads may spend considerable time waiting for others in the same warp, a phenomenon known as **warp divergence**.

A classic example of warp divergence occurs with conditional branches. If threads in a warp split between the `if` and `else` branches, all threads execute both paths sequentially. Threads not taking a branch stall, waiting for others to complete it.

This behavior can be demonstrated with the following kernel:

```
@cuda.jit
def warp_divergence(output):
    t_id = cuda.grid(1)

    if t_id % 2 == 0:
        val = 1.0
        cuda.nanosleep(1000)
    else:
```

```
        val = 0.0
        cuda.nanosleep(1000)

    output[t_id] = val
```

This kernel generates an alternating sequence of 1s and 0s, where even-numbered threads execute the first branch and odd-numbered threads execute the second. With 16 threads per warp in each branch, warp divergence is expected.

Note

Why cuda.nanosleep?

Compilers often optimize away branch divergence by removing conditional branches in the generated assembly. Here, `cuda.nanosleep` is added to force branching and prevent such optimizations.

Branch efficiency, measured via `ncu`, quantifies the fraction of non-divergent branching instructions. For this example, where half the threads diverge, ~50% efficiency is expected. The code can be profiled with the following:

```
ncu --section SourceCounters python warp_divergence_script.py
```

This kernel was run on a grid of 10,000 blocks and 256 threads per block. For the full code in `warp_divergence_script.py`, see the code repository associated with this book.

The results are captured in the following table:

```
Section: Source Counters
------------------------ ----------- ------------
Metric Name              Metric Unit Metric Value
------------------------ ----------- ------------
Branch Instructions Ratio          %         0.17
Branch Instructions             inst      640,000
Branch Efficiency                  %           50
Avg. Divergent Branches                    294.12
------------------------ ----------- ------------
```

A divergence-free version replaces the condition with `(t_id // 32) % 2 == 0`, ensuring all threads in a warp follow the same branch. While this alters the output (32-element blocks of 1s and 0s), it demonstrates the effect on branch efficiency. Profiling shows the following:

```
Section: Source Counters
------------------------ ---------- -----------
Metric Name              Metric Unit Metric Value
------------------------ ---------- -----------
Branch Instructions Ratio          %        0.11
Branch Instructions             inst     360,000
Branch Efficiency                  %         100
Avg. Divergent Branches                        0
------------------------ ---------- -----------
```

As expected, there are no divergent branches, and branch efficiency is 100%. However, the overall performance gain is negligible: from 0.166 s to 0.163 s. This is because `cuda.nanosleep` is considered warp stall, which allows the scheduler to mask divergence effects. Compute-heavy branches might yield different results.

The main takeaway from this section is to avoid strong variation in control flow within warps if possible. The only way to know whether control flow results in warp divergence is by profiling the kernel. For simple `if-else` clauses, the compiler automatically optimizes out the branches. Different warps can execute different code paths without any penalty on performance.

Efficient global memory access patterns

When a thread requests data from global memory, it fetches more than just this data. Data read and write requests from all threads in a warp are bundled into **transactions**. Transactions always fetch a fixed amount of data from fixed places in memory.

Think of memory like a very long line of boxes, each representing a byte (=8 bits) of data. Very often, a piece of data required by a thread will be 4 consecutive bytes (for 32-bit floats or integers) or 8 consecutive bytes (for 64-bit floats or integers). Now think of memory transactions like a container crane, packaging multiple of these boxes for shipment. The crane is only able to stop at well-defined positions along the line and is only able to put a fixed number of consecutive boxes in the container. Only entire containers can be shipped from memory to the SMs. The idea is visualized in *Figure 5.6*:

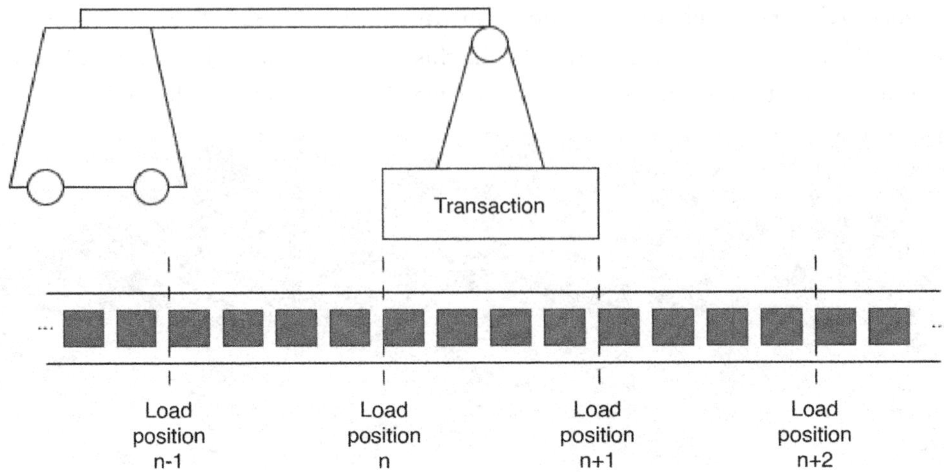

Figure 5.6 – An analogy for memory transactions. Units of data are represented by dark boxes. The figure is not to scale with the size of an actual transaction

Load transactions either span **32 bytes** or **128 bytes**, depending on the type of load instruction that is used. Note that 32 bytes = 8 × 4 bytes and 128 bytes = 32 × 4 bytes, so one transaction can load **8 or 32 single-precision floats** from global memory. Loads can only be performed starting from memory addresses that are a multiple of the transaction size (i.e., where `<memory address> % <32 or 128> == 0`). If every thread in a warp loads one 32-bit float from a contiguous stretch of memory starting from a transaction load position, this data request could global memory access patterns be serviced with four 32-byte transactions or a single 128-byte transaction. If this happens, the load is said to be **coalesced** (threads in a warp use contiguous data from memory) and **aligned** (with a transaction load position). The situation is illustrated for a 128-byte load in *Figure 5.7*:

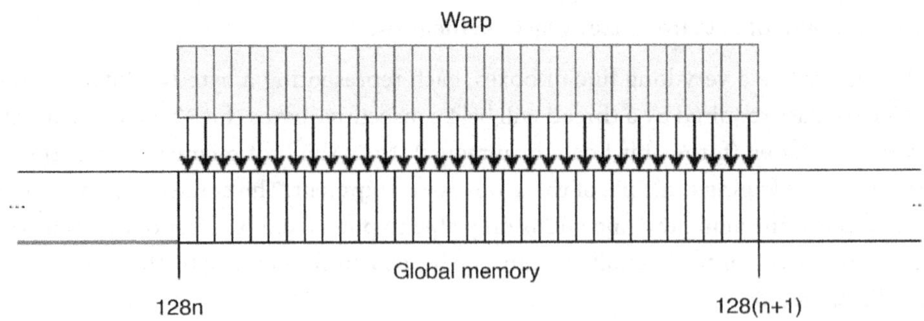

Figure 5.7 – Coalesced and aligned data access from one warp. A single 128-byte memory transaction can service all the data needs. One box in memory represents 4 bytes of data (e.g., a single-precision float)

Coalesced and aligned data access yields optimal use of the memory system and available bandwidth. Non-coalesced and/or non-aligned data access will always require more memory transactions, which puts pressure on the memory system and sends data that is not used. *Figure 5.8* illustrates an example of coalesced but non-aligned data access for a 128-byte transaction. In this case, two transactions are necessary and 50% of the data is unused:

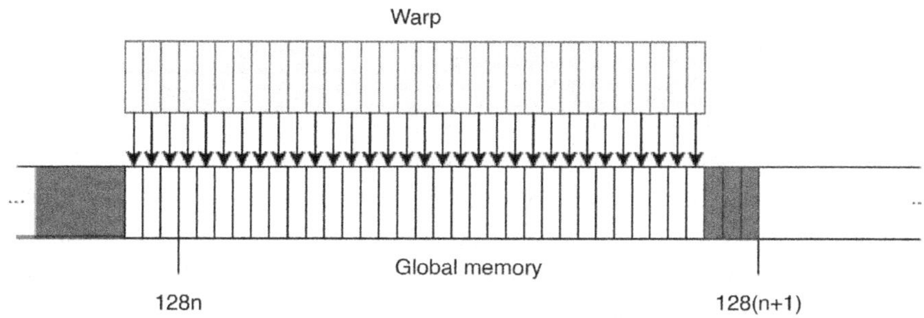

Figure 5.8 – Coalesced but not aligned data access from a warp. Two 128-byte memory transactions are needed. One box in memory represents 4 bytes of data

Figure 5.9 illustrates one example of aligned but non-coalesced data access for a 128-byte transaction. In this example, two transactions are needed to load the data, but only 50% of the data is used:

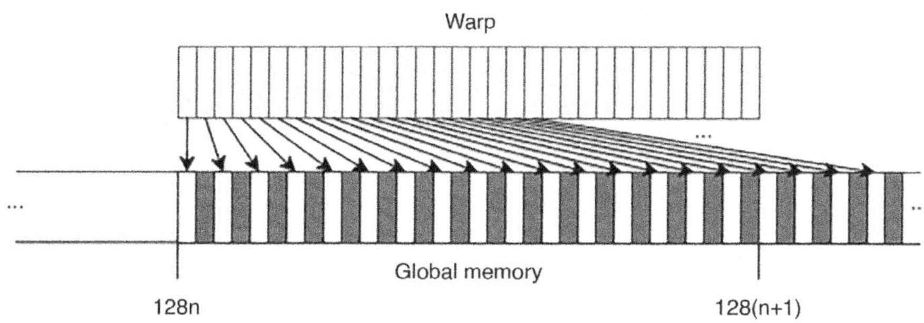

Figure 5.9 – Aligned but non-coalesced data access from a warp. Two 128-byte memory transactions are needed. One box in memory represents 4 bytes of data

In the worst case, data access is not coalesced and not aligned in such a way that each thread in a warp requires its own memory transaction. In this case, for a 128-byte transaction, (31 × 4 bytes)/(32 × 4 bytes) = 97% of the loaded data is wasted. With the smaller 32-byte transactions, bad data access patterns are more forgiving; in the worst case, (7 × 4 bytes)/(8 × 4 bytes) = 87.5% of data is unused.

How are good data access patterns implemented? The data in a device array is automatically aligned (i.e., the pointer to the start of the array will be a multiple of 128). This can be verified as follows:

```
arr = cuda.device_array(1024, dtype=np.float32)
ptr = arr.device_ctypes_pointer.value
assert ptr % 128 == 0
```

In a one-dimensional device array, all the values in the array are stored sequentially (i.e., the data is **contiguous**), making coalesced data access very natural. In a multi-dimensional array, the data is also stored sequentially in memory. However, for coalesced memory access on the GPU, it's important to know which dimension is the "inner" one – that is, the dimension along which elements are laid out contiguously in memory. This depends on the array's memory layout convention: in **C-order** (row-major), elements are contiguous along the last axis, while in **Fortran-order** (column-major), they are contiguous along the first axis. Warps should be aligned with the axis along which data is contiguous.

Let's illustrate non-aligned data access using a modified version of the simple kernel for adding two arrays element-wise:

```
@cuda.jit
def add_arrays(
    x: NDArray,
    y: NDArray,
    z: NDArray,
    shift: int,
) -> None:
    t_id = cuda.grid(1)
    inx = (t_id + shift) % x.shape[0]
    z[inx] = x[inx] + y[inx]
```

An extra `shift` parameter was added that controls which index in the array each thread maps to. By using `% x.shape[0]`, the index wraps around to the beginning of the array for indices that are out of bounds.

This kernel was profiled with

```
ncu --metrics smsp__sass_average_data_bytes_per_sector_mem_global_op_ld.pct,
l1tex__t_sectors_pipe_lsu_mem_global_op_ld.sum
```

The first metric represents the efficiency of the load operations (i.e., how much data was loaded versus how much was required). The second metric contains the total number of load operations. For arrays of 25.6 million elements and a shift of 0, which is equivalent to the unmodified kernel, there are 6.4 million load operations and 100% load efficiency. The observation that there are 6.4 million load operations indicates that the transaction size is 32 bytes: there are 25.6M / 32 = 800K warps, and each must perform 6.4M / 800K = 8 transactions. Two elements are loaded per thread, so a warp needs 2 × 4 × 32 = 256 bytes of data, which means 256 / 8 = 32 bytes per transaction.

Therefore, when the `shift` parameter is a multiple of `32 // 4 = 8`, 100% load efficiency is measured, because each warp is aligned with a transaction boundary. However, the total transactions are different unless `shift` is a multiple of 32 (i.e., 128 bytes). This is related to the way loads happen through the different layers of the cache.

Selecting a `shift` parameter that is not a multiple of 8 (i.e., 32 bytes), the efficiency drops to the expected 80%, and the number of loads increases by 20%.

Does this impact performance? Timing this kernel with different values of `shift` shows no significant change to performance. For this very simple kernel, the device is able to hide the latency associated with the small inefficiency.

So, let's make the situation worse by using non-coalesced access to add two 2D arrays. Consider the following kernel:

```
@cuda.jit
def add_arrays_2D(
    x: NDArray,
    y: NDArray,
    z: NDArray,
) -> None:
    t_x, t_y = cuda.grid(2)
    z[t_y, t_x] = x[t_y, t_x] + y[t_y, t_x]
```

Ideally, warps are aligned with the data: consecutive threads should access consecutive elements in the array. Let's run this kernel with different grid configurations, using blocks with 256 threads but with different shapes. The profiling and timing results for 16K by 16K arrays are shown in *Figure 5.10*:

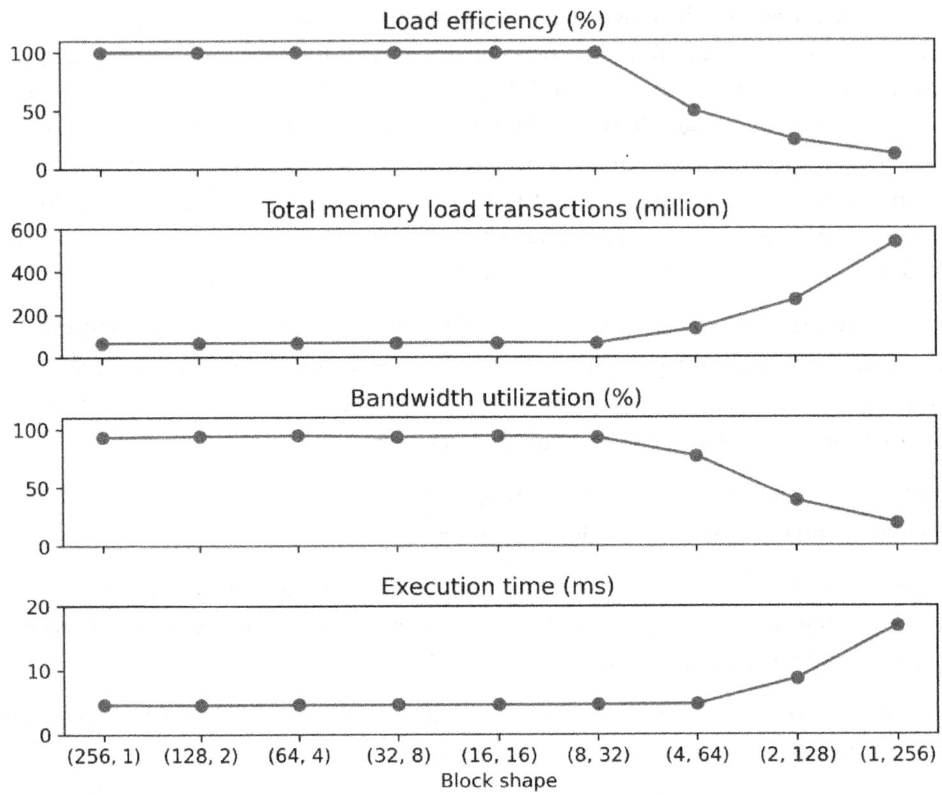

Figure 5.10 – Profiling and timing results for adding two 2D arrays for different block shapes

On the left are results for blocks that are long in the x direction and short in the y direction. Going to the right, blocks become narrower in x and longer in y. Up until a block width of 8, all metrics and execution times are nearly identical. When the block width becomes smaller than 8, the load efficiency halves, and the number of transactions doubles each time the width halves. In the extreme case of (1, 256), the load efficiency is only 12.5%, and there are nearly 600 million load transactions. In addition, the bandwidth utilization nosedives from nearly 93% to about 20%. Finally, execution time increases from 5 ms to 18 ms in the worst case.

What is going on? Remember that x is the inner dimension, which means that threads are scheduled into warps row by row. When the block is of shape (8, 32), the threads belonging to the same warp can be viewed as eight (8, 4) sub-blocks stacked on top of each other. The first row of 8 threads fetches $8 \times 4 = 32$ consecutive bytes from the first row of each matrix. So does the second, third, and fourth. Hence, each warp can service all its data loading needs with four 32-byte transactions (per matrix), even though the data between transactions is far apart.

When the block is of shape (1, 256), the warps can be viewed as eight (1, 32) sub-blocks. In this case, all threads in the warp read from a different row, so each warp sends 32 load instructions per input array. Of the 32 bytes in each transaction, only 4 bytes are used, leading to the measured efficiency of 12.5%.

Because warps need to send 32 times more requests for data, they stall much more often, and the memory system becomes overloaded with requests, which eventually leads to the bandwidth not being fully utilized; the amount of parallelism can no longer hide all the latency. For a problem that is very clearly memory-bound, this has a measurable impact on performance.

Store operations also happen through transactions. Like load operations, it is also important to consider aligned and coalesced access for store operations. Store transactions are either 128 bytes, 64 bytes, or 32 bytes; the optimal size will be chosen depending on how well data is coalesced. For example, if a warp writes 32 floats to a contiguous and aligned 128-byte range in VRAM, this can be serviced with a single 128-byte transaction. Store operations also contribute to bandwidth utilization and in-flight instructions, so it is important to be able to profile these as well. Use:

```
ncu --metrics smsp__sass_average_data_bytes_per_sector_mem_global_op_st.pct,
l1tex__t_sectors_pipe_lsu_mem_global_op_st.sum
```

to get store efficiency and the total number of store transactions. Details for store operations are omitted here, since the optimization logic is the same as for load operations.

> Note
>
> **Store and load efficiency trade-off**
>
> In the example used here, store operations follow the same pattern as load operations. However, for some kernels, efficient loads come at the cost of efficient stores, for example, in transposing a matrix. In this case, an appropriate trade-off needs to be found for optimal performance.

Accessing global memory efficiently is very important due to the very high latency of fetching data. Global memory bandwidth is used optimally when the fetching of unused data is avoided. This can be achieved by designing kernels and launch configurations with the intent to maximize aligned and coalesced data access. Furthermore, maximizing parallelism by launching many threads and making use of ILP also enhances bandwidth utilization and performance.

Avoiding frequent global memory data access

Accessing global memory is slow, which is why there are two layers of cache in between to reduce the effective latency. L1 and L2 caches cannot be explicitly programmed; their behavior is controlled indirectly via data access patterns, through configuration, and by using specific load and store operations. However, some algorithms with predictable data access patterns and frequent data reuse benefit from low-latency memory that is explicitly controlled. This section explains two mechanisms that reduce global memory requests and cache pressure: **shared memory** and **warp intrinsics**.

Effectively using shared memory

Shared memory is memory that lives on the same hardware as the L1 cache. Each SM has its own L1 cache, with data access that is about 20-30 times faster than accessing VRAM.

As the name implies, shared memory is shared by all threads in a block. Therefore, it is useful as a programmable scratch space for keeping data that needs to be reused by multiple threads.

> Note
>
> **Sharing data between blocks**
>
> Inter-block data sharing is only possible through global memory. However, sharing data between threads often requires synchronization. There is no primitive for syncing blocks.

In the case of the array addition kernel, there is no benefit to using shared memory, since each element of each array is used only once by one thread. However, there are many algorithms where shared memory can be of tremendous benefit. Consider the following kernel for calculating a moving average:

```
@cuda.jit
def moving_average(
    data: NDArray,
    avg: NDArray,
) -> None:
    g_id = cuda.grid(1)

    if g_id < WINDOW - 1 or g_id >= data.size:
        return

    acc = float32(0.0)
    for i in range(WINDOW):
        acc += data[g_id - i]
    avg[g_id] = acc / float32(WINDOW)
```

The moving average calculates the average of an element and the elements that precede it, for each element. The number of elements included in the average is specified by a `WINDOW` parameter. So, for example, if `WINDOW=2` and the data is `[2, 4, 6, 8, 10]`, the moving averages will be `[?, 3, 5, 7, 9]`. Moving averages are often used as a tool for analyzing the price evolution of financial instruments.

To calculate the moving average of an array with CUDA, one thread is mapped to each element in the output array. In the straightforward kernel, there is first a check whether the thread ID is in bounds. Then, all the elements in the window are summed, with the result stored in the output array. The `WINDOW` parameter is a global parameter initialized outside the kernel, for reasons that will soon become apparent.

Notice that this kernel loads the same data multiple times for different threads: thread `n` needs the data from `[n - WINDOW + 1, n]` and thread `n+1` needs the data from `[n - WINDOW + 2, n+1]`; except for 1 element, all the data overlaps. As the window size increases, the duplicate data loads increase. Since the data access pattern is well defined, shared memory can help reduce the pressure on global memory.

To use shared memory, it must be allocated inside a kernel as follows:

```
shared = cuda.shared.array(SHARED_SIZE, dtype=float32)
```

`SHARED_SIZE` is a global constant that must be declared outside the kernel. For **static shared memory**, the size of shared memory must be known at compile time. Shared memory is shared among all threads in a block, so a good starting point is to size the shared memory array such that it can hold all the data needed by all the threads in the block. For the moving average kernel, this means the following:

```
SHARED_SIZE = BLOCK_SIZE + WINDOW - 1
```

Since `SHARED_SIZE` must be defined outside the kernel, `WINDOW` must also be declared outside the kernel.

The most common pattern is to first use the threads in each block to load data into shared memory. Then, a calculation is performed on the data in shared memory. Data is loaded from global memory only once in a coalesced way; for repeated use in the calculation, data is loaded from the much faster shared memory instead.

The following code loads data into the shared array for the moving averages kernel:

```
t_id = cuda.threadIdx.x

if g_id >= SHARED_SIZE:
    stop = g_id - SHARED_SIZE
else:
    stop = -1

for i in range(g_id, stop, -BLOCK_SIZE):
    j = i - g_id + t_id + WINDOW - 1
    shared[j] = data[i]
```

To illustrate what is going on in this snippet, *Figure 5.11* shows the data flow for one block with BLOCK_SIZE=4 and WINDOW=3:

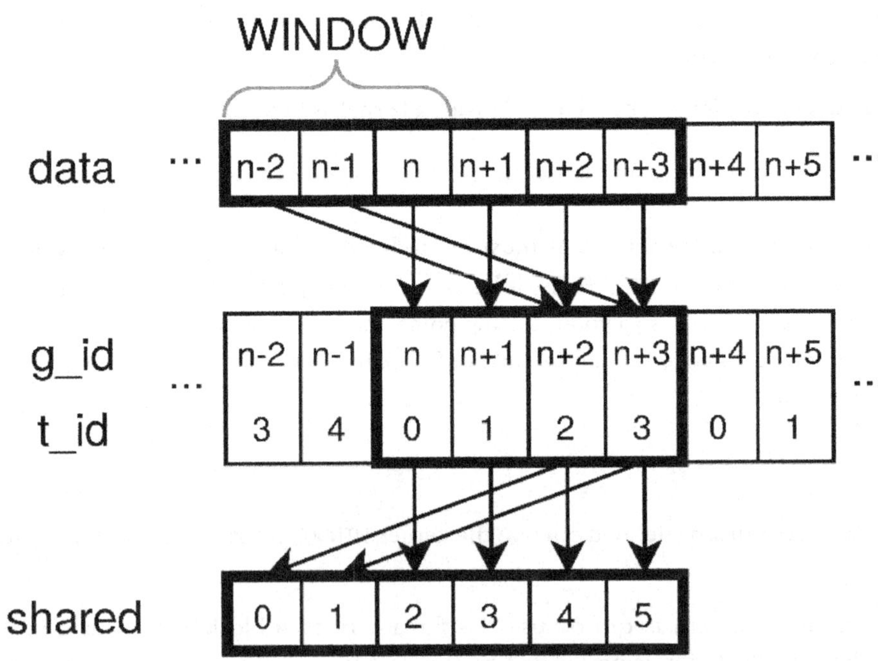

Figure 5.11 – Illustration of loading moving window data into shared memory

The pattern used here is similar to the grid-stride-loop approach discussed in *Chapter 3*. Each thread in the block is responsible for loading elements [g_id, g_id - BLOCK_SIZE, g_id - 2*BLOCK_SIZE, ...] from global memory, where g_id is the global thread index in the grid. When the window is smaller than the block size, most threads only load a single element, and some will load two, as illustrated in the figure. Thanks to the striding-loop approach, the algorithm works for any block and window size. Slightly tricky is mapping the index `i` of the data element in global memory to the corresponding index `j` in the shared memory array. Verifying that the given expression in the code is correct is left as an exercise.

The `if` statement before the `for` loop serves to deal with the edge case of the first few blocks that might attempt to load out-of-bounds data before the start of the array.

Before moving on to calculating the moving average, it is crucial that all threads in the block have finished loading the data into shared memory. Otherwise, some threads may begin calculating moving averages with incomplete data. Thus, after loading data in shared memory, threads in the block need to be **synchronized**, using the following statement in the kernel:

```
cuda.syncthreads()
```

When warps reach this statement, they wait until all other warps in the block have reached the same point.

The final part of the kernel serves to calculate the moving average like before:

```
if g_id < WINDOW - 1:
    return

acc = float32(0.0)
for i in range(WINDOW):
    acc += shared[t_id + i]
avg[g_id] = acc / float32(WINDOW)
```

The only changes compared to the original kernel are that the array from which data is read was replaced, and the indexing was modified. The full kernel can be found in the code repository associated with this chapter. This kernel produces the same result as the simple kernel.

Using shared memory does not automatically improve performance. Firstly, using shared memory often leads to more complexity and therefore more instructions and branches. Secondly, an explicit thread synchronization step is often needed, which stalls warps and constrains the warp scheduler. Third, shared memory is a limited resource that may restrict the number of blocks that can be scheduled on the SM. These effects can offset the beneficial effects of fetching data from low-latency memory.

Applying this logic to the moving averages kernel, the window size determines how often a data element is needed. So, the benefit of shared memory should be larger when the window size is large. However, the size of blocks also determines the size of the shared memory array. Larger blocks imply fewer re-loads of the same data into shared memory (by different blocks), but also less parallelism (since more warps need to synchronize) and higher resource requirements from each block.

The best way to find out how all these effects influence performance is to profile the kernel. *Figure 5.12* shows the timing results for different combinations of window sizes and block sizes:

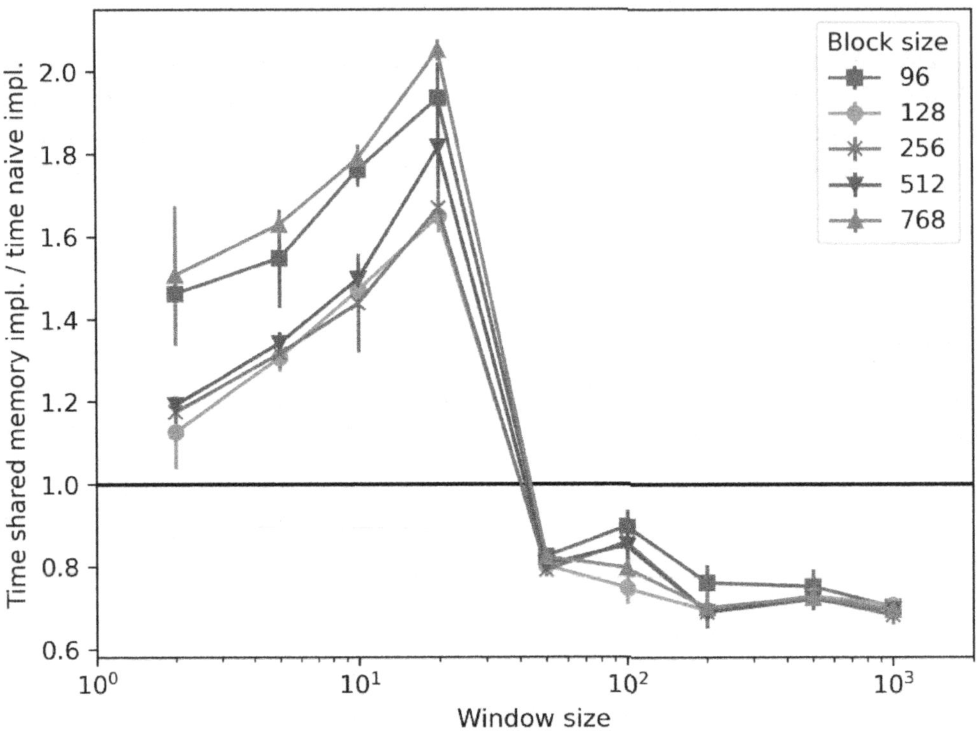

Figure 5.12 – Comparative timing results for shared memory versus naive implementation for different window and block sizes

The window size is represented on a log scale *x* axis, and the *y* axis represents the ratio of the time for the kernel that uses shared memory versus the kernel that does not. Different curves represent different block sizes. When the *y* value is larger than 1, the shared memory implementation is slower than the naive kernel; when the *y* value is smaller than 1, the shared memory implementation is more performant.

As expected, larger windows make the shared memory implementation more performant compared to the naive implementation. Between a window size of 20 and 50 elements, the shared memory kernel suddenly becomes more performant. However, performance improvement seems limited to 30-40%. The block size has no significant effect on the relative improvement, likely because the increased resource requirements counteract the beneficial effect of a larger block.

Understanding the shape of the graph and the sudden drop would require a deep profiling investigation and is outside the scope of this discussion. The main takeaway is that, while using shared memory can overcome the bottleneck of global memory data accesses, it comes at the cost of a more complicated kernel that may not always show improved performance due to extraneous effects.

Note

Dynamic shared memory

In the previous example, static shared memory with a known size at compile time was used. It is also possible to use **dynamic shared memory arrays** by declaring the size of the array to be 0 in the kernel. The size of the array then needs to be supplied as an extra parameter in the kernel launch configuration. Instead of launching the kernel with `kernel[grid_size, block_dim]`, it must be launched with `kernel[grid_dim, block_dim, stream, dyn_shared_mem_size]`, where `dyn_shared_mem_size` is the size of the dynamic memory in bytes and `stream` is the CUDA stream (more details in *Chapter 6*). Using dynamic shared memory is tricky when the kernel requires multiple shared memory arrays; in this case, `dyn_shared_mem_size` must be the sum of the size of all arrays. Whereas static shared memory arrays can be 2D or 3D, dynamic shared memory arrays are limited to 1D.

The final element to discuss with regard to shared memory and performance is **bank conflicts**. When threads access shared memory, they do so through 32 **banks**, each 4 bytes (one 32-bit float) wide. Think of an analogy with 32 chambers over which the data is divided. For each request, the door of each chamber allows 4 bytes of data to pass. The bank in which data resides is deterministic, and is given by the following expression:

```
bank index = (byte address / 4) % 32
```

So, for an array of 32-bit floats or integers, this simplifies to the following:

```
bank index = element index % 32
```

When a thread accesses data in a bank, the process is akin to opening the door, getting the data, and closing the door again. Bank conflicts occur when multiple threads in a warp all access different data in the same bank. This means there will be congestion at one of the doors, and multiple requests are required to fetch the data. The desired methods of data access are as follows:

- All threads in a warp access data in different banks. This can be handled by one request of a warp to shared memory.
- All threads in a warp access the same value. This can also be handled by one request per warp; the value is broadcast to all threads.

All other forms of data access result in bank conflicts, which can reduce performance.

Good shared data access practices are illustrated in the following kernel:

```
@cuda.jit
def bank_no_conflicts(
    output: NDArray,
) -> None:
    shared = cuda.shared.array((32, 32), float32)

    g_idx, g_idy = cuda.grid(2)
    t_idx = cuda.threadIdx.x
    t_idy = cuda.threadIdx.y

    lin_id = t_idx + t_idy * cuda.blockDim.x
    shared[t_idy, t_idx] = float32(lin_id)

    output[g_idy, g_idx] = shared[t_idy, t_idx]
```

This simple kernel produces a 2D array, with the linear thread ID `lin_id` stored in each element. The kernel must be called with a 32 by 32 thread block. Instead of simply storing `lin_id` directly in `output`, the result is first stored in a 32 by 32 shared memory array. Then the data is copied from shared memory to global memory. Since the threads don't share data, there is no need for thread synchronization after loading data into shared memory.

The worst way to use shared memory is achieved by swapping the indices on the `shared` array, from `shared[t_idy, t_idx]` to `shared[t_idx, t_idy]`. The output kernel is the same, the global memory store operations are the same; the only difference is that the intermediate shared memory array is transposed:

```
@cuda.jit
def bank_conflicts(
    output: NDArray,
) -> None:
    shared = cuda.shared.array((32, 32), float32)

    g_idx, g_idy = cuda.grid(2)
    t_idx = cuda.threadIdx.x
    t_idy = cuda.threadIdx.y

    lin_id = t_idx + t_idy * cuda.blockDim.x
    shared[t_idx, t_idy] = float32(lin_id)

    output[g_idy, g_idx] = shared[t_idx, t_idy]
```

For a 16k by 16k output array, the `no_bank_conflicts` kernel runs in 2.0 ms, while the `bank_conflicts` kernel takes 3.4 ms. The runtime nearly doubled! Since everything else about the kernel remained the same, this can only be the result of bank conflicts.

This can be verified using `ncu`, using metrics such as `l1tex__data_bank_conflicts_pipe_lsu_mem_shared_op_ld.sum`, which measures the total number of bank conflicts when loading from shared memory, and `l1tex__data_bank_conflicts_pipe_lsu_mem_shared_op_st.sum`, which measures the total number of bank conflicts when storing to shared memory. For the `no_bank_conflicts` kernel, both of these metrics are 0, as expected. For the `bank_conflicts` kernel, `l1tex__data_bank_conflicts_pipe_lsu_mem_shared_op_st.sum = 260,046,848`. This is exactly equal to the total number of warps in the grid times 31 (i.e., each warp has a 31-way bank conflict because all threads access different data in the same bank).

Interestingly, there are 0 bank conflicts for `l1tex__data_bank_conflicts_pipe_lsu_mem_shared_op_ld.sum` (i.e., there are no bank conflicts when loading from shared memory). This can be explained by inspecting the PTX assembly of the `bank_conflicts` kernel. The PTX assembly shows a `st.shared.f32` instruction, but no `ld.shared` instruction. The kernel ends with the following:

```
st.global.f32   [%rd31], %f1;
```

This means the compiler realized that there is no need to load the value from shared memory to store it in global memory; the value stored in `shared[t_idx, t_idy]` was also stored in a register, and global memory is updated using the register value.

In summary, shared memory is a programmable cache with low latency that can help with kernel performance if many threads need to reuse data from global memory. However, effectively using shared memory significantly complicates kernel logic and makes debugging much harder. The added complexity can reduce performance in some instances, so be sure that loading from global memory is the bottleneck. When shared memory is used in the kernel, avoid access patterns that induce bank conflicts. This can easily happen accidentally by swapping indices when using 2D or 3D shared memory arrays.

Exchanging register data using warp shuffle instructions

Besides shared memory, there is a method with even lower latency in which threads can share data: **warp shuffle instructions**. These allow threads in the same warp to exchange data directly via registers. There are four variants: `shfl_sync`, `shfl_up_sync`, `shfl_down_sync`, and `shfl_xor_sync`. The `shfl_*` instructions all take a `mask` argument, a value argument, and an additional parameter that parametrizes the shuffle.

Consider the following dummy example that uses `shfl_sync`:

```
@cuda.jit
def shfl_sync_example(
    output: NDArray,
    source_lane: int,
) -> None:
    g_id = cuda.grid(1)
    lane = cuda.threadIdx.x % 32

    val = g_id
    new_val = cuda.shfl_sync(cuda.activemask(), val, source_lane)

    output[g_id] = new_val
```

This kernel stores the global thread ID in the `val` variable. With `shfl_sync`, each thread gets the value of `val` from the thread in the same warp corresponding to the `source_lane` lane. The lane of the thread is the index of the thread in the warp, which goes up from 0 to 31. The shuffled `val` is stored in the output array.

Running this kernel with `source_lane = 1` results in elements 0-31 of the output being equal to the ID of thread 1, elements 32-63 will be equal to the ID of thread 33, elements 64-95 will be equal to the ID of thread 65, and so on. In this example, each thread sees the same `lane` parameter, but this can also be different for each thread for more interesting behavior.

The `mask` parameter is a 32-bit integer from 0 to $2^{32} - 1$ that represents a bitmask for which threads take part in the instruction. Each bit represents a thread; 1 represents active participation of the thread in the lane of that bit position. Most of the time, all threads take part in the instruction, and `cuda.activemask()` should be used. This is equal to $2^{32} - 1$ for most warps, except for warps at the edges of the grid.

The purpose of `mask` is to deal with the situation where the `shfl_*` instruction is used inside a branch. When some threads in a warp do see the instruction, the program could hang. Therefore, it is important to set the mask appropriately based on the logic of the kernel.

Note

Masks are not control logic

The `mask` parameter is used for thread synchronization within a warp. It is not a replacement for control logic (i.e., it cannot be used to prevent threads from executing the shuffle instruction).

The `shfl_up_sync` and `shfl_down_sync` instructions shift a value up or down the warp by a given `delta`. So, for example, the following code returns the value of `val` from the previous thread in the warp (without wraparound):

```
cuda.shfl_up_sync(cuda.activemask(), val, 1)
```

The result, if the shuffled value is stored, is that the values of `val` are shifted up the warp to higher thread lanes. The situation is analogous for `shfl_down_sync`, but in the opposite direction.

The most complex operation is `shfl_xor_sync`. It takes a `lane_mask` parameter, and each thread gets the value from the thread with the lane index equal to `XOR(lane, lane_mask)`. The end result is a swapping of values in a cross-over pattern. If `lane_mask` is 1, then neighboring pairs are swapped. If `lane_mask` is 2, then groups of two neighboring pairs are swapped.

Let's illustrate this with a real example of summing all elements in a warp:

```
MASK = 0b11111111111111111111111111111111

@cuda.jit
def sum_in_warp(data: NDArray, output: NDArray) -> None:
    g_id = cuda.grid(1)
    val = data[g_id]

    val += cuda.shfl_xor_sync(MASK, val, 16)
    val += cuda.shfl_xor_sync(MASK, val, 8)
    val += cuda.shfl_xor_sync(MASK, val, 4)
    val += cuda.shfl_xor_sync(MASK, val, 2)
    val += cuda.shfl_xor_sync(MASK, val, 1)

    output[g_id] = val
```

The first 32 elements of the output array contain the sum of the first 32 input elements, and so on for each group of 32 consecutive elements. *Figure 5.13* illustrates how the kernel works for one warp. The values in the array represent `val` for one warp. In the illustration, the values are the integers 0 to 31. To keep the image interpretable, only half of the warp is shown after the first addition, and only one-fourth of the warp after that.

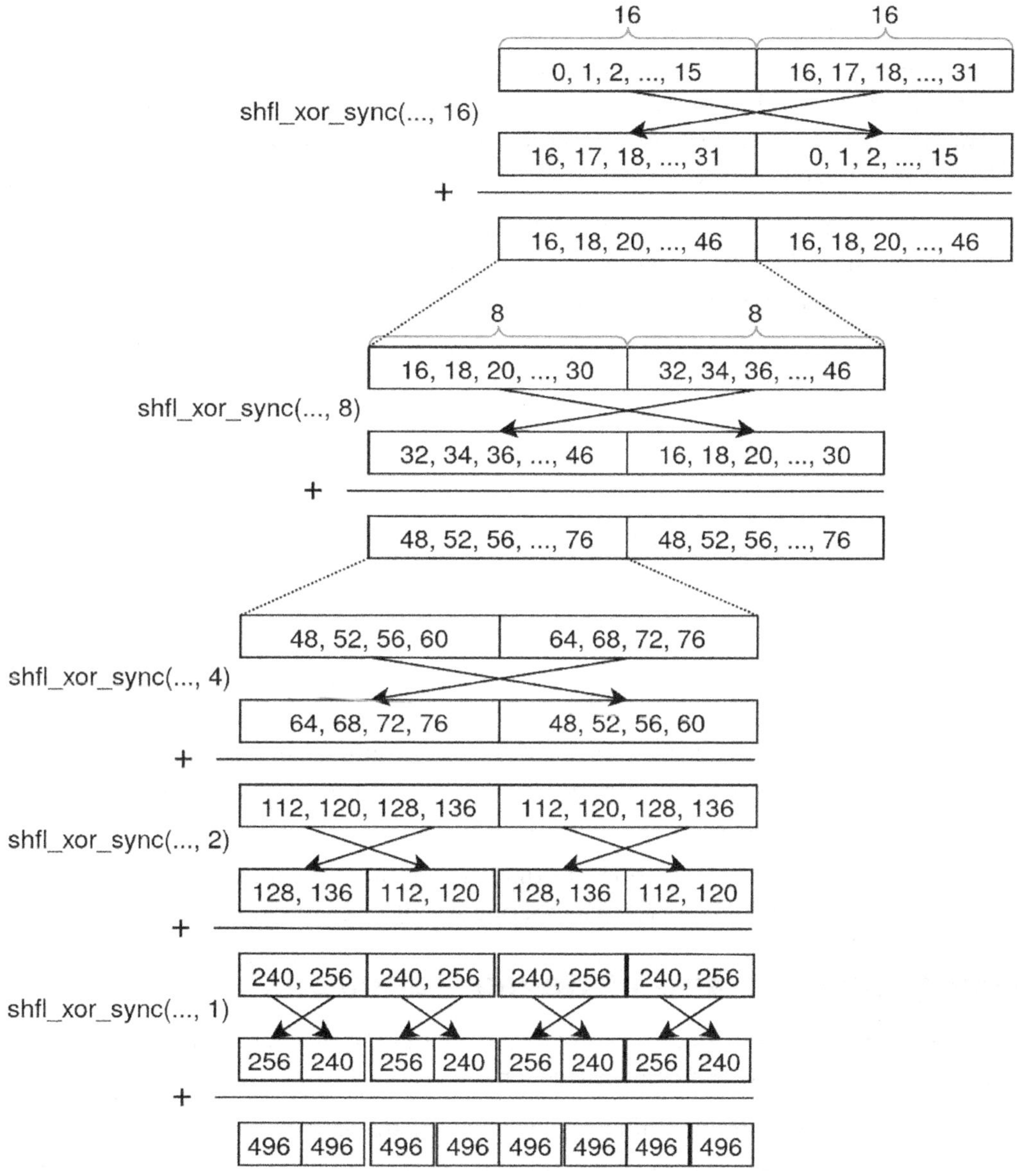

Figure 5.13 – Illustration of the sum_in_warp kernel for one warp

To see how this works, a helpful way to think about it is imagining the values corresponding to a warp as a long piece of paper with 32 numbers, representing `val` in each thread. Assume the perspective of the first thread. Shuffle XOR 16 plus addition is like cutting the strip of paper in half and stacking the second piece on top of the first. Shuffle XOR 8 plus addition afterwards is like cutting the 2 stacked strips in half, then stacking the 4 pieces. The process repeats until the stack is 32 numbers high (i.e., all the numbers in the warp have been added).

In this example, 32 numbers have been added using only 5 shuffle operations and 5 additions. Compare this to the following naive implementation, whereby elements are summed directly in threads with IDs that are a multiple of 32:

```
@cuda.jit
def sum_in_warp_global_mem(data: NDArray, output: NDArray) -> None:
    g_id = cuda.grid(1)
    lane = g_id % 32

    if lane == 0:
        s = 0.0
        for i in range(32):
            s += data[g_id + i]
        output[g_id] = s
```

For arrays of size 50M, the naive implementation takes around 14 ms, while the warp shuffle implementation takes only 620 microseconds. Warp shuffle instructions are often used as part of optimized reduction kernels.

Warp shuffle instructions can be tricky to think about and use effectively. Consider it another specialized tool that enables very fast data sharing among threads within the same warp.

Using intrinsic and libdevice functions

Sometimes, the bottleneck is in the compute operations themselves. Maybe there is a faster way to do the same thing with a different instruction.

A very common operation is multiplication followed by addition: `xy + z`. For this specific situation, there exist **intrinsic** functions that perform this in a single operation: **fused multiply add** or **FMA**. This single operation can be substantially faster than two separate arithmetic operations, which can make a meaningful performance difference if the kernel performs many of these instructions. Different flavors of FMA exist, for different `dtypes` and with different rounding behaviors.

Many other intrinsics exist for common operations – for example, to calculate the cube root of a number. It is impossible to list all operations here; consult the official CUDA documentation for an up-to-date list: `https://docs.nvidia.com/cuda/libdevice-users-guide/function-desc.html`. All these functions are wrapped in `numba.cuda`, for which the documentation can be found here: `https://nvidia.github.io/numba-cuda/reference/libdevice.html`.

Using cooperative groups instead of multiple kernel launches

Explicit synchronization between threads is only possible at the level of blocks, not entire grids.

Some problems require more control over synchronization. For these problems, one solution is launching the kernel multiple times, since kernel completion implicitly synchronizes all blocks. Alternatively, **cooperative groups** allow for thread synchronization at a higher level. The mechanism is similar to `cuda.syncthreads()`. At the time of writing, the implementation of cooperative groups in Numba-CUDA is quite limited and only allows for synchronization across all threads in the grid.

This is illustrated with an example that can also be found in the Numba-CUDA documentation. Consider a 1D grid where each thread is responsible for filling in one column of a 2D matrix according to some rule. The rule is that each thread must use the value on the other side of the matrix and increment by 1 to get the value for the next row. When a row of zeros is passed to the kernel, each thread produces a column with row numbers. It is important that threads depend on data that is produced by other threads on the other side of the grid. Therefore, all threads in the entire grid must move row-by-row in lockstep.

The following kernel implements this idea with cooperative groups:

```
@cuda.jit
def sequential_rows(M: NDArray):
    column = cuda.grid(1)
    cg = cuda.cg.this_grid()

    n_rows = M.shape[0]
    n_cols = M.shape[1]

    for row in range(1, n_rows):
        other_side = n_cols - column - 1
        M[row, column] = M[row - 1, other_side] + 1
        cg.sync()
```

The group is obtained through the `cuda.cg.this_grid()` function, which represents the group of all threads in the grid. In the loop, each thread attempts to update each element in the column row by row. In each iteration of the loop, all threads in the cooperative group are synced to ensure all threads move in lockstep.

Without cooperative groups, all the threads process the rows at different speeds, so the output is non-deterministic. The only other way to avoid undefined behavior would be with a new kernel launch for every row. Thanks to the cooperative group abstraction, this complexity can be avoided. As with any type of synchronization, it should only be used when necessary for maximum performance.

Summary

This chapter examined the CUDA execution model and GPU hardware architecture, analyzing how metrics such as occupancy, warp divergence, and memory bandwidth utilization impact performance. Since no single metric fully explains performance issues, and each may have multiple root causes, optimization often requires systematic investigation.

For peak performance, parallelism should be maximized to keep compute and memory operations in flight, hiding latency. Key strategies include the following:

- Distributing work across as many threads as possible
- Selecting grid configurations that maximize occupancy
- Using loop unrolling for ILP, if the compiler hasn't already

In addition, coalesced and aligned global memory access is critical for minimizing waste. While shared memory and warp shuffle instructions can accelerate kernels that require data reuse, they add complexity and may not always improve performance. Efficient intrinsics should also be prioritized. Ultimately, timing, profiling, and experimentation are essential to diagnose kernel behavior and identify optimizations. Reading PTX assembly further aids in understanding low-level execution.

Having explored how GPUs execute kernels, the next chapter introduces CUDA streams, a tool for parallelizing data transfers and kernel executions.

Questions

1. In the occupancy graph of *Figure 5.3*, why, for the block size of 1,024, is there nearly perfect agreement with the theoretical occupancy for all problem sizes?
2. What information is needed to calculate theoretical occupancy?
3. What is the advantage of large blocks over small blocks and vice versa?

4. Someone opines that it is better to use fewer threads and give more work to individual threads. Is this good advice? Why or why not?
5. If each thread in a warp needs to load one f64 from global memory, how many 32-byte transactions are needed in the best case? What about the worst case?
6. Is shared memory beneficial in a kernel that multiplies two matrices?

Answers

1. For a block size of 1,024 threads (32 warps), each SM can host only one block due to thread limits. Since 1,024 threads occupy 32 of the 48 possible warps per SM (for RTX 3080), the theoretical occupancy is 66%. When the problem size is large enough, all SMs are saturated with one block, so the occupancy matches the theoretical value. Smaller problem sizes leave some SMs idle, but occupancy is calculated per active SM, so the average remains consistent. To measure reliable occupancy, the number of blocks must exceed the number of SMs to ensure full device utilization.
2. To calculate theoretical occupancy per SM, hardware limits per SM (max resident threads, blocks, registers, and shared memory), kernel resource requirements (registers per thread and shared memory per thread/block), and block size are required. For device-wide occupancy, the number of SMs and grid size (to ensure enough blocks exist to saturate the GPU) are also required.
3. Large blocks are advantageous when kernels rely on shared memory or thread communication, as they reduce the overhead of launching many blocks and can improve data locality within a block. Small blocks, however, are better for load balancing across SMs and in cases where warps within a block frequently synchronize, as smaller blocks give the warp scheduler more flexibility to switch to other warps when stalls occur. Ultimately, the optimal block size depends on the kernel's specific requirements, and profiling is the only reliable way to determine the best choice.
4. This is generally poor advice because GPUs hide latency by rapidly switching between warps, and fewer threads reduce the scheduler's ability to mask latency. Maximizing parallelism by distributing work across many threads is almost always better. However, there are exceptions: kernel launch overhead (the time required to start a kernel on the GPU) can become significant for very small workloads, where the cost of launching many blocks outweighs the benefits of parallelism. For memory-bound kernels, if each thread's additional work is compute-intensive rather than memory-intensive, bundling work into fewer threads might help, but this is rare and should always be validated through profiling.

5. One `f64` takes up 8 bytes, so 4 doubles can be loaded per 32-byte transaction if they are loaded in an aligned and coalesced way. If 32 threads need to load one double, at least 8 transactions are needed. In the worst case, each thread loads a double from a different place in memory, in which case 32 transactions are needed.
6. Yes. Matrix multiplication involves reusing elements from both input matrices (e.g., in tiled algorithms). Shared memory caches tiles of the matrices, drastically reducing global memory accesses and improving performance. This will be explored further in an upcoming chapter.

Get this book's PDF version and more

Scan the QR code (or go to `packtpub.com/unlock`). Search for this book by name, confirm the edition, and then follow the steps on the page.

UNLOCK NOW

Note: Keep your invoice handy. Purchases made directly from Packt don't require an invoice.

6

Enabling Concurrency Using CUDA Streams

This chapter introduces **CUDA streams**, a powerful feature of the CUDA programming model designed to increase GPU performance by overlapping tasks. GPU operations by default are carried out sequentially. This sequential execution can lead to underutilization of GPU resources, as the GPU may remain idle while waiting for data transfers or computation to be completed. CUDA streams address this limitation by enabling multiple tasks to proceed concurrently. This is potentially useful for applications involving repetitive data processing or requiring real-time responsiveness. In this chapter, we begin with an overview of CUDA streams, then explore how to implement stream concurrency in Numba-CUDA. We will then see how CUDA **events** can be used to coordinate dependencies between streams, and how streams can be combined with multithreading to maximize performance.

By the end of this chapter, you will have a solid understanding of the following concepts:

- Key concepts of CUDA streams
- Creating and managing streams in Numba-CUDA
- Asynchronous data transfers between the host and the device
- Overlapping kernel execution with data transfers for improved efficiency
- Analyzing performance improvements using stream profiling
- Timing streams and handling stream dependencies using CUDA events
- Learning how to use multithreading together with CUDA streams

Technical requirements

To be able to run the provided example codes in this chapter, you will need a system equipped with an NVIDIA GPU. We use `pixi` as a dependency management tool that installs all required packages, including the Numba-CUDA library. To set up the environment, simply run `pixi install` in the root directory of the book's GitHub repository. This will ensure that all dependencies are installed. Once the installation is complete, you can activate the environment using `pixi shell`.

To use JupyterLab, run the following command:

```
pixi run jupyter-lab
```

You will also need to install **NVIDIA Nsight Systems** separately to enable profiling and visualization of the CUDA stream timeline. You can always get the latest version from NVIDIA's official Developer site (`https://developer.nvidia.com/tools-downloads`), available for different platforms such as Linux, Windows, and macOS.

The chapter's code is available on GitHub and can be accessed via this link: `https://github.com/PacktPublishing/GPU-Accelerated-Computing-with-Python-3-and-CUDA`. We recommend cloning the repository and following the instructions in the README file to get started on building the environment.

Why CUDA streams are needed

CUDA streams are a programming abstraction used to improve scheduling work on a GPU. A stream represents a sequence of operations, such as kernel launches and memory transfers, that execute in order relative to each other. By default, all GPU work runs on a single stream, which enforces a strict, sequential execution order. Using multiple streams allows expressing which operations must be ordered and which are independent, allowing the CUDA runtime and hardware scheduler to overlap data transfers and independent kernels. This leads to better GPU utilization and often performance gains. Streams are especially valuable when memory movement is a bottleneck. By placing **host-to-device** (**H2D**) copies, kernel execution, and **device-to-host** (**D2H**) copies in different streams, applications can overlap data transfers with computation. This is common in real-time signal processing, video pipelines, and large scientific simulations. Streams also provide finer-grained **synchronization** through **events**, helping avoid costly global device synchronizations that stall all GPU work. These topics will be discussed in more detail later in this chapter.

Nevertheless, it is important to note that CUDA streams are not always beneficial and can sometimes make things worse. If your application launches only a single large kernel that already fully occupies the GPU, additional streams won't increase performance and may add overhead or complexity. Streams also provide little benefit when kernels have strong data dependencies, or when memory transfers cannot overlap due to hardware limitations (e.g., old GPUs). They're best avoided when concurrency is limited, unnecessary, or adds more complexity than value. We will return to this later and will introduce profiling tools for identifying exactly when CUDA streams can be beneficial.

Key concepts in CUDA streams

We begin by discussing key concepts related to CUDA streams and addressing common challenges that may arise when working with them. These challenges often involve understanding how concurrency is achieved, recognizing when synchronization can limit performance, learning techniques on how to avoid it, and managing how tasks are scheduled and executed on the GPU hardware.

Streams and concurrency

A **stream** can be thought of as a *logical* queue of operations to be executed on the GPU. Streams heavily rely on **concurrency**, which is the ability of multiple tasks to run at the same time, even if they are not completing simultaneously. Concurrency is not the same as parallelism. Parallelism means executing multiple kernels simultaneously using different GPU resources. Concurrency with streams refers to overlapping different types of operations, in particular, performing data transfers between the host and device while execution kernels. CUDA allows operations from multiple streams to execute concurrently when the hardware supports asynchronous execution. Most GPUs have a single copy engine, but some (e.g., A100) support two separate engines, allowing H2D and D2H memory transfers to overlap with each other and with kernel execution. When we launch kernels or perform memory transfers, all operations are placed into the **same stream**. Within this stream, operations always run sequentially in the order submitted by the host. However, by creating and using multiple streams, we can enable **concurrency**, overlapping data transfers with kernel executions, which helps hide data transfer latency and improves overall performance.

Common data processing applications require transferring different datasets to the device, running an operation on it, and transferring results back. The straightforward way to implement this is to rely on a single stream. The following diagram visualizes how using a single stream enforces sequential execution. Instead, using multiple streams allows concurrency between data transfers and kernel execution, leading to significant performance gains, as demonstrated here:

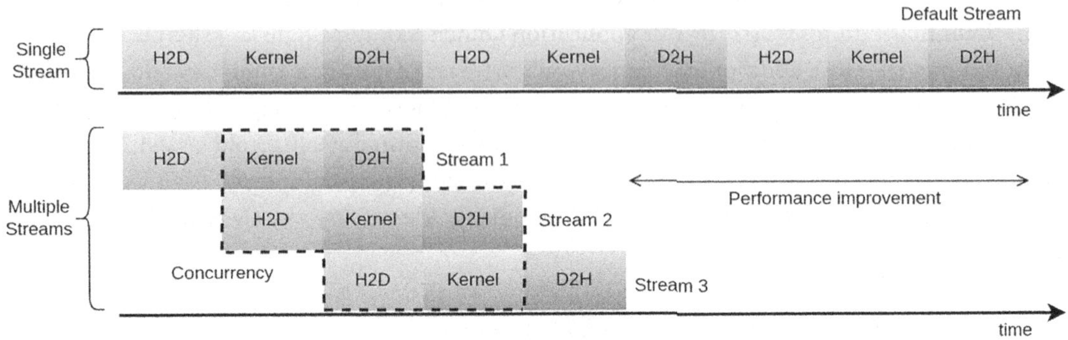

Figure 6.1 – A schematic diagram of how multiple CUDA streams enable concurrency

The top part is the single stream workflow. All operations, including H2D copy, kernel execution, and D2H copy, are placed in one stream. Since this stream executes sequentially, each operation must wait for the previous one to finish. Memory transfers and kernel execution cannot overlap, which often leads to underutilization of GPU resources.

In the case of multiple streams (bottom part), operations are split across different streams (Stream 1, Stream 2, and Stream 3). CUDA allows operations from different streams to run concurrently, provided the GPU has enough resources. For example, while Stream 1 is running a kernel, Stream 2 can already start a memory transfer. Stream 3 can further overlap its copy with Stream 1 and Stream 2's kernels. This overlapping creates concurrency, where H2D/D2H data transfers and computations run side by side. GPU idle time is reduced, which results in higher throughput and faster overall execution. It is important that we distinguish overlapping kernel executions using multiple streams from the GPU's ability to run independent kernels concurrently, in which the latter depends on hardware support and is available for compute capability ≥ 2.0. The streams overlap results in increased processing throughput of the GPU. Without this concurrency, the GPU might sit idle during memory transfers, which can degrade performance.

Furthermore, CUDA streams are a tool, not a requirement, and their benefits depend on the characteristics of your application. In practice, we should consider using streams when there is an opportunity to overlap tasks, including kernel execution and memory transfers (H2D, D2H, or both). If your workload consists of a single large kernel, highly sequential dependencies, or one-time large data movement, then using streams may not provide a meaningful benefit. Profiling and experimentation are usually required. You often start with a single stream to verify correctness, then introduce additional streams incrementally while measuring performance improvements. We will follow the same approach when working on an example processing pipeline.

The next important concept that we should know about is implicit synchronization and how it affects CUDA streams.

Implicit synchronization

In CUDA, **synchronization** refers to the process of coordinating the execution of tasks between the GPU and CPU, or among different GPU tasks, to ensure that certain operations complete before others begin. There are two types of synchronization between the device and host: implicit and explicit. With **explicit synchronization**, we deliberately wait for specific operations to finish before proceeding. We have already seen explicit synchronization in previous chapters when using `cuda.synchronize()`. In contrast, **implicit synchronization** happens automatically when certain CUDA API calls or operations force the GPU to complete all preceding tasks, even if no explicit synchronization was requested. Stream concurrency relies on the asynchronous (non-blocking) execution of operations. However, synchronization enforces serialization, which can limit the advantages of using multiple streams. Therefore, we must minimize or avoid unnecessary synchronization to be able to fully leverage concurrency.

When working with streams, synchronization often occurs during data transfer operations, as kernel launches are inherently asynchronous and thus non-blocking on the host. In practice, implicit synchronization often creates hidden bottlenecks by preventing the overlap of computation and data transfers, thereby reducing overall performance.

Common causes of implicit synchronization can be listed as follows:

- Memory transfers using synchronous APIs (e.g., `cuda.cuda.to_device` in the default stream)
- Device memory allocation (e.g., `cuda.device_array`), which forces all preceding GPU tasks to finish before allocation proceeds
- Host memory allocation, which may block if not handled carefully
- Kernel launches in the `NULL` stream, which has special synchronizing behavior with all other streams

In traditional CUDA, all operations in the legacy default stream are also implicitly synchronized with other streams. This can create a dependency because even unrelated kernels or memory transfers are forced to wait for each other. A per-thread default stream is a feature started from CUDA Toolkit 7 that changes how the default stream behaves in multithreaded programs. Each host thread gets its own private default stream. Operations in one thread's default stream are ordered within that thread, but they do not automatically synchronize with operations in other threads' default streams. This allows multiple host threads to launch GPU work independently and still get the convenience of the default stream without forcing unnecessary serialization.

GPU work queue

The number of streams that can run concurrently is limited by the hardware. Even though hundreds of streams can be created in software, the GPU can only manage a fixed number of hardware work queues (usually 8 but can be increased up to 32, depending on the GPU model), and when the number of streams exceeds this capacity, they are multiplexed onto the same queues. A **work queue** is an internal hardware-managed queue, where operations (including kernel launches, memory copies, and synchronization) are submitted for execution on the GPU. The work queue can be seen as a buffer between the host, which issues commands, and the device, which executes them.

Early NVIDIA GPUs (pre-Kepler architectures) had a single hardware work queue; regardless of streams and their independence, they were directed to this single queue. As a result, operations from multiple streams were serialized, even if they targeted different parts of memory or performed unrelated tasks. This serialization often created *false dependencies*, where two operations appeared to depend on each other only because they shared the same queue and not because they shared actual data or resources. Suppose Stream A launches a kernel operating on Buffer X, and Stream B initiates an H2D copy for Buffer Y. On older hardware with a single queue, the copy in Stream B would wait until the kernel in Stream A finishes, even though X and Y are independent. **Hyper-Q technology** addresses this issue by providing multiple hardware work queues, allowing independent streams to be executed concurrently if sufficient resources are available.

The Numba-CUDA APIs support working with streams, and in the next section, we explore how to use them.

Creating and managing streams

CUDA operations, including kernel launches and memory copies, are by default placed into the *null* or *default* stream. This particular stream enforces sequential execution, which prevents overlapping between kernels or between data transfers and computation. To achieve concurrency, we explicitly create non-default streams in Numba-CUDA, using `cuda.stream()`. Once created, these streams behave as independent task queues, and operations enqueued in different streams can potentially execute concurrently.

For example, two streams (`stream1` and `stream2`) can be created with the following:

```
from numba import cuda

stream1 = cuda.stream()
stream2 = cuda.stream()
```

With such streams available, we can launch kernels in parallel on different streams, given that the GPU has the necessary resources, such as free compute units and sufficient memory bandwidth.

A kernel launch associated with a particular stream looks like this:

```
my_kernel[blocks, threads, stream1](device_array_1)
my_kernel[blocks, threads, stream2](device_array_2)
```

The additional stream argument tells CUDA to schedule the kernel in a non-default stream. Using multiple streams allows overlapping operations. It must be noted that these launches are *non-blocking* for the host thread, meaning the CPU can continue performing other tasks immediately after dispatching them. If no stream is specified, the launch goes into the default stream, which then serializes execution and often synchronizes implicitly with host code, thereby limiting the chance for concurrency.

Each non-default stream can also be synchronized independently when needed. Calling `stream1.synchronize()` or `stream2.synchronize()` makes the host wait only until all operations queued in that specific stream are complete. This is different from a device-wide `cuda.synchronize()`, which blocks until every stream on the device has finished its work. Stream-level synchronization provides finer control over execution order and allows overlapping operations to proceed in other streams without unnecessary stalling.

Next, we shift our attention toward asynchronous data transfer between host and device to see how they interact with streams.

Asynchronous data transfers

Synchronous copies such as `cuda.to_device()` and `cuda.copy_to_host()` block the CPU thread until the transfer is complete via enforcing implicit synchronization. This means that the CPU cannot schedule kernels or additional transfers while waiting, which prevents overlap between data movement and computation. To allow such overlap, we must instead use *asynchronous* copies, using `cuda.to_device(..., stream=stream)` or `device_array.copy_to_host(stream=stream)`, which return control to the CPU immediately and let it continue scheduling kernels or further transfers while the data transfer proceeds in the background.

The following snippet of code illustrates how two asynchronous transfers can be issued on two separate streams:

```
device_array_1 = cuda.to_device(array_1, stream=stream1)
device_array_2 = cuda.to_device(array_2, stream=stream2)
```

On most GPUs, only one transfer in each direction (either H2D or D2H) can overlap with computation. More recent GPUs (e.g., A100), however, are equipped with separate copy engines and can carry out H2D and D2H transfer simultaneously, in addition to running kernels concurrently.

For asynchronous transfers to overlap with computation, the host memory involved must be **pinned**, or page-locked. Pinned memory cannot be paged out by the operating system, ensuring that the GPU can access it directly via **direct memory access** (**DMA**) without hidden staging or implicit synchronization. Without pinned memory, transfers that appear asynchronous in code will still force synchronization under the hood. In Numba-CUDA, pinned host arrays are easily allocated using `cuda.pinned_array` or `cuda.pinned_array_like`, which return objects that behave like regular NumPy arrays but are backed by page-locked memory.

Here is an example of preparing a pinned array and populating it with values for GPU transfers:

```
pinned_array = cuda.pinned_array((1000,), dtype=np.float32)
pinned_array[:] = np.arange(1000, dtype=np.float32)
```

From NumPy's perspective, there is no distinction between pageable and pinned memory. So NumPy arrays with a pinned memory backend behave exactly the same as regular arrays. Nevertheless, NumPy by default always uses regular host allocation mechanisms and has no concept of pinned memory, which is entirely a CUDA-specific optimization.

Moreover, allocating memory on the GPU itself also implicitly enforces synchronization, thus eliminating concurrency. A common strategy is to allocate required device buffers in advance and then reuse them for subsequent transfers and kernel launches. This, in principle, avoids synchronization overhead and keeps data movement and computation flowing simultaneously.

In short, to enable concurrency, the following conditions must be met:

- Using non-default streams
- Performing memory copies asynchronously
- Using pinned host memory to enable non-blocking transfers
- Pre-allocating device and host memory to prevent implicit synchronizations

Since we have already covered the basics of streams and data movement, we are now ready to work on building a practical example that demonstrates how to overlap image transfers and processing on the GPU using CUDA streams.

Speeding up image processing with CUDA streams

To demonstrate how CUDA streams can be applied in practice, we will build an image processing pipeline for retina image analysis using the concepts we have discussed so far. Since this use case often consists of large collections of high-resolution images, CUDA streams allow us to overlap different phases of computation and data movement, making better use of GPU resources than a single-stream workflow.

This pipeline highlights vascular structures through an *average filter* followed by *Sobel edge detection*. The average filter suppresses noise and softens fine details that may otherwise interfere with edge detection. Sobel edge detection emphasizes gradient information along the vasculature, helping to delineate veins and artery paths. The following figure shows example retina images after applying these two image filters. Identifying vascular networks is useful for diagnosing diabetic retinopathy, whether through specialist examination or by supporting deep learning models during the screening stage:

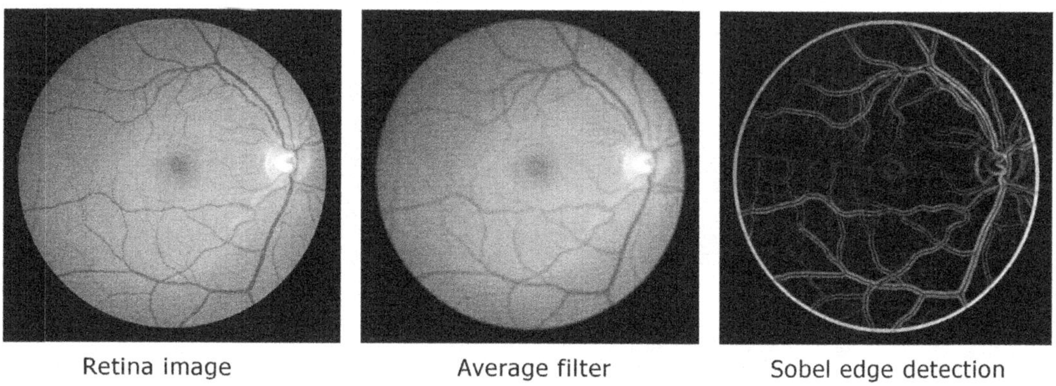

Figure 6.2 – An example retina image after applying filters

How would streams improve performance? Suppose we divide a sequence of images across four streams. An ideal scenario would be like this: one stream handles the average blur on the first image, and another stream can simultaneously transfer the second image from the host to the device. Yet another stream might already be performing the Sobel operation on a previously blurred image, while a fourth stream could be copying the final edge-detected result of an earlier image back to the host. The GPU schedules these independent tasks concurrently, effectively hiding transfer latency.

Defining CUDA kernels

In this section, we will implement the required CUDA kernels needed to build the image processing pipeline and then demonstrate how to use these kernels with multiple streams.

It should be kept in mind that understanding the exact implementation of the average filter or Sobel edge detection is not central to our discussion. The focus better lies on how to enable concurrency with CUDA streams to increase GPU utilization and increase the overall performance.

Average filter

We begin by implementing a CUDA kernel for the average filter required to operate on a grayscale image. The **average filter** computes the value of each pixel as the average of the pixel values in a local neighborhood around it. If the window has size $(2s+1) \times (2s+1)$, where s is the blur size, then the formula for the new pixel intensity at location (x, y) is the following:

$$I_{\text{blur}}(y,x) = \frac{1}{(2s+1)^2} \sum_{dx=-s}^{s} \sum_{dy=-s}^{s} I(y+dy, x+dx)$$

Here, $I(y, x)$ is the intensity of the input image at a certain pixel, and $I_{\text{blur}}(y, x)$ is the blurred output intensity. Boundary conditions (e.g., pixels near the edges) are usually handled by ignoring out-of-bound neighbors, mirroring, or padding:

```
from numba import cuda
from numba.cuda.cudadrv.devicearray import DeviceNDArray

@cuda.jit
def average_filter_kernel(
    gray_image: DeviceNDArray,
    blurred_image: DeviceNDArray,
) -> None:
    x, y = cuda.grid(2)
    if (
        x < gray_image.shape[1]
        and y < gray_image.shape[0]
    ):
        blur_size = 5
        sum_val = 0.0
        for dx in range(-blur_size, blur_size + 1):
            for dy in range(-blur_size, blur_size + 1):
                x_idx = x + dx
```

```
                y_idx = y + dy
                if (
                    0 <= x_idx < gray_image.shape[1]
                    and 0 <= y_idx < gray_image.shape[0]
                ):
                    sum_val += gray_image[y_idx, x_idx]
        blurred_image[y, x] = sum_val / (2 * blur_size + 1) ** 2
```

This kernel operates on a two-dimensional grid of threads, where each thread is responsible for computing the blurred intensity value of a single pixel. For each pixel, the kernel computes the average intensity within a square neighborhood centered on that pixel. The neighborhood size is determined by `blur_size`, which, in this case, is set to 5, so each thread looks at a window of 11 × 11 pixels. This kernel expects two arguments: `gray_image`, the input image in grayscale, and `blurred_image`, the output array where the blurred result will be stored. Both are represented as `DeviceNDArray`, meaning they reside in GPU memory.

Each CUDA thread is responsible for computing the blurred value of a single pixel. The call to `cuda.grid(2)` generates a unique `(x, y)` coordinate for each thread in a 2D grid layout, corresponding to the column and row of a pixel in the image. The actual blurring is performed using a square neighborhood filter. The nested loops over `dx` and `dy` iterate through this neighborhood. For each offset, the code checks whether the neighboring pixel falls inside the image boundaries. If so, the pixel value is added to `sum_val`. After accumulating all valid neighboring pixel values, the kernel computes the average by dividing the sum by the total number of pixels in the window, `(2 * blur_radius + 1) ** 2`. This averaged value is then stored in `blurred_image[y, x]`. As a result, this filter reduces noise and fine details in the input image.

Next, we define a Numba-CUDA kernel for applying Sobel edge detection.

Sobel edge detection kernel

Sobel edge detection is a classic image processing technique that highlights edges by detecting intensity gradients in both the horizontal and vertical directions.

It computes the gradient of image intensity by convolving the image with two 3 × 3 filters: one for detecting horizontal changes (G_x) and one for vertical changes (G_y).

The Sobel operators are as follows:

$$G_x = \begin{bmatrix} -1 & 0 & 1 \\ -2 & 0 & 2 \\ -1 & 0 & 1 \end{bmatrix}, \quad G_y = \begin{bmatrix} 1 & 2 & 1 \\ 0 & 0 & 0 \\ -1 & -2 & -1 \end{bmatrix}$$

For each pixel, the gradients are computed as follows:

$$G_x(y,x) = \sum_{dx=-1}^{1} \sum_{dy=-1}^{1} G_x[dy+1, dx+1] \cdot I(y+dy, x+dx)$$

$$G_y(y,x) = \sum_{dx=-1}^{1} \sum_{dy=-1}^{1} G_y[dy+1, dx+1] \cdot I(y+dy, x+dx)$$

Here, *I(y, x)* is the grayscale intensity of the input image. The edge magnitude is then given by the following:

$$M(y,x) = \sqrt{G_x(y,x)^2 + G_y(y,x)^2}$$

M(x, y) is then used to produce the edge map, highlighting areas of strong intensity change:

```
import math
import numpy as np

SOBEL_X = np.array(
    [[-1, 0, 1],
     [-2, 0, 2],
     [-1, 0, 1]],
     dtype=np.float32,
)
SOBEL_Y = np.array(
    [[1, 2, 1],
     [0, 0, 0],
     [-1, -2, -1]],
     dtype=np.float32,
)

@cuda.jit
def sobel_edge_detection_kernel(
    gray_image: DeviceNDArray,
    edge_image: DeviceNDArray,
) -> None:
    x, y = cuda.grid(2)
    if (
        x < gray_image.shape[1]
        and y < gray_image.shape[0]
```

```
    ):
        const_sobel_x = cuda.const.array_like(SOBEL_X)
        const_sobel_y = cuda.const.array_like(SOBEL_Y)

        sum_val_x, sum_val_y = 0.0, 0.0
        for dx in range(-1, 2):
            for dy in range(-1, 2):
                x_idx = x + dx
                y_idx = y + dy
                if (
                    0 <= x_idx < gray_image.shape[1]
                    and 0 <= y_idx < gray_image.shape[0]
                ):
                    sum_val_x += const_sobel_x[dy + 1, dx +
 1] * gray_image[y_idx, x_idx]
                    sum_val_y += const_sobel_y[dy + 1, dx +
 1] * gray_image[y_idx, x_idx]
        edge_image[y, x] = math.sqrt(sum_val_x**2 + sum_val_y**2)
```

At the top, two small 3 × 3 convolution operators (`SOBEL_X` and `SOBEL_Y`) are defined as NumPy arrays. These represent the standard Sobel masks, where one emphasizes horizontal gradients and the other emphasizes vertical gradients. These matrices are later placed into constant memory via `cuda.const.array_like`, which provides fast, read-only access to all threads. The `sobel_edge_detection_kernel` kernel similarly takes two arguments: `gray_image`, the input image that has typically been smoothed (with the average filter from the previous step), and `edge_image`, the output array that will hold the gradient magnitudes representing edges.

Each thread again corresponds to one pixel, where coordinates are determined by `cuda.grid(2)`. It performs a 3 × 3 convolution around its pixel. It loops over the `dx` and `dy` offsets in the `[-1, 1]` range, corresponding to the neighborhood of the pixel. For each valid neighbor, it multiplies the pixel value by the corresponding Sobel filter coefficient. Contributions are accumulated separately into `sum_val_x` and `sum_val_y`. Once the neighborhood has been processed, the gradient magnitude is computed. This value reflects the strength of an edge at that pixel, regardless of its orientation, and is written to `edge_data[y, x]`. In our case, this kernel transforms a smoothed grayscale image into an edge map that highlights vessel boundaries and other structural transitions in the retinal scan.

We will focus next on generating images, creating streams, and pre-allocating arrays.

Preparing memory and CUDA streams

We first define the generate_images function to produce synthetic random image data, optionally in pinned memory for efficient GPU transfers. The purpose is to simulate a stream of images (i.e., retinal scans) for our pipeline benchmarking later:

```
import numpy as np
from typing import Iterator
from numpy.typing import NDArray

def generate_images(
        num_images:int = 1,
        shape: tuple[int, int] = (1024, 1024),
        dtype: np.dtype = np.float32,
        pinned_memory: bool = True,
    ) -> Iterator[NDArray]:
    empty = cuda.pinned_array if pinned_memory else np.empty
    rng = np.random.default_rng()
    for _ in range(num_images):
        buf = empty(shape, dtype=dtype)
        rng.random(buf.shape, dtype=buf.dtype, out=buf)
        yield buf
```

This function accepts several parameters, such as the number of images to generate (`num_images`), `shape`, `dtype`, and, more importantly, the `pinned_memory` Boolean flag. The latter indicates whether the arrays should be allocated in page-locked memory, which is essential for asynchronous data transfers in CUDA. We conditionally choose the array allocation method and use `cuda.pinned_array` to create arrays in page-locked memory. Otherwise, it defaults to the standard `np.empty`.

A random number generator (`np.random.default_rng()`) is initialized to fill the images with data. We first allocate a buffer (`buf`) and initialize it with random values using `rng.random` in the `[0, 1]` range. The output values are then directly copied into the allocated array using the `out=buf` parameter. Finally, the function yields each generated image one by one, rather than returning all images at once. In more advanced cases, this approach is memory-efficient even for an infinite number of images and allows processing pipelines to start consuming images immediately as they are generated.

Host memory allocated with NumPy by default is pageable, meaning the operating system is free to move it around in physical RAM. Before the GPU can access data in pageable memory, the

CUDA driver must first copy it into a temporary pinned buffer behind the scenes, then initiate the transfer to device memory. This extra step makes transfers slower and, more importantly, prevents them from overlapping with kernel execution. Pinned memory, on the other hand, is locked in physical RAM, so the OS cannot move it. When pinned memory is used, transfers can overlap with computation kernels on other streams. Otherwise, if pageable memory is used, the driver forces synchronization, destroying concurrency.

We next set up the memory and streams needed for our multi-stream GPU processing pipeline:

```
import time
from tqdm import tqdm

NUM_IMAGES = 100
NUM_STREAMS = 4

# images = [image]  # retina
images = [m for m in generate_images(NUM_IMAGES)]
streams = [cuda.stream() for _ in range(NUM_STREAMS)]
outputs = [cuda.pinned_array(m.shape, dtype=m.dtype) for m in images]

shape, dtype = images[0].shape, images[0].dtype
preallocated_device_arrays = [
    (
        cuda.device_array(shape, dtype=dtype, stream=stream),
        cuda.device_array(shape, dtype=dtype, stream=stream),
    )
    for stream in streams
]
```

We first initialize a list of `NUM_IMAGES` synthetic images using the previously defined generator function. Each image is a NumPy array in pinned memory, simulating high-resolution retinal scans. We create `NUM_STREAMS` CUDA streams, which are independent queues of GPU operations. The `outputs` allocate host-side pinned memory for storing the results. Each output buffer corresponds to one input image, allowing the results of the GPU computations to be copied back efficiently.

We also allocate device memory arrays for each stream in advance. Using `cuda.device_array(..., stream=stream)`, it creates GPU-resident arrays to hold both the intermediate results for each image in that stream. The `preallocated_device_arrays` represents a tuple of two device arrays per stream to be used later as scratch storage for the CUDA kernel. These preallocations of host and device memory prevent implicit synchronization, which is essential for multi-stream CUDA applications to ensure each stream has dedicated buffers for pipeline execution.

Processing images

We proceed with defining a function called process to process a given image on a specific CUDA stream:

```
from numba.cuda.cudadrv.driver import Stream
import math

def process(
    image: NDArray,
    stream: Stream,
    preallocated_device_arrays: tuple[DeviceNDArray, ...],
    output: NDArray,
) -> None:
    d_array1, d_array2 = preallocated_device_arrays
    cuda.to_device(image, stream=stream, to=d_array1)

    threads = (16, 32)
    blocks_x = math.ceil(image.shape[1] / threads[0])
    blocks_y = math.ceil(image.shape[0] / threads[1])
    blocks = (blocks_x, blocks_y)

    average_filter_kernel[blocks, threads, stream](d_array1, d_array2)
    sobel_edge_detection_kernel[blocks, threads, stream](d_array2, d_array1)

    d_array1.copy_to_host(output, stream=stream)
```

This function takes four arguments, including `image` as a NumPy array, `stream` in which all GPU operations for this image will be enqueued, `preallocated_device_arrays`, which holds the intermediate device arrays, and `output`, a NumPy array where the final edge-detected image will be copied to the host. The input image is first copied to the GPU using `cuda.to_device`, placing it into the first preallocated device array (`d_array1`) within the given stream. Using the `stream` input ensures that this transfer is asynchronous and can overlap with other operations queued in different streams.

Next, the kernel launch configuration is computed. `threads = (16, 32)` defines the number of threads per block in a 2D layout, and `blocks_x` and `blocks_y` are calculated to cover the full image dimensions, using `math.ceil` to ensure complete coverage. These values define a 2D grid of CUDA blocks for both the blur and Sobel kernels.

The GPU computation then proceeds in two steps. First, `average_filter_kernel` is launched on the preallocated `d_array1` to produce the blurred image in `d_array2`. Second, `sobel_edge_detection_kernel` is then launched, taking `d_array2` as input and writing the final edge map back into `d_array1`. Both kernel launches are associated with the same stream, ensuring that they execute sequentially within that stream but can still run concurrently with other streams on the GPU.

The resulting edge-detected image is copied back to the host memory (`output`) using `d_array1.copy_to_host`, also within the same stream. This completes the processing of one image, with all data transfers and computation confined to a single stream.

Finally, we process images on multiple CUDA streams to overlap computation and data transfers:

```
%%time

for index, (image, output) in tqdm(
        enumerate(zip(images, outputs))
):
    stream_index = index % len(streams)
    result = process(
            image,
            streams[stream_index],
            preallocated_device_arrays[stream_index],
            output,
    )
for stream in streams:
        stream.synchronize()
```

The first loop iterates over the input images and their corresponding output buffers simultaneously. Within the loop, the `stream_index = index % len(streams)` variable assigns each image to a CUDA stream in a round-robin fashion. This ensures distributing the workload across multiple streams so that data transfers and kernel executions can overlap. The `process` function is then called for each image with the corresponding stream, preallocated arrays, and output parameters. After the loop, the code explicitly synchronizes all streams. `stream.synchronize()` ensures that all operations enqueued in each individual stream are complete. This ensures that by the time the program continues, all images have been fully processed, and their results are safely available in host memory.

Benchmarking results

For a batch of 1,000 images, using 4 streams on the A100 GPU reduces processing time to 285 ms, delivering a 2.1× speedup compared to the single-stream execution time of 600 ms. To gain deeper insight into this improvement, we profile the stream with *NVIDIA Nsight Systems*, as illustrated here:

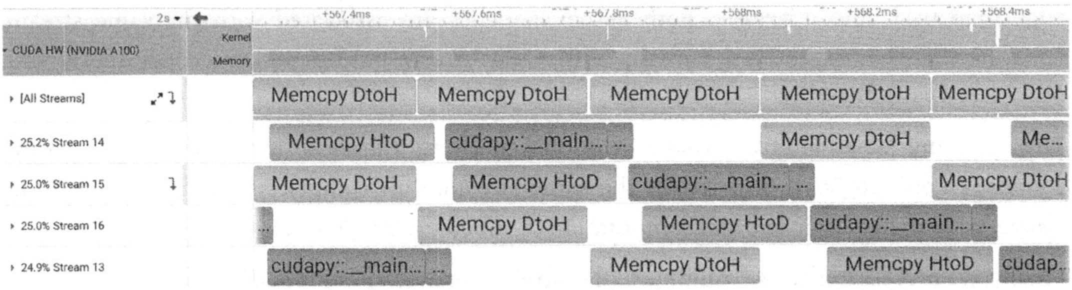

Figure 6.3 – Profiling of the image processing pipeline using four CUDA streams (concurrency)

This profiling visualizes GPU activity with multiple CUDA streams running concurrently. The purple regions represent D2H transfers, the green regions correspond to H2D transfers, and the blue regions indicate kernel executions. At the top, the aggregated bar summarizes overall kernel and memory activity, while the lower section provides a per-stream breakdown.

From the top bar, it is evident that kernel execution overlaps with both H2D and D2H transfers, which demonstrates that computation and communication are pipelined. This view gives an immediate sense of how well the GPU pipeline is balanced, and it serves as the first place to assess efficiency and identify potential bottlenecks.

In the lower section, each stream shows interleaved activity, where memory transfers and kernel launch occur in an overlapping manner. This concurrency indicates an intentional effort to hide data transfer latency behind computation. However, certain intervals (bubbles) reveal that transfers dominate execution, which could limit overall throughput. These regions highlight where optimizations might focus, such as improving data staging or better distributing workloads across streams.

You can simply profile a CUDA application using `nsys` as follows:

```
nsys profile -o report python your_script.py
```

This generates a `report.nsys-rep` file, which can then be visualized using the NVIDIA Nsight Systems GUI:

```
nsys-ui report.nsys-rep
```

Each CUDA stream is displayed as its own timeline track, where kernel launches, data transfers, and synchronization events are arranged chronologically. The corresponding CPU-side API calls that triggered these operations are also shown in alignment with the GPU timeline.

To understand how multiple streams influence data movement, we measured PCIe throughput, which reflects the communication between host and device. The following figure shows GPU PCIe throughput for the pipeline, comparing single-stream execution with the use of four streams.

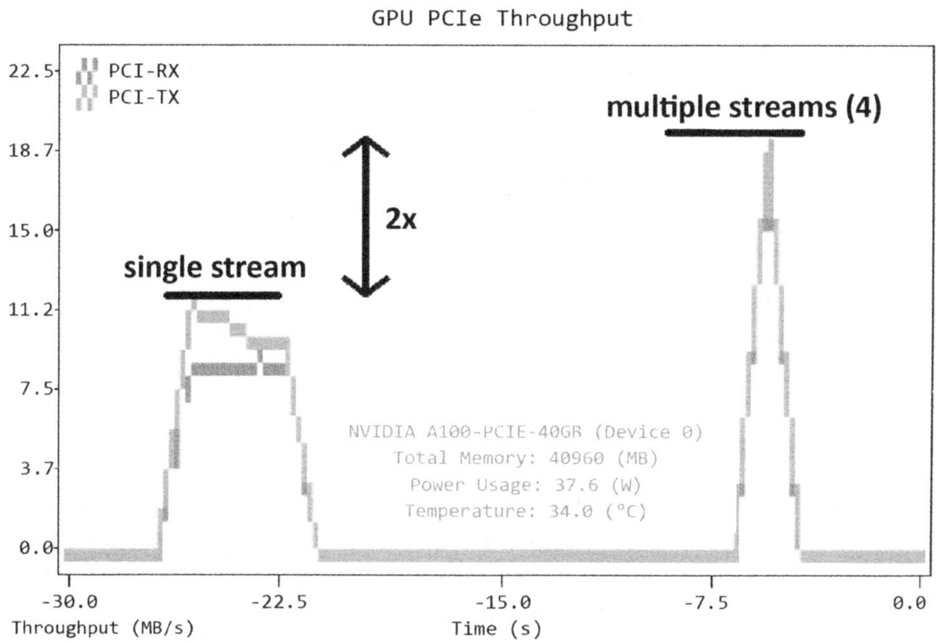

Figure 6.4 – PCI throughput variation during pipeline execution with one stream (left) and four streams (right)

In the single-stream case, the plot shows **PCI-RX** (H2D) and **PCI-TX** (D2H) transfers, with throughput peaking around 11 MB/s. When using 4 streams, the throughput nearly doubles, reaching about 22 MB/s, clearly demonstrating the benefit of overlapping data transfers across multiple streams.

As a reference, we also provide the GPU activity when we use only a single CUDA stream (`NUM_STREAMS=1`):

Figure 6.5 – Stream activity when using only a single CUDA stream (no concurrency)

The timeline shows a sequential pattern where data transfers and kernel executions occur one after the other rather than overlapping. The data transfers alternate with kernel launches, but there are noticeable idle gaps between operations, meaning that the GPU cannot overlap computation with communication. The top-level view indicates that memory transfers occupy more time than kernels, with about 59% of the activity dedicated to data movement compared to 41% spent on execution. This imbalance suggests that in the single-stream configuration, throughput is limited by PCIe communication, and the GPU's ability to hide transfer latency behind computation is underutilized.

In the next section, we will explore CUDA events, demonstrating how they can be applied for fine-grained stream time profiling while also serving as a mechanism for introducing dependencies between streams.

CUDA events

CUDA events are lightweight GPU trackers that provide both accurate timing and fine-grained synchronization. This allows measuring kernel execution time or coordinating the ordering of tasks. Because they are placed directly into the GPU's command queue, they reflect actual device execution rather than just the moment when the host issues work. In Numba-CUDA, we can create events in Numba with `cuda.event()` and record them on a specific stream. For example, by placing one event before a kernel launch and another after, then querying the elapsed time between them, we can obtain precise performance measurements for a single kernel or for a sequence of kernels. This makes CUDA events particularly useful when analyzing how kernels overlap or when comparing alternative implementations.

Events are also a powerful synchronization mechanism. For example, one stream can record an event, and another stream can be instructed to wait for it, ensuring a specific order of execution without forcing a full device-wide barrier such as `cuda.synchronize()`. On the host side, calling `event.synchronize()` blocks until all GPU work up to that point has been completed, which is helpful when results need to be retrieved or when subsequent operations depend on the completion of earlier GPU tasks.

Timing individual streams

In the following example, we show how CUDA events can be used for measuring per-stream execution time:

```
%%time

events_begin = [cuda.event() for _ in streams]
events_end = [cuda.event() for _ in streams]

[event.record(stream) for event, stream in zip(events_begin, streams)]
for index, (image, output) in tqdm(
        enumerate(zip(images, outputs))
):
    stream_index = 0 if index < 50 else index % len(streams)
    process(
        image,
        streams[stream_index],
        preallocated_device_arrays[stream_index],
        output,
    )
[event.record(stream) for event, stream in zip(events_end, streams)]
[stream.synchronize() for stream in streams]
stream_elapsed_times = [eb.elapsed_time(ee)*0.001 for eb, ee in zip(events_begin,
events_end)]
for index, elapsed_time in enumerate(stream_elapsed_times):
    print(f"Stream {index+1} finished after {elapsed_time:<.2f} s")
```

Each stream gets a pair of events (`begin` and `end`), so we can measure elapsed time. The `events_begin` sets markers for when each stream starts, and `events_end` sets markers for when each stream finishes (after calling the `process` function). We insert each `events_begin[i]` at the current position in `streams[i]`. This indicates when the time measurement starts for streams. We iterate over `images` and `outputs` just like the previous example.

For educational purposes, we choose a stream index so that the first 50 items always go to stream index `0`, and after that, use round-robin distribution across all streams. After all work is submitted, insert `events_end[i]` at the tail of each stream. This means that each `events_end[i]` will complete only after that stream has finished all its queued tasks. `stream.synchronize()` waits for all streams to finish before moving on. Without this, the CPU might continue before the GPU has completed work. `ee.elapsed_time(ee)` gives the time in milliseconds between `events_begin[i]` and `events_end[i]` for each stream; multiply this by 0.001 to convert it to seconds.

Finally, we measure and report the active duration of each stream, which helps profile how evenly the workload is distributed. In the same way, we can also time individual kernel execution or memory transfers.

```
Stream 1 finished after 2.41 s
Stream 2 finished after 1.10 s
Stream 3 finished after 1.16 s
Stream 4 finished after 1.17 s
Wall time: 2.42 s
```

The output gives the execution time for each stream. Stream 1 takes noticeably longer, completing in 2.41 seconds, while the other three streams finish in just over 1.1 seconds. This imbalance occurs because Stream 1 carries additional work, handling the processing of the first 50 images before the rest of the streams can proceed. As a result, its timeline dominates the total wall-clock duration, even though the other streams complete earlier.

We introduce dependencies in the next section; this will force the other streams to wait until Stream 1 completes its initial workload.

Synchronizing across streams

CUDA events also allow creating dependencies so that some streams don't start until another stream reaches that point. The following example code distributes work across multiple CUDA streams but enforces a dependency barrier so that all other streams can only start processing after Stream 0 has finished the first 50 images:

```
%%time

events_begin = [cuda.event() for _ in streams]
events_end = [cuda.event() for _ in streams]
event_done = cuda.event()

[event.record(stream) for event, stream in zip(events_begin, streams)]
for index, (image, output) in tqdm(
        enumerate(zip(images, outputs))
):
    s_index = 0 if index < 50 else index % len(streams)
    process(
        image,
```

```
            streams[s_index],
            preallocated_device_arrays[s_index],
            output,
        )
        # Add stream dependencies
        if index == 50:
            event_done.record(streams[0])
            [event_done.wait(stream) for stream in streams[1:]]
    [event.record(stream) for event, stream in zip(events_end, streams)]

    [stream.synchronize() for stream in streams]
    stream_elapsed_times = [eb.elapsed_time(ee)*0.001 for eb, ee in zip(events_begin,
    events_end)]
    for index, elapsed_time in enumerate(stream_elapsed_times):
        print(f"Stream {index+1} finished after {elapsed_time:<.2f} s")
```

The only difference this time is that when image 50 is reached, `event_done.record(streams[0])` inserts an event into the queue of `stream[0]`. Other streams (`streams[1:]`) are waiting until this event is complete. In practice, Streams 1, 2, 3 ... are blocked until Stream 0 reaches the 50-image milestone.

The output shows that all streams take a similar time due to inserted dependencies:

```
Stream 1 finished after 2.30 s
Stream 2 finished after 2.30 s
Stream 3 finished after 2.31 s
Stream 4 finished after 2.34 s
Wall time: 2.34 s
```

As illustrated in the following figure, the stream profiling timeline is different. All other streams this time wait for Stream 1 to finish, after which concurrent execution on all streams begins.

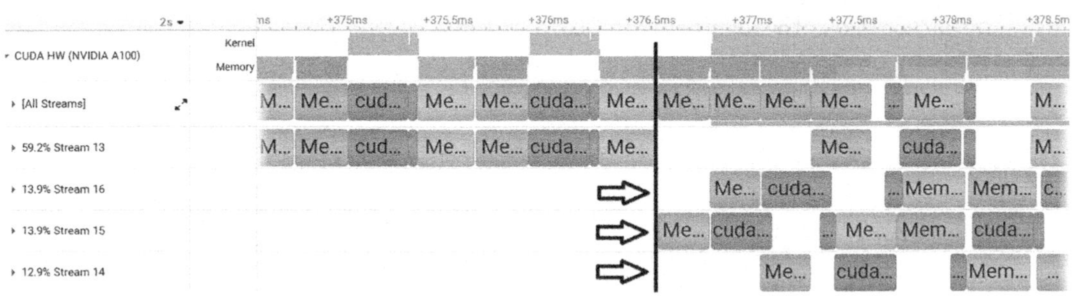

Figure 6.6 – Timeline of stream activity with cross-stream synchronization

Multiple CPU threads with CUDA streams

In our previous example, all CUDA operations queued on multiple streams were issued from a single CPU thread. This can potentially create a computational bottleneck if preparing and submitting tasks to the streams requires significant CPU processing or if the host is blocked on I/O. In such cases, multiple CPU threads can issue work to the GPU concurrently, as shown in the following schematic diagram. Multithreading is especially useful when I/O or host-side preparation would otherwise serialize GPU work if only a single thread were responsible. The CUDA runtime API is thread-safe, so each CPU thread can independently create and use its own CUDA stream. This allows the CPU to keep feeding work to the GPU while other streams are still processing data:

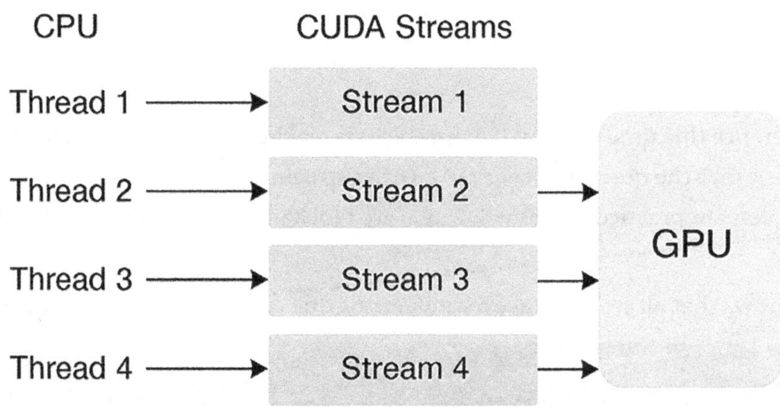

Figure 6.7 – Multiple CPU threads supplying data to each CUDA stream

For Python, the **Global Interpreter Lock** (**GIL**) must be taken into account. Although the GIL restricts parallel execution of pure Python code, multithreading remains valuable, particularly when workloads are dominated by I/O, such as reading and writing to disk or network.

The following code snippet demonstrates how to overlap CPU-side I/O and GPU computation using `ThreadPoolExecutor` together with CUDA streams:

```
from concurrent.futures import ThreadPoolExecutor, wait

start = time.perf_counter()
futures = []
with cuda.defer_cleanup():
    with ThreadPoolExecutor(max_workers=len(streams)) as executor:
        for index, output in tqdm(enumerate(outputs)):
            s_index = index % len(streams)
```

```
            futures.append(
                executor.submit(
                    load_and_process,
                    f"tmp/image{index}.npy",
                    streams[s_index],
                    preallocated_device_arrays[s_index],
                    output,
                )
            )
        wait(futures)
    cuda.synchronize()
```

Each thread is responsible for loading a subset of input files, transferring them to the GPU, and performing computation using a specific stream and pre-allocated device buffers. The mapping from tasks to streams is again round-robin, ensuring that work is evenly distributed across the available streams. The `cuda.defer_cleanup()` context manager defers device memory cleaning up (deallocation) to avoid implicit synchronization. `ThreadPoolExecutor` creates a pool of worker threads with one thread per CUDA stream. This allows the CPU to prepare and submit work to multiple streams simultaneously. `executor.submit(...)` schedules the `load_and_process` function to run in a worker thread. This function loads an image from disk, copies it into pinned memory, and feeds it to the `process` function.

As tasks are submitted to the thread pool, their `future` objects are collected in a list. Once all tasks have been launched, `wait(futures)` ensures that the host does not exit early and waits until all threads have completed their work. Afterward, `cuda.synchronize()` blocks until all GPU work across all streams has finished. This pattern allows multiple CPU threads to concurrently stage data and launch kernels on different CUDA streams, keeping the GPU busy while other threads continue I/O or host-side preprocessing.

Summary

In this chapter, we began with an overview of CUDA streams, including the concept of concurrency, when to use streams to improve performance, implicit synchronization, and how streams are executed on the GPU. We then demonstrated how to create streams in Numba-CUDA and outlined the requirements for performing asynchronous data transfers between the host and device, including pinned memory and creating non-default streams.

Next, we built a retina image processing pipeline using multiple streams, illustrating how streams can enhance overall performance. We further analyzed, based on profiling results, why and how streams contribute to speedup.

We then introduced CUDA events, showing how they can be used to measure execution time for individual streams and to establish dependencies between streams. Finally, we explored combining multithreading with CUDA streams for scenarios where CPU data preparation becomes a bottleneck.

In the next chapter, we will explore how to scale our computations to multiple GPUs.

Questions

1. What is the impact of setting `pinned_memory=False` when generating images? Verify your answer using stream profiling results.
2. What would the performance be if we skipped pre-reallocating arrays in the pipeline?
3. How would a larger number of streams (e.g., eight) affect performance?
4. How can we measure the execution time of the edge detection kernel using CUDA events?

Answers

1. This flag determines whether the image array is allocated in pinned memory. If `pinned_memory` is set to `False`, H2D data transfers can cause implicit synchronization.
2. Because device and host memory allocations introduce implicit synchronization, pre-allocating memory ensures that all required arrays are available when multiple streams are executing.
3. Streams are a CUDA programming abstraction, and using a larger number of streams does not necessarily lead to performance improvements. If the streams cannot execute concurrently at the hardware level, they only add overhead.
4. By wrapping this kernel with two CUDA events (`start` and `end`), we can measure its execution time accurately. This can be done separately for each stream or by reporting the average execution time across all streams.

Get this book's PDF version and more

Scan the QR code (or go to `packtpub.com/unlock`). Search for this book by name, confirm the edition, and then follow the steps on the page.

UNLOCK NOW

Note: Keep your invoice handy. Purchases made directly from Packt don't require an invoice.

7

Scaling to Multiple GPUs

In this chapter, we will explore how to use multiple GPUs when the limitations of a single GPU become a bottleneck. We will begin by highlighting the importance of multi-GPU computing, providing an overview of multi-GPU systems and two commonly used parallelism approaches. Next, we will present practical examples using Numba-CUDA to introduce core concepts such as data partitioning, memory data movement, and distributed computing. We will then scale these examples to a multi-node environment using a Dask cluster, which enables us to orchestrate computation across multiple GPUs and machines. Finally, we will demonstrate multi-GPU computing in JAX and how to perform distributed training of a machine learning model.

By the end of this chapter, you will have a solid understanding of the following:

- Multi-GPU computing fundamentals and parallelism approaches
- Performing multi-GPU computing with Numba-CUDA
- Distributing workloads across GPU systems using a Dask-CUDA cluster
- Analyzing parallel execution performance using the Dask dashboard
- Training machine learning models in a distributed setting using JAX

Technical requirements

To be able to run the example code provided in this chapter, you will need a system equipped with at least two NVIDIA GPUs. We use Pixi as a dependency management tool that installs all of the required packages, including the Numba-CUDA and Dask-CUDA packages. To set up the environment, simply run `pixi install` in the root directory of the book's GitHub repository. This will ensure that all dependencies are installed. Once the installation is complete, you can activate the environment using `pixi shell`.

To use JupyterLab, run the following command:

```
pixi run jupyter-lab
```

The chapter's code is available on GitHub and can be accessed via this link: `https://github.com/PacktPublishing/GPU-Accelerated-Computing-with-Python-3-and-CUDA`. We recommend cloning the repository and following the instructions in the `README` file to get started with building the environment.

All of the example code throughout this chapter will use RTX 2080 Ti GPUs with PCIe inter-GPU communication, unless stated otherwise.

Introduction to multi-GPU computing

A single GPU often becomes insufficient as computational problems grow in scale, for example, when the model is too large to fit into the memory of one GPU, or when fitting model parameters is so computationally demanding that distributing the load becomes necessary to achieve reasonable performance or time. In such cases, **multi-GPU computing** becomes unavoidable as it allows distributing the workload across several GPUs, enabling more data to be processed or simulations that would otherwise be impractical to run to be accelerated.

In the following two sections, we will briefly discuss the architecture of multi-GPU systems and elaborate on popular parallelism strategies for utilizing multiple GPUs.

Multi-GPU systems architecture

A system with multiple GPUs is designed to utilize the combined computational power of several GPUs. The way these GPUs are arranged and connected within the system affects how efficiently they can share data and coordinate work. Broadly, such systems are classified into two main network topologies. In a **single-node** setup, multiple GPUs typically communicate via in-node high-bandwidth interfaces such as **PCI Express** (**PCIe**) or NVIDIA's NVLink buses, and all GPUs are located on the same main board (machine). PCIe is widely supported, with support for duplex communication in addition to unidirectional. It is, however, relatively slower with higher latency (up to 64 GB/s total bandwidth in PCIe 5.0), while NVLink, available on selected NVIDIA GPUs, offers faster bandwidth (up to 900 GB/s NVLink 4.0) and lower latency. This architecture typically supports the interconnection of up to 10 GPUs for fast data sharing. For setups requiring more than that, multiple-node systems are needed.

In a **multi-node** configuration, where GPUs are spread across several interconnected single nodes, communication happens over a network optimized for low latency and high throughput, such as **Ethernet** or **InfiniBand**. Software frameworks designed for distributed computing manage this communication, enabling seamless workload distribution despite the physical separation of hardware. Furthermore, technologies such as **GPUDirect RDMA** (**RDMA** stands for **remote direct memory access**) enable InfiniBand or Ethernet network interfaces to directly access memory via PCIe inside a node, bypassing the classical CPU involvement. Across nodes, the interconnected pathways natively supported by InfiniBand and most clusters use InfiniBand RDMA between nodes.

The following figure shows a simplified schematic representation of a multi-GPU system architecture:

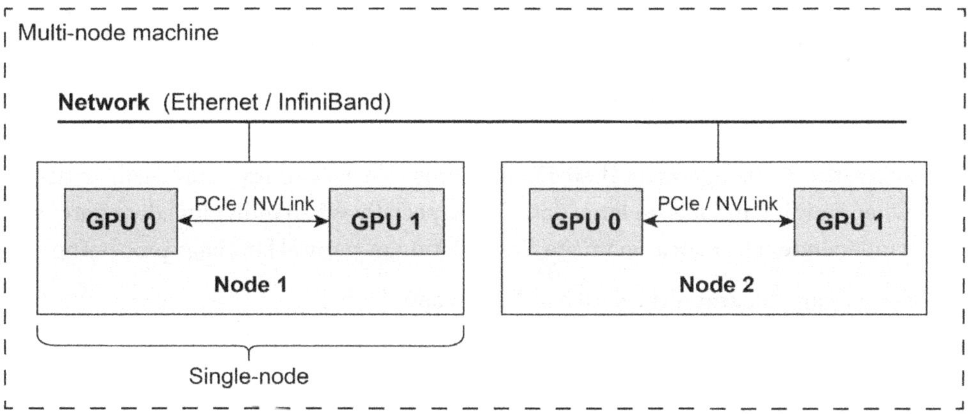

Figure 7.1 – An overview of a multi-GPU system network architecture

Each node contains GPUs (**GPU 0** and **GPU 1**) that are connected to each other via PCIe or NVLink, enabling high-speed intra-node communication. The nodes themselves are connected over a network, such as Ethernet or InfiniBand, which facilitates inter-node communication. In most scenarios, a single multi-GPU node is sufficient for running computations. It has the advantage of minimal network-induced latency compared to multi-node setups.

A multi-GPU system introduces complexity such as efficiently splitting workloads, synchronizing computations, and minimizing communication overhead. We must consider hardware compatibility, interconnect bandwidth, and software support to be able to fully leverage the potential of multiple GPUs. The good news is that modern programming models and libraries such as CUDA and Dask, as well as frameworks such as JAX, provide tools to abstract much of this complexity, allowing developers to focus on solving the core problems while the system handles parallel execution and resource management. But how should we approach parallelizing tasks for a specific problem? In the next section, we will explore two common methods.

Parallelism strategies

Performing multi-GPU computing additionally requires selecting the right parallelization strategy based on the nature of the problem, the size of the model or dataset, and the performance goals. At the core of multi-GPU computing are different approaches designed to split workloads in a way that maximizes efficiency while minimizing overhead, such as data movement or synchronization.

Two of the most common strategies are the following:

- **Data parallelism** replicates the same model on multiple GPUs and distributes different portions of the dataset to each GPU for parallel processing
- **Model parallelism** splits the model itself across multiple GPUs, allowing different parts of the model to run on different devices

Data parallelism

The more intuitive strategy is data parallelism. In this approach, each GPU maintains a complete copy of the model and processes a different chunk of the input data. After performing computations, the GPUs *aggregate* their results across devices. Data parallelism is particularly effective when training models on large datasets, especially when individual data batches can be processed independently, such as in image classification or natural language processing.

The following figure illustrates the data parallelism approach.

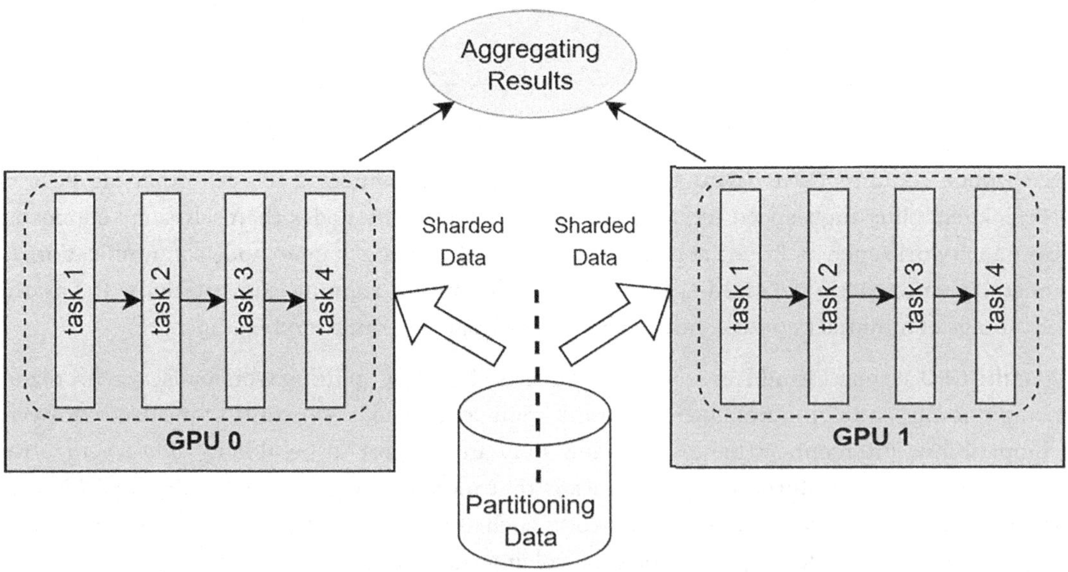

Figure 7.2 – Data parallelism method including data partitioning, model replication, and aggregation

It shows a dataset partitioned into smaller, independent shards that are distributed across multiple GPUs. Each GPU receives its portion of the data and performs the same sequence of tasks in parallel, processing its shard independently of the others. Once all GPUs have completed their computations, the results are aggregated to form the final output.

There are also cases where the problem itself consists of many independent tasks, *without aggregating* results at the end. In these situations, **task parallelism** can be employed. Each GPU performs a completely different computation, often unrelated to what the others are doing. This is common in hyperparameter tuning, ensemble modeling, or running independent simulations. Because tasks do not need to communicate, this approach is relatively simple to implement and avoids synchronization overhead.

Model parallelism

Another powerful strategy is model parallelism, which is used when the model itself is too large to fit into the memory of a single GPU. Instead of duplicating the model across GPUs, model parallelism divides the model into smaller parts, with each part assigned to a different GPU. During inference, data flows *sequentially* through the GPUs, each handling only a portion of the computation.

This figure shows the model parallelism approach when multiple GPUs are available.

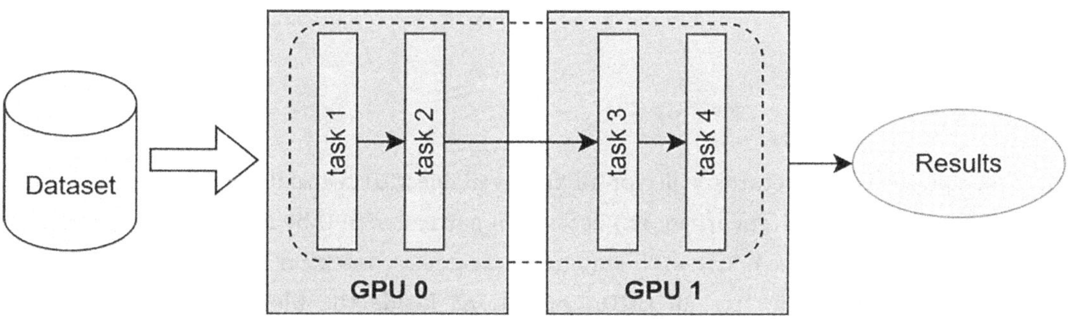

Figure 7.3 – Model parallelism method

The model is partitioned across several GPUs, so its components are placed on different devices and executed sequentially. This is often due to the memory constraints of an individual GPU, which the entire model cannot fit into, so it must be broken into smaller sub-modules; each GPU holds and computes only its assigned segments.

In real-world systems, it's common to see hybrid approaches that combine multiple strategies to optimize performance and scale. For instance, a system might use data parallelism across nodes in a cluster and model parallelism within each node to further increase GPU utilization. Choosing the right combination depends on the architecture of the hardware, the size of the problem, and the tools or frameworks being used. Libraries such as JAX and Dask provide abstractions to help implement these patterns more flexibly. Ultimately, the choice of parallelism strategy can significantly affect both performance and scalability.

It is not feasible for us to cover all of these concepts in detail in this chapter. However, we will provide a few illustrative examples using Numba-CUDA and Dask, primarily focused on task parallelism. We will then introduce data parallelism in the context of distributed training of a linear regression model using JAX. We strongly encourage anyone who is interested to conduct their own research using the keywords and software packages that will be mentioned throughout this chapter.

Let us begin with the basics of multi-GPU computing in Numba in the next section.

Multi-GPU techniques with Numba

Numba-CUDA supports multi-GPU programming by providing low-level APIs. Unlike JAX or CuPy, we must explicitly handle device context, memory allocation, data transfer, and kernel launches for each GPU. This offers fine-grained control over GPU processing and makes it easier to implement non-standard parallelism patterns.

Some generic code for targeting a specific GPU with Numba-CUDA looks like this:

```
from numba import cuda


with cuda.gpus[gpu_id]:
  data_device = cuda.to_device(data)
```

Here, `numba.cuda.gpus` returns a list of all the available CUDA-capable GPUs on the system detected by Numba. `cuda.gpus[gpu_id]` accesses a particular GPU by its ID (e.g., `0` for the first GPU, `1` for the second, etc.). The `with` statement creates a context in which the selected GPU becomes the active device for all CUDA operations inside the block. Inside this context, `cuda.to_device(data)` transfers the `data` from the CPU to the memory of the currently active GPU. This ensures that memory allocations and data transfers are directed to the correct GPU. Once the block is completed, the active GPU context is automatically restored to whatever it was before. To share data between GPUs, we must copy data from one GPU to the host and then from the host to another GPU.

> Note
>
> **Inter-GPU communication and data transfer**
>
> The host-mediated transfer method is supported by default; however, it can be slow due to the overhead of memory movement through the CPU. More efficient **peer-to-peer (P2P)** communication, such as that available via NVLink, or **unified memory** features for shared access between devices, is not natively supported in Numba, although it may be achievable through lower-level libraries or interoperability with CUDA C extensions. While Numba allows multi-GPU programming, its inter-GPU communication

> capabilities are still relatively low-level and manual, best suited for workloads where GPU tasks can remain largely independent.

Multi-GPU matrix multiplication with Numba

Matrix multiplication is an example of a use case that can benefit from multi-GPU computing. In a multi-GPU scenario, following the task parallelism approach, we can split the output matrix into horizontal blocks and distribute them to different GPUs, with each GPU calculating a segment of the final output matrix.

Let's assume that we want to compute $C = A \times B$, where A is a matrix sharded across devices by row, and B is fully replicated on each device. The following figure illustrates how matrix multiplication can be distributed across two GPUs using row-wise sharding:

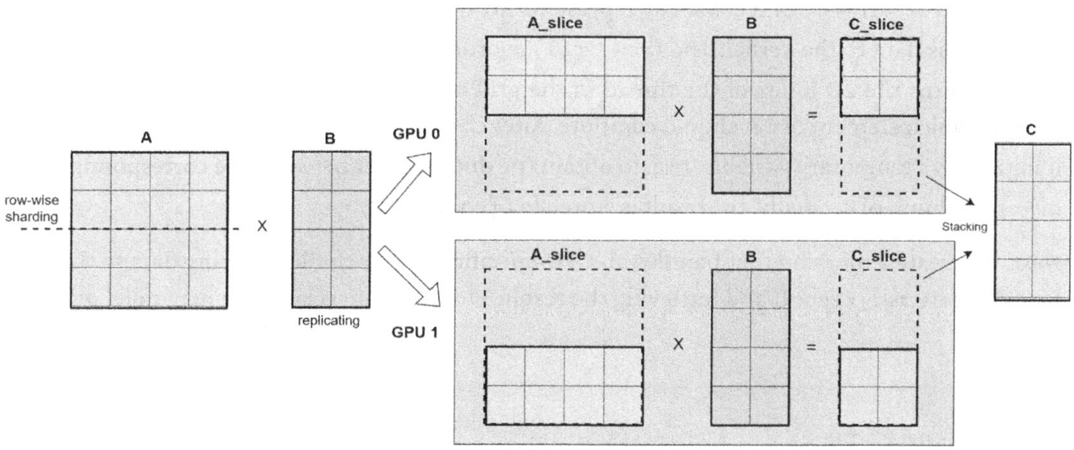

Figure 7.4 – Row-wise sharding of matrix multiplication across two GPUs

Matrix A is split row-wise so each GPU processes a distinct portion, while matrix B is replicated on both devices. Each GPU performs its local multiplication of `A_slice × B`, producing partial outputs that are then stacked to form the final matrix, C.

We will present an implementation of multi-GPU matrix multiplication using Numba-CUDA. To achieve this, we first define a CUDA kernel function, `matmul_kernel`, as shown here:

```
from numba import cuda
from numba.cuda.cudadrv.devicearray import DeviceNDArray

@cuda.jit
def matmul_kernel(
```

```
    A: DeviceNDArray,
    B: DeviceNDArray,
    C: DeviceNDArray,
) -> None:
    row, col = cuda.grid(2)
    if row < C.shape[0] and col < C.shape[1]:
        tmp = 0.0
        for k in range(A.shape[1]):
            tmp += A[row, k] * B[k, col]
        C[row, col] = tmp
```

`@cuda.jit` indicates that it will be compiled and executed on the GPU using Numba's CUDA JIT compiler. This kernel is designed to compute the matrix product `C = A × B`, where `A`, `B`, and `C` are expected as 2D arrays. `DeviceNDArray` represents arrays allocated on the GPU (device memory), used to pass data to the kernel. The `(row, col)` coordinates are computed using `cuda.grid(2)`, which returns the 2D index of the thread in the grid of CUDA threads. It allows each thread to identify which element of `C` it should compute. After checking the out-of-bounds memory access, it initializes a temporary variable, `tmp`, to obtain the **dot product** between the corresponding row of `A` and column of `B`. Finally, the result is stored in `C[row, col]`.

Next, we create a function that handles all GPU-specific tasks, including moving data to the GPU, launching `matmul_kernel`, and retrieving the result. This function is later run in parallel on one of the GPUs:

```
import math
from numpy.typing import NDArray

def run_on_gpu(
    gpu_id: int,
    A_slice: NDArray,
    B: NDArray,
    C_slice: NDArray
) -> None:

    with cuda.gpus[gpu_id]:
        A_dev = cuda.to_device(A_slice)
        B_dev = cuda.to_device(B)
        C_dev = cuda.to_device(C_slice)

        threads = (16, 16)
```

```
        blocks_x = math.ceil(
            C_dev.shape[0] / threads[0]
        )
        blocks_y = math.ceil(
            C_dev.shape[1] / threads[1]
        )
        blocks = (blocks_x, blocks_y)
        matmul_kernel[blocks, threads](A_dev, B_dev, C_dev)
        cuda.synchronize()

        C_slice[:] = C_dev.copy_to_host()
```

The `run_on_gpu` function takes three arguments: `gpu_id`, identifying which GPU to use; `A_slice`, a portion of matrix `A` assigned to this GPU; and `B`, the full matrix to be multiplied. A 2D block of CUDA threads is set to `(16, 16)`, and the number of blocks is computed based on the dimensions of the output matrix to ensure all elements are covered. After the kernel execution, `cuda.synchronize()` is called to ensure all GPU operations are complete before continuing.

We could also avoid copying the resulting array (`C_dev`) to the host. In that case, the calling function would be responsible for handling the data transfer from the device to the host. If needed, the return type of this function would be a `DeviceArray`.

Finally, we define our multi-GPU matrix multiplication function as follows:

```
import numpy as np
from typing import Optional
from concurrent.futures import ThreadPoolExecutor, wait

def multi_gpu_matmul(
    A: NDArray,
    B: NDArray,
    num_gpus: Optional[int] = None,
) -> NDArray:

    if num_gpus is None:
        num_gpus = len(cuda.gpus)

    assert A.shape[1] == B.shape[0]
    C = np.empty((A.shape[0], B.shape[1]), dtype=A.dtype)
    rows_per_gpu = math.ceil(A.shape[0] / num_gpus)
```

```
    with ThreadPoolExecutor(num_gpus) as executor:
        futures = []
        for gpu_id in range(num_gpus):

            start = gpu_id * rows_per_gpu
            end = min(A.shape[0], (gpu_id + 1) * rows_per_gpu)
            A_slice = A[start:end, ...]
            C_slice = C[start:end, ...]

            futures.append(
                executor.submit(
                    run_on_gpu, gpu_id, A_slice, B, C_slice
                )
            )
        wait(futures)

    return C
```

The `multi_gpu_matmul` function begins by determining the number of available GPUs. If not explicitly provided, it defaults to using all GPUs detected by the system. It then verifies that the input matrices, `A` and `B`, have compatible dimensions for matrix multiplication, specifically that the number of columns in `A` matches the number of rows in `B`. The `np.empty(...)` allocates the output `C` matrix. To parallelize the computation, the rows of matrix `A` are divided across the available GPUs. Each GPU is responsible for processing a distinct slice of `A` (`A_slice`) and performs its portion of the matrix multiplication with the full matrix `B`, using the `run_on_gpu` function. The result is stored in a slice of `C` (`C_slice`).

`ThreadPoolExecutor` is used to manage parallel execution, with one thread per GPU. This design choice respects the CUDA context restriction that ties each GPU to a single host thread. Within this thread pool, the `executor.submit(...)` call schedules the `run_on_gpu` function for execution, passing in the GPU identifier, the assigned slice of matrix `A`, the full matrix `B`, and the slice of output matrix `C`. The `futures` list serves as a container to keep track of all the GPU tasks that have been submitted for execution via the thread pool. Instead of returning the result immediately, `submit` yields to a `Future` object, an abstraction representing a result that will become available once the computation completes.

Each GPU computation runs concurrently in its own thread, enabling parallel processing across devices. After all tasks have been submitted, the program waits for their completion using `wait(futures)`. Once finished, it returns the full result matrix, `C`.

> **Note**
>
> Python's **Global Interpreter Lock (GIL)** doesn't affect CUDA kernels. This is because kernel launches happen through native code (compiled LLVM/PTX), and Numba uses `nogil` signatures for device interaction. Furthermore, each thread will get its own CUDA **context**, and Numba tracks this safely. This makes it possible to write Python programs where each thread controls a different GPU concurrently. This is why we use multi-threading (instead of multi-processing) to run tasks on multiple GPUs in Numba-CUDA without being limited by the GIL.

For example, a matrix multiplication workload between two random `float32` matrices with sizes of `A (4048, 4048)` and `B (4048, 8096)`, utilizing two GPUs instead of one, results in a performance improvement with >90% GPU utilization on each device. When executed on a single GPU, the operation takes 1.37 seconds to complete. By distributing the computation across two GPUs, the runtime is reduced to 0.72 seconds, resulting in a 1.90x speed-up in execution. Also, the performance improvement ratio remains similar for both `float32` and `float64` precisions.

Up to this point, we've used a thread pool, and no data sharing between executor workers has been necessary. This approach works well for single-node GPU systems, where multiple GPUs can still be managed in parallel using separate threads within the same process. While we could have used a process pool instead, doing so would introduce **inter-process communication (IPC)** overhead, which can negatively impact performance. However, if we want to scale our GPU workloads to a multi-node setup, where GPUs are distributed across different machines, using processes becomes essential, as threads cannot span multiple nodes. In this case, Python's `ProcessPoolExecutor` could still be used, but we would then need to explicitly handle IPC for data sharing between processes and machines, which adds significant complexity.

A more scalable and convenient alternative is to use a Dask cluster, which abstracts much of the communication and task scheduling involved in distributed computing. Therefore, in the next section, we will introduce how to use a Dask cluster to easily enable distributed GPU computing even across multiple machines.

Distributed computing with Dask

Distributed computing can introduce significant technical complexity, particularly when managing parallel tasks across multiple machines. To simplify this process, we will use **Dask**, which abstracts much of the underlying parallelism while providing a flexible and familiar interface for Python users.

Dask overview

Dask is a powerful parallel computing ecosystem that supports local and distributed computing on both CPUs and GPUs. Dask works by breaking down computations into smaller tasks, organizing them into a **task graph**, and then executing them using a scheduler. This allows Dask to execute tasks independently or in sequence, depending on their dependencies, which makes it suitable for a wide range of applications, including data processing, machine learning, and custom parallel workflows. Dask supports two execution modes. **Lazy execution** defers computation until requested. When we create or transform data, Dask builds the task graph instead of computing the results immediately. Actual computation only happens when we explicitly trigger it using the `compute()` method. This allows Dask to optimize the task graph before execution. **Eager execution** happens when we use `client.submit()`. These functions immediately schedule tasks for execution on the cluster and return `Future` objects. Unlike lazy mode, the work starts as soon as the task is submitted.

Numba is best used in combination with tools such as Dask clusters when trying to scale GPU workloads beyond a single node. Numba-CUDA alone currently offers limited built-in support for distributed computing for inter-node communication. Dask fills this gap by enabling automatic data handling, coordinated GPU task execution, and efficient multi-node communication. Ideally, Dask manages task distribution and data movement, while Numba handles custom GPU kernels, giving us the best of both performance and scalability.

We are particularly interested in using a Dask cluster for distributed GPU computing. In the following section, we will discuss how to set up and use such a cluster.

Setting up a Dask-CUDA cluster

To use Dask with GPUs, we rely on **Dask-CUDA**, which extends Dask to be CUDA-aware. Setting up a Dask-CUDA cluster involves launching a Dask **scheduler** and, in principle, multiple Dask **workers**. Often, each worker is assigned exclusively to a specific GPU device, but further adjustments are also possible. Dask handles data partitioning, task scheduling, and inter-worker communication, making it seamless to scale computations across all available GPUs.

The following figure shows an overview of key Dask components, including the Dask scheduler and GPU-enabled Dask workers:

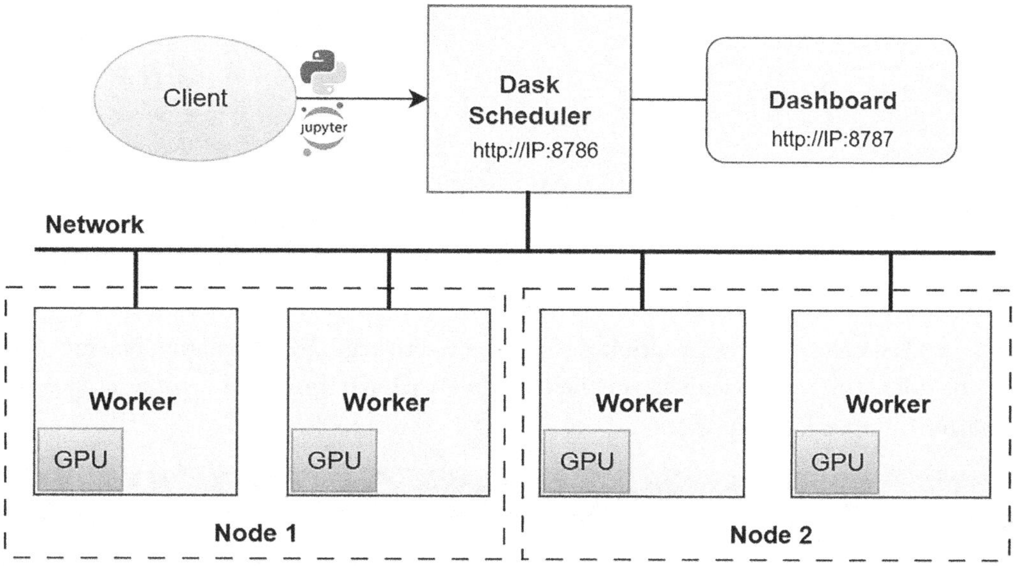

Figure 7.5 – An overview of key Dask cluster components

At the core of Dask's distributed GPU execution are workers, each managing one or more GPUs. A central scheduler coordinates task execution across all workers using `tcp://<IP>:8786`. Each worker is by default pinned to a single GPU to avoid conflicts and maximize memory locality. Tasks are sent to workers with available resources and data proximity.

Setting up a Dask cluster locally

A typical local (single-node) setup involves importing `LocalCUDACluster`, which automatically detects available GPUs and configures the cluster accordingly. It gives a multi-process Dask cluster on your local machine:

```
from dask_cuda import LocalCUDACluster

cluster = LocalCUDACluster()
```

Here's what the Dask cluster output would look like:

Figure 7.6 – Screenshot of a Dask cluster output in a Jupyter notebook

Setting up a multi-node Dask cluster

To set up a Dask cluster across multiple nodes, we need to begin by designating one machine as the scheduler. On that machine, you launch the scheduler process by running the `dask-scheduler` command, as follows:

```
$ pixi run dask-scheduler
```

This starts the central coordinator responsible for managing task distribution and communication between the workers. When the scheduler starts, it displays an address (usually starting with `tcp://`) that the workers will use to connect. After the scheduler is running, you move on to each of the other nodes that have GPUs and start the workers using the `dask-cuda-worker` command, followed by the address of the scheduler. This command initializes a set of GPU-aware workers on the node, automatically detecting the available GPUs and assigning each worker to a specific device. The workers will connect back to the scheduler and register themselves, making their compute resources available to the cluster:

```
$ pixi run dask-cuda-worker tcp://<scheduler-ip>:8786
```

You can optionally configure the workers by adding flags to control how much GPU memory they allocate or how many threads each one uses, but this is not strictly necessary for a basic setup. Once all workers have connected, the Dask cluster is fully operational and ready to accept tasks.

Dask client

Once the cluster is created, a Dask `Client` is used to connect to it and submit computational tasks:

```
from dask.distributed import Client

client = Client(cluster)
client
```

The first line imports the `Client` class from the `dask.distributed` module. The `Client` class is responsible for connecting to the Dask distributed cluster. Calling `Client(cluster)` creates a client on the input cluster. Alternatively, `Client('tcp://DASK-SCHEDULER-IP:8786')` can be used to create a client on a distributed Dask cluster setup.

The `client` object in an interactive environment such as Jupyter Notebook, displays useful information about the cluster, such as the number of workers, available resources, and current task status.

An example output looks like this:

Figure 7.7 – Dask client displaying information in the Jupyter notebook

Combining Numba-CUDA and Dask

Using Numba, we can write custom GPU functions, compile them with `@cuda.jit`, and apply them to data chunks managed by Dask. This approach allows us to scale user-defined GPU kernels across multiple devices without rewriting code for multi-GPU execution. Dask handles the distribution of data and tasks, while Numba ensures execution on the GPU.

The following example shows how to build a simple pipeline using Numba-compiled CUDA functions, with Dask managing distributed execution across GPUs. For simplicity, we define a helper function, `run_on_worker`, that abstracts away the details of data preparation, kernel launching, and result retrieval for multiple kernels, as illustrated here:

```
from typing import Callable

def run_on_worker(kernel: Callable) -> Callable:
    def wrapper(d_arr: DeviceNDArray) -> DeviceNDArray:
        d_out = cuda.device_array_like(d_arr)
        threads_per_block=256
        blocks_per_grid = math.ceil(d_arr.size / threads_per_block)
        kernel[blocks_per_grid, threads_per_block](d_arr, d_out)
        cuda.synchronize()
        return d_out
    return wrapper
```

The run_on_worker function is a **decorator** to wrap element-wise CUDA kernel functions. It takes a kernel function and returns a wrapper function that handles preparing data for GPU execution. Within this wrapper, it assumes the input array (d_arr) is already on the GPU and allocates output memory on the device using cuda.device_array_like. It computes the number of blocks needed to launch the kernel and invokes the kernel on the input data. After the kernel completes, it calls cuda.synchronize() to ensure the GPU finishes execution before returning the result. It finally returns the result as a device array (d_out).

We also define a simple data loader that splits the input array into multiple chunks, as follows:

```
from typing import Generator

def get_chunks(
    arr: NDArray, num_chunks: int
) -> Generator:
    chunk_size = math.ceil(arr.size / num_chunks)
    for i in range(num_chunks):
        start = i * chunk_size
        end = min(arr.size, (i+1) * chunk_size)
        yield arr[start:end, ...]
```

The get_chunks function is a **generator** that divides an array into a specified number of chunks along its first axis. It computes the size of each chunk based on the total size and number of chunks, then yields slices of the array accordingly. This function will be useful for distributing data across GPUs or Dask workers.

Next, we define two dummy CUDA kernels:

```
@run_on_worker
@cuda.jit
def square_kernel(
    x: DeviceNDArray, out: DeviceNDArray
) -> None:
    i = cuda.grid(1)
    if i < x.size:
        out[i] = x[i] ** 2


@run_on_worker
@cuda.jit
def sin_kernel(
    x: DeviceNDArray, out: DeviceNDArray
```

```
) -> None:
    i = cuda.grid(1)
    if i < x.size:
        out[i] = math.sin(x[i])
```

The `square_kernel` and `sin_kernel` functions are decorated with both `@cuda.jit` and `@run_on_worker`. These kernels define element-wise operations to be applied to GPU arrays. `square_kernel` squares each element of the input, while `sin_kernel` computes the sine of each element. Both kernels use `cuda.grid(1)` to determine the thread's global index and ensure threads do not access out-of-bound memory by checking `i < x.size`.

To build a simple pipeline, we define a few additional functions. Rather than using a single function call, we structure the computation as a pipeline to observe later how individual tasks are scheduled and executed within the Dask scheduler:

```
def to_gpu(x: NDArray) -> DeviceNDArray:
    return cuda.to_device(x)

def to_host(x: DeviceNDArray) -> NDArray:
    return x.copy_to_host()

def process_step_1(x :NDArray) -> NDArray:
    return square_kernel(x)

def process_step_2(x: NDArray) -> NDArray:
    return sin_kernel(x)

pipeline = (to_gpu, process_step_1, process_step_2, to_host)
```

The to_gpu function transfers a NumPy array from host memory to GPU device memory using `cuda.to_device`, while `to_host` retrieves the data back to host memory using `copy_to_host`. These functions are defined as being called separately on each worker, ensuring that each worker manages its own data transfer to and from the GPU. This enables concurrent data loading across workers. Moreover, if the host array is too large to fit into a single GPU's memory, this allows the array to be divided into smaller chunks and distributed across multiple GPUs. The `process_step_1` and `process_step_2` functions apply the GPU-accelerated kernels to a chunk of data. Each of these functions assumes the input is already on the GPU and applies either the square or sine transformation accordingly. `pipeline` encapsulates a sequence of operations in the form of a tuple.

Finally, we are ready to execute our data-processing pipeline using Dask:

```
from distributed import Future

def run(
    pipeline: tuple[Callable, ...],
    client: Client,
    data: NDArray
) -> Future:
    x = data
    for fn in pipeline:
        x = client.submit(fn, x)
    return x

num_workers = len(client.scheduler_info()['workers'])
futures = []
for chunk in get_chunks(arr, num_workers):
    futures.append(
        run(pipeline, client, chunk)
    )
client.gather(futures);
```

The `run` function takes three arguments, including a pipeline, a Dask client, and some input data. It iteratively submits each function in the pipeline to the Dask scheduler using `client.submit`. This constructs a task graph where each stage of computation depends on the previous one. For a complex pipeline, Dask automatically runs independent tasks concurrently.

`len(client.scheduler_info()['workers'])` queries the connected Dask cluster to determine how many active workers are available, which is used to split the workload accordingly. The main loop iterates over chunks of a larger dataset, `arr`, dividing it into as many parts as there are workers. For each chunk, it calls the `run` function to submit the pipeline of computations to Dask, as we have seen before, collecting the resulting `Future` in a list named `futures`. Finally, `client.gather(futures)` blocks execution until all the futures have completed and gathers the final results from all the workers back to the local process. This approach allows parallel processing of large datasets, with each chunk being processed independently and concurrently through a customizable sequence of functions, distributed across the Dask GPU-enabled workers.

Dask dashboard

Dask additionally provides a real-time diagnostic dashboard (typically accessible at `http://localhost:8787`) that visualizes task graphs, memory usage, GPU utilization, and performance bottlenecks in real time. This helps us analyze the efficiency of parallel executions and fine-tune workflows. If tasks are unevenly distributed or memory limits are exceeded, the scheduler dashboard makes it easy to detect and address these issues.

The following screenshot shows a Dask dashboard visualizing the execution of our simple processing pipeline. For illustration purposes, we have set `num_chunks=200`, which distributes more chunks across the workers:

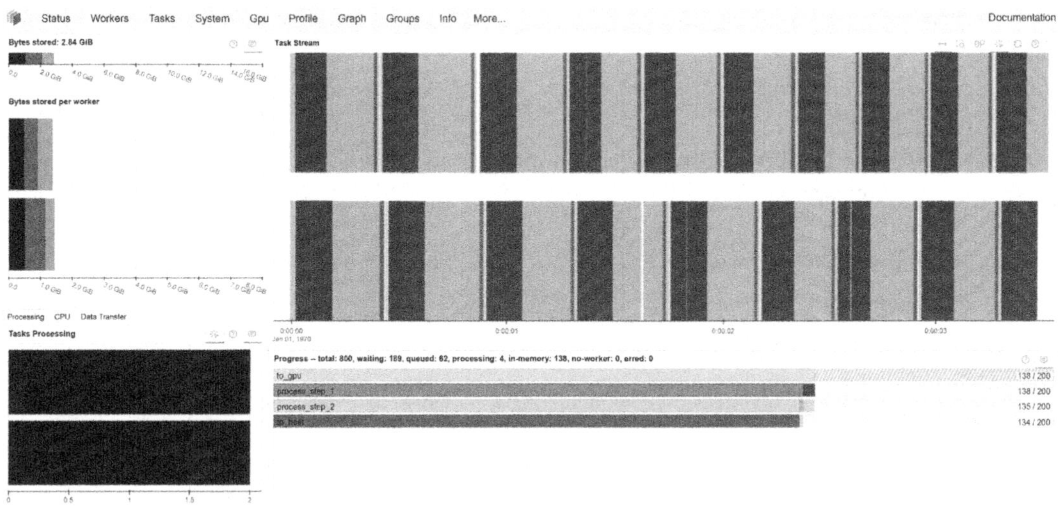

Figure 7.8 – Dask dashboard visualizing execution of the pipeline

The task stream indicates that both workers are fully utilized with continuous task execution, as shown by the alternating green and purple blocks representing different processing steps. The absence of large white gaps suggests minimal idle time. Memory usage is balanced across workers, with each storing a similar amount of data, totaling 2.84 GiB. The **Tasks Processing** panel confirms that both workers remain consistently active. Progress bars illustrate how tasks flow through the pipeline stages, with a steady progression across steps such as transferring data to the GPU, processing, and sending results back. For our simple element-wise pipeline, the dashboard reflects an efficient and well-balanced workload, with effective resource utilization and steady task throughput. However, real-world scenarios are often more complex, and such a dashboard can help with visually identifying bottlenecks and optimizing pipeline performance.

Dask array API

Beyond Numba, **Dask arrays** extend NumPy-like APIs to work with larger-than-memory data by breaking it into chunks and scheduling computations in parallel. Using Dask arrays, which natively support CuPy, we can effortlessly process large GPU-resident arrays in parallel across multiple GPUs or nodes:

```
import dask.array as da
import cupy as cp

def make_array(
    chunk_size: int, value: float
) -> NDArray:
    return cp.full(chunk_size, value)

chunk_size = (1_000_000,)
workers = client.scheduler_info()['workers']
futures = []
for i, worker in enumerate(workers):
    future = client.submit(make_array, chunk_size, i + 1, workers=[worker])
    futures.append(future)

chunks = [da.from_delayed(f, shape=chunk_size, dtype=cp.float32) for f in futures]

dask_array = da.concatenate(chunks, axis=0)
dask_array
```

This code constructs a Dask array distributed across multiple workers, with each chunk stored as a CuPy array on the GPU. A helper `make_array` function generates an array filled with a constant value. For each available worker, a task is submitted to create a chunk filled with a unique number, and the task is pinned to that specific worker. These futures are wrapped as delayed Dask array chunks with predefined shapes and data types. Finally, all chunks are concatenated into a single Dask array. The result is a Dask array composed of multiple CuPy-backed chunks, each allocated to a distinct worker, enabling controlled distribution and GPU acceleration.

The following figure represents an overview of the output Dask array, summarizing its structure and memory usage:

	Array	Chunk
Bytes	7.63 MiB	3.81 MiB
Shape	(2000000,)	(1000000,)
Dask graph	2 chunks in 3 graph layers	
Data type	float32 numpy.ndarray	

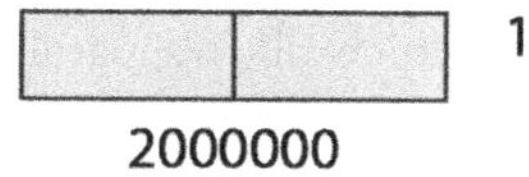

Figure 7.9 – An example Dask array representation

The array has a total of 2,000,000 elements, divided into 2 chunks, each containing 1,000,000 elements. The overall memory usage of the array is approximately 7.63 MiB, while each chunk individually consumes 3.81 MiB. The Dask graph underlying this array consists of two chunks organized within three computational graph layers, indicating some intermediate steps in the computation. The small diagram shows the array divided into two equally sized chunks, giving a clear visual representation of how the data is partitioned.

This chunked Dask array can now be used much like a NumPy array, allowing integration into a processing pipeline. Operations applied to it will be lazily evaluated and distributed across the workers:

```
pipeline = lambda x: da.sin(x**2)
dask.compute(pipeline(dask_array))
```

Here, we defined and executed a Dask-based computation pipeline. The `lambda` function represents a simple transformation pipeline. When this function is applied to the previously constructed `dask_array`, it returns a new Dask array representing the computation graph, but does not execute it immediately. The call to `dask.compute(...)` triggers the actual execution of this computation. Dask schedules and runs the operations across the distributed workers, processes the data in parallel, and returns the final computed result as a CuPy array.

Also, processing **DataFrames** is similarly possible using **cuDF**, a GPU-accelerated DataFrame library with a pandas-like API. Curious readers are encouraged to check out the *RapidAI* official documentation for more in-depth information.

In the next section, we will shift our focus to machine learning applications and explore the distributed training of a model on multiple GPUs using JAX.

Multi-GPU computing with JAX

JAX offers a clean path to distributed machine learning. As far as using a high-level API is concerned, JAX automatically manages device allocation, parallel computation, and gradient synchronization. This facilitates data processing or machine learning model training across multiple GPUs with minimal changes to the code. We will specifically use the `jax.pmap` (parallel map) function, which allows parallelizing a computation across multiple devices. JAX also handles **data sharding** for inputs, so we can basically pass a full batch and it will divide it evenly across the GPUs, enabling synchronous data parallel training with very little boilerplate. This chapter focuses on multi-GPU computing; readers new to JAX should refer to *Chapter 10* for an introduction.

Matrix multiplication

We will demonstrate how the previous matrix multiplication example can be executed across multiple GPUs using JAX. We follow the same parallelization strategy by distributing the rows of one input matrix across available GPU devices. Each GPU independently processes its assigned row segment to compute a portion of the final result.

The following code snippet showcases this multi-GPU implementation in JAX.

We first need to define a `matmul` function that performs a dot product for any two given input matrices:

```
import jax
import jax.numpy as jnp
from jax import Array

@jax.jit
def matmul(A: Array, B: Array) -> Array:
    return jnp.dot(A, B)
```

This function is decorated with `@jax.jit`, meaning it is compiled with XLA for optimized execution. It takes two matrices, `A` and `B`, and performs a standard dot product (`jnp.dot`).

Then, we define the `multi_gpu_matmul_jax` function, as follows:

```
from typing import Optional
from numpy.typing import NDArray

def multi_gpu_matmul_jax(
    A: NDArray,
    B: NDArray,
    num_gpus: Optional[int] = None,
) -> NDArray:
```

```
    devices = jax.devices()
    if num_gpus is not None:
        devices = devices[:num_gpus]

    A_chunks = np.split(A, len(devices), axis=0)
    A_sharded = jax.device_put_sharded(A_chunks, devices)
    B_replicated = jax.device_put_sharded([B] * len(devices), devices)

    parallel_matmul = jax.pmap(matmul, devices=devices)

    for _ in range(100):
        result_sharded = parallel_matmul(A_sharded, B_replicated)

    return np.concatenate(result_sharded)
```

In this function, the input matrix `A` is first split into equal chunks along the first axis using `np.split`. This means `A_chunks` has a shape of `(num_gpus, rows / num_gpus, cols)` instead of `(rows, cols)`. The `A_chunks` is then converted into a JAX **sharded** array using `jax.device_put_sharded`, placing each chunk on its respective GPU devices. Matrix `B` is **replicated**, meaning it is broadcasted for each GPU so that every device can multiply its chunk of `A` with the same `B` (see *Figure 7.4*).

Next, `jax.pmap` wraps the `matmul` function, creating a parallelized version that runs across multiple devices in lockstep. This tells JAX to feed each GPU with the corresponding sharded matrix, `A_sharded`, and replicated matrix, `B`, along the first index.

The matrix multiplication, again between the two random matrices with sizes of `A (4048, 4048)` and `B (4048, 8096)`, results in a speed-up of 1.95x in JAX. Additionally, our JAX implementation for the base single GPU execution gives a runtime of 200 ms, which is noticeably faster than our Numba implementation (750 ms). This is because JAX traces the function and sends the computation graph to XLA, and XLA fuses, reorders, and optimizes the operations. Also, for matrix multiplication specifically, XLA delegates vector or matrix operations to highly tuned vendor libraries such as **cuBLAS**. This library uses low-level optimizations, such as cache blocking, vectorization, and specialized GPU kernels, that are far more efficient than our basic implementation. But with careful profiling of the Numba-CUDA implementation and applying the optimization techniques that we have learned in the previous chapter, we expect to achieve performance that is reasonably close to the JAX implementation. Note that, for performance benchmarking, the computation is repeated 100 times to increase GPU utilization to 90%.

In the following section, we will focus on a practical example of distributed training for a machine learning model using JAX.

Distributed machine learning training

Distributed training of a linear regression model using `jax.pmap` is a great way to demonstrate how JAX enables scalable machine learning across multiple GPUs. In linear regression, the model learns two key trainable parameters: weights (`w`) and bias (`b`). These parameters define the relationship between input data (`X`) and predicted outputs (`y_pred`), calculated as `y_pred = X @ w + b`. The goal is to minimize the **mean squared error**, a loss function that measures the average squared difference between predicted and true target values (`y`). This optimization process often relies on **gradient descent**, where the model iteratively adjusts `w` and `b` based on gradients of the loss with respect to these parameters.

We have adopted the data parallelism strategy for this distributed training and used `jax.pmap`, where the dataset is divided into smaller subsets and distributed across multiple GPUs. Each GPU processes its assigned shard of data independently, while the model parameters are replicated across all devices (see *Figure 7.2*). After each GPU computes its local gradients, a collective all-reduce `pmean` (which stands for parallel mean) operation is performed to average the gradients across devices. This step ensures that the final parameter updates reflect the combined information from all the shards, rather than being limited to a single shard. The average gradients are then used to update the replicated model parameters on each device, maintaining consistency across the distributed system.

The following code defines a simple linear regression model and its parameters:

```
from typing import NamedTuple

class Params(NamedTuple):
    weight: Array
    bias: Array

def model(params: Params, xs: Array) -> Array:
    """Linear regression model."""
    return params.weight * xs + params.bias
```

The `Params` class is a typed container holding two JAX arrays: `weight` and `bias`, representing the parameters. Using `NameTuple` is an organized way to manage the model parameters and ensures immutability. The `model` function takes the parameters and an input array, `xs`, and computes the linear transformation.

Next, we implement the loss function to quantify the model's performance by comparing its parameterized predictions against the target values, ys, for the input observations, xs:

```
def loss_fn(
    params: Params, xs: Array, ys: Array
) -> Array:
    predictions = model(params, xs)
    return jnp.mean((predictions - ys) ** 2)
```

It takes the model parameters, `params`; input data, `xs`; and target values, `ys`. First, it uses the `model` function to compute `predictions` for the inputs. Then, it calculates the mean squared error, which is the squared difference between the predictions and the actual targets, averages these squared errors with `jnp.mean`, and returns the result as a single scalar JAX array.

We also define the `initialize_params` function, which randomly initializes the model parameters prior to the training loop:

```
def initialize_params(rng) -> Params:
    weights_key, bias_key = jax.random.split(rng)
    weight = jax.random.normal(weights_key, ())
    bias = jax.random.normal(bias_key, ())
    return Params(weight, bias)
```

This function accepts a random number generator key, `rng`, as input and splits it into two independent keys (`weights_key` and `bias_key`) so that the weight and bias are initialized with separate random keys. The `jax.random.normal` function then samples each parameter from a standard normal distribution. These values are returned as a `Params` object, which holds the model's weight and bias in a structured and type-safe way.

We can now initialize the parameters and replicate those parameters across the GPU devices:

```
devices = jax.devices()
key=jax.random.PRNGKey(123)
params = initialize_params(key)

params_replicated = jax.tree.map(
    lambda x: jnp.array([x] * len(devices)),
    params,
)
```

This first sets up the initial model parameters. `jax.local_devices()` retrieves the available devices on the machine. A reproducible random number generator key is then created with `jax.random.PRNGKey(123)` and passed to `initialize_params` to generate the model's initial weight and bias. As each device expects to receive its own identical copy of the parameters, `jax.tree.map` is used to transform the `Params` structure. For each leaf value (weight or bias), it creates a JAX array containing `len(devices)` identical copies, one for each device. This `params_replicated` is now ready to be fed into a parallelized function, ensuring that all devices start with exactly the same parameters.

We also need to generate a small synthetic dataset with added noise for training our linear regression model:

```
from numpy.typing import NDArray

def generate_data(
    true_weight: float = 2.0,
    true_bias: float = -1,
    samples: int = 256,
) -> tuple[NDArray, NDArray]:
    xs = np.random.normal(size=(samples, 1))
    noise = 0.5 * np.random.normal(size=(samples, 1))
    ys = true_weight * xs + true_bias + noise
    return xs, ys

xs, ys = generate_data()
```

Like the matrix multiplication example, we split the data and move it to different devices using `jax.device_put_sharded`:

```
xs_sharded = jax.device_put_sharded(
    np.split(xs, len(devices)),
    devices,
)

ys_sharded = jax.device_put_sharded(
    np.split(ys, len(devices)),
    devices,
)
```

Now that the model, loss function, and data are all in place, we can proceed and define an `update` function that performs each step of training in parallel. In each training step, we provide the `xs_sharded` inputs and their corresponding `ys_shared` targets, where each device gets its own portion of the training data:

```
from functools import partial

@partial(jax.pmap, axis_name="device")
def update(
    params: Params,
    xs_sharded: Array,
    ys_sharded: Array,
) -> tuple[Params, Array]:

    loss, grads = jax.value_and_grad(loss_fn)(
        params, xs_sharded, ys_sharded
    )

    updated_params = jax.tree.map(
        lambda param, grad: param - grad * 0.005,
        params,
        jax.lax.pmean(grads, axis_name="device"),
    )

    return (
        updated_params,
        jax.lax.pmean(loss, axis_name="device"),
    )
```

Let's go through this function in more detail.

The `@partial(jax.pmap, axis_name="device")` decorator both JIT-compiles and parallelizes the function across all available GPU devices. The `axis_name="device"` label creates a named parallel axis, which is later used to coordinate collective operations, such as averaging gradients or losses across devices. When the `update` function runs under `jax.pmap`, each device gets its own identical copy of the parameters, as well as the sharded input data, so that each device processes only its assigned slice. Inside the function, `jax.value_and_grad(loss_fn)` evaluates both the scalar **loss** and its **gradient** with respect to the model parameters for the current data batch (`xs`) and targets (`ys`).

Since each device computes gradients independently,

```
jax.lax.pmean(grads, axis_name="device")
```

performs an all-reduce mean over the "`device`" axis, ensuring that the gradients from all devices are averaged together. This is essential for synchronous data parallel training; without it, each GPU would update its parameters using only its local gradient and not benefit from the combined information from other GPUs. `axis_name="device"` in `pmean` must match the name given in the `@partial(..., axis_name="device")` decorator so that JAX knows exactly which group of devices participates in the reduction.

Once the averaged gradients are available, `jax.tree.map` applies the **gradient descent** update to every parameter in the `Params` structure, subtracting `grad * 0.005` (where `0.005` is the chosen learning rate) from the current value. Finally, the function returns the updated parameters along with the mean loss value across devices for monitoring reasons, which is computed with `jax.lax.pmean(loss, axis_name="device")` in the same way as the gradients.

If all goes well, the distributed training loop, which parallelizes computations across multiple GPU devices, can be implemented as follows:

```
for i in range(1000):
    params_replicated, loss = update(
        params_replicated, xs_sharded, ys_sharded
    )
    if i % 100 == 0:
        print(
            f"Step {i:3d}, loss: {loss[0]:.3f},
            {get_params(replicated_params)}"
)
```

This loop runs 1,000 training steps, calling `update` each time to compute the loss, average gradients across devices, and update the model parameters for distributed learning. The following results show the training progress of a linear regression model over 1,000 steps:

```
Step   0, loss: 6.304, Params(weight=-0.4665026, bias=-0.78407454)
Step 100, loss: 1.058, Params(weight=1.0769118, bias=-0.8888425)
...
Step 900, loss: 0.209, Params(weight=1.991673231, bias=-1.0042194)
Step 1000, loss: 0.209, Params(weight=1.99226288, bias=-1.0044189)
```

The model successfully learns a linear relationship in the data, with parameters converging to values close to y=2x-1. The loss plateaus at ~0.209, indicating that the model has reached a good fit but may not fully capture all patterns due to our model's simplicity or introduced data noise.

Finally, the following figure shows a scatter plot of the generated data for the linear regression example:

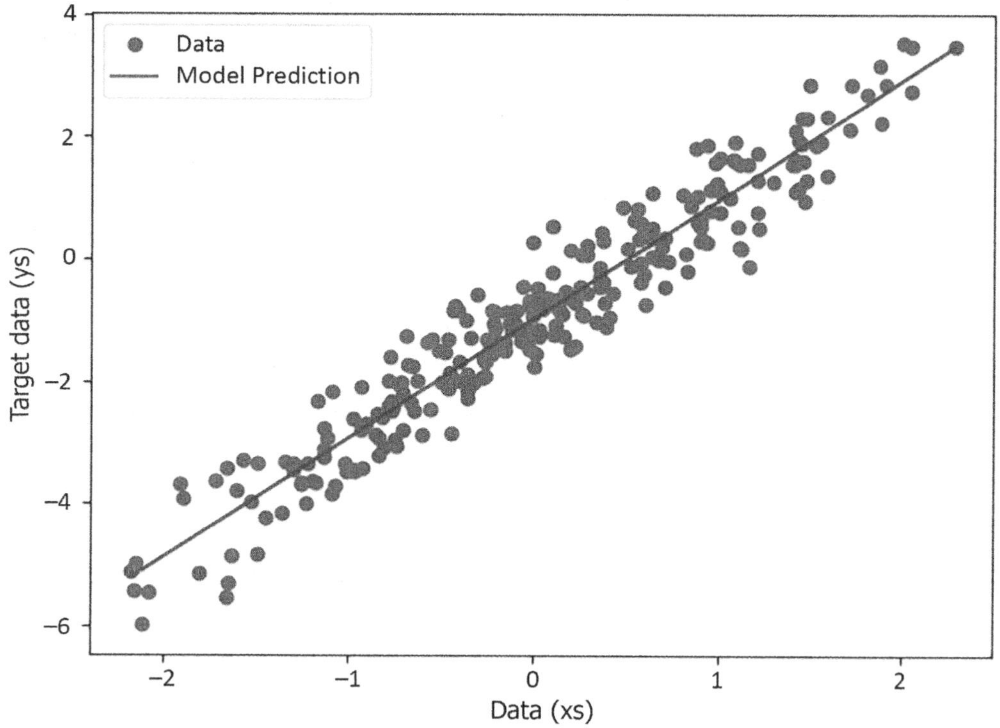

Figure 7.10 – Visualization of data and model predictions after the distributed training

The line represents the model's predicted linear relationship between xs and ys after training. The close alignment of the line with the dense region of blue points indicates that the model has successfully learned the underlying linear pattern in the data.

JAX also provides support for multi-node computation through its distributed runtime, enabling large-scale execution across multiple machines. However, configuring and managing such setups can be complex and is indeed beyond the scope of this chapter. But the examples provided here should give you a basic understanding and the essential tools for using JAX in distributed training.

Summary

We focused on overcoming the limitations of single-GPU computing by using multiple GPUs. We began by introducing the basics of multi-GPU computing, including an overview of multi-GPU systems, particularly their network topology. Then, we discussed two common parallelism approaches: data parallelism and model parallelism. To illustrate these concepts, a simple example of matrix multiplication was used to demonstrate how to implement a multi-GPU version using Numba-CUDA. This example showcased the core concepts of data partitioning, memory data movement, and distributed computing.

We then further scaled up to a multi-node environment by utilizing a Dask-CUDA cluster, which enabled orchestrating computation across multiple GPUs and machines. A simple pipeline was introduced to demonstrate task dependencies in the Dask dashboard, providing insights into performance analysis using the Dask scheduler.

Finally, we switched to JAX, re-implementing the multi-GPU matrix multiplication example and demonstrating distributed training of a machine learning model, a linear regression model.

In the next chapter, we will focus on high-level CuPy library to bring NumPy and SciPy to the GPU.

Questions

1. As the number of GPUs used in multi-GPU computation increases, what potential computational bottlenecks may arise and how can they be addressed?
2. When working with large datasets, what parallelization methods are most effective for achieving efficient multi-GPU computation, and why are they recommended?
3. How can the `multi_gpu_matmul_jax` function be modified to handle matrices of any size, particularly when the number of rows is not a multiple of the number of GPUs available?

Answers

1. As the number of GPUs increases in multi-GPU computation, bottlenecks, including communication overhead and data transfer limitations, between the CPU and GPU can arise. They can be addressed using high-bandwidth interconnection, such as NVLink and InfiniBand, and utilizing direct memory access (i.e., NVIDIA RDMA).
2. Data parallelism is recommended as long as the model fits in the memory of a single GPU because it scales well with large datasets, as it utilizes the GPU with almost independent computations and low communication overhead. Note that the

aggregation step can become a bottleneck as the number of GPUs increases (see the answer to the previous question).

3. Instead of `np.split`, which requires equal-sized splits, we can simply use `np.array_split`, as it automatically distributes the remaining rows across chunks.

Get this book's PDF version and more

Scan the QR code (or go to `packtpub.com/unlock`). Search for this book by name, confirm the edition, and then follow the steps on the page.

UNLOCK NOW

Note: Keep your invoice handy. Purchases made directly from Packt don't require an invoice.

Part 3

Using High-Level Python Libraries for GPU Computation

This part pivots to GPU computing with high-level libraries that mimic the API of familiar Python libraries. These libraries let us focus on quickly prototyping solutions rather than implementing every low-level detail from scratch. We'll use CuPy to replace NumPy and SciPy workflows, RAPIDS (cuDF/cuML) for pandas and scikit-learn tasks, and JAX for optimization and machine learning. Each chapter bridges high-level APIs with GPU performance and explores interoperability with custom low-level CUDA kernels.

This part of the book includes the following chapters:

8

Bringing NumPy and SciPy to the GPU with CuPy

The previous chapters focused on interacting with the GPU using low-level CUDA primitives: kernels, threads, grids, blocks, streams, and more. This chapter and those that follow build on these low-level foundations to move up a level of abstraction. This chapter introduces CuPy, a library that implements a plethora of routines for manipulating N-dimensional arrays on the GPU. For readers familiar with NumPy and SciPy, CuPy brings the functionality of both these libraries to the GPU, with a near-identical API.

The learning outcomes for this chapter are as follows:

- Using CuPy to perform NumPy-like array manipulations on the GPU
- Using CuPy to perform routines from SciPy on the GPU
- Converting CPU code based on NumPy and SciPy to run on the GPU
- How to combine CuPy with other libraries
- Understanding the benefits, drawbacks, and use cases of CuPy versus Numba-CUDA versus CPU implementations.
- Writing GPU-agnostic code
- Writing performant CuPy code

Technical requirements

To run the code in this chapter, an NVIDIA GPU with compute capability 7.5 or more is required. The CUDA Toolkit, Python 3, and a number of Python packages must also be installed. As explained in *Chapter 2*, it is recommended to create a `pixi` environment based on the `pixi.lock` file in the GitHub repository associated with this book:

https://github.com/PacktPublishing/GPU-Accelerated-Computing-with-Python-3-and-CUDA

The details for getting set up are explained in the `README.md` file. To run the code snippets in this chapter, an A100 GPU was used; timing results will differ depending on the specific device that is used to run the examples.

What CuPy offers

To implement custom algorithms, such as calculating a Julia set fractal in *Chapters 3* and *5*, the best approach is to implement it from scratch using low-level CUDA primitives. However, many algorithms can be decomposed into smaller operations that appear repeatedly in many different problems; examples include matrix multiplication, linear algebra routines, and discrete Fourier transforms, just to name a few. Highly optimized implementations of these common routines can be found in various libraries, and it makes no sense to re-implement these algorithms. A problem is solved faster by connecting existing routines, and performance may even be better than a solution coded from scratch.

This philosophy explains the popularity of libraries such as **NumPy** and **SciPy**. Arguably, NumPy and SciPy are responsible for making Python the dominant language in data, (data) science, and AI. Vanilla Python is an extremely slow language for numerical computation. NumPy and SciPy wrap highly optimized routines, written in compiled languages such as C, C++, and Fortran, with a convenient-to-use Python interface. By combining these elementary operations, sophisticated and reasonably fast numerical algorithms can be composed with only a few lines of code.

What NumPy and SciPy are for computation on the CPU, CuPy is for computations on the GPU. Indeed, CuPy aims to have a near-identical API as SciPy and NumPy, which makes transforming a CPU implementation into a GPU implementation trivial.

Let's illustrate with the very common example of **matrix multiplication**. The applications of matrix multiplications are too numerous to list; it is used everywhere. Therefore, people have spent an enormous amount of effort over decades to make the multiplication of matrices as fast as possible.

For readers who need a refresher, the M-by-K matrix, A, can be multiplied by the K-by-N matrix, B, to produce the M-by-N matrix, C. The elements in C ($c_{i,j}$, where i is the row index and j is the column index) are computed in accordance with Equation:

$$c_{i,j} = \sum_{p}^{k} a_{i,p} b_{p,j}$$

Conceptually, each element of *C* is produced by multiplying corresponding elements in a row of *A* and a column of *B* and summing up the products; this is equivalent to a dot product between vectors. *Figure 8.1* works through this process for a small example matrix:

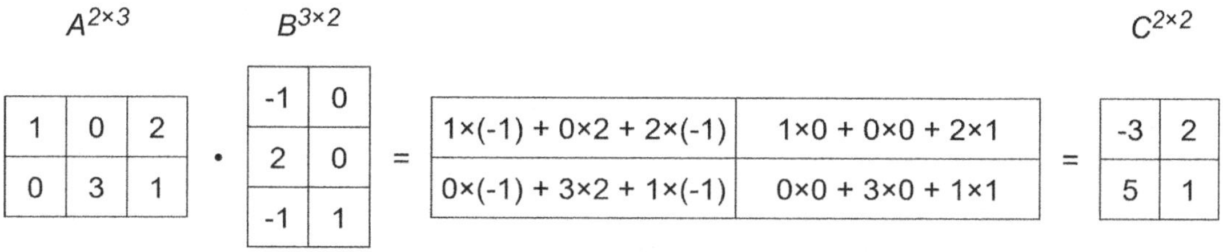

Figure 8.1 – Illustration of matrix multiplication

The time complexity of matrix multiplication is roughly *O(MKN)*, because computing each element in *C* requires *K* multiplications. If *N*=*M*=*K*, then the time complexity is cubic with respect to the matrix dimension, which means that as matrices grow, the computation time increases very fast. Matrices in real applications often contain thousands of elements, so it's very important that matrix multiplication is optimized.

Let's write a CUDA kernel for matrix multiplication with `numba.cuda`. For a full breakdown of how to write CUDA kernels, refer to *Chapter 3*. The following is a straightforward implementation:

```
@cuda.jit
def matmul(A: NDArray, B: NDArray, C: NDArray) -> None:
    j, i = cuda.grid(2)
    if i >= C.shape[0] or j >= C.shape[1]:
        return
    temp = float32(0.)
    for p in range(A.shape[1]):
        temp += A[i, p] * B[p, j]
    C[i, j] = temp
```

In this kernel, each thread in the grid is responsible for calculating one element of `C`. After checking whether the thread is in bounds, *Equation 1* is used to calculate $c_{i,j}$.

To use the kernel, random arrays, `A` and `B`, are created on the host and transferred to the device:

```
import numpy as np

M, N, K = 2000, 2000, 2000
```

```
A = cuda.to_device(np.random.rand(M, N).astype(np.float32))
B = cuda.to_device(np.random.rand(N, K).astype(np.float32))
```

An empty C array is allocated directly on the device:

```
C = cuda.device_array((M, K), dtype=np.float32)
```

Note

Note on float precision

By default, numpy and numba use double precision, so to use single precision, an explicit conversion is required.

Additionally, the block and grid dimensions must be defined. After some trial and error, timing the kernel with different launch configurations, a block size of (128, 4) was chosen. The grid dimensions are calculated accordingly:

```
block = (128, 4)
grid = (
    (K + block[0] - 1) // block[0],
    (M + block[1] - 1) // block[1],
)
```

Finally, the kernel can be executed as follows:

```
matmul[grid, block](A, B, C)
```

The calculation takes slightly less than 22 ms on an A100 GPU for 2,000 by 2,000 arrays. Without context, this looks good. However, let's now compare this to CuPy.

CuPy has its own array type, through which most of CuPy's functionality is exposed. One of the ways to create CuPy arrays from existing numba arrays is by using the cupy.asarray function:

```
import cupy as cp
A_cp = cp.asarray(A)
B_cp = cp.asarray(B)
```

The asarray function accepts many different types of objects and attempts to convert them to CuPy arrays. For example, it also accepts NumPy arrays; CuPy automatically handles the host-to-device data transfer. For Numba-CUDA arrays that already exist on the device, creating a CuPy array is a **zero-copy** operation; `A_cp` and `A` are different objects, but they point to the same buffer of memory containing the array data in the device's main memory.

Multiplying `A_cp` and `B_cp` is achieved using the following function:

```
C_cp = cp.matmul(A_cp, B_cp)
```

The resulting array is identical to the result of the custom kernel. However, CuPy performs the calculation in 1 ms, an improvement of more than 20 times!

CuPy achieves this impressive performance by wrapping the `cuBLAS` (and sometimes `cuTENSOR`) library written by NVIDIA, which contains highly optimized linear algebra routines that are precompiled. The `matmul` kernel could be improved a bit by using **shared memory**, since the same data is reused many times across multiple threads. However, the performance will never come close to `cupy.matmul`.

Now that the power of CuPy has been illustrated, let's learn how to use it.

How to use CuPy arrays

To explain every operation implemented in CuPy would require a separate book. This section is not a substitute for the official API documentation, which can be found here: `https://docs.cupy.dev/en/stable/reference/index.html`. The aim of this section is to provide a high-level overview of the most important features, illustrated with some simple examples, to serve as a starting point for further reading. Most of the content in this section will be very familiar to readers who have extensive NumPy experience.

Creating CuPy arrays

CuPy arrays are objects that point to array data in device **global memory**. Unlike Numba-CUDA arrays, where data creation on the host and host-to-device copies are separate steps, CuPy arrays filled with data can be created directly on the device in a single step:

```
my_1d_array = cp.array([1, 2, 3])
my_2d_array = cp.array([
    [1, 2, 3],
    [4, 5, 6],
])
```

CuPy also exposes a number of array creation routines with different initialization logic. The following are the most common:

- `cp.empty(shape)` creates an array with uninitialized elements. `shape` is a tuple of integers.
- `cp.zeros(shape)` creates an array with all elements initialized to `0`.
- `cp.full(shape, fill_value)` creates an array with all elements initialized to `fill_value`.
- `cp.arange(start, stop, step)` creates a 1D array with evenly spaced values bounded by `start` (inclusive) and `stop` (exclusive), spaced by `step`. For example, `cp.arange(1, 7, 2)` creates an array with the elements `1`, `3`, and `5`. By default, `start=0` and `step=1`, so the function follows the same conventions as Python's built-in `range` function.
- `cp.linspace(start, stop, num)` creates a 1D array with `num` evenly spaced values bounded by `start` (inclusive) and `stop` (inclusive). For example, `cp.linspace(1, 5, 3)` creates the same array as the one created with `arange`. `num` defaults to `50`.

Note

Array initialization

Under the hood, initializing an array with values is performed in two steps: memory allocation and writing data to this memory. Filling an array with values carries a small performance penalty. Therefore, if the initialized values are not needed, `cp.empty` is the preferred way to initialize an array.

All these array creation methods accept the optional `dtype` argument. It is recommended to always pass `np.float32`, `np.int32`, or `np.uint32`, since the default `dtype` is `np.float64`, which is suboptimal for performance on most GPU devices. For an overview of the available data types, please consult the official NumPy documentation here: `https://numpy.org/doc/stable/user/basics.types.html`.

Another very useful creation method is `cupy.meshgrid`. It is a convenient way to create arrays that represent coordinates in N dimensions. The arguments to `meshgrid` are 1D arrays containing the coordinates in each dimension. `numpy.meshgrid` was used in *Chapters 3* and *5* to create a coordinate grid for calculating the Julia set.

Let's illustrate the CuPy implementation with another example. The goal is to generate a 2D distance map, where each entry represents the distance to the origin. The easiest way to do this is to create a 2D grid of coordinates and compute the distance from all the coordinates to `(0, 0)`. A 2D coordinate grid from -10 to 10 on both axes, sampled with 100 by 100 points, is generated as follows:

```
resolution = 100
x, y = cp.meshgrid(
    cp.linspace(-10, 10, resolution),
    cp.linspace(-10, 10, resolution),
)
```

The (Euclidean) distance map to the origin is calculated as follows:

```
d = cp.sqrt(cp.square(x) + cp.square(y))
```

The `square` and `sqrt` functions are examples of **ufuncs**, or operations that are applied on an element-by-element basis. These will be discussed in more detail in the next section.

The distance array can be visualized by mapping each value to a color or grayscale and plotting it as an image. This can be done using, for example, Matplotlib's `imshow` method. The result is shown in *Figure 8.2*. Darker tones represent small distance values close to the origin (the center of the image); light tones represent greater distances:

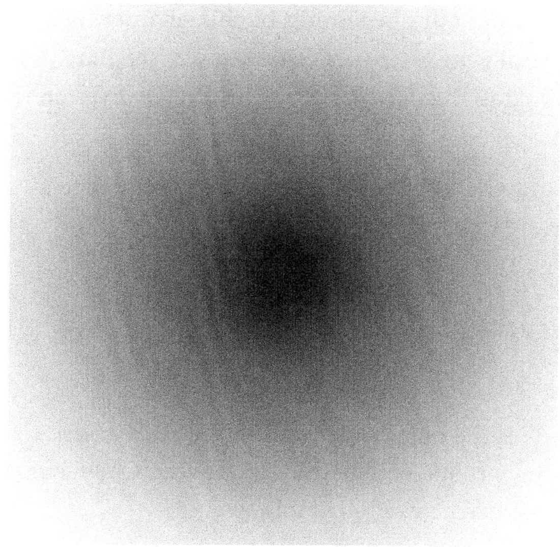

Figure 8.2 – Visualization of the distance array

Finally, CuPy also supports creating **random arrays**. Many different sampling distributions are supported, but the most common are uniform sampling with `cupy.random.rand`, integer range sampling with `cupy.random.randint`, choice sampling with `cupy.random.choice`, and normal distribution sampling with `cupy.random.randn`. Most of these functions accept a `size` argument, which is equivalent to shape in other functions. For a full breakdown of the available sampling functions, consult the official documentation: `https://docs.cupy.dev/en/stable/reference/random.html`.

> Note
>
> **Reproducibility of randomness**
>
> Even when working with random numbers, it is desirable to be able to reproduce calculations that use those random numbers. One way to make random number generation deterministic is to set the random seed to a chosen integer with `cupy.seed(integer)` before generating any random numbers.

Data transfers and converting other objects to CuPy arrays

Not all data can materialize directly on the device; some of it originates from the host as data from files or external services.

`cupy.asarray` was discussed at the beginning of this chapter, and in most cases, this is the preferred way to create a CuPy array from another array. If the data lives on the host, a copy will automatically be transferred to the device. If the data already lives on the device, a CuPy array is created without copying.

It is very important to know when data is copied versus referenced, especially when mutating data. Consider the following example:

```
host_array = np.array([1, 2, 3])
cupy_array = cp.asarray(host_array)
cupy_array += 1
```

A NumPy array is created on the host, and a copy of the data is sent to the device. When all the elements in the CuPy array are incremented by 1, only the CuPy array is modified; the NumPy array is left unchanged. This can be verified as follows:

```
assert (host_array == np.array([1, 2, 3])).all() # True
assert (cupy_array == cp.array([2, 3, 4])).all() # True
```

To assert whether two arrays are the same, each corresponding element needs to be compared for equality. This is done using the == operator, which calls the `cupy.equal` ufunc under the hood. The output is an array of Booleans. The `all` method is a **reduction** operation, which checks whether all elements in the array are `True` and returns a single `True` or `False` value.

The example is modified to first transfer the data to the device with Numba-CUDA. The CuPy array is then created from the Numba-CUDA array:

```
device_array = cuda.to_device(host_array)
cupy_array = cp.asarray(device_array)
cupy_array += 1
```

In this case, the data in the original Numba-CUDA array is changed:

```
assert (device_array.copy_to_host() == np.array([2, 3, 4])).all()
```

By only copying data when it is strictly necessary, CuPy can efficiently use the limited resource of the device's global memory. However, be mindful of when data is copied versus referenced, as this can lead to all kinds of unexpected bugs. To force CuPy to make a copy, use the `cupy.array` function instead. By using `cupy.array` in the previous example, the data in `device_array` is not modified:

```
device_array = cuda.to_device(host_array)
cupy_array = cp.array(device_array)
cupy_array += 1
assert (device_array.copy_to_host() == np.array([1, 2, 3])).all()
```

To transfer CuPy arrays back to the host and convert them to NumPy arrays, use this:

```
cp.asnumpy(cupy_array)
```

Alternatively, use the `get` method on the array:

```
cupy_array.get()
```

Elementwise operations (ufuncs)

The most common type of operation performed on arrays is **ufuncs**: an operation applied on an element-by-element basis. The function accepts one or multiple arrays of the same shape and returns an array of the same shape. The most common types of ufuncs are as follows:

- **Arithmetic operations**: These include addition, subtraction, multiplication, division, remainder, raising to a power, taking roots, and a few more obscure ones. These are available through functions such as cupy.add, cupy.subtract, and so on, but also more simply through the usual Python operators, +, -, *, /, %, and **. When two equally sized CuPy arrays are added together, this corresponds to adding them elementwise.
- **Mathematical functions**: These include most mathematical functions that can be found on a calculator, including trigonometric functions such as sine (cupy.sin), cosine (cupy.cos), tangent (cupy.tan), and their inverses (cupy.arcsin, cupy.arccos, and cupy.arctan), hyperbolic functions such as cupy.sinh, cupy.cosh, and cupy.tanh, logarithmic functions (cupy.log, cupy.log2, and cupy.log10), and exponential functions (cupy.exp, cupy.exp2).
- **Comparison operations**: These include cupy.greater or the > operator, cupy.less or the < operator, and cupy.equal or the == operator. These return arrays of bool, where each element represents whether the condition was True or False for each element.
- **Miscellaneous functions**: These include various ways of rounding, such as cupy.floor, cupy.ceil, cupy.round, and cupy.rint.
- **Bit manipulation functions**: More niche, but these can be convenient in some cases. Included are cupy.left_shift or the << operator, cupy.right_shift or the >> operator, cupy.bitwise_xor, cupy.bitwise_and and cupy.bitwise_or. Most of these only work on arrays of integers or Booleans.

A full overview of available ufuncs can be found in the official documentation at https://docs.cupy.dev/en/stable/reference/ufunc.html.

Note that for some operations, there exist specialized functions with improved performance. For example, square (cupy.square), square root (cupy.sqrt), and cube root (cupy.cbrt) are roughly 50% faster than using the ** operator with the exponents 2, 1/2, and 1/3, respectively.

By default, ufuncs allocate new arrays for the output and return them. When multiple ufuncs are chained, this can have a negative impact on performance. Most ufuncs accept an optional out parameter, in which a pre-allocated array can be passed to which the output is written. This avoids repeated and unnecessary memory allocations.

There are also implementations of many more obscure mathematical functions, such as Bessel functions, spherical harmonics, functions for statistics and probability, and more. A full overview can be found at `https://docs.cupy.dev/en/stable/reference/scipy_special.html`. These are not accessible directly from the `cupy` namespace, but instead from `cupyx.scipy.special`.

To create custom ufuncs, the most accessible method is to use the `cupy.vectorize` decorator. Let's illustrate by revisiting the Julia set example from *Chapters 3* and *5*. The details and mathematics behind the kernel have been thoroughly explained in those chapters; refer back if interested. In this instance, it serves as an example of a complicated function that needs to be applied to all elements of an array.

The following is an implementation of the Julia set kernel with `cupy.vectorize`:

```
@cp.vectorize
def julia_set_vectorize(
    z: complex,
    max_iter: int,
    R: float,
    c: complex,
) -> int:
    for iteration in range(1, max_iter + 1):
        if cp.abs(z) > R:
            return iteration
        z = cp.square(z) + c
    return 0
```

Note the similarity to the kernel created in *Chapter 3* using `numba.cuda.vectorize`. The main difference is that operations such as `abs` and `** 2` were replaced with `cp.abs` and `cp.square`, respectively. Arbitrary functions cannot be used in functions decorated with `cp.vectorize`; only functions with CuPy ufunc equivalents are accepted.

Before calling the ufunc, the `z` input array is created using `cupy.linspace` and `cupy.meshgrid` as follows:

```
a = cp.linspace(-1.7, 1.7, 1024, dtype=np.float32)
b = cp.linspace(-1.7, 1.7, 1024, dtype=np.float32)
A, B = cp.meshgrid(a, b)
z = A + 1j * B
```

The ufunc is called like a normal function:

```
c = -0.8+0.156j
R = 0.5 + 0.5 * np.sqrt(1 + 4 * abs(c))
result = julia_set_vectorize(z, 3000, R, c)
```

Recall that c is just a parameter that determines the shape of the fractal, and R is a parameter that depends on c.

The first time this function is called, it is slow. This is because underneath the hood, the function is **JIT compiled** to a CUDA kernel. This is the reason there are limitations on the functions that can be used in a function decorated with `cupy.vectorize`. Calling the ufunc a second time is fast.

As expected, the result is the familiar Julia set image shown in *Figure 8.3*:

Figure 8.3 – Julia set calculated with cupy.vectorize

Ufuncs must be compiled to a CUDA kernel to achieve acceptable performance. Looping over the elements using the Python interpreter and processing the data with arbitrary functions results in terrible performance; individual elements are fetched from the device, and all computation happens on the host without any acceleration. The use case for CuPy is accelerating data processing with CUDA kernels under the hood.

Reduction operations

Reduction operations have been mentioned multiple times throughout this book. Reductions combine elements in one array and collapse them to a single value. Examples include calculating a sum, maximum, minimum, and so on.

Writing performant reduction kernels with Numba-CUDA is not straightforward. CuPy makes reduction operations easy and intuitive. Moreover, CuPy reductions are flexible and can be applied over a subset of the axes.

The set of built-in reduction operations is limited. The most important ones are as follows:

- **Sum and product**: `cp.sum` and `cupy.prod`.
- **Minimum and maximum**: `cupy.min` and `cupy.max`. Also, `cupy.argmin` and `cupy.argmax` exist, which return the index of the minimum and maximum instead. If `axis` is not specified, the index will be the index in the flattened array; otherwise, it is the index of the minimum/maximum along that axis.
- **Logical reductions**: `cupy.all` and `cupy.any` return whether all or any element is `True`, respectively.
- **Statistical reductions**: `cupy.mean`, `cupy.std`, `cupy.median`, `cupy.var`, and `cupy.percentile` serve to calculate summary statistics along specific axes.

Many of these reductions are also available as methods directly on the CuPy array objects.

Scan operations

Scan or accumulate operations perform an associative operation in a cumulative fashion over the elements in an array. The most used scan operation is the **cumulative sum**. The cumulative sum of an array `[a_0, a_1, a_2, ..., a_n]` is `[a_0, a_0 + a_1, a_0 + a_1 + a_2, ..., a_0 + a_1 + ... + a_n]`.

In CuPy, the cumulative sum is available through `cupy.cumsum`. Also, `cupy.cumprod` is available for the cumulative product.

Ufuncs (also called **map** operations), reductions, and scans are three essential building blocks to build other parallel algorithms like filtering and sorting.

Broadcasting

Ufuncs apply an operation element by element. Some ufuncs, such as the basic arithmetic operations, accept multiple inputs. Normally, these inputs have to be of the same shape.

However, input arrays can be of different shapes while remaining compatible under the **broadcasting** rules. This is very convenient when values must be reused across multiple axes without duplicating data.

Earlier in this chapter, a form of broadcasting was already used by combining an array and a constant. Multiplying an array by a constant, which could be considered a zero-dimensional array, broadcasts the constant over all elements in the array.

However, broadcasting is much more powerful and flexible. The general rules are as follows:

- For arrays with the same number of dimensions, all axes with a length of `1` are broadcast. For example, an array of the `(1, 2)` shape can be multiplied with an array of the `(3, 1)` shape; it will produce an array of the `(3, 2)` shape:

```
a = cp.array([[2, 3]])               # shape (1, 2)
b = cp.array([[5], [7], [11]])  # shape (3, 1)
expected = cp.array([
    [10, 15],
    [14, 21],
    [22, 33],
])
assert (a * b == expected).all()  # True
```

- Arrays without the same number of dimensions will be padded with dimensions of length of `1` from right to left until it has an equal number of dimensions as the array with the most dimensions. In the previous example, an array of the `(2,)` shape can be multiplied with an array of the `(3, 1)` shape: the `(2,)` array will automatically be padded to the `(1, 2)` shape during the multiplication:

```
a_2 = cp.array([2, 3]) # shape (2,) -> padded to (1, 2)
assert (a_2 * b == expected).all()
```

- Corresponding axes (after a potential dimension padding) must either have equal length or a length of 1. Any other scenario results in an invalid operation. There is no way to multiply a `(3, 1)` array with a `(2, 2)` array, for example, since the outer dimension is a size of 3 for the first array and 2 for the second array:

```
a_3 = cp.array([[2, 3], [2, 3]])
a_3 * b  # throws ValueError
```

Using broadcasting creatively can save a lot of GPU memory and unnecessary operations.

Array indexing and slicing

Array slicing and indexing are operations to select a subset of arrays. There are many different ways to slice and index, and the behavior can be non-intuitive in some situations.

Throughout this book, indexing has been used extensively to access single elements of arrays in CUDA kernels. CuPy arrays behave the same way. In an n-dimensional array, each element can be accessed through its coordinate, which is an n-tuple. Indices start at `0`. Coordinates are ordered from the outer dimension to the inner dimension.

Consider the following simple 2D example:

```
A = cp.array([
    [1, 2, 3, 4],
    [5, 6, 7, 8],
    [9, 10, 11, 12],
])
assert A[0, 0] == 1
assert A[1, 2] == 7
```

To select multiple connected elements in an array (i.e., create a **slice**), use **range indices**. Similar to Python's built-in `range` function, the range index follows the syntax `(start):(end)(:step)`. In contrast to Python's `range` function, `start`, `stop`, and `:step` are all optional; if not provided `start=0`, `end` is the length of the axis, and `step=1`. Range indices in some dimensions can be combined with single-value indices in other dimensions. The following examples illustrate slicing a CuPy array with ranges and single-value indices:

```
assert (A[:2, 2:] == cp.array([
    [3, 4],
    [7, 8],
])).all()
assert (A[:, 1] == cp.array([2, 6, 10])).all()
assert (A[1, 1:3] == cp.array([6, 7])).all()
assert (A[2, :3:2] == cp.array([9, 11])).all()
assert (A[2, ::-1] == cp.array([12, 11, 10, 9])).all()
```

Multiple non-connected elements can be selected using arrays or lists of coordinates:

```
assert (A[[0, 2, 1], [2, 0, 3]] == cp.array([3, 9, 8])).all()
```

Whereas slicing with the range syntax retains dimensions, using lists of coordinates always returns a 1D array.

Finally, elements can be selected based on a Boolean mask array, which must be broadcast-compatible (see the previous section on broadcasting). In the simplest case, the mask is the same size as the original array:

```
is_div_by_5_mask = (A % 5 == 0)
assert (A[is_div_by_5_mask] == cp.array([5, 10])).all()
```

However, this is also valid:

```
assert (A[cp.array([False, True, False]), 1::2]
        == cp.array([6, 8])
       ).all()
```

With regards to data copying, there is a big difference between range indices on the one hand, and a list of coordinate indices and Boolean masks on the other hand. When using range indices, a **view** of the data is returned, not a copy. When elements in the view are mutated, the original data is also mutated, since the view points to the same data as the original object. This is demonstrated by the following example:

```
a = cp.ones(5)
b = a[::2]
b[:] = 2
assert (a == cp.array([2, 1, 2, 1, 2])).all()
```

When selecting data with coordinate indices or Boolean masks, a copy of the data is returned. Mutating the output does not change the original data. Here is an example:

```
a = cp.ones(5)
b = a[[0, 2, 4]]
b[:] = 2
assert (a == cp.ones(5)).all()
```

All types of indexing can be used for assignment. For example, here, we are using a list of indices:

```
a = cp.ones(5)
a[[0, 2, 4]] = 2
assert (a == cp.array([2, 1, 2, 1, 2])).all()
```

Always be aware of these subtle differences in implicit data sharing versus data copying.

Why does range indexing produce views? The data for a CuPy array of any dimension is stored in a 1D contiguous block of GPU memory (a buffer). The *illusion* of n-dimensionality is created using a list of **stride** values, which is stored as part of the object. Stride information enables CuPy to quickly calculate memory addresses of data in the buffer from n-dimensional coordinates. The reason range indices don't have to copy data is that a view is a CuPy array pointing to the same buffer but with updated strides.

With an arbitrary list of coordinates, elements are no longer regularly spaced, and the stride concept breaks down. Therefore, data needs to be copied to a new buffer.

Whether an array is a view can be verified using the `base` property. If it is `None`, it is not a view; if it is a view, it returns the original array on which the view is based.

Indexing into non-existing dimensions is also possible, using the `None` index. This will create the non-existing dimension. Consider the following example:

```
a = cp.array([1, 2, 3])
assert a[:, None].shape == (3, 1)
assert a[None, :, None].shape == (1, 3, 1)
assert a[None, :, None, None].shape == (1, 3, 1, 1)
```

Dimensions can also be inserted between existing dimensions:

```
assert A[:, None, :, None].shape == (3, 1, 4, 1)
```

This can be very helpful for arrays of incompatible shapes or misaligned dimensions that need to be broadcast together.

> **Tip**
>
> The `start:stop:step` notation for slices is a convenient short-hand syntax for a `slice` object, a Python built-in. A `slice` object can be created with `slice(start, stop, step)` and it can be used for indexing into arrays. The advantage is that `slice` objects can be passed around like any other object, which offers more flexibility.

Reshaping, combining, and reordering arrays

Underneath the hood, CuPy arrays are just a contiguous block of data in GPU memory with some metadata that resides on the host, such as the strides and the data type. This means that reshaping an array is a very inexpensive operation, since it only modifies the strides. The most common reshaping methods are `cupy.ravel` and `cupy.reshape`.

With `cupy.ravel`, a 1D view of the array is returned. This is a flattened view into the contiguous block of data. In C-ordered arrays, the data is contiguous with the last (innermost) axis varying fastest, and the first (outermost) axis varying slowest. Consider the following 3D array:

```
A = cp.array([
    [
        [1, 2],
        [3, 4],
    ],
    [
        [5, 6],
        [7, 8],
    ],
])
```

The numbers in the elements correspond to their relative position in memory:

```
assert (A.ravel() == cp.array([1, 2, 3, 4, 5, 6, 7, 8])).all()
```

The opposite is true when the array is F-ordered: the first (outermost) axis varies fastest, and the last (innermost) axis varies slowest:

```
A_f = cp.asfortranarray(A)
assert (A_f.ravel(order="F")
        == cp.array([1, 5, 3, 7, 2, 6, 4, 8])
       ).all()
```

Note

Ravel

`cupy.ravel` does not give a direct 1D view into the buffer of data; `ravel` can unroll a C-ordered array into F-ordering, and vice versa.

The `cupy.reshape` operation takes as arguments an array and a new shape, and rolls up the array elements according to the new shape. Of course, the new shape needs to be compatible with the total number of array elements. Reshaping can be tricky to think about when attempting to transform one shape into another; it can help to think about a flattened array as an intermediate step and how the data elements will roll up into the new shape. Like `ravel`, C or F ordering can be chosen in `reshape`.

Let's illustrate the utility of `reshape` with a **binning** example. The goal is to downsample a 2D image by averaging x-by-x tiles of neighboring pixels. This produces an image that is x times smaller than the original. It can be assumed that both dimensions of the image are divisible by x.

The approach is to reshape the original array of the `(w, h)` shape to a 4D array with a shape of `(w // x, x, h // x, x)`. Each image dimension is broken into two dimensions: an axis to retain and an axis to reduce. Because of the way the data is laid out, taking the mean over axes 1 and 3 produces the desired result.

> **Tip**
>
> If it is difficult to visualize how this works with a 2D array that is turned into a 4D array, try visualizing it with a 1D array that turns into a 2D array.

To demonstrate, consider the following 4-by-6 array, which represents an image:

```
A = cp.array([
    [0, 0, 0, 0, 0, 0],
    [0, 1, 2, 2, 1, 0],
    [0, 1, 2, 2, 1, 0],
    [0, 0, 0, 0, 0, 0],
])
```

To downsample the array by a factor of 2, the array is reshaped and averaged over two axes as follows:

```
x = 2
downsampled = A.reshape(
    A.shape[0] // x, x, A.shape[1] // x, x
).mean(axis=(1, 3))
```

On this small array, the result can be verified manually:

```
expected = cp.array([
    [0.25, 1, 0.25],
    [0.25, 1, 0.25],
])
assert (expected == downsampled).all()
```

Arrays can be combined with `cupy.stack` and `cupy.concatenate`. Both these functions take a list of CuPy arrays. `stack` adds a new dimension and combines arrays along a specified dimension (by default, the new outer dimension). `concatenate` glues arrays together along an existing dimension. In both cases, a new array with copied data is created.

Finally, there are operations to rearrange the order of axes:

- `cp.moveaxis` moves one or multiple axes to other positions, leaving other axes in the same order
- `cp.swapaxes` swaps two axes
- `cp.transpose` reverses the order of axes

There is also `cp.rollaxis`, but it is older, and `cp.moveaxis` is generally preferred. None of these operations copies or changes the underlying data buffer; they only modify the strides (i.e., the view on the buffer), so they are very fast and inexpensive.

Other operations

This includes all array operations that can't be classified as any of the previous types of operations. Technically, this is the largest class of operations, as it includes most SciPy routines. The following is a rough classification:

- **Linear algebra**: This includes operations for multiplying matrices and vectors (`cupy.matmul` and `cupy.dot`), decomposing matrices (`cupy.linalg.qr` for QR decomposition, `cupy.linalg.svd` for singular value decomposition, and `cupyx.scipy.linalg.lu` for LU decomposition), calculating eigenvalues and eigenvectors (`cupy.linalg.eigh`), calculating the determinant (`cupy.linalg.det`), and operations for solving linear systems (`cupy.linalg.solve` for an exact solution and `cupy.linalg.lstsq` for a least-squares solution). For more information, consult the official documentation here: `https://docs.cupy.dev/en/stable/reference/linalg.html` and `https://docs.cupy.dev/en/stable/reference/scipy_linalg.html`.
- **Sparse linear algebra**: Sparse matrices are matrices that are too large to fully represent in memory but contain relatively few non-zero elements. There are efficient ways to represent, store, and work with these types of matrices. Functionality for creating and performing basic operations on sparse matrices can be found in the `cupyx.linalg.sparse` namespace. Linear algebra routines (matrix multiplication, solving linear systems, and matrix decomposition) for sparse matrices can be found under the `cupyx.linalg.sparse.linalg` namespace. Consult the documentation here:

`https://docs.cupy.dev/en/stable/reference/scipy_sparse.html` and `https://docs.cupy.dev/en/stable/reference/scipy_sparse_linalg.html`.

- **Discrete Fourier transforms**: The Fourier transformation converts data into its frequency components, which is a very useful concept in image processing and multi-dimensional signal processing. The basic methods for transforming an array to the frequency domain are `cupy.fft` (when the transform needs to be computed along a single axis), `cupy.fft2` (when the transform needs to be computed along two axes, which is relevant for images) and `cupy.fftn` (when the transform needs to be computed along `n` axes). These all have a corresponding inverse transform function: `cupy.ifft`, `cupy.ifft2`, and `cupy.ifftn`. There are more specialized and optimized functions for specific input types, for example, when it is known that all elements in the input array are real numbers or when the input array is Hermitian. Consult the documentation here: `https://docs.cupy.dev/en/stable/reference/fft.html`.
- **Sorting**: Arrays can be sorted along an axis with `cupy.sort`. Alternatively, `cupy.argsort` produces indices in the order that would sort the array.
- **Interpolation and resampling**: If an array represents values sampled from a continuous function, a common problem is to estimate the value of the function between the samples. This problem is called interpolation, and there are many different approaches. To perform interpolation on CuPy arrays, have a look at the `cupyx.scipy.interpolate` namespace and at the SciPy documentation here: `https://docs.cupy.dev/en/stable/reference/scipy_interpolate.html`.
- **Convolutions and signal processing**: The convolution is a very important operation whereby two functions are "folded" together. Applied to arrays of which the values represent regularly spaced samples of a function, this can be thought of as one array sliding across the other. At each position, corresponding elements are multiplied, and the result is summed. An illustration is shown in *Figure 8.4* for the convolution of `[1, 0, 2, 2, 1]` and `[1, 0, 1]` arrays, as implemented in `cupy.convolve`. At the edges, the arrays are padded with zeros. Convolutions are intricately linked to Fourier transforms, since convolving two functions is equivalent to multiplying them in Fourier space. Almost everything in signal processing builds on convolutions and Fourier transforms. Signal processing is a field of its own, and discussing all the types of operations is outside the scope of this chapter. Signal processing functionality is available under the `cupyx.scipy.signal` namespace; the documentation can be consulted here: `https://docs.cupy.dev/en/stable/reference/scipy_signal.html`.

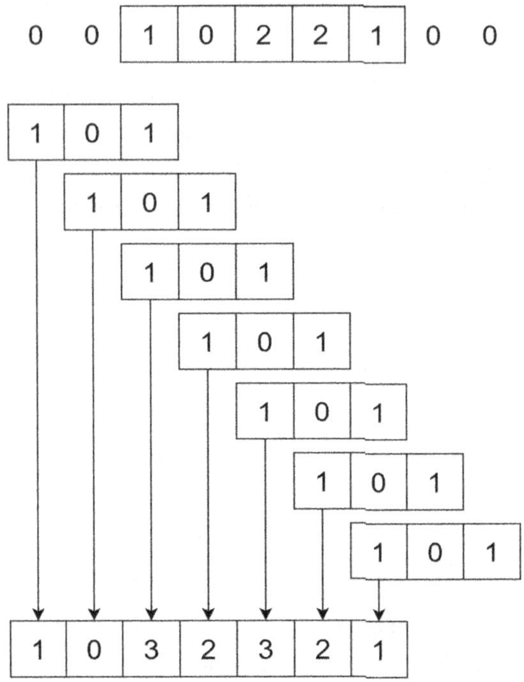

Figure 8.4 – Illustration of the convolution of arrays [1, 0, 2, 2, 1] and [1, 0, 1]. The second array is slid across the first, element by element. Corresponding elements are multiplied, and the products are added to produce the output array element. The output array has an element for each position of the sliding array.

- **Image processing**: images can be represented by n-dimensional arrays, with elements representing pixel values. A grayscale image can be represented with a 2D array, while an RGB image can be represented with a 3D array with two spatial dimensions and one channel dimension, with a size of 3, representing the different colors. In the most general case, images can have any number of spatial dimensions and have a channel dimension; think of satellite imagery or 3D medical images. The goal of image processing is to extract, label, and measure features of interest. To do so, filters (convolutions) can be applied to images to bring out parts of the signal or reduce noise. Rotating, cropping, distorting, shifting, or zooming are also common operations. There are also algorithms for grouping and labeling different pixels based on some criteria. All this type of functionality can be found under the `cupyx.scipy.ndimage` namespace, for which the documentation can be found here: `https://docs.cupy.dev/en/stable/reference/scipy_ndimage.html`. *Chapter 12* presents a case study of image processing on the GPU.

Saving and loading data

To store an array on disk for later processing, there exists the `cupy.save` method, which saves the array to a binary `.npy` file. This is the file format NumPy also uses. Here is an example:

```
cp.save("my_array.npy", cp.array([1, 2, 3, 4, 5]))
```

The data can be loaded again as follows:

```
cp.load("my_array.npy")
```

Since the file format is identical, the same file can be loaded as a NumPy array:

```
assert isinstance(np.load("my_array.npy"), np.ndarray)
```

CuPy supports alternative storage formats such as text, but performance for reading and writing is worse. As of the time of writing, there is no dominant standard in file formats for multidimensional arrays, though some scientific disciplines have standardized on HDF5 or the newer ZARR format.

This section provided a condensed overview of CuPy's core functionality. However, knowing the available operations is only half the challenge. The other half lies in decomposing problems into smaller steps, each solvable with a CuPy function. This requires thinking in terms of vectorized operations. While most problems can be solved in multiple ways, using different chains of operations, not all approaches yield equal performance. Choosing the right sequence of operations is key to efficiency.

How to use CuPy with other libraries

CuPy seamlessly interoperates with most libraries in the numerical Python ecosystem. This flexibility means that tools can be combined based on specific requirements.

Using CuPy with NumPy

CuPy aims to mimic the entire API of NumPy. That means that, in an ideal world, a CuPy array should behave in exactly the same way as a NumPy array, except the former lives in GPU memory and is processed through wrapped CUDA kernels. If a CuPy array behaves identically to a NumPy array, then converting NumPy code to run on the GPU should be as simple as changing NumPy's `import` statement to the following:

```
import cupy as np
```

While this works surprisingly often, it can result in unexpected problems. As of writing, not all of NumPy's functionality has been implemented in CuPy; the following GitHub issue tracks which NumPy functions still need a CuPy equivalent: `https://github.com/cupy/cupy/issues/6078`.

In addition, some code may need to use both `numpy` and `cupy` to perform some operations on the host and some on the device.

In most scenarios, NumPy functions can be passed CuPy arrays. When this happens, NumPy automatically delegates the operation to CuPy, and the output is a CuPy array. Here is an example:

```
a_np = np.ones((3, 3))
a_cp = cp.ones((3, 3))
assert isinstance(np.matmul(a_cp, a_cp), cp.ndarray)
```

The opposite, passing a NumPy array to a CuPy function, sometimes works but often fails. Here is an example:

```
cp.matmul(a_np, a_np)  # raises TypeError
```

Combining NumPy and CuPy arrays in a single operation does not work, since it would entail either copying the NumPy array to the device or copying the CuPy array back to the host. In general, CuPy tries to block operations that entail implicit data transfers. For example, CuPy arrays cannot be plotted with Matplotlib; they must first be transferred to the host.

Using CuPy with Numba

CuPy arrays can be used directly as inputs to Numba-CUDA kernels due to their implementation of `__cuda_array_interface__`. This compatibility enables a hybrid approach: optimized standard operations via CuPy and custom kernels via Numba-CUDA. As demonstrated earlier, CuPy arrays can also be created directly from Numba device arrays without copying underlying data.

However, CuPy functions cannot be called within Numba-CUDA kernels. CuPy functions are not purely CUDA kernels; some high-level logic remains in Python, which Numba cannot compile.

Using CuPy with SciPy

CuPy arrays are incompatible with SciPy routines. Instead, GPU-equivalent routines under the `cupyx.scipy` namespace must be used. However, as of the time of writing, many SciPy routines lack equivalents in `cupyx`, particularly for calculus and analysis tasks such as root finding, optimization, integration, and **ordinary differential equation** (**ODE**) solving.

When to use CuPy

As demonstrated earlier in this chapter, CuPy delivers outstanding performance for highly optimized elementary routines, such as matrix multiplication. Compared to manually written kernels, CuPy achieved an order of magnitude better performance with minimal effort. However, CuPy is not a universal solution. Numba, Numba-CUDA, NumPy, and SciPy each have their own strengths and use cases. This section explores when to choose CuPy over these alternatives.

CuPy versus NumPy

Earlier in this chapter, the performance of `cupy.matmul` was compared to a naive CUDA kernel implemented with Numba-CUDA. However, this comparison was not entirely balanced.

A more meaningful benchmark is against `numpy.matmul`, which leverages highly optimized CPU-based routines available in libraries such as **BLAS** for matrix multiplication. *Figure 8.5* presents a log-log plot comparing the performance of `cupy.matmul` and `numpy.matmul`. The time required to multiply two $N \times N$ square matrices was measured. The x axis represents the matrix dimension, N, while the y axis shows the execution time in milliseconds:

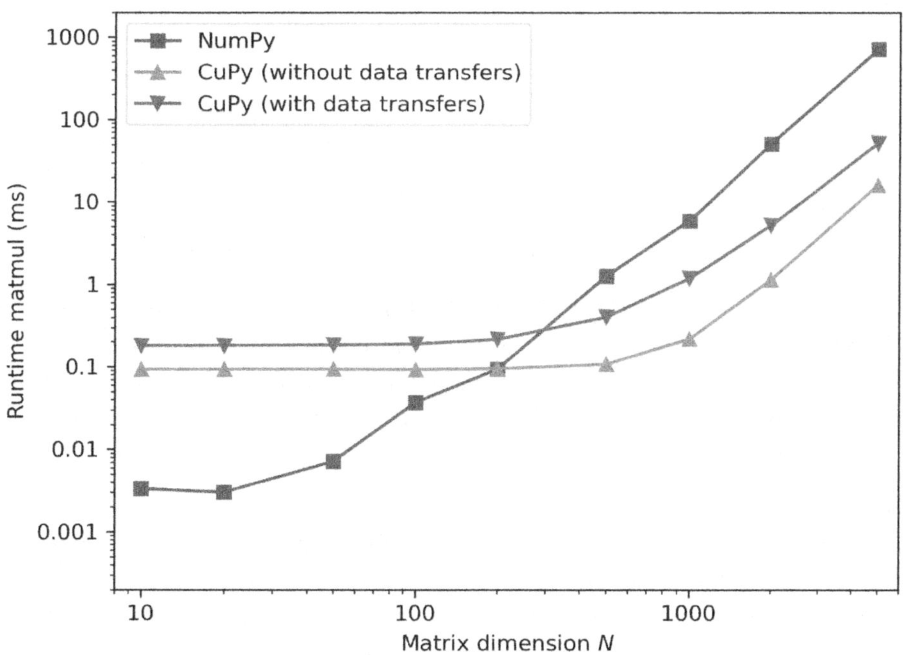

Figure 8.5 – Timing results for matrix multiplication using NumPy and CuPy

NumPy's performance is more than 20 times better than CuPy for small matrices. Only when N is larger than 200 does CuPy surpass the performance of NumPy.

An important consideration when doing work on the GPU is the time for data transfers between the host and the device. When data transfers are included in the timing, the benefit of CuPy over NumPy is further reduced. This can be seen more clearly in *Figure 8.6*, which shows the speedup of CuPy versus NumPy for `matmul`, including and excluding data transfers:

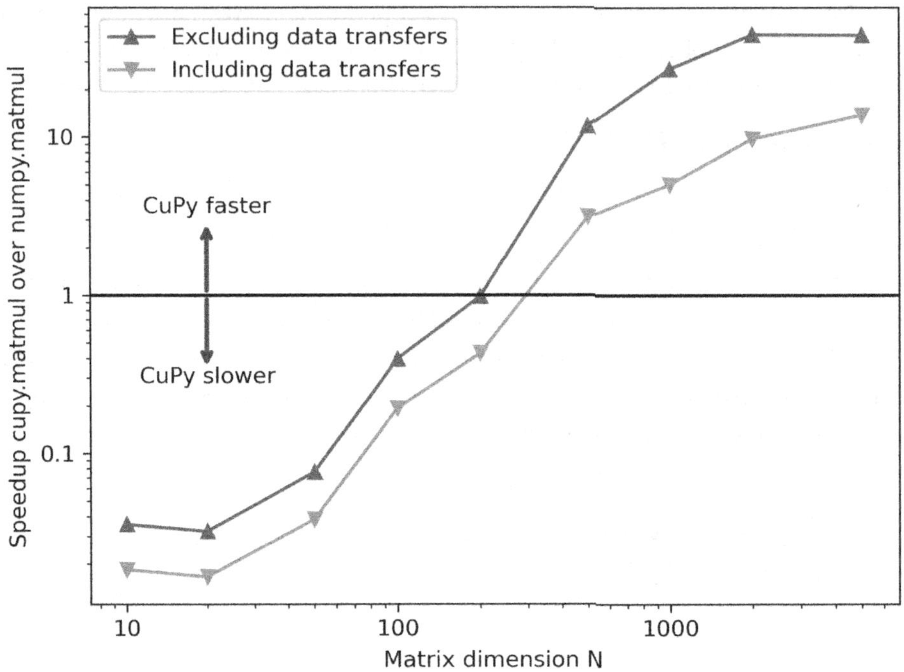

Figure 8.6 – Speedup of CuPy's matmul over NumPy's matmul

When data transfers are excluded from the timing, `cupy.matmul` is up to 40 times faster for large matrices. Including data transfers, CuPy is only slightly more than 10 times faster. This again highlights the importance of minimizing device and host data transfers, which can sometimes be difficult to track when using high-level libraries. Doing more work on data residing in GPU memory amortizes these transfer costs.

In summary, operations on small matrices generally execute faster on the host, and transferring such workloads to the GPU can even result in significant performance degradation. The size threshold at which GPUs outperform CPUs varies by operation; this analysis focused solely on `matmul`, but other operations behave differently. While a rough guideline suggests GPUs become competitive for arrays with 10^5–10^6 elements, the only reliable method to assess GPU benefits for a specific problem is through direct performance measurement.

CuPy versus Numba-CUDA

Once there is a case for running a workload on the GPU, the choice between CuPy, Numba-CUDA, or a hybrid approach remains. CuPy excels in highly optimized elementary routines such as matrix multiplication, often outperforming custom implementations by an order of magnitude. However, for non-standard workloads, it is not always clear whether performance will benefit more from chaining optimized operations or writing custom kernels. Even with `cupy.vectorize`, custom ufuncs can deliver surprisingly good performance.

Numba-CUDA may still be preferred over CuPy in specific cases:

- **Flexibility and simplicity**: While CuPy's API is streamlined, some problems resist vectorized solutions. Loops and explicit indexing can be easier to reason about for certain tasks.
- **Minimizing intermediate allocations**: CuPy operations that do not create views often generate temporary copies. For example, elementwise addition of 10 arrays creates 8 intermediate arrays before producing the final result. A custom Numba kernel can fuse operations without intermediate allocations.
- **Custom logic and output shapes**: When an operation cannot be expressed as a ufunc or in a vectorized manner, a custom Numba kernel is often the best solution. For instance, computing histograms along a specific axis in an *n*-dimensional array is unsupported in CuPy, difficult to vectorize, and not a ufunc.

Consider the Julia set example, previously treated as a ufunc that maps a grid of complex values, z, to an integer array. Strictly speaking, constructing the grid of z is unnecessary; instead, two coordinates defining a bounding box on the complex plane can be provided. Each thread calculates its corresponding z value based on its index and the bounding box. The following Numba-CUDA kernel demonstrates this approach:

```
@cuda.jit
def generating_julia(
    bbox: tuple[complex, complex],
    max_iter: int,
    R: float,
    c: complex,
    out: NDArray,
):
    j, i = cuda.grid(2)
    w, h = cuda.gridsize(2)

    x0 = bbox[0].real
```

```
    y0 = bbox[0].imag
    x1 = bbox[1].real
    y1 = bbox[1].imag

    real = (x1 - x0) * j / w + x0
    imag = (y1 - y0) * i / h + y0
    z = real + 1j * imag

    for iteration in range(1, max_iter + 1):
        if abs(z) > R:
            out[i, j] = iteration
            return
        z = z * z + c
    out[i, j] = 0
```

This refactoring transforms the Julia set example from a ufunc into an array-generating kernel, achieving significantly higher efficiency. For a 1,024×1,024 fractal image, the `cupy.vectorize` implementation required approximately 7 ms on an A100, excluding the time to construct the input z array. The Numba-CUDA kernel completed in just 1 ms.

Further optimization, such as explicitly expanding complex number operations, can push performance even further. The authors reduced execution time to 380 µs, nearly 20 times faster than `cupy.vectorize`. This solution is available in the book's GitHub repository.

CuPy lacks this level of flexibility, as it requires preconstructing the input z array and applying a ufunc. For custom, performance-critical algorithms, a Numba-CUDA kernel often remains the optimal solution.

How to write GPU-agnostic code

Given CuPy's API similarity to NumPy, it's natural to consider writing hardware-agnostic code: code that runs on the GPU (using CuPy) when available, and otherwise falls back to the CPU (using NumPy).

To achieve this, CuPy should be treated as an **optional dependency**, ensuring users without a GPU are not forced to install it.

The following code snippet can be used to import CuPy when available, or else fall back to NumPy:

```
import numpy as np
try:
```

```
    import cupy as xp
    CUPY_IS_INSTALLED = True
except ImportError:
    xp = np
    CUPY_IS_INSTALLED = False
```

Based on the value of `CUPY_IS_INSTALLED`, different code paths can be followed. Additionally, `xp` can be used as the hardware-agnostic **dispatcher** that points to `cupy` when it is available and to `numpy` when it is not. `xp` should be used instead of `cp` throughout the code.

The dispatcher can be inferred at runtime from the array type by checking whether it is of the `numpy.ndarray` type, and otherwise assuming it's a `cupy.ndarray` type. Since most `numpy` functions delegate automatically to `cupy` when CuPy arrays are passed as arguments, using `numpy` as the default dispatcher should work most of the time.

SciPy functions will *not* automatically delegate to `cupyx.scipy`. Unfortunately, in this case, an explicit check on the type of the array is required to delegate to the correct function. The following example shows how to make LU factorization hardware-agnostic:

```
from scipy import linalg
if CUPY_IS_INSTALLED:
    from cupyx.scipy import linalg as culinalg
else:
    culinalg = linalg

if isinstance(a, np.ndarray):
    lu = linalg.lu(a)
else:
    lu = culinalg.lu(a)
```

Performance tips

CuPy abstracts much of the underlying complexity of GPU computing, enabling high-performance operations without low-level management. However, this abstraction does not eliminate the need for performance awareness. This section highlights key considerations to optimize CuPy-based code effectively.

Be mindful of dtypes

By default, CuPy arrays use the `np.float64` data type for compatibility with NumPy. However, as alluded to multiple times, performance on most GPUs is better when using single precision. When investigating performance, always look at the data types of arrays.

Special attention should be paid to **silent casting**. Multiplying a `float32` array with a `float64` array results in a `float64` array because `float32` is silently upcast to `float64`.

The `dtype` of an existing array can be changed with the `astype` method. However, this will copy the data, which can be an expensive operation. Provide the `dtype` of an array at creation time, whenever possible.

Preallocate, don't concatenate

Python programmers often write code that dynamically creates and mutates data structures. However, CuPy arrays are not lists, and treating them as such leads to significant performance degradation.

For example, consider a scenario with a list of 100 grayscale images, each represented as a 1,000×1,000 2D array:

```
n_images = 100
size = 1000
images = [cp.ones((size, size)) for _ in range(n_images)]
```

These images need to be stacked into a 3D array to calculate the average pixel values. This could be done by looping over the images and concatenating them onto a growing stack as follows:

```
stack = images[0][None, :, :]
for image in images[1:]:
    stack = cp.concatenate((stack, image[None, :, :]))
```

Alternatively, since the size of the stack is known, the output array can be allocated ahead of time and filled with images, as follows:

```
stack = cp.empty((n_images, size, size), dtype=images[0].dtype)
for i, image in enumerate(images):
    stack[i, :, :] = image
```

The former solution takes almost 60 ms; the second solution takes less than 2 ms, an improvement of roughly 30 times. The reason is that in the first implementation, a new stack array is allocated and all data is copied every loop iteration.

Of course, this is a contrived example, because the list of images can be passed directly to `cupy.stack` as follows:

```
stack = cp.stack(images)
```

This takes 1.8 ms, similar but slightly better than the manual solution with preallocation. It demonstrates that, underneath the hood, CuPy is likely following a similar preallocation strategy.

The goal of this section is not to discourage the use of `cupy.stack` or `cupy.concatenate`; for combining arrays in a list, these are the best options. The point is to be aware when new arrays are allocated, and data is being copied, and to minimize this whenever possible. Additionally, operating on CuPy arrays in Python loops should be avoided whenever possible.

Not every axis is created equal

CuPy simplifies GPU programming by abstracting away low-level details such as CUDA kernels, grids, and hardware mechanics. This allows developers to focus on data and operations rather than implementation specifics.

However, beneath this abstraction, CuPy still executes CUDA kernels using threads, blocks, and grids. These kernels are still subject to the same performance constraints discussed in *Chapter 5*. Especially significant is the data memory layout and, consequently, the data access patterns. While there is no direct control over the execution grid with CuPy, performance can be influenced by carefully choosing the axes over which operations are applied.

To illustrate, consider the performance difference between summing all columns of a 2D array versus summing all rows. First, a large array is created as follows:

```
big_array = cp.ones((10000, 10000))
```

The columns are summed as follows:

```
col_sum = big_array.sum(axis=1)
```

Similarly, the rows are summed as follows:

```
row_sum = big_array.sum(axis=0)
```

The column sum takes 570 µs, and the row sum takes 660 µs, an increase of roughly 15%. In `C`-ordered 2D arrays, data is contiguous along rows, meaning that it is easier to perform coalesced reads when reducing over this dimension. Changing the `big_array` ordering, `F` (`C` is the default), precisely the opposite timings are found.

This demonstrates that the underlying memory layout of the data has a significant impact on the performance of operations, and performance varies when performing operations over different axes. This should inform how the data should be ordered for optimal performance.

Summary

This chapter introduced CuPy as the GPU-equivalent of NumPy and SciPy, enabling high-level yet performant code for *n*-dimensional array operations. Effective use of CuPy demands vectorized thinking, much like NumPy.

As a library rather than a framework, CuPy integrates seamlessly with NumPy and Numba-CUDA, offering flexibility in code design. For standard operations such as `matmul`, CuPy's optimizations make it the preferred choice. However, for custom operations that don't fit the ufunc model, Numba-CUDA kernels can deliver superior performance. For small-scale problems, NumPy outperforms CuPy due to data transfer overheads and low device occupancy.

CuPy's high-level abstraction does not negate the importance of GPU fundamentals such as memory layout and data access patterns. The chapter concluded with practical performance tips.

In the next chapter, the focus shifts to GPU-accelerated dataframes and machine learning using RAPIDS.

Questions

1. Are the two arrays of the `(600, 1, 3, 4, 5, 1)` and `(3, 1, 4, 1, 600)` shapes broadcastable?
2. The task is to sum 1,000 arrays elementwise. Which is faster: stacking them and summing over the new axis, or adding them together individually using the + operator?
3. `cupy` arrays are passed into the `np.block` function. What happens?
4. Why is matrix multiplication for small matrices faster on the CPU?
5. Why is the `generating_julia` kernel faster than kernels that operate on an array of z?
6. When images are stacked by looping over them and concatenating, why is `cupy.concatenate` used and not `cupy.stack`?
7. Why is reduction fastest along the inner dimension of an array?

Answers

1. Yes. The first array is six-dimensional, and the other is five-dimensional. The second array will be padded on the left with an additional axis of a length of `1`. Then, all corresponding axes are either the same number or `1`.
2. Stacking them and summing over the new axis. Adding them with 99 + operations will create 98 intermediate arrays.

3. The answer may depend on when you read this. At the time of writing, `cupy` does not have an implementation of `block`. That means an exception will be raised, because `numpy` cannot delegate to `cupy` for this function. If `cupy.block` exists at the time you read this, then `numpy.block` will delegate `cupy` and the function will work like `cupy.block`.
4. The speed of the GPU comes from being able to do parallel operations. With small matrices, occupancy on the device is too low to hide latency.
5. There are two main reasons. Firstly, threads no longer need to perform one or two `load` operations from global memory, which are slow; threads only need to perform a single `store` operation. Secondly, this kernel uses `z * z` instead of `z ** 2`, which is faster.
6. After stacking the first two images, the stack is a 3D array. Stacking a 2D array on a 3D array is not allowed. Therefore, the 2D arrays are converted to 3D arrays by prepending an empty axis and concatenating them along this axis.
7. Data is contiguous along the inner dimension. Threads in the same warp will load contiguous data elements in coalesced reads. When operating over another axis, this is not possible.

Get this book's PDF version and more

9

Bringing pandas and scikit-learn to the GPU with Rapids

This chapter introduces high-level libraries for manipulating tabular data and training classic machine learning models on the GPU. **RAPIDS** is a GPU-accelerated data science framework that includes libraries for data manipulation and training machine learning models. The focus in this chapter is on two RAPIDS libraries: cuDF, the GPU equivalent of pandas for manipulating tabular data, and cuML, the GPU-accelerated equivalent of scikit-learn for classical machine learning tasks.

The learning outcomes for this chapter are as follows:

- Performing data manipulation on the GPU using cuDF
- Applying cuML to accelerate machine learning models
- Converting pandas and scikit-learn workflows to RAPIDS
- Understand the benefits, drawbacks, and use cases of RAPIDS versus the CPU implementations

Technical requirements

To run the code in this chapter, an NVIDIA GPU with compute capability 7.5 or more is required. The CUDA Toolkit, Python 3, and a number of Python packages must also be installed. As explained in *Chapter 2*, it is also recommended to create a `pixi` environment based on the `pixi.lock` file in the GitHub repository associated with this book:

`https://github.com/PacktPublishing/GPU-Accelerated-Computing-with-Python-3-and-CUDA`

The setup details are explained in the `README.md` file. To run the code snippets in this chapter, an A100-PCIE-40GB GPU was used; timing results will differ depending on the specific device that is used to run the examples.

Accelerating data science on the GPU with RAPIDS

Data science has become an integral part of informed decision-making in most organizations. By combining statistics, computer science, and domain expertise, data scientists distill insights from operational data. Concretely, a significant portion of data science work involves cleaning, transforming, and analyzing **structured (tabular) data**, before training machine learning models to uncover patterns, make predictions, or automate tasks.

While many datasets fit comfortably in RAM, modern applications increasingly involve data volumes and computational workloads that exceed what a single CPU can handle efficiently. This is where GPU-accelerated libraries such as those bundled in RAPIDS come in, enabling data scientists to run familiar workflows orders of magnitude faster on the GPU.

The next section explores cuDF, RAPIDS' GPU DataFrame library, for performing common data manipulations directly on the GPU.

How to use cuDF: pandas on the GPU

In the real world, data is rarely in a form that can be fed directly to a machine learning algorithm. Data needs to be combined from multiple sources, cleaned, and transformed. This type of work is typically performed using a **DataFrame** library such as pandas, Polars, or PySpark.

The most popular DataFrame library among data scientists is pandas. pandas builds on NumPy, inheriting its CPU-bound limitations and restricted parallel execution capabilities, which constrain performance scaling. cuDF aims to replicate the pandas API but run on CUDA-enabled GPUs, just like CuPy does for NumPy.

This section summarizes the essential capabilities of cuDF. It is not a substitute for reading the official documentation. For those already familiar with pandas, most of this section will be a review.

Introducing the DataFrame

A DataFrame in pandas and cuDF represents a 2D table in memory. Each column is represented by a **Series**, a wrapper for a 1D array. Different columns in the same table can have different data types. In pandas, column data is stored by default in a NumPy array. cuDF uses wrapped device arrays to store column data. Conceptually, a DataFrame acts like a dictionary that maps column names to Series objects, with all Series sharing the same length to preserve the 2D structure.

There are many ways to create a new DataFrame. One way is to pass a dictionary of lists:

```
import cudf

df = cudf.DataFrame({
    "col1": [1, 2, 3],
    "col2": ["a", "b", "c"],
    "col3": [1.0, 2.0, 3.0],
})
```

Each column has a different data type, which can be viewed with `print(df.dtypes)`:

```
col1      int64
col2     object
col3    float64
dtype: object
```

The data types are automatically inferred from the input data. For numerical data, the highest-precision data type (`int64` and `float64`) is automatically selected. On the GPU, single precision is preferred for performance. To set the `dtype` of a column, it must be passed explicitly by creating the DataFrame out of a `dict` of `Series`:

```
df = cudf.DataFrame({
    "col1": cudf.Series([1, 2, 3], dtype="int32"),
    "col2": cudf.Series(["a", "b", "c"], dtype="string"),
    "col3": cudf.Series([1.0, 2.0, 3.0], dtype="float32"),
})
```

Note

The string and object data types

The `string` and `object` data types are synonymous in cuDF: both represent strings. In pandas, `object` is the data type for a column that stores arbitrary Python objects. In the past, this included strings. Recently, the `string` data type was added to pandas to support fast vectorized string operations. cuDF only supports columns of strings, not columns of arbitrary Python objects; the `object` data type alias exists for compatibility with pandas.

The names of columns can be viewed as follows:

```
print(df.columns)
```

This prints the following:

```
Index(['col1', 'col2', 'col3'], dtype='object')
```

The columns are packed into an `Index` object, which is very similar to a `Series` object. `Index` objects are used for efficient lookups along rows and columns. pandas and cuDF DataFrames have an implicit index on the rows, accessed through `df.index`. DataFrames support multiple layers of indices with `MultiIndex`.

The number of rows in the DataFrame is obtained using the `len` function:

```
print(len(df))
```

In this case, the result is `3`.

Let's examine the data in an individual column and demonstrate that the data exists on the device. A column (`Series`) can be selected as follows:

```
col1 = df["col1"]
```

Using the built-in `type(..)` function on `col1` shows it is a `cudf.core.series.Series` object. It implements the `__cuda_device_array__` attribute, which contains the following dictionary:

```
{'shape': (3,),  # 3 elements
'strides': (4,),
```

```
'typestr': '<i4',  # single precision int
'data': (140062855530496, False),  # pointer
'version': 1}
```

This dictionary contains a pointer to the buffer of data (the large integer associated with the `data` key), as well as metadata to interpret the buffer as an n-dimensional array (data type, length, and strides). All objects that implement the `__cuda_device_array__` interface can be easily converted to other types of arrays (e.g., CuPy or Numba-CUDA device arrays), and they can be passed directly to custom CUDA kernels written with Numba-CUDA.

Note

Where does data live?

While the data of a cuDF DataFrame resides in device memory, the metadata (column names, dtypes, etc.) resides on the host. cuDF objects are host-resident metadata structures that reference and orchestrate operations on device-resident data.

Columns containing strings such as `col2` are implemented differently, because the length of this data type is not fixed. Therefore, `df["col2"]` does not implement `__cuda_device_array__`, meaning this column cannot directly be passed to custom CUDA kernels.

Exchanging data between the host and the device

A cuDF DataFrame can be created from a pandas DataFrame as follows:

```
import pandas as pd

df_pd = pd.DataFrame({"a": [1, 2, 3]})
df_cudf = cudf.from_pandas(df_pd)
```

Under the hood, this constitutes a host-to-device copy for the data in the column buffers. The reverse is achieved as follows:

```
df_host = df_cudf.to_pandas()
```

Importing and exporting data

Real-world data that needs to be processed with DataFrames usually lives in files on disk or on cloud storage. DataFrame libraries such as cuDF include helper functions to read and write data in a variety of file formats.

A common file format for tabular data is **comma-separated values (CSV)**. A CSV file is just a text file in which rows of tabular data are stored as text. Columns are separated by commas. A small CSV file can be created as follows:

```
csv_file = "my_file.csv"
with open(csv_file, "w") as f:
    f.write("""
col1,col2,col3
1,a,1.0
2,b,2.0
3,c,3.0""")
```

This data can be imported as a cuDF DataFrame as follows:

```
df_imported = cudf.read_csv(csv_file)
```

Since the CSV format does not store the column data type, column `dtypes` are inferred automatically by cuDF unless a list of dtypes is passed to the `read_csv` function.

> Note
>
> **CSV variants**
>
> The CSV format is not standardized, so many variants exist. For example, sometimes the column delimiter is a semicolon instead of a comma. Sometimes the file contains an unstructured header or footer (i.e., some regular text at the top or bottom of the file). The `read_csv` function has lots of optional arguments to deal with all these variants.

A DataFrame is written to a CSV file as follows:

```
df_imported.to_csv("data_export.csv", index=False)
```

By default, the row index is included as the first column; this behavior is negated with `index=False`. When the data is read, a new row index is created automatically.

Other formats that can be read from and written to by cuDF out of the box include the following:

- **JSON**: The most common format for data exchange on the web. REST APIs typically return data in this format. It is human-readable.
- **Text**: A plaintext file, similar to CSV.

- **Parquet**: Currently the most popular format to persist structured data for analytical workloads. It is a binary format in which data is stored column-wise, which enables efficient compression and I/O. The schema, which includes column data types, is stored directly in the file. This is a big advantage over CSV, where the schema is ambiguous.
- **ORC**: Another binary format. An alternative to Parquet, which is less commonly seen.
- **Feather**: A binary format that is a disk representation of Apache Arrow, a widely used in-memory format for structured data. This yields very efficient I/O when working with Arrow, but makes it less suited for long-term storage compared to Parquet.
- **Avro**: A binary row serialization format commonly seen in streaming applications. It is an alternative to JSON, with an embedded schema.
- **HDF**: A binary hierarchical data format, commonly seen in scientific applications when dealing with large, complex datasets. HDF is akin to a filesystem in a single file and supports storing multiple *N*-dimensional arrays and metadata.

For most of these methods, reading directly from remote storage (e.g., cloud blob storage) is supported.

Note

I/O performance

Using the cuDF I/O functionality is more efficient than reading the data first from disk with pandas and then copying the data to the device. cuDF uses **KvikIO**, a library that wraps **GPUDirect Storage** (**GDS**) for high-performance file I/O from the device. This enables the device to bypass the CPU and RAM to interact directly with files on disk, which saves CPU cycles and memory. Additionally, some (de)serialization and/or (de)compression steps are performed on the GPU with increased performance.

Exchanging data with other libraries

cuDF DataFrames and Series have useful conversion methods to interoperate with other libraries. Numerical columns can be converted to CuPy arrays (see *Chapter 8*), as follows:

```
import cupy as cp

col1.to_cupy()
# or
cp.asarray(col1)
```

Both of these operations are zero-copy, because the data in the column already resides in device memory.

Conversion in the other direction is performed by passing a CuPy array as an argument to the `cudf.Series` constructor:

```
cudf.Series(col1.to_cupy())
```

Alternatively, a CuPy array can be directly converted into a new column for an existing DataFrame:

```
df["col4"] = cp.array([10, 11, 12])
```

cuDF automatically handles the conversion to a Series.

Series with variable-length data types, such as strings, cannot be converted to CuPy arrays, since CuPy does not support these data types. On the other hand, data types such as `datetime64[ns]` are supported since they are fixed length and just wrap an integer.

Series can also be converted to NumPy arrays with the `to_numpy` method. NumPy supports more data types than CuPy, but the data is copied back to the host in this conversion.

A highly relevant data format in the context of DataFrames is the **Apache Arrow** format. Arrow is a columnar, in-memory format for representing structured data that many tools have standardized around. Its design allows data exchange between different libraries and processes without serialization and deserialization overhead, often allowing zero-copy data sharing. Most DataFrame libraries, including pandas, Polars, and PySpark, and query engines such as DuckDB provide Arrow interoperability, and some use it for internal data representation. Similarly, cuDF supports conversion to Arrow, as follows:

```
arrow_table = df.to_arrow()
```

A cuDF DataFrame is created from an Arrow table as follows:

```
cudf.DataFrame.from_arrow(arrow_table)
```

cuDF uses a very similar data layout as Arrow, but with data buffers residing in GPU memory. This means that exchanging data between the host and the device is significantly faster if the DataFrame on the host uses Arrow. With pandas DataFrames, the user can choose whether the underlying data is backed by Arrow or NumPy. A pandas DataFrame that uses `pyarrow` as the backend can be converted to a cuDF DataFrame more than 10 times faster than a DataFrame using the default `numpy` backend. In the other direction, converting a cuDF DataFrame to a pyarrow-backed pandas DataFrame is about five times faster than converting to a numpy-backed DataFrame. A demonstration benchmark can be found in the notebook accompanying this chapter, which can be found in the GitHub repository referenced at the beginning of this chapter.

Selecting data in a DataFrame

Filtering, selecting a subset of the data in a DataFrame, is an elementary operation in data processing. One way of selecting a subset of data is selecting one column using the `df[<column_name>]` syntax. Multiple columns can be selected by passing a list of column names, as follows:

```
df[["col1", "col3"]]
```

This selects the first and third columns:

```
   col1  col3
0     1   1.0
1     2   2.0
2     3   3.0
```

To filter the rows, a list or array of Booleans (a row mask) must be passed with a length equal to the number of rows. Here is an example:

```
df[[False, True, False]]
```

This selects the second row from the previously defined three-row DataFrame:

```
   col1  col2  col3
1     2     b   2.0
```

Typically, this Boolean mask is created using Boolean conditions on columns of the table. For example, the mask that selects the rows where `col2` is equal to `"b"` or where `col1` is larger than `2` is expressed as follows:

```
selection = (df["col1"] > 2) | (df["col2"] == "b")
```

The `|` operator performs an element-wise logical `OR`. For element-wise logical `AND`, use the `&` operator.

The `selection` variable contains a Series of Booleans, which can be used for selecting rows like before:

```
df[selection]
```

	col1	col2	col3
1	2	b	2.0
2	3	c	3.0

Note

Boolean logic with Series

A common mistake is to use the `or` and `and` keywords for expressing row selection logic. These keywords should not be used because they treat Series as a single `True` or `False` value, instead of broadcasting over the elements. Underneath the hood, they call the `__bool__` special method. In older versions of pandas, this method would return `True` unless the Series was empty. In modern versions of pandas and cuDF, `__bool__` raises an exception.

Rows can also be filtered by referencing the row index, using the `loc` attribute. With `loc`, rows and columns can be filtered simultaneously in a way that is similar to array slicing and indexing, as discussed in *Chapter 8*. For example, the following selects rows with an index between 1 and 2 and the `col1` and `col3` columns:

```
df.loc[1:2, ["col1", "col3"]]
```

	col1	col3
1	2	2.0
2	3	3.0

Note that, unlike indexing into arrays, the upper bound in a row range is inclusive.

Finally, data can also be selected using position-based numerical indexing using `iloc`. This treats the values in the DataFrame like a 2D array, and indexes into this array accordingly. The following is equivalent to the previous example using `loc`:

```
df.iloc[1:3, [0, 2]]
```

When using ranges in `iloc`, the upper bound is exclusive.

> Note
>
> **Indexing performance**
>
> In general, index and position-based filtering has the best performance since it directly slices contiguous regions of memory. Boolean row filters require more processing and are less memory efficient (since the row mask is also a buffer that takes up space). However, Boolean indexing is more intuitive, readable, and similar to the way data is filtered in SQL using the `WHERE` clause. For these reasons, it is often still preferred.

Transforming data in columns

A data-processing pipeline usually includes data transformation. For example, a new column is calculated based on the data in other columns. In a text column, all entries may need to be capitalized. From a column with dates, the day of the week may need to be extracted. In all these examples, the most commonly used class of operations is **element-wise** operations, which are identical to **ufuncs** for arrays, which were discussed in *Chapter 8*.

For numeric columns, these include all the expected basic arithmetic operations (+, -, *, /, etc.) and logical operations (>, <, >=, ==, !=, <=). For example, two columns can be added element-wise and assigned to a new column in a DataFrame as follows:

```
df["col4"] = df["col1"] + df["col3"]
```

The logical operations have already been discussed in the context of Boolean indexing.

Unlike CuPy and NumPy, the cuDF and pandas libraries do not wrap more advanced mathematical ufuncs. Fortunately, the functions available in CuPy or NumPy can be applied directly to a Series with a numerical dtype. For example, the sine of `col1` is calculated as follows:

```
import cupy as cp

df["col1_sin"] = cp.sin(df["col1"])
```

Since a Series implements `__cuda_array_interface__`, CuPy can directly operate on this data without copying. The output of `cp.sin` is a `cupy.ndarray`. On assignment to the new `col1_sin` column, cuDF automatically converts it to a `Series` object. Since both `cupy.ndarray` and a Series from cuDF are essentially wrappers for data buffers in device memory, this is also a zero-copy operation.

Functionality for operating on string columns can be found under the `Series.str` namespace. For example, the first letter of the entries in `col2` is capitalized, as follows:

```
df["col2"] = df["col2"].str.capitalize()
```

Most operations that are implemented for Python `str` objects are also implemented in pandas and cuDF.

Functionality for operating on `datetime` columns can be found under the `Series.dt` namespace. For example, to get the day of the week from a `datetime` column, use the following:

```
cudf.Series(
    ["2025-11-09", "2025-11-10", "2025-11-12"],
    dtype="datetime64[ns]",
).dt.dayofweek
```

Returned is a Series of `int16`, where `0` maps to Monday and `6` maps to Sunday:

```
0    6
1    0
2    2
dtype: int16
```

Most functions in the built-in `datetime` library are implemented in pandas and cuDF.

It is also possible to define a custom element-wise function, a **user-defined function** (**UDF**). A UDF can be applied to a Series using the `apply` method. For pandas Series, this can be an arbitrary Python function. Here is an example:

```
def my_udf(x):
    if x % 2 == 0:
        return 42
    else:
        return x

df_pd["b"] = df_pd["a"].apply(my_udf)
```

However, this is discouraged for performance reasons; underneath the hood, this involves a Python loop over all the elements, and there is no acceleration from compiled code.

In cuDF, arbitrary Python functions cannot be used, since the data resides in device memory. However, `my_udf` can be applied to a column in the cuDF DataFrame:

```
df["col_udf"] = df["col1"].apply(my_udf)
```

The reason this works is that cuDF tries to compile the UDF to a CUDA kernel via Numba-CUDA under the hood. This means that if Numba-CUDA cannot compile the UDF to a kernel, an exception will be raised. For example, the following UDF will not work because a `dict` is created inside the function, which is not supported in CUDA kernels:

```
def my_other_udf(x):
    k = {}
    if x % 2 == 0:
        return 42
    else:
        return x

df_pd["a"].apply(my_other_udf) # pandas: works
df["col1"].apply(my_other_udf) # cudf: raises exception
```

At the time of writing, cuDF only fully supports UDFs on columns with numeric data. There is experimental support for UDFs on `str` columns. The list of supported string operations that can be used in a UDF can be found here: `https://docs.rapids.ai/api/cudf/stable/user_guide/guide-to-udfs/#string-data`.

For full control, data can be processed using a custom Numba-CUDA kernel (see *Chapter 3* and *Chapter 5*). Because numerical `cudf.Series` implement the `__cuda_array_interface__` interface, they can be passed directly as inputs to a kernel. The following is a kernel that implements the same logic as the previous UDF:

```
from numba import cuda

@cuda.jit
def my_udf_kernel(in_col, out_col):
    idx = cuda.grid(1)
    if idx >= in_col.size:
        return
    value = in_col[idx]
    if value % 2 == 0:
        out_col[idx] = 42
```

```
    else:
        out_col[idx] = value
```

To launch the kernel, a buffer to write the output to must be pre-allocated. With cuDF, a new column of a specific type can be created as follows:

```
from numba import int32

df["col_kernel"] = int32(0)
```

The kernel can then be launched by directly passing in the cuDF Series as input:

```
tpb = 256
bpg = (len(df) + tpb - 1) // tpb
my_udf_kernel[tpb, bpg](df["col1"], df["col_kernel"])
```

So far, this section has been concerned with element-wise operations. There are also operations that take multiple rows as input to produce an output. The most common in this class of operations is a **rolling window** or **sliding window**, with an **expanding window** being a special subclass of these functions. These come up often in the context of time-series analysis. An example is calculating the average of a quantity over the previous week for each point in time. Mathematically, this is identical to the 1D convolution discussed in *Chapter 8*.

cuDF exposes a number of sliding window operations through `Series.rolling`. For example, the sum of the three preceding elements (including the element itself) can be calculated as follows:

```
col = cudf.Series(
    [1, 2, 1, 0, 1],
    dtype="int32",
)
col.rolling(3).sum()
```

The result looks as follows:

```
0    <NA>
1    <NA>
2       4
3       3
4       2
dtype: int64
```

Notice that the original data type is not conserved. Additionally, the first two elements are `<NA>`, which means not a number. For these elements, there is no valid three-element window.

The `rolling` method accepts additional arguments to customize the window behavior. For example, the window can be centered instead of the default right-aligned. Additionally, the behavior for incomplete windows can be adjusted with the `min_periods` argument. Consider this modification:

```
col.rolling(3, min_periods=0, center=True).sum()
```

The result looks as follows:

```
0    3
1    4
2    3
3    2
4    1
dtype: int64
```

Besides `sum`, averages or standard deviations can also be calculated over a window. The available methods on the rolling window can be found in the official documentation: `https://docs.rapids.ai/api/cudf/stable/user_guide/api_docs/window/`. Just like elementwise operations, it is possible to write a custom rolling window UDF; see the documentation here: `https://docs.rapids.ai/api/cudf/stable/user_guide/guide-to-udfs/#rolling-window-udfs`. Of course, with custom Numba-CUDA kernels, any kind of operation can be implemented.

Expanding windows are a special case of the rolling window whereby the window size starts at 1 and grows to the size of the Series. An example would be the cumulative sum, which is implemented directly as a method on `Series`.

```
col.cumsum()
```

This produces the following Series:

```
0    1
1    3
2    4
3    4
4    5
dtype: int64
```

Currently, the available expanding window operations are `cumsum`, `cummin`, `cummax`, and `cumprod`. An expanding window can be implemented using a rolling window, as in this example:

```
col.rolling(len(col), min_periods=1).sum()
```

Aggregating data across rows

The previous section looked at operations that transform one or multiple Series of length `N` to another Series of length `N`. This section focuses on **aggregations**, which combine multiple rows into fewer rows.

Aggregating the rows in a column to a single value is equivalent to a **reduction**, as was discussed for arrays in *Chapter 8*. For example, to calculate the mean of a Series, use the following:

```
col.mean()
```

More interesting aggregations in the context of DataFrames are **split-apply-combine** operations. First, the rows in a DataFrame are partitioned based on some rules. Second, a reduction operation is applied over each of these partitions separately. Finally, the results are recombined into one DataFrame.

Consider the following DataFrame:

```
df = cudf.DataFrame({
    "group": ["a", "b", "a", "b", "c"],
    "value_1": [1, 2, 5, 3, 4],
    "value_2": [2, 0, 3, 0, 1],
})
```

The goal is to calculate the mean of `value_1` for each group in the group column. The first step is to perform a partitioning with the group_by operation:

```
grp = df.groupby(by="group")
```

The rows in `df` are partitioned by the value in the group column. Partitions can be inspected as follows:

```
grp.get_group("a")
```

```
  group  value_1  value_2
0     a        1        2
2     a        5        3
```

The mean of `value_1` in each group is calculated as follows:

```
grp["value_1"].mean()
```

The result is a Series with an index that matches the groups:

```
group
c    4.0
b    2.5
a    3.0
Name: value_1, dtype: float64
```

Note

Ordering

The default behavior of aggregation with cuDF is that the index is randomly ordered, which yields the best performance. To force ordering of the index at the cost of performance, set `sort=True` in the groupby method.

A list of the available aggregation methods can be found in the official documentation: `https://docs.rapids.ai/api/cudf/stable/user_guide/groupby/#aggregation`. Aggregation methods can also be supplied to the `GroupBy.agg` method. At the time of writing, user-defined aggregation methods are supported and can be supplied to agg, but the available functionality is limited.

For some aggregation methods, for example, `first` and `last`, the order of the rows is important. To get the desired result, the original DataFrame should be pre-sorted. For example, if the goal is to find `value_1` in each group where `value_2` is the largest, the DataFrame should first be sorted as follows:

```
sorted_df = df.sort_values(["group", "value_2"])
```

This ensures that the rows are sorted first by group, then by `value_2` within each group, both in ascending order. Now, the `value_1` value corresponding to the largest `value_2` value in each group is obtained as follows:

```
sorted_df.groupby("group")["value_1"].last()
```

This yields the following result:

```
group
a    5
b    3
c    4
Name: value_1, dtype: int64
```

Besides aggregation, `GroupBy` also has a `transform` method. `transform` accepts operations that can be performed on a Series and applies them per partition. The output of `transform` is a Series of the same length as the input. For example, the cumulative sum of `value_1` can be calculated on a group-by-group basis and added as a new column, as follows:

```
sorted_df["value_1_cumsum"] = (
    sorted_df
    .groupby("group")["value_1"]
    .transform("cumsum")
)
```

`sorted_df` now looks as follows:

```
  group  value_1  value_2  value_1_cumsum
0     a        1        2               1
2     a        5        3               6
1     b        2        0               2
3     b        3        0               5
4     c        4        1               4
```

`transform` also accepts aggregation methods; the result of the reduction is broadcast over the original rows. Here is an example:

```
sorted_df.groupby("group")["value_1"].transform("sum")
```

This yields the following output:

```
0    6
2    6
1    5
3    5
4    4
Name: value_1, dtype: int64
```

The sum of each group is written to each row in the group. At the time of writing, `transform` does not support arbitrary UDFs.

Combining DataFrames

There are two main ways to combine DataFrames. Firstly, multiple DataFrames that have the same columns can be combined into a single DataFrame by stacking the rows with `concat`, as follows:

```
df_concat = cudf.concat([df, df])
assert len(df_concat) == len(df) * 2
```

> Note
>
> **concat does more**
>
> `concat` can do more than only stack rows from DataFrames with identical columns. When columns differ across DataFrames, `concat` takes the union of columns and fills missing entries with `cudf.NA`. The function can also stitch DataFrames side by side by combining columns and aligning rows by index. However, to keep DataFrame operations conceptually clear and SQL-like, it is recommended to use `concat` only for stacking rows (similar to SQL `UNION ALL`) and using `merge` for combining DataFrames by keys (similar to SQL `JOIN`).

The second method for combining DataFrames involves matching rows based on shared column values. In SQL, this is accomplished using the `JOIN` operation. In cuDF and pandas, `JOIN` is implemented in the `merge` function. Consider the following pair of DataFrames:

```
df1 = cudf.DataFrame({
    "key_1": [1, 2, 2, 3],
    "value_1": ["a", "b", "c", "d"],
```

```
})
df2 = cudf.DataFrame({
    "key_2": [2, 2, 3, 4],
    "value_2": ["w", "x", "y", "z"],
})
```

The rows of `df1` can be joined with `df2` where `key_1 == key_2`, as follows:

```
cudf.merge(df1, df2, left_on="key_1", right_on="key_2")
```

The resulting DataFrame is as follows:

```
   key_1 value_1  key_2 value_2
0      2       b      2       w
1      2       b      2       x
2      2       c      2       w
3      2       c      2       x
4      3       d      3       y
```

The output contains all possible row combinations for duplicate keys, in this case, where `key_1 == key_2 == 2`. The data type of the matching column can be anything; it does not have to be an integer like in this example.

By default, the "join mode" is `"inner"`, which removes rows in both DataFrames for which there is no match between keys. In this example, rows where `key_1 == 1` and `key_2 == 4` were removed. The most commonly used alternate join modes are `"left"`, `"right"`, and `"outer"`, which should be supplied to the `mode` argument. Here is an example:

```
cudf.merge(df1, df2, left_on="key_1", right_on="key_2", how="left")
```

A left join keeps all the keys from the left DataFrame, even if there is no match with the right DataFrame. For rows that don't have a match (`key_1 == 1`), the columns originating from the right DataFrame are filled with `cudf.NA` (see the next section). `"outer"` keeps all keys from both DataFrames and fills missing values in columns with `cudf.NA`. At the time of writing, right join is not implemented in cuDF; right join is achieved by swapping the DataFrames and using `mode="left"`.

The type of join that should be used is context-specific and depends on the question, as well as the semantics of the data that is being represented in the DataFrames.

Dealing with missing elements

Most real-world data contains missing values. In relational database systems, missing values are often represented by `NULL`. In cuDF, the equivalent of `NULL` is `cudf.NA`. When creating a DataFrame or Series, `None`-like objects are all converted to `cudf.NA`:

```
cudf.Series([cudf.NA, np.nan, None])
```

This produces the following Series:

```
0    <NA>
1    <NA>
2    <NA>
dtype: object
```

When dealing with missing data, a choice must be made on how to handle it. Machine learning models often cannot deal with missing values, so in this case, they must be removed somehow. Checking whether values are `NA` is achieved as follows:

```
cudf.Series([1, None, 1]).isna()
```

This returns the following Boolean Series:

```
0    False
1     True
2    False
dtype: bool
```

This Series can be used as a row mask. To select rows that are *not* `NA`, the Series can be inverted using the `~` operator. Alternatively, `notna` can be used instead of `isna`. If the only goal is to remove rows with `NA`, the `dropna` method is most efficient.

> Note
>
> **NA is not NA**
>
> Checking for NA should never be done using the == operator. The result will always be False, since cuDF considers NA!=NA.

Instead of removing NA rows, sometimes it makes sense to fill in a value, which can be done using the `fillna` method. For example, NA rows in a column can be filled with the mean of the non-NA values, as follows:

```
data = cudf.Series([1, 4, 1, None, 5], dtype="float32")
data.fillna(data.mean())
```

The `fillna` method also supports filling in NA with the first non-NA value before or after the NA row, using the `method` argument.

The built-in transformation and aggregation methods automatically deal with NA values. When performing arithmetic operations among columns, NA values propagate; any operation with NA outputs another NA. In aggregation methods, NA rows are usually ignored; this behavior can sometimes be modified using the `skipna` argument.

External transformation functions, such as those implemented in CuPy, may not work as expected, especially on a Series of integers. The following raises an exception:

```
cp.sin(cudf.Series([1, 2, None], dtype="int32"))
```

A workaround is to store data in `float` columns and represent missing values with `np.nan` instead of NA. CuPy and other libraries can work with `np.nan`. The NA and `np.nan` options are not the same. NA uses a separate validity mask to mark the absence of a value, whereas `np.nan` is an actual floating-point number (just like `np.inf`) with its own arithmetic behavior. NA and `np.nan` also differ semantically: NA means "a value is missing," while `np.nan` means "a value exists but is not a valid number" (for example, the result of dividing 0 by 0).

The previous example can be fixed as follows:

```
cp.sin(cudf.Series([1, 2, np.nan], nan_as_null=False, dtype="float32"))
```

The `nan_as_null` argument ensures cuDF does not silently convert `np.nan` to `NA`. None is still treated like `NA`, and `NA` and `np.nan` can be combined in columns with a `float` dtype. However, cuDF still treats `np.nan` like a `NULL` value and will return `True` when testing for `isna`. Rows with `np.nan` are also dropped with `dropna`.

Currently, there is no obvious way to distinguish between `NA` and `np.nan` when they exist in the same column. To ensure all `NA` values are converted to `np.nan`, either use `fillna(np.nan)` or convert the Series to a CuPy array with the `to_cupy` method.

Reshaping DataFrames

In some corporate environments, being able to create a **pivot table** in Excel promotes a person to the status of data wizard. In this section, let's demystify the **pivot** operation using cuDF.

Consider the following DataFrame:

```
df = cudf.DataFrame({
    "stock": ["NVDA", "NVDA", "AMD", "AMD"],
    "datetime": cudf.Series(
        ["2025-11-15", "2025-11-16", "2025-11-15", "2025-11-17"],
        dtype="datetime64[ns]",
    ),
    "price": [190, 200, 250, 230],
})
```

It contains prices of different stocks at different points in time. The table is in **long form**; that is, all the data is stacked on top of each other. The long-form table is a very popular way to store data, since the schema almost never changes; new stocks can be added without changing the structure of the table.

However, this form is less convenient for analyzing data. For example, to compare the prices of different stock over time, it is more convenient to present the prices side by side in different columns. This can be done using the `pivot` function:

```
cudf.pivot(df, columns="stock", index="datetime", values="price")
```

This produces the following result, a **wide table** that is much more convenient for analysis:

```
stock        AMD  NVDA
datetime
2025-11-15   250   190
```

```
2025-11-16   <NA>    200
2025-11-17    230   <NA>
```

The `price` column has been split into different columns based on the value in the `stock` column. In this format, missing values are immediately revealed.

A wide table can be converted to a long table using the `melt` function:

```
cudf.melt(wide_df, var_name="stock", value_name="price", ignore_index=False)
```

The only difference from the original DataFrame is that the `melt` function preserves the `NA` rows and retains `datetime` as an index (instead of a regular column). This can be fixed using the `dropna` and `reset_index` methods.

One additional capability of Excel pivot tables is to perform simultaneous pivoting and aggregation; this is not possible with `pivot` but is possible with the `pivot_table` function. With `pivot`, each combination of `(index, column)` must be associated with a unique value. In the preceding example, if the long table contains multiple rows with a price for the same stock on the same date, `pivot` will not work because the value that should be entered into the wide table is ambiguous. `pivot_table` accepts an aggregation method, which aggregates over duplicate values. Here is an example:

```
extra_row = cudf.DataFrame({
    "stock": ["NVDA", "AMD"],
    "datetime": cudf.Series(
        ["2025-11-16", "2025-11-15"],
        dtype="datetime64[ns]",
    ),
    "price": [200, 140],
})
df_with_extra = cudf.concat([df, extra_row])
cudf.pivot_table(df_with_extra, columns="stock", index="datetime",
                 values="price", aggfunc="mean")
```

Although `pivot_table` is powerful and convenient, it combines aggregation and reshaping into a single operation, which can obscure what is happening under the hood. A clearer and often more maintainable approach is to first perform any required aggregation using groupby, and then apply `pivot` to reshape the data. This separates the logic into simpler, more explicit steps.

This section has introduced DataFrames and how to interact with them. All of these operations are abstractions on top of complex CUDA kernels. These abstractions allow data scientists to focus on data-processing logic by composing a few basic logical steps, at the cost of a loss of low-level control.

The next section explores the benefits of cuDF over alternatives.

When to use cuDF

cuDF is fast, especially when dealing with large datasets. Performance comparisons to other DataFrame libraries can be found in the official documentation here: `https://docs.rapids.ai/api/cudf/stable/user_guide/performance-comparisons/performance-comparisons/#`. In these benchmarks, cuDF significantly outperforms all DataFrame libraries and query engines that run on the CPU, including DuckDB and Polars.

However, the official benchmarks are performed on very large DataFrames (hundreds of millions of rows) on a device with a very large amount of VRAM. Additionally, host-device data transfers are not included in the benchmarks. This significantly skews the results in favor of cuDF.

cuDF DataFrames are an abstraction over collections of device arrays that are processed with CUDA kernels. Therefore, they are subject to the same performance considerations as arrays. Worse performance is expected on the GPU for small DataFrames compared to the CPU. Relative performance should increase with increased DataFrame size. However, the maximum size of the DataFrame is limited by the size of the global memory.

As was done in *Chapter 8*, let's compare the performance of pandas to cuDF for different DataFrame sizes. Not every operation can be compared, so let's focus on operations that are DataFrame-specific: transformation of string columns, `groupby` aggregation, and `merge`. For operations on numerical columns, the guidance from *Chapter 8* applies.

Figure 9.1 shows the speedup of cuDF relative to pandas for an aggregation, join, and string transformation for DataFrames of different sizes on a log-log plot:

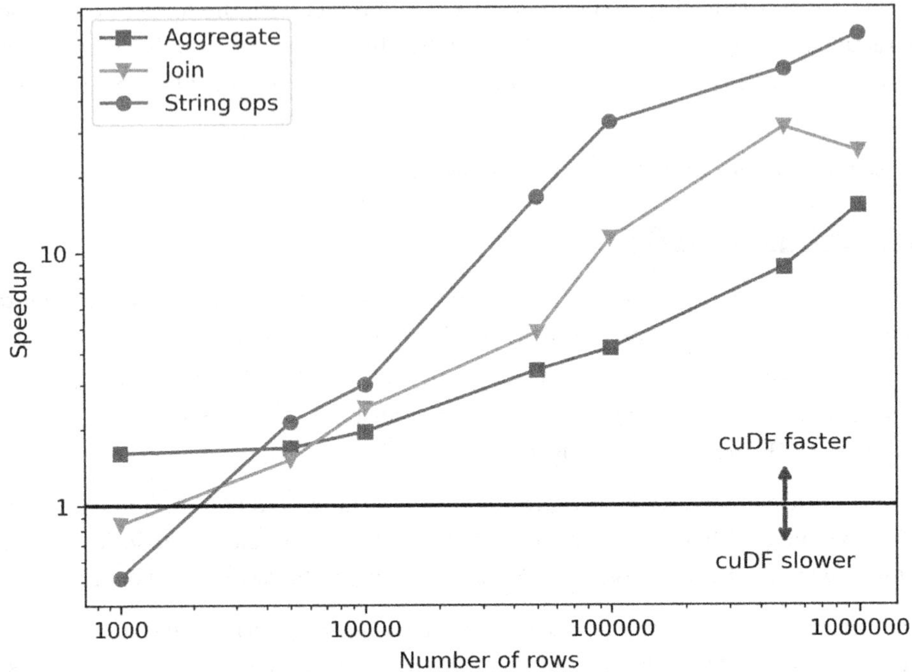

Figure 9.1 – Speedup of cuDF's aggregation, joining, and string transformation operations compared to pandas excluding data transfers

These benchmarks do not include the time for data transfers between the host and the device. For the full details of these benchmarks, consult the GitHub repository associated with this book. As expected, the relative benefit of cuDF increases as the DataFrame gets larger. For large DataFrames, speedups range from a factor of 10 to almost 100, depending on the operation. Only for the smallest DataFrames (fewer than 1,000 rows) is pandas slightly faster or equally fast as cuDF. For small DataFrames, the absolute difference in timing is very small, so the choice between pandas and cuDF is irrelevant.

If the time to convert a pandas DataFrame to a cuDF DataFrame (which serves as a proxy for host-to-device data transfer time) is included, the results (shown in *Figure 9.2*) look very different:

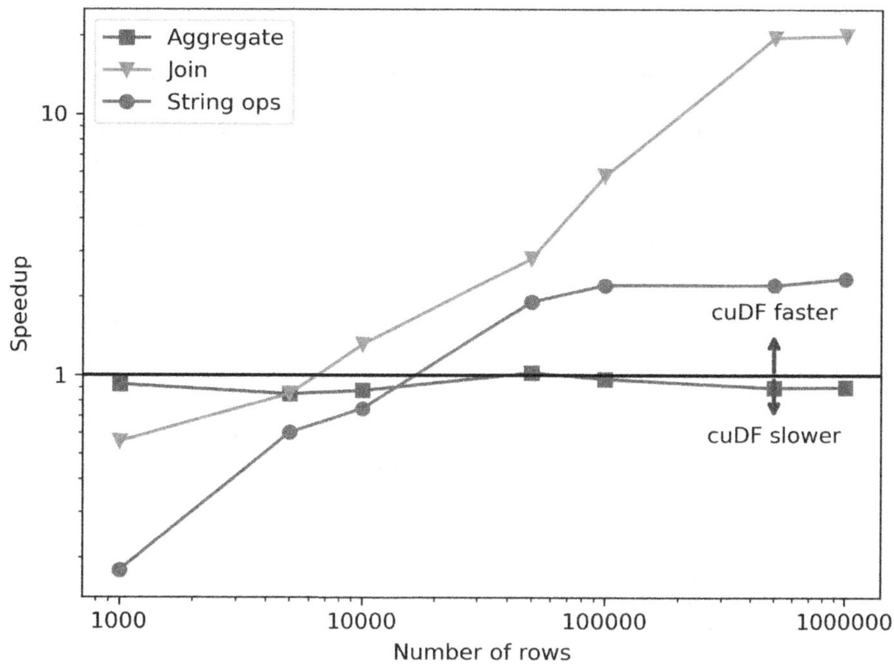

Figure 9.2 – Speedup of cuDF's operations compared to pandas, including time to convert the DataFrame from pandas to cuDF

When the time to convert to a cuDF DataFrame is included in the benchmark, cuDF is only faster than pandas when DataFrames exceed about 10,000 rows. For the aggregation, the benefit of GPU acceleration is cancelled out by the conversion. Total speedups are strongly reduced to between 2 and 10 times. Results would be even worse if the cuDF DataFrame needs to be converted back to a pandas DataFrame.

Fortunately, this is close to the worst-case scenario and highlights a pattern that should be avoided. Converting from pandas to cuDF is not a pure host-to-device copy but also includes serialization overhead to convert NumPy arrays to Arrow. Therefore, this type of transformation should be avoided, and data should be transferred into device memory as directly as possible. That means using cuDF's built-in I/O functionality (see earlier in this chapter) to read data from disk. To get the best I/O performance, choose data formats that can be easily converted to and from Arrow, mainly Parquet and Feather. Using these techniques, the host-to-device time contribution becomes vanishingly small. Additionally, the importance of host-to-device transfer is amortized as more work is performed on the data in device memory.

Note

Working with datasets that are larger than memory

The GPU becomes relatively more efficient for larger datasets. Unfortunately, on average, GPU VRAM is quite limited, especially compared to the size of many real-world datasets. This is why frameworks such as PySpark, which can process very big datasets across multiple nodes, are so popular in the industry. Fortunately, cuDF can be scaled to multiple nodes and devices using **Dask cuDF**, which is also part of the RAPIDS ecosystem. Dask was introduced in *Chapter 7* of this book, but multi-GPU computing is beyond the scope of this chapter.

How to write GPU-agnostic DataFrame manipulation code

cuDF aims to mirror the pandas API as closely as possible. In most cases, the following pattern that was introduced in *Chapter 8* works:

```
import pandas as pd
try:
    import cudf as xd
    CUDF_IS_INSTALLED = True
except ImportError:
    xd = pd
    CUDF_IS_INSTALLED = False
```

However, cuDF is not an exact replacement for pandas. Not all functions, arguments, and options have been implemented. If a code base relies on more exotic pandas functionality, cuDF may not replace it.

For these cases, there is `cudf.pandas`. This `cudf.pandas` keeps a pandas code base entirely unchanged. The operations that are supported by cuDF will automatically run on the GPU. Operations that are not supported by cuDF will fall back to pandas automatically. The only requirement is that the following lines are added to the code before importing or using pandas:

```
import cudf.pandas
cudf.pandas.install()
```

In a Jupyter notebook, the following line should be run at the top of the notebook:

```
%load_ext cudf.pandas
```

`cudf.pandas` builds on CUDA **Unified Memory** (also known as managed memory), a memory model that provides a single shared address space for both the CPU and GPU. This allows the host and the device code to use the same pointer to access data, greatly simplifying memory management. The trade-off is that Unified Memory can obscure where data physically resides and may trigger implicit data migrations between the host and the device, which can be expensive. For the highest performance, it is generally preferable to use `cudf` directly and keep most computation on the GPU to avoid such migrations.

Beyond its near drop-in acceleration benefits, a key use case of `cudf.pandas` is processing DataFrames that are larger than the available GPU memory. cuDF requires the entire DataFrame (and intermediate results) to fit in VRAM. Unified Memory, however, allows the GPU to access data residing in system memory. This incurs some overhead but makes it possible to process datasets larger than device memory as long as they fit in host memory.

> Note
>
> **cudf.pandas versus dask_cudf**
>
> `cudf.pandas` requires workloads to fit inside the memory of a single host with a single device. Dask is more flexible and scalable, supporting multi-GPU and multi-node execution, as well as spilling to disk when data exceeds host RAM. This comes with additional complexity and some overhead, especially on a single machine.

Alternatives to cuDF

Processing structured data is a fundamental task in analytics and machine learning, so many libraries and systems exist to address this workload. In Python, pandas is the most widely used tool by data scientists, and cuDF follows its API to provide GPU acceleration.

However, the pandas API often receives criticism for being too messy, with many overlapping features and multiple ways to accomplish the same task. In addition, both pandas and cuDF evaluate operations **eagerly**: each method call immediately computes its result. This makes some types of optimization impossible, and because each intermediate result must be materialized, this wastes both computation and memory usage.

A relatively new alternative to pandas is Polars, a DataFrame library written in Rust. Its expression-based query language is more compact and declarative than pandas. Polars takes a **lazy** execution approach, where operations build up a query plan or task graph that is executed only when the final result is needed. This allows the query engine to optimize how the task will be executed, which can significantly enhance performance. Polars also provides an eager API, but the lazy API is recommended for writing analytical queries. Polars is often much faster than pandas on CPU workloads. RAPIDS includes a GPU engine for Polars that can accelerate queries by up to an order of magnitude; see the official documentation: `https://docs.rapids.ai/api/cudf/stable/cudf_polars/`.

Apache Spark is another popular framework for processing structured data, particularly at a large scale. Built on the **Java Virtual Machine (JVM)**, Spark supports distributed execution across clusters, exposes both a DataFrame API and full SQL, and evaluates computations lazily. RAPIDS provides a Spark GPU accelerator plugin that enables many Spark SQL and DataFrame operations to run on NVIDIA GPUs; see `https://nvidia.github.io/spark-rapids/`.

DataFrame libraries serve to process data. Now it's time to learn how to train machine learning models on this data.

How to use cuML: scikit-learn on the GPU

Just like cuDF is the GPU counterpart to pandas, cuML is the GPU counterpart to scikit-learn. Scikit-learn is a very popular library that packages hundreds of classical machine learning algorithms and exposes all of them through a uniform interface.

This section goes over the very basics of training a machine learning model on the GPU.

The basics of machine learning

In traditional software, programmers specify exact instructions for the computer to follow. Unfortunately, some tasks are too complex to express as explicit rules. A classic example is distinguishing images of cats and dogs. Hardcoding logic for this task is nearly impossible.

Machine learning takes a data-centric approach. Instead of encoding all the rules explicitly, a model is **trained** to perform the task by showing it many **labeled** examples. In the cats-and-dogs scenario, many images are provided to the model, along with their correct labels. After training, the goal is for the model to generalize to images it has never seen before; this phase is called **inference**. Because this process parallels how humans learn from examples, it is known as **machine learning**, a sub-field of **artificial intelligence**.

On a technical level, this workflow is a generalization of **function fitting**, such as **linear regression**. The aim of linear regression is to fit a line through a cloud of points. The line is the model. It has parameters, the slope and intercept, that need to be adjusted to minimize the difference between the model's predictions and the known outcomes. The inputs (x values) are the **features**, and the outputs (y values) are the **labels**. Once the model is trained (the best-fitting slope and intercept have been found), the model can be passed new x values to obtain y-value predictions.

Real-world data is often multi-dimensional and better fit by more complex models (such as neural networks), though simple linear models are still surprisingly useful. However, the basic idea remains the same:

- Data consists of features (X) and labels (y), and a model is a function, f, with internal parameters
- Training (or fitting) means adjusting those parameters to minimize the difference between the model's predictions, $f(X)$, and the true labels, y
- Once trained, the model can make predictions for new X values where y is unknown

Scikit-learn and cuML embody this workflow in their APIs. All models provide a `fit` method to learn parameters from data, and a `predict` (or `transform`) method to compute $f(X)$. In the next sections, these concepts are applied to the California housing dataset.

> Note
>
> **Unsupervised learning**
>
> The workflow described in this section is **supervised learning**, where models are trained on labeled data, that is, where the desired output is known. Machine learning also includes **unsupervised learning**, where the model is trained on data without labels. Common unsupervised tasks include clustering, dimensionality reduction, density estimation, anomaly detection, and generative modeling. A full treatment of machine learning is beyond the scope of this book.

Deciding on an objective

The first step in a machine learning project is deciding on what needs to be achieved. This will determine the type of model that needs to be trained and how it will be trained.

As a guiding example, this section explores the California housing dataset and trains a machine learning model on it with cuML. The dataset comprises median house prices for districts in California, as well as other data about each district: the population size, location, average income levels, and so on. The goal is to predict the median house price in a district based on other information about the district. This is a **regression** problem: the output that needs to be predicted is a continuous variable. The cats-and-dogs problem is a **classification** problem: the desired output is a category.

Note

Regression versus classification

Classification and regression are closely related. Many classification problems can be framed as learning a continuous score (similar to regression) and then applying a threshold or decision rule to convert that score into discrete classes.

Since the dataset is a well-known dataset often used in tutorials, it is made directly available through scikit-learn. The dataset is fetched as follows:

```
from sklearn.datasets import fetch_california_housing

dataset = fetch_california_housing(as_frame=True)
```

The dataset contains a pandas DataFrame with the data in the `frame` attribute:

```
df_cpu = dataset.frame
```

To use cuML and ensure computations are performed on the GPU, the DataFrame is converted to a cuDF DataFrame, thereby transferring the data to the device:

```
df = cudf.from_pandas(df_cpu)
```

The dataset also includes a description with an explanation of all the columns:

```
print(dataset.DESCR)
```

This reveals that the data has the following columns, which may correlate with the median house price:

- `MedInc`: Median income in the district
- `HouseAge`: Median house age in the district
- `AveRooms`: Average number of rooms per household
- `AveBedrms`: Average number of bedrooms per household
- `Population`: District population
- `AveOccup`: Average number of household members

- `Latitude`: District latitude
- `Longitude`: District longitude

The description also mentions that there are 20,640 districts, which should correspond to the number of rows.

Data exploration and preprocessing

Once the goal is clear, the next step in training a machine learning model is to explore the data and transform it into a form that can be passed to a model to train it. Often, this is the most time-consuming part of a machine learning project.

Most cuML regression models expect features *X* to be in the form of a 2D matrix or a DataFrame, and *Y* to be in the form of a 1D array or Series. Some models also accept a 2D *Y*, in cases where the model needs to predict multiple outputs at once. Most models require all the values in *X* and *Y* to be numerical.

In the California housing dataset, all columns are numerical features, and the desired output is a single value. So, *X* and *Y* are extracted from the DataFrame as follows:

```
X = df.drop(columns=["MedHouseVal"])
y = df["MedHouseVal"]
```

> Note
>
> **Dealing with non-numerical data**
>
> In many real-world datasets, *X* contains **categorical** variables (for example, `"city"` or `"zip code"`), which may carry useful information for the model. Several strategies exist to convert these into a numerical form. A common technique is **one-hot encoding**, which creates a binary indicator column for each category. Textual data for which the semantic meaning needs to be quantified can be converted to vectors using **embeddings**. Some columns may appear numerical but do not represent meaningful quantities, for example, ID numbers. These columns should be dropped, since they may teach the model erroneous relationships.

Once the data is in a useful form, it should be explored to *get a feel* for it. A good starting point is calculating summary statistics, visualizing the data to get a feel for the distribution, and estimating how much predictive power features have by calculating metrics such as correlation coefficients. This process brings out artifacts in the data that may need to be mitigated, for example, missing data or impossible values. For a DataFrame with all numerical columns, the most important summary statistics can be calculated quickly, as follows:

```
df.describe()
```

This produces the table in *Figure 9.3*.

	Medinc	HouseAge	AveRooms	AveBedrms	Population	AveOccup	Latitude	Longitude	MedHouseVal
count	20640.000000	20640.000000	20640.000000	20640.000000	20640.000000	20640.000000	20640.000000	20640.000000	20640.000000
mean	3.870671	28.639486	5.429000	1.096675	1425.476744	3.070655	35.631861	-119.569704	2.068558
std	1.899822	12.585558	2.474173	0.473911	1132.462122	10.386050	2.135952	2.003532	1.153956
min	0.499900	1.000000	0.846154	0.333333	3.000000	0.692308	32.540000	-124.350000	0.149990
25%	2.563400	18.000000	4.440716	1.006079	787.000000	2.429741	33.930000	-121.800000	1.196000
50%	3.534800	29.000000	5.229129	1.048780	1166.000000	2.818116	34.260000	-118.490000	1.797000
75%	4.743250	37.000000	6.052381	1.099526	1725,000000	3.282261	37.710000	-118.010000	2.647250
max	15.000100	52.000000	141.909091	34.066667	35682.000000	1243.333333	41.950000	-114.310000	5.000010

Figure 9.3 – Summary statistics table of the California housing dataset

`count` shows that all the rows are complete, and there are no missing values. The `max` row reveals some interesting artifacts, for example, districts with 141 rooms per household. The dataset description provides the following explanation for these anomalies: *these columns may take surprisingly large values for block groups with few households and many empty houses, such as vacation resorts*. In real-world datasets that have not been extensively analyzed, explaining data anomalies is part of the job for a data scientist.

To visualize how the data is distributed, it is useful to plot a **histogram**. The pandas DataFrame has a convenient method for this; cuDF does not. Therefore, the histograms for all columns are plotted using the pandas DataFrame, as follows:

```
df_cpu.hist(bins=50, figsize=(10, 10))
```

This produces the plots shown in *Figure 9.4*:

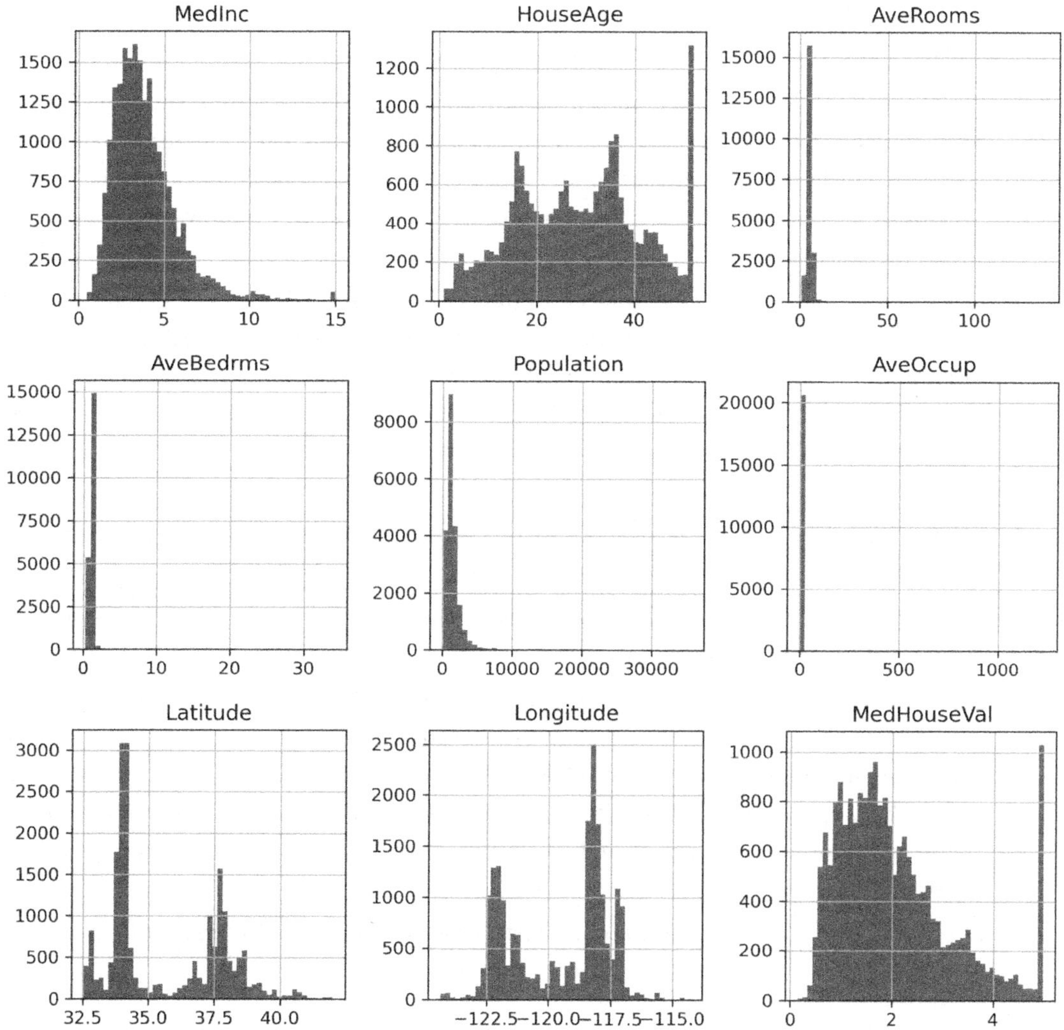

Figure 9.4 – Histograms of the columns in the California housing dataset

This reveals the following useful information:

- Many features (median income, average rooms, population, etc.) show a **skewed distribution** with a long right tail. This means some models, such as linear models, will perform poorly on the dataset unless features are transformed, for example, with a logarithm or square root. Tree-based models are not sensitive to feature distribution, so these models are easy to try first.
- The average age of the house shows a number of peaks, probably reflecting past building booms. However, there is a very narrow peak around 50 years old, which indicates that all houses older than this cutoff were simply assigned this age. The last bin, therefore, has a different meaning; it means the house is *50 years old or more*. This is another aspect that will make linear models behave poorly but should not be a large problem for tree-based models.
- There are some very large outliers in the rooms and occupancy due to the reason mentioned in the dataset description.
- The latitude and longitude show two large peaks, probably corresponding to two large urban centers with lots of districts.
- The labels (median house value) also show a skewed distribution and a similar cut-off artifact at the right of the distribution. A skewed distribution and a data cut-off in the labels are problematic for most models. If this were a real data science project, the data would be preprocessed to deal with these data issues. However, since our primary goal is walking through a small practical data science example, the data will be used as is to see how well the model performs.

Since the data is geographic in nature, it is also instructive to plot a "map" of the data, as follows:

```
df_cpu.plot(kind="scatter", x="Longitude", y="Latitude",
            alpha=0.3, c=df_cpu["MedHouseVal"],
            s=df_cpu["Population"] / 100,
            colormap="grey_r", colorbar=False)
```

Here is what the map looks like:

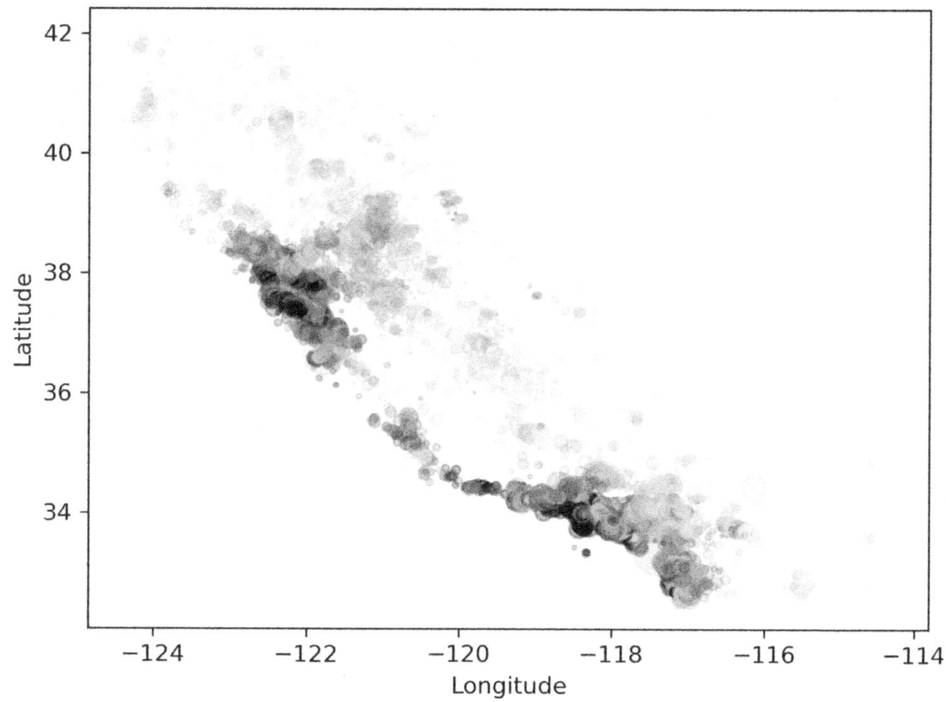

Figure 9.5 – Map of the California housing dataset

The point cloud clearly resembles the outline of California. The house prices are mapped to a color, with darker being more expensive housing and lighter being less expensive. This reveals that the most expensive housing is found near the two big cities (San Francisco and Los Angeles) and near the coast. Most markers also cluster near the two big cities, which explains the peaks in latitude and longitude in the histograms. The population size of the district was mapped to the size of the marker, but this does not reveal any obvious trends.

Finally, let's calculate how much each feature **correlates** with the label. This is done as follows:

```
df.corr()["MedHouseVal"].sort_values()
```

The output looks as follows:

```
Latitude      -0.144160
AveBedrms     -0.046701
Longitude     -0.045967
Population    -0.024650
AveOccup      -0.023737
```

```
HouseAge        0.105623
AveRooms        0.151948
MedInc          0.688075
MedHouseVal     1.000000
Name: MedHouseVal, dtype: float64
```

Correlation is a measure of the degree to which variables are linearly related. A random point cloud will have a correlation near 0: one variable does not predict the other. A correlation near 1 means that increasing one variable is associated with an increase in the other variable. A negative correlation means that increasing one variable is associated with a decrease in the other. As the saying goes, correlation does not imply causation. However, correlation indicates which features are most associated with a change in the target, and therefore carry the most predictive power. In this case, the median income is the feature that correlates most strongly with the median house value.

Note

Feature scaling

For many regression models, it is beneficial or even necessary to **scale** the features such that they span roughly the same range. Feature scaling ensures that all features contribute proportionally to the model's loss function and gradient updates. Without scaling, features with larger magnitudes dominate, leading to slow convergence or biased parameter estimates. Therefore, it is often an essential part of the preprocessing pipeline. Different methods of scaling are available as Scaler classes in the `cuml.preprocessing` module. However, for tree-based models, which will be used for this example, feature scaling is not so important.

Splitting the dataset into training and test sets

A well-trained model should generalize to unseen data. To verify this, part of the data should be held out as a **test set**, which the model never sees. Then, the model is trained on the rest of the data. At the end, the performance of the model can be tested using the test set, since the labels are known for this data. If the error is low, it is assumed that the model generalizes well.

cuML has handy utility functions to split a dataset into test and training datasets:

```
from cuml.model_selection import train_test_split

X_train, X_test, y_train, y_test = train_test_split(X, y=y, test_size=0.2,
random_state=42)
```

The test dataset must be held out until the very end. If any information from the test data is used during training (known as **data leakage**), the model tends to become tuned to fit the test data better. When this happens, it becomes impossible to estimate how well the model will perform on completely unseen data.

Training a model

Finally, the time has come to train a machine learning model. The most challenging part is choosing an appropriate model for the project objective and the data. This type of knowledge distinguishes a seasoned data scientist from someone who is just familiar with the scikit-learn API. Given the previous discussion, a **decision tree-based** model is likely a good starting point.

Tree-based models are machine learning models that make predictions by repeatedly asking simple yes/no questions about the features. Imagine a flowchart where each question splits the data into smaller and smaller groups until the final question yields a prediction. These models are very flexible, can handle numerical and categorical data, and capture complex patterns without needing the data to be scaled or transformed. The two most popular tree-based models are **random forests** and **gradient-boosted trees**. These models are also known to perform well in general on structured data, often better than neural networks, and are often the first pick to establish a baseline.

cuML provides an implementation of the random forest model, which can be instantiated as follows:

```
from cuml.ensemble import RandomForestRegressor

model = RandomForestRegressor()
```

Training the model on the training dataset is as simple as running the following:

```
model.fit(X_train, y_train)
```

That's it. All the complexity of optimizing the model parameters is hidden. All that remains is evaluating how well the model performs.

Evaluating the model

Regression models are most commonly evaluated using the **mean squared error** (**MSE**) and the **coefficient of determination** or $\mathbf{R}^2$ metric.

The MSE is the mean of the squares of the differences between the predictions and the ground truths. Often, this is also the metric that is optimized under the hood when training the model; "training" actually means finding the model parameters that minimize the MSE on the training data. A lower MSE implies better model fit. The downside of the MSE is that the absolute value is meaningless, since it is sensitive to the label scaling; it is only meaningful in relative terms (comparing one model to another).

The R^2 statistic has a more complicated formula, but it can be roughly interpreted as: how much better is the model at predicting the label compared to just using the mean of the labels? When R^2 is 1, the model predicts the labels perfectly. When it is 0, the model has no predictive power; just outputting the mean for every input is equally good. When R^2 is negative, the model performs worse than just using the mean. In short, an R^2 metric close to 1 is desirable in a regression problem.

These metrics can be evaluated using functions built into cuML. First, the model is used to predict labels. This is done both for the training set and the test set, as follows:

```
y_prd_train = model.predict(X_train)
y_prd_test = model.predict(X_test)
```

Then, the MSE and R^2 are calculated for both sets of labels as follows:

```
from cuml.metrics import mean_squared_error, r2_score

mse_train = mean_squared_error(y_train, y_prd_train)
r2_train = r2_score(y_train, y_prd_train)
mse_test = mean_squared_error(y_test, y_prd_test)
r2_test = r2_score(y_test, y_prd_test)
```

For the training data, the model performs extremely well, with an MSE of 0.05 and an R^2 of 0.96. This means the model was successfully fit to the data. If performance metrics for the training data are bad, it means either that the model is **undertrained** or that the model cannot fit the data well.

The model performs slightly worse on the test data, with an MSE of 0.25 and an R^2 of 0.8. Random forest models tend to show slightly better performance on the training dataset compared to the test dataset (i.e., they are typically **overtrained**). Still, this performance is quite good and demonstrates that the model generalizes well to unseen data. The performance metrics on the test dataset are what really count for evaluating whether the model is useful.

Evaluating model performance using these simple metrics is helpful as a quick check and for comparing the performance of different models. However, to fully investigate how the model performs, the error distribution should be analyzed in more detail. One quick and convenient approach is to plot the predictions versus the ground truth in one plot, as in *Figure 9.6*:

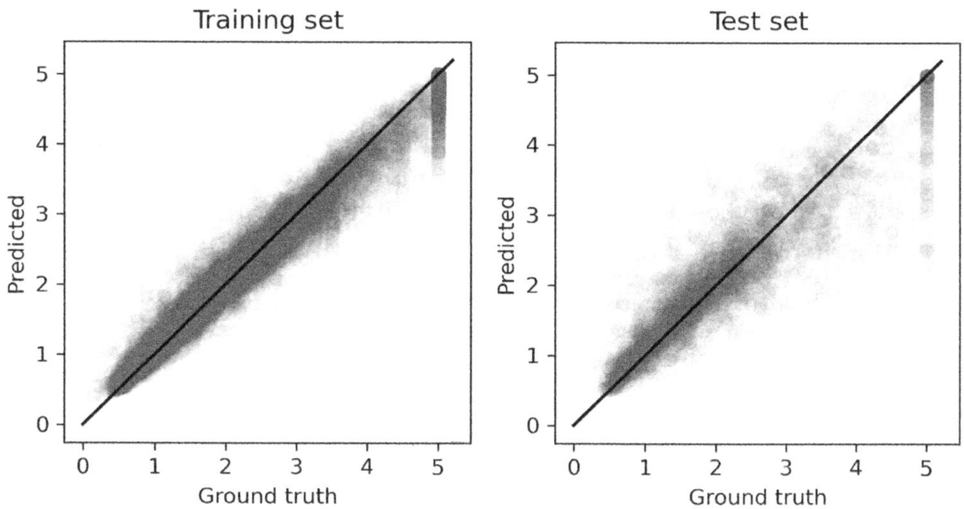

Figure 9.6 – Predictions versus ground truth, revealing the error distribution

For a perfect model, all the points should lie on the $y=x$ line; any deviation is an error of the model. This is much more informative for analyzing the model behavior. The plot reveals that the model performs best for districts with cheaper housing, probably because this is also where the bulk of the data is situated. It also reveals that the model, as expected, has problems with the artificial price cut-off. These insights can be used to strategize on how to further improve the model.

Storing the model

In real-world contexts, training models and using them for inference are distinct phases in the model life cycle, and they tend to happen in different environments. Training is relatively slow and may require a lot of data and computational resources; retraining a model is not a continuous process. Inference happens when the model is part of a software system and should be fast and efficient. Inference may even need to happen in real time; think of robotics with computer vision systems.

Therefore, it's important to be able to store the model after training and to load it again in a different environment for inference. The random forest model can be exported using the built-in `pickle` library, as follows:

```
import pickle

with open("housing_model.pkl", "wb") as output_file:
    pickle.dump(model, output_file, protocol=5)
```

The model can be loaded again as follows:

```
with open("housing_model.pkl", "rb") as input_file:
    loaded_model = pickle.load(input_file)
```

In many cases, training may happen on a GPU, whereas inference happens on a CPU. To enable this, the cuML model should be converted to a scikit-learn model on the host with the `as_sklearn` method. Then, the model can be exported with `pickle`.

Pickle is Python's built-in binary format for saving and loading arbitrary Python objects. It is fast and convenient, but it is not designed for long-term or cross-environment storage. Pickle files may break between Python versions, since the underlying format can change without guaranteed backward compatibility. In addition, objects created by third-party libraries may not unpickle correctly if loaded with a different library version, leading to errors or unexpected behavior.

For this reason, alternative formats for persisting models have been developed, but to date, no universal standard exists. For decision-tree-based models, there is Treelite (see `https://github.com/dmlc/treelite`), which is directly supported as an output format by cuDF:

```
model.as_treelite().serialize("model.tl")
```

In the deployment environment, the model can be loaded with the Treelite library:

```
import treelite

model = treelite.Model.deserialize("model.tl")
```

Predictions can be made as follows:

```
predictions = treelite.gtil.predict(model, X, pred_margin=True)
```

The advantage is that only the Treelite library is needed in the production environment.

Performance tips

In this example, the cuML model was passed cuDF DataFrames for training and inference. cuML is flexible with regard to the model input data type. However, internally, most models represent data as 1D and 2D arrays. Therefore, the best performance can be obtained by passing CuPy arrays instead of cuDF DataFrames.

Additionally, some models may perform better when the arrays use F-ordering, whereby data in columns is contiguous. Use benchmarking to verify whether this is the case for the model of choice.

Finally, since cuML also runs on the GPU, the general advice of using mainly `float32` as a data type still applies.

The next steps

This section demonstrated that training a machine learning model with cuML is straightforward. However, this example barely scratches the surface of real-world machine learning. Topics such as hyperparameter tuning, feature engineering, model interpretability, deployment, monitoring, and detecting data drift were not explored. Libraries such as scikit-learn and cuML make it easy to fit and use models, but as illustrated in this chapter, that is only a very small part of a full workflow. Most of the effort lies in preparing the data, designing experiments, interpreting results, and iterating based on what the data reveals. While modern models seem to behave like powerful black boxes, relying on them without understanding their limitations can be risky. A skilled practitioner goes beyond the abstractions and develops an intuition for how models work and how to apply them responsibly.

When to use cuML

This section compares cuML to other libraries and frameworks for building and training machine learning models.

cuML versus scikit-learn

According to the official documentation, cuML can speed up scikit-learn models by a factor of 10–50 times. This was confirmed by quick benchmarks performed by the authors. *Figure 9.3* plots training and inference times in `RandomForestRegressor` from scikit-learn and cuML for different DataFrame sizes on log-log axes. As always, the benefits of the GPU become greater with larger datasets to process.

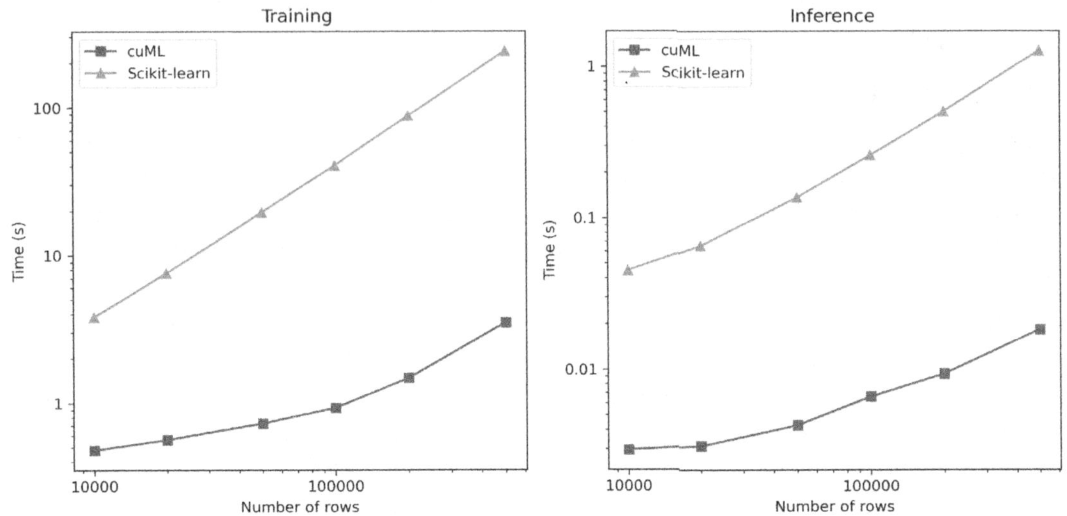

Figure 9.7 – Time to train and perform inference using a RandomForestRegressor model from cuML and scikit-learn

For realistic datasets, cuML is always the most performant and thus preferred option if the hardware is available. DataFrames smaller than 10,000 rows are usually too small for training useful machine learning models. Since inference is relatively fast and is often performed on small data, scikit-learn may be preferred from a cost perspective.

cuML versus Pytorch, JAX, or TensorFlow

If the task at hand requires neural networks and deep learning, cuML is not the appropriate library. cuML and scikit-learn focus on models with relatively few parameters that can be packaged in a class with a uniform interface. Neural networks are too customizable to fit into this framework. Even though neural networks receive a lot of attention, the tree-based models available in cuML are the simplest and often best models for fitting structured data.

How to write GPU-agnostic cuML code

Similar to the `cudf.pandas` accelerator shipped with cuDF, cuML ships `cuml.accel`, which enables scikit-learn code to be accelerated on the GPU without code changes. To enable it, run the following lines before importing or using scikit-learn:

```
import cuml
cuml.accel.install()
```

Alternatively, in a Jupyter notebook, add and run the following line at the top of the notebook:

```
%%load_ext cuml.accel
```

Just like the `cudf.pandas` accelerator, if functionality is not available in cuML, `cuml.accel` falls back on scikit-learn. Therefore, implicit data transfers are possible.

Summary

This chapter introduced two libraries from the RAPIDS ecosystem: cuDF and cuML. cuDF provides a familiar, pandas-like API for high-performance data manipulation on GPU, while cuML offers GPU-accelerated implementations of common machine learning algorithms. Effective use of these libraries requires thinking in terms of GPU-friendly workflows: keeping data on the GPU, choosing appropriate data types, and avoiding unnecessary memory transfers.

While cuDF and cuML make GPU acceleration accessible, they do not replace the need for careful data preparation, feature engineering, and thoughtful experimentation. For small datasets, CPU-based libraries such as pandas and scikit-learn may still be faster, and understanding the limitations of black-box models remains important. Common pitfalls and performance considerations were highlighted for both libraries. Underneath the hood, these libraries are built on top of CUDA kernels, so all the concepts from the previous chapters still apply.

The next chapter introduces JAX, a library for high-performance tensor computations, optimization, and deep learning. JAX offers built-in automatic differentiation and **just-in-time (JIT)** compilation, and can run seamlessly on both the CPU and GPU. It provides a flexible, high-level foundation for a wide range of numerical and machine learning tasks, making it a powerful tool for research and production workflows alike.

Questions

1. In the California housing dataset, can the cut-off data be removed?
2. Suppose there is an extra column, `district_id`, in the California housing dataset, which refers to the `id` column in another table containing information about the district (such as `name`, `city`, `zip_code`, etc.). How can a DataFrame be constructed that contains the largest median district house price per city?
3. What is the general workflow for training a machine learning model using cuML?
4. Why does cuDF support both `NaN` and `NA` in a column of `float`, but pandas does not?
5. Why can't cuDF data be plotted directly with `matplotlib`?

Answers

1. Use filtering, that is, `df[df["MedHouseValue"] < cutoff]`, where `cutoff` is determined by examining the data.
2. First, use `cudf.merge(df_housing_dataset, df_districts, left_on="district_id", right_on="id")` to join the DataFrames. Then, aggregate using `groupby("city")["MedHouseValue"].max()`.
3. Determine the objective, prepare the data with a DataFrame library such as cuDF, explore the data with summary statistics and visualizations, split the data into training and test sets, choose an appropriate cuML model and instantiate it, call `.fit(X_train, y_train)` to fit the model, evaluate the model with metrics and visualize error distributions, and call `.predict(X)` to make inferences.
4. cuDF, built on Apache Arrow, uses null masks to track missing values, enabling explicit support for both `NA` (a true null) and `NaN` (a float). pandas traditionally relied on `NaN` for floats, though newer nullable dtypes (e.g., Float64) now support `pd.NA`.
5. `matplotlib` runs on the CPU and requires data to be resident on the host. Therefore, data needs to be implicitly transferred from the device to the host, which CuPy and cuDF forbid in most scenarios.

10

Solving Optimization Problems on the GPU with JAX

In this chapter, we will focus on JAX, a Python library designed for scientific computing, to solve optimization problems on the GPU. We'll use JAX to develop both a linear regression model and a neural network from scratch. Additionally, we'll construct a **physics-informed neural network** by incorporating physical laws into the training process. All these tasks are made possible by JAX's automatic differentiation capabilities. Furthermore, we'll showcase the benefits of utilizing JAX's automatic vectorization and **Just-In-Time** (**JIT**) compilation features. By the end of this chapter, you will have gained the knowledge and skills to build gradient-based solutions that can be applied to various machine learning problems.

We will cover the following topics:

- JAX's key features, including automatic differentiation, automatic vectorization, and JIT compilation
- Identifying optimization problems that are suited for automatic differentiation
- Implementing gradient-based optimization in both machine learning and scientific computing contexts
- Using JAX to execute complex tasks on the GPU

Introduction to JAX's key features

JAX is an open source framework available in Python for array-oriented computation, making it ideal for machine learning applications. JAX offers an API like NumPy and is optimized for modern hardware accelerators.

Here's how to create arrays in JAX:

```
import jax
import jax.numpy as jnp

x = jnp.array([1, 2, 3])  # Create an array
y = jnp.zeros((2, 2))     # Create a zero matrix
z = jnp.ones((3, 3))      # Create a matrix of ones
```

We import the `jax.numpy` module, which is an almost drop-in replacement for NumPy. Most NumPy operations have direct counterparts in JAX, such as the following:

- **Basic arithmetic**:

  ```
  a = jnp.array([1, 2, 3])
  b = jnp.array([4, 5, 6])
  c = a + b
  d = a * b
  ```

- **Reduction operations**:

  ```
  sum_a = jnp.sum(a)
  mean_a = jnp.mean(a)
  ```

If a GPU is available, JAX typically defaults to using it for computations; otherwise, it runs on the CPU. We can explicitly place arrays in a specific device using the following:

```
x = jax.device_put(
    jnp.array([1.0, 2.0]),
    device=jax.devices("gpu")[0]
)
```

Here, `jax.device_put` transfers an array to a device, and `jax.devices("gpu")` returns a list of all available GPUs (empty if none are detected). Selecting `[0]` chooses the first GPU.

Unlike NumPy, JAX arrays are **immutable**, which means that operations on JAX arrays produce new arrays rather than modifying existing ones. This immutability aligns with functional programming principles and enables safe parallel execution and optimization during JIT compilation. For instance, JAX uses immutability for efficient parallel execution, as multiple threads can work on the same array simultaneously. This makes JAX an excellent choice for machine learning applications that heavily rely on array computing.

In the following sections, we will separately elaborate on JAX's key features.

JIT compilation

Like Numba, JAX supports JIT compilation. This feature allows for the automatic conversion of Python code into optimized accelerator code at runtime. Underlying JAX's JIT functionality is the **Accelerated Linear Algebra (XLA)** compiler developed by Google. XLA is specifically designed to optimize linear algebra and tensor computations. Additionally, XLA is a single compiler that lets the same JAX program run unchanged on CPU, GPU, and **tensor processing unit (TPU)**.

Let's explore how JAX's JIT compilation works. First, we define a dummy kernel as follows:

```
def kernel(x):
  result = 0
  for index in range(10):
      result += index * jnp.sin(jnp.cos(x))
  return jnp.sum(result)
```

Then, we generate a random array as input data:

```
x = jax.random.normal(jax.random.key(2024), shape=(100_000, ))
print(f"{x.shape=}, {x.dtype=}, {x.device=}")
```

```
x.shape=(100000,), x.dtype=dtype('float32'), x.device=CudaDevice(id=0)
```

We measure the execution time of the implemented function call without JIT compilation:

```
%timeit kernel(x).block_until_ready()
```

```
2.39 ms ± 104 µs per loop (mean ± std. dev. of 7 runs, 100 loops each)
```

As JAX uses *asynchronous dispatch*, calling the `block_until_ready()` method on JAX arrays locks Python program execution until those arrays are finished computing. This is recommended when writing micro-benchmarks for computation times. The reported result shows 2.4 ms, the average time taken per loop.

Now, we create a JIT-compiled version of the same function and measure its execution time:

```
jitted_kernel = jax.jit(kernel)
jitted_kernel(x) # Warm-up call
```

```
%timeit jitted_kernel(x).block_until_ready()
```

```
67.5 µs ± 808 ns per loop (mean ± std. dev. of 7 runs, 10,000 loops each)
```

A warmup call for the JIT function is generally executed to compile and optimize its performance before assessing its speed. We could also use `jax.jit` with Python's @ decorator syntax instead. The compiled function runs 35 times faster compared to the non-compiled version, showcasing the significant performance enhancement achieved through JIT compilation.

Under the hood, JAX uses **JAX expressions (jaxprs)**, which are JAX's internal **intermediate representation (IR)** of primitive operations of JAX programs. Think of jaxprs as the internal *blueprint* that JAX uses to understand and manipulate Python code.

`jax.max_jaxpr` can be used to inspect the jaxpr representation of a function as follows:

```
jax.make_jaxpr(lambda x: jnp.sin(x)*2 + 1)(jnp.array([1, 2]))
```

The output of JAX's internal representation for the preceding lambda function is shown here:

```
{ lambda ; a:i32[2]. let
    b:f32[2] = convert_element_type[new_dtype=float32 weak_type=False] a
    c:f32[2] = sin b
    d:f32[2] = mul c 2.0
    e:f32[2] = add d 1.0
  in (e,) }
```

This will output a symbolic representation of the computation graph (jaxpr), showing primitive operations and data dependencies rather than executing the actual numeric computation. This jaxpr defines a computation that takes an integer array with a length of 2 as input, converts it to floating-point, applies the sine function, scales by 2, and then adds 1. The output is a two-element array of floating-point numbers.

Jaxprs allow code execution across various hardware platforms. This capability is particularly valuable when applying transformations such as `jax.jit`, which breaks down complex tasks into a sequence of low-level operations, allowing the compiler to apply optimizations via constant folding, loop unrolling, vectorization, and parallel execution. Once the jaxpr has been optimized, it is converted into machine code that can be executed by a target hardware, such as a CPU or GPU. Furthermore, jaxprs enable JAX to trace and record the underlying flow of instructions to build a computational graph. This is essential for automatic differentiation features in JAX, which we will discuss in the next section.

Automatic differentiation

Automatic differentiation **(autodiff)** is a computational technique used to automatically calculate the derivatives of functions. Unlike numerical differentiation, which approximates derivatives using finite differences, or symbolic differentiation, which manipulates expressions to find derivatives, autodiff evaluates derivatives exactly and efficiently by applying the chain rule of calculus systematically. Nowadays, autodiff plays a pivotal role in deep learning frameworks such as PyTorch, TensorFlow, and JAX. Efficient computation of gradients of complex functions is valuable for optimization algorithms such as gradient descent, which forms the basis for much of machine learning. Autodiff is the core feature of JAX that simplifies and accelerates the process of computing gradients. It provides several functions to perform differentiation, the most prominent being `jax.grad`, which computes gradients of scalar-valued functions with respect to their inputs.

Let's consider the previous example kernel. Using `jax.grad`, we can easily calculate the gradient of the kernel function with respect to each input using the following code:

```
gradient_kernel = jax.grad(kernel)

%timeit gradient_kernel(x).block_until_ready()
```

```
20.5 ms ± 549 µs per loop (mean ± std. dev. of 7 runs, 10 loops each)
```

The `gradient_kernel` function takes the same input as the original kernel and calculates the gradient of the function with respect to one of the input arguments. By default, the gradient is with respect to the first input argument, but this can be adjusted via the `argnums` argument.

JAX allows us to combine `jax.grad` with `jax.jit` in any order to create a function that automatically calculates the gradient of the kernel. By doing so, we utilize JAX's automatic differentiation to compute gradients, while also benefiting from JIT compilation:

```
jitted_gradient_kernel = jax.jit(gradient_kernel)

%timeit jitted_gradient_kernel(x).block_until_ready()
```

```
59.5 µs ± 1.25 µs per loop (mean ± std. dev. of 7 runs, 10,000 loops each)
```

This code further JIT-compiles the `gradient_kernel` function with JAX and then benchmarks its execution time on the `x` input. This application of `jax.jit` resulted in a significant increase in performance, up to 32 times. We can still achieve better performance by utilizing vectorization, as we'll discuss in the next section.

Automatic vectorization

Vectorized computation refers to the process of applying operations to an entire array rather than individual elements. This is like the `vectorize` feature in Numba, which we discussed in *Chapter 3*. Automatic vectorization utilizes the capabilities of modern CPUs and GPUs to perform computations in parallel, resulting in faster execution times. To write efficient code in Python, we already know that we should avoid using explicit loops on the Python level most of the time and instead rely on the efficient implementation of the universal functions that operate on arrays, which are optimized for us by JAX/NumPy developers. While low-level implementations, such as those that we have previously used in Numba-CUDA, employ numerous loops, the approach in numerical Python with JAX, or NumPy-like API libraries in general, emphasizes avoiding loops and translating logic into vector functions. The `jax.vmap` transformation is designed to generate a vectorized implementation of a function automatically, making it easier to apply a function over arrays in parallel. Also, it simplifies the code by removing the need for explicit loops.

An example of calculating distances between arrays of positional vectors is particularly relevant in this context, as determining the distances between points is often needed in scientific calculations. Assume that we have two arrays, `x` and `y`, each containing positional vectors. Both arrays have dimensions, `(N, 3)`, where `N` represents the number of points, and each vector in the array contains 3D coordinates. We want to compute a distance matrix of the `(N, N)` shape that describes the distances between every pair of points from these arrays.

The following function returns this matrix of distances between the two input arrays:

```
def calculate_distances(x, y):
    distances = []
    rows, _ = x.shape
    for i in range(rows):
        distances_from_single_point = jnp.sqrt(
            ((x[i] - y)**2).sum(axis=1)
        )
        distances.append(distances_from_single_point)
    return jnp.array(distances)
```

This task can be automatically and efficiently vectorized in JAX. Using `jax.vmap`, we can transform the function that operates on a single point into one that processes the entire array of position vectors in parallel. To achieve this, we first define the function to handle a single point, namely, `calculate_distances_from_single_point`. Then, using `jax.vmap`, we generalize this function to apply it across the first index of the input arrays, enabling efficient computation over batches without any for loops. This approach not only simplifies the code but also takes advantage of JAX's optimization capabilities for faster execution:

```
def calculate_distances_from_single_point(xi, y):
    return jnp.sqrt(((xi - y)**2).sum(axis=1))

vmapped_calculate_distances = jax.vmap(
    calculate_distances_from_single_point,
    in_axes=(0, None),
)
```

Here, in_axes=(0, None) specifies the input axes for the vectorized function. In this case, the first argument (xi) is mapped along with the first axis (0), while the second argument (y) remains unchanged (None), indicating that it remains unchanged across all computations. We check that both implementations produce identical results:

```
x = jax.random.normal(
    jax.random.key(1234),
    shape=(100, 3),
)

assert jnp.allclose(
  calculate_distances(x, x),
  vmapped_calculate_distances(x, x),
)
```

The assertion statement ensures that the distances computed by the for loop implementation are equal to those computed by the vectorized implementation. However, the performance of the mapped function is significantly faster due to better vectorization. Additionally, the implementation is more readable. Note that, unlike the stateful pseudorandom number generators that users of NumPy may be accustomed to, JAX random functions all require an explicit state to be passed as a first argument. The random state is described by a special array element type that we call a key, usually generated by jax.random.key.

The time profiling results clearly demonstrate these differences, as follows:

```
%timeit calculate_distances(x, x).block_until_ready()
65.4 ms ± 979 µs per loop (mean ± std. dev. of 7 runs, 10 loops each) %timeit
vmapped_calculate_distances(x, x).block_until_ready()
```

```
920 µs ± 10.9 µs per loop (mean ± std. dev. of 7 runs, 1,000 loops each)
```

We can now again combine JIT compilation with `jax.vmap` to achieve improved performance:

```
jitted_vmapped_calculate_distances = jax.jit(vmapped_calculate_distances)
jitted_vmapped_calculate_distances(x, x)  # warmup call

%timeit jitted_vmapped_calculate_distances(x, x).block_until_ready()
```

```
59.2 µs ± 1.95 µs per loop (mean ± std. dev. of 7 runs, 10,000 loops each)
```

This combination maximizes the efficiency of our computations up to three orders of magnitude by taking full advantage of JAX.

In what follows, we'll explore how to use these JAX capabilities to solve some of the optimization problems in practical scenarios. To begin, we'll start with a simple example – building a linear regression model.

Building a linear regression model with JAX

Linear regression is a statistical method used for modeling the relationship between a dependent variable (target) and one or more independent variables (features). Linear regression assumes a linear relationship between the input features and the target output. It can be mathematically represented as follows:

$$y = \sum_{i=1}^{n} w_i \, x_i + b$$

Here, y is the target output that we are trying to predict. x_i refers to input features that influence y, and n is the total number of features. w_i is the weights associated with each input feature, and b is the value of y when all x_i features are zero. The objective is to estimate these parameters (*w1*, *w2*, ..., *wn*, and *b*) in such a way that the function fits the data as closely as possible. In two dimensions, this function represents a line. In higher dimensions, this function is a hyperplane.

Linear regression as an optimization problem

Linear regression is fundamentally an optimization problem that aims to find the parameters that minimize a loss function. The loss indicates how well the model fits the data. The **mean squared error** (**MSE**) is often used as a loss function for regression tasks, which can be defined as follows:

$$L = \frac{1}{m}\sum_{j=1}^{m}[y^{(j)} - \left(\sum_{i=1}^{n} w_i\, x_i^{(j)} + b\right)]^2$$

Index j refers to each observed training data point, and m is the total number of training data points. Once the parameters are estimated, the linear regression model can be used to predict the dependent variable for new values of the input features.

We utilize the **gradient descent** (**GD**) algorithm to find the best-fitting parameters for our model due to its simplicity, efficiency, and ease of implementation. GD iteratively updates the values of w_i and b based on the gradients of the loss function, minimizing the error in each step:

$$w_i \leftarrow w_i - \eta\frac{\partial L}{\partial w_i}$$

$$b \leftarrow b - \eta\frac{\partial L}{\partial b}$$

Here, $\partial L/\partial w_i$ and $\partial L/\partial b$ refer to the gradient of the loss function with respect to the corresponding w_i and b parameters. The parameters are iteratively updated in the direction opposite to the gradient to reduce the loss function. The step size is controlled by the learning rate, η.

Now that we have learned about the basic mathematical requirements, let's consider an example of implementing a linear regression model in practice using JAX.

Calculating electrical resistance with noisy measurements

As an example, we will build a model based on the measurements of current (A) versus voltage (V) in a circuit (*Figure 10.1*) to estimate the resistance, R:

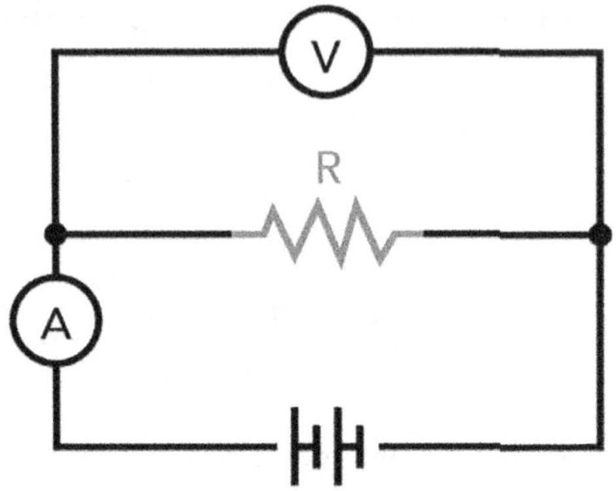

Figure 10.1 – A simple circuit diagram to verify Ohm's law

The diagram illustrates Ohm's law, which relates measured current, voltage, and resistance values in an electrical circuit.

The linear relation between current and voltage can be theoretically described by Ohm's law:

$$V = IR$$

However, if we assume some noise or errors in our measurements, we might not get exact values. Instead, we collect data points of I and V. Suppose we have the following data (in arbitrary units):

```
import numpy as np
from numpy.typing import NDArray

true_w, true_b = 2.0, 1.0
def generate_data() -> tuple[NDArray, NDArray]:
    xs = np.random.uniform(size=(128, 1))
    noise = np.random.normal(size=xs.shape) * 0.1
    return xs, xs * true_w + true_b + noise

xs, ys = generate_data()
```

The inputs (xs) are generated from a uniform distribution, and the outputs (ys) are calculated using predefined parameters and the input values. A normal (Gaussian) distribution of random noise is added to the linear relationship to simulate real-world conditions.

The following figure illustrates the current/voltage data along with measurement errors:

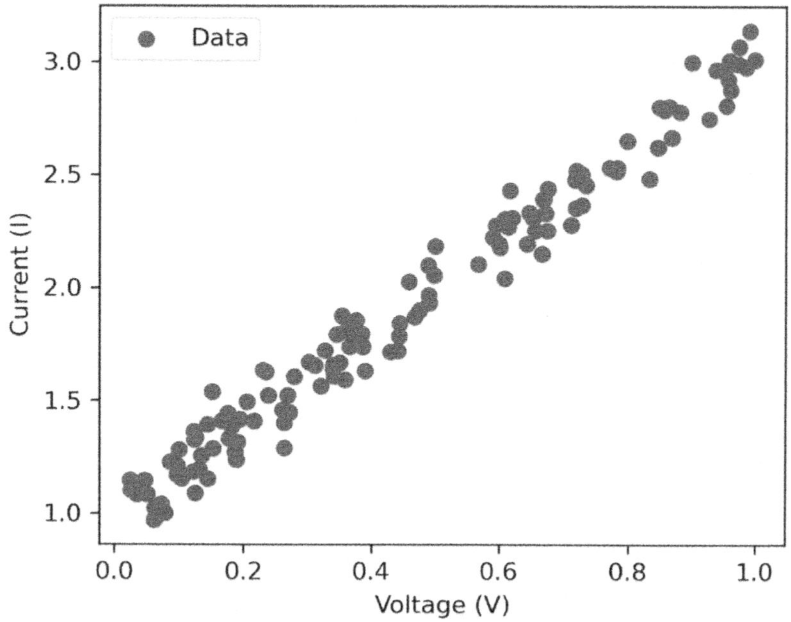

Figure 10.2 – Current/voltage measurements

We suspect that there is a linear relationship between I and V, but it might be slightly off due to measurement errors or other factors. We can set up a linear regression model with two features, as follows:

$$I = w * V + b$$

To find w and b, we can use our data points to solve the linear regression problem. The goal is to minimize the loss function. Once we find w, we know that resistance, R, can be obtained via the following:

$$R = \frac{1}{w}$$

First, we need to import `jax` and `jax.numpy`. We also define a type alias named `Array` that refers to `jnp.ndarray` as follows:

```
import jax
import jax.numpy as jnp
from typing import TypeAlias

Array: TypeAlias = jnp.ndarray
```

Next, we implement a simple linear regression model using JAX and its NumPy-like interface:

```
Params: TypeAlias = tuple[Array, Array]

def linear_regression(params: Params, x: Array) -> Array:
    weight, bias = params
    return weight * x + bias
```

The `Params` type alias is defined to represent model parameters, comprising two arrays for unknown weights and biases. The `linear_regression` function then utilizes this parameter structure to perform linear regression calculations.

Let's now implement the MSE loss function as follows:

```
def loss(params: Params, x: Array, y: Array) -> Array:
    y_pred = linear_regression(params, x)
    return jnp.mean((y - y_pred) ** 2)
```

This calls the linear regression model to compute the predicted outputs (`y_pred`) based on the given input data, `x`, and `params`. We then compute the MSE between the actual target outputs, `y`, and the predicted outputs using `jnp.mean`.

The `update` function, shown as follows, calculates the gradient of the loss function and performs one step of GD update for our linear regression model:

```
@jax.jit
def update(
    params: Params,
    x: Array,
    y: Array,
    lr: float,
) -> Params:
    """Performs one step GD update."""
    grads = jax.grad(loss)(params, x, y)
    return jax.tree.map(
        lambda param, grad: param - grad * lr, params, grads
    )
```

The `@jax.jit` decorator compiles the `update` function using JIT compilation and allows for more efficient execution by transforming the Python code into machine code that is optimized for performance. We don't need to manually JIT-compile every function that is called from inside a jitted function. When we apply the `jax.jit` decorator to a function, JAX will automatically handle compiling any functions it calls as part of its compilation process. General advice is to use `jax.jit` on top-level functions in the call stack when we have nested JIT-compiled functions. This will avoid the overhead associated with individual function compilations. By compiling all relevant functions together, JAX can optimize the entire computation graph and take advantage of various compiler optimizations.

`jax.grad(loss)(params, x, y)` computes the gradients of the loss with respect to the parameters using JAX's `grad` function. Note that the result is a named tuple containing the gradients for each parameter. `jax.tree.map` updates the parameters using the computed gradients and the specified `learning_rate`. This applies a function element-wise to each node in a nested PyTree (in this case, the parameter tuple). The `lambda param, grad: param - grad * learning_rate` lambda function takes each parameter and its corresponding gradient and updates it by subtracting the product of the gradient and the learning rate from the current parameter value.

`jax.tree.map` is a utility function in JAX that applies a given function to each node in a nested **PyTree** and constructs a new PyTree with the results. A PyTree is a nested collection of arrays, lists, dicts, named tuples, tuples, or any other hashable Python objects.

Finally, we iteratively update the model parameters as follows:

```
learning_rate = 0.005
params = 0.0, 0.0
for step in range(10_000):
    if step % 1000 == 0:
        w, b = params
        print(f"w_pred: {float(w):<0.8f}, b_pred: {float(b):<0.8f}")
    params = update(params, xs, ys, learning_rate)

print(f"Estimated resistance (1/w) is {1/params[0]:<0.8f}")
```

```
Estimated resistance (1/w) is 0.51942104
```

This initializes parameters, updates them using the `update` function over many epochs (10,000 in this case), and prints intermediate results to monitor convergence. This approach helps ensure that the model learns from the training data by adjusting its parameters to minimize the **MSE** loss.

The following figure shows model predictions:

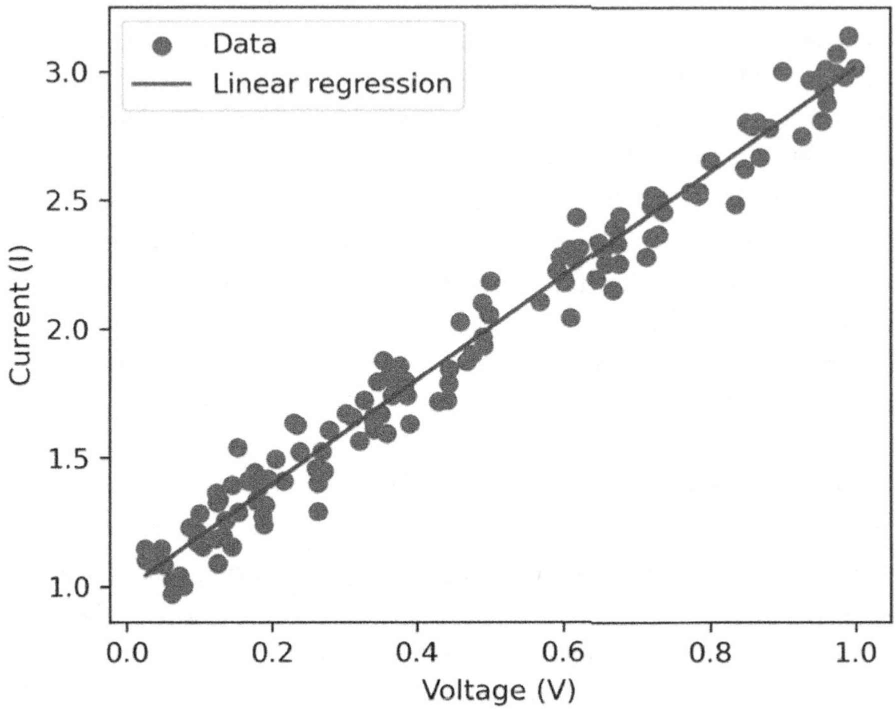

Figure 10.3 – Linear regression predictions on current/voltage measurements

By optimizing the model parameters, we minimize the distance between the linear regression model and the actual data. This enables us to accurately estimate resistance parameters with a value of `0.52` (exact value is `0.50`). The linear model can also be used to predict current values for a new voltage. Our trained linear regression model can also be used for predictions of unknown current or voltage. This example demonstrates how linear regression can be used in practical applications to estimate desired physical quantities.

Let's now move on and investigate the world of neural networks and learn how to create a network on the GPU from scratch using JAX.

Building a neural network

Artificial neural networks (**ANNs**) are a powerful type of machine learning algorithm inspired by the structure and function of the human brain. ANNs learn from data by identifying patterns and relationships, allowing them to perform tasks such as image recognition, natural language processing, time series forecasting, and more. We'll focus on building a **multi-layer perceptron** (**MLP**), which is a specific type of ANN that consists of multiple layers of neurons.

How MLP works

MLPs are commonly used for supervised learning tasks such as classification and regression. The following figure shows a schematic representation of an MLP:

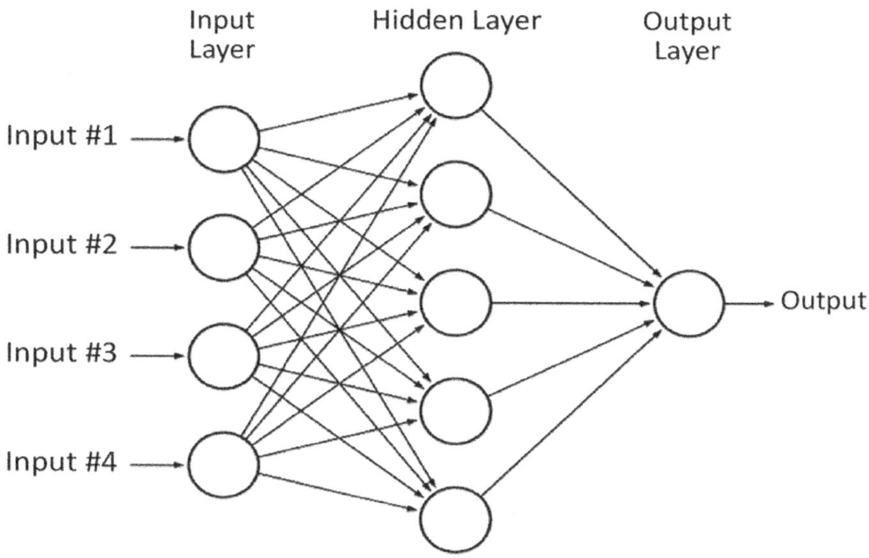

Figure 10.4 – MLP including input, hidden, and output layers

Each connection between neurons has a *weight* associated with it. This weight determines how strongly one neuron influences another. Think of it like the strength of a synapse in our brain.

Neurons in MLPs are organized into stacked layers, including the *input* layer, which receives the initial data, *hidden* layers, which process the information through multiple stages, and the *output* layer, which produces the result. The greater the number of hidden layers, the deeper the neural network becomes, allowing it to recognize increasingly complex patterns. The **universal approximation theorem** mathematically proves that an MLP with at least one hidden layer with a sufficient number of neurons that use a non-linear activation function can approximate any continuous function to arbitrary accuracy.

In a single layer, each neuron computes a weighted sum of its inputs via a linear transformation, as we discussed before. Then, it applies a non-linear **activation function** and sends the result to the next layer:

$$z^{[l]} = W^{[l]}a^{[l-1]} + b^{[l]}$$

Here $z^{[l]}$ is the weighted sum of inputs pre-activation, $W^{[l]}$ is the weight matrix, $a^{[l-1]}$ is the activation from the previous layer, and $b^{[l]}$ is the bias vector. Subsequently, a non-linear activation function is applied to all the outputs of a layer element-wise:

$$a = \text{ActivationFunction}(z)$$

A common activation function is the `tanh` function. No activation ($a^{[l]} = z^{[l]}$) will be applied to the output layer.

The weight matrix for each layer has dimensions equal to the number of inputs (rows) by the number of neurons in the layer (columns). Each element in this matrix corresponds to the strength of the connection between a specific pair of neurons. MLPs also use a bias vector where each element represents the bias for one neuron. The bias allows the neuron to shift the decision boundary or threshold, effectively allowing for more flexibility in separating different classes or patterns in the input data. The input data progresses through successive layers, where each neuron applies a transformation using a weight matrix and a bias vector. Ultimately, this process results in an output prediction in the final layer.

Just like in linear regression, an MSE loss function is used to measure the error between the predicted output and the actual target. Training an MLP relies on minimizing loss, *L*, by updating the parameters for each layer using (backpropagated) gradients and updating the parameters using GD.

The following section provides details on building an MLP model that can predict the behavior of an example RLC circuit, contains three electronic – components a resistor (**R**), an inductor (**L**), and a capacitor (**C**), based on given measurement data.

Predicting damped oscillation in an RLC circuit

Let's consider an example of an electrical circuit, where the current variation over time, *I(t)*, exhibits more complex behavior. Here is a schematic representation of the RLC circuit:

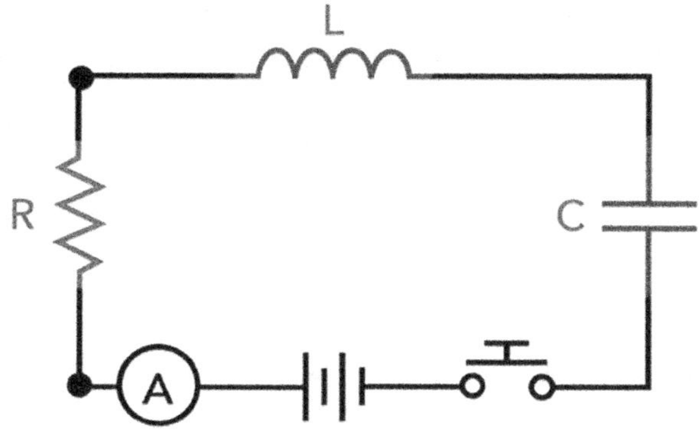

Figure 10.5 – RLC circuit

The interaction between these components in specific cases gives rise to oscillating dynamics, influencing the measured current. Instead of using linear regression, we'll employ a neural network to model these dynamics.

The RLC circuit is governed by a second-order differential equation derived from Kirchhoff's voltage law:

$$\frac{d^2I(t)}{dt^2} + \frac{R}{L}\frac{dI(t)}{dt} + \frac{1}{LC}I(t) = 0$$

For simplicity, we generate synthetic data (x and y) that represents the expected response of the circuit. The goal would then be to use this data to train a network to approximate the RLC circuit's behavior:

```
R, L, C = 0.1, 0.032, 0.1

def rlc_solution(x: NDArray) -> NDArray:
    w0 = np.sqrt(1/(L*C) - R**2/(4*L**2))
    return np.exp(-R * x / (2 * L)) * np.cos(w0 * x)

x = 0.7 * np.random.rand(50, 1)
y = rlc_solution(x)
```

The `rlc_solution` function generates the exact solution for an RLC circuit that is initially charged and operates in a *damped oscillation* mode, given by the following condition:

$$R < \sqrt{4L/C}$$

`w0` is known as the *natural frequency* of the circuit. The output of the function is the current as a time-dependent quantity, without delving into the mathematical method used to derive this solution.

The following figure illustrates the current response of the RLC circuit over time:

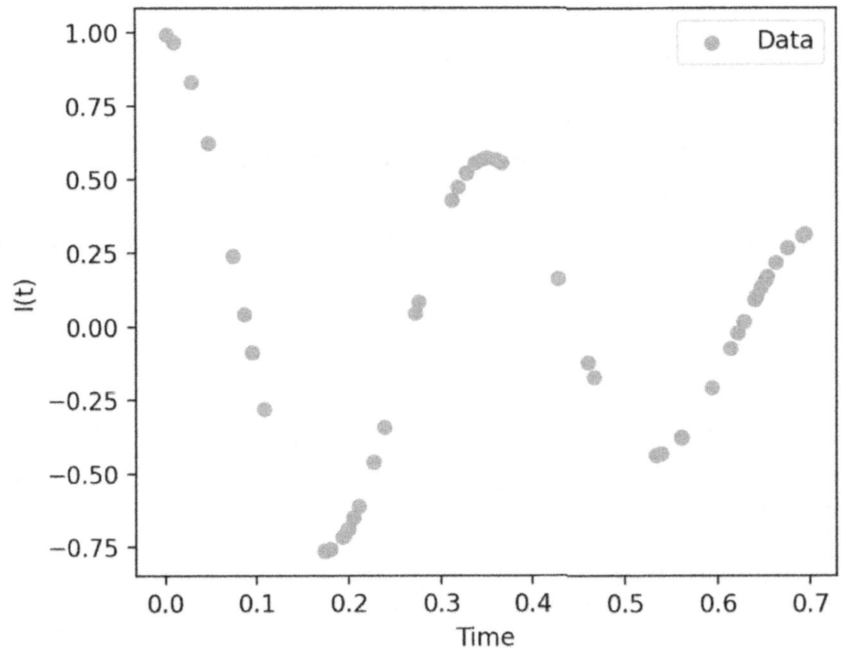

Figure 10.6 – RLC circuit damped oscillation

To proceed with building the neural network model, we set up an MLP with specified hidden layer sizes and initialize its weights and biases using random normal distributions. The following commands define a few useful type aliases to enhance the readability of our implementation:

```
LayerParams: TypeAlias = tuple[Array, Array]
NetworkParams: TypeAlias = tuple[LayerParams, ...]
KeyArray: TypeAlias = jax._src.prng.PRNGKeyArray
```

LayerParams is a tuple containing two Array types, including weights and biases. NetworkParams represents all the parameters in the network. KeyArray is a type alias for a random key for JAX:

```
def initialize_layer(
  input_size: int,
  num_neurons: int,
  key: KeyArray,
) -> LayerParams:
  w_key, b_key = jax.random.split(key)
  return (
    jax.random.normal(w_key, (num_neurons, input_size)),
    jax.random.normal(b_key, (num_neurons,)),
  )
```

The initialize_layer function initializes a single layer of neurons based on the number of inputs and the number of neurons. We split the provided random key into two keys using jax.random.split. These two keys are then used to generate a *pseudorandom* weight matrix and bias vector using jax.random.normal.

We finally initialize the network layers as follows:

```
def initialize_network(
    hidden_sizes: tuple[int, ...],
    key: KeyArray,
    input_size: int = 1,
    output_size: int = 1,
  ) -> NetworkParams:
  sizes = input_size, *hidden_sizes, output_size
  keys = jax.random.split(key, len(sizes))
  return tuple(
    initialize_layer(m, n, k)
    for m, n, k in zip(sizes[:-1], sizes[1:], keys)
)
```

Here, hidden_sizes represents the number of neurons in each hidden layer, and input_size and output_size are the number of inputs to the network and the number of outputs from the network, respectively. This function first creates a tuple of sizes, then it similarly splits the provided key into multiple keys. Splitting the given input key is essential; otherwise, all layers would be initialized with the same random values. Ultimately, we create a tuple of LayerParams for each layer in the network. The number of inputs and outputs for each layer is determined by consecutive elements in the `sizes` tuple, along with the corresponding random key for each layer. Here, we set the number of neurons for each hidden layer, 32 neurons per layer and 3 hidden layers in total, and initialize network parameters with a given random key:

```
hidden_sizes = (32, 32, 32)
params = initialize_network(hidden_sizes, key=jax.random.key(0))
```

We define the activation function for use in our neural network:

```
def activation_function(x: Array) -> Array:
    return jnp.tanh(x)
```

The *hyperbolic tangent* is a common choice for activation functions in neural networks because it squashes the input values between `-1` and `1`, which can help with vanishing gradient issues during training. It also introduces non-linearity into the model. Without a non-linear element, an MLP is identical to linear regression.

Let's now define a function that calculates the output of the neural network for a single input:

```
def neural_network_single(
    params: NetworkParams,
    x: Array
) -> Array:
    inputs = x
    *hidden, last = params
    for w, b in hidden:
        outputs = jnp.dot(w, inputs) + b
        inputs = activation_function(outputs)

    last_w, last_b = last
    logits = jnp.dot(last_w, inputs) + last_b
    return logits
```

This takes two arguments: `params`, which is a `NetworkParams`, and `x`, which is the input data. The parameters are unpacked into a list of tuples containing weights and biases for each hidden layer (`hidden`) and the parameters for the final layer (`last`). A loop iterates over each hidden layer, computing the linear transformation (`jnp.dot(w, inputs) + b`) followed by applying the activation function to the result. After processing all hidden layers, the computation moves to the last layer. The linear transformation is performed (without applying the activation function) to produce the raw unnormalized scores (`logits`).

Now, we can use JAX's auto-vectorization feature (`jax.vmap`) to vectorize `neural_network_single` across multiple inputs:

```
neural_network = jax.vmap(neural_network_single, in_axes=(None, 0))
```

The `(None, 0)` argument specifies that the first argument (`params`) should be broadcast (i.e., not changed), while the second argument (x) should be mapped over its leading dimension (batch size). This allows the neural network to handle a *batch* of inputs simultaneously.

We define (as in the linear regression example) an MSE loss function for evaluating the performance of a neural network during training. Lower loss values indicate better performance:

```
def loss(
    params: NetworkParams,
    x: Array,
    y: Array,
) -> Array:
    y_pred = neural_network(params, x)
    loss_data = jnp.mean((y_pred - y)**2)
    return loss_data
```

Here, `y_pred` computes the predicted outputs from the neural network by calling the `neural_network` function with the given parameters and input data. Also, `loss_data` calculates the MSE between the predicted outputs (y_pred) and the true target values (y). The mean is taken across all elements of the array, giving a scalar value representing the average loss over the batch.

The `update_network` function updates the parameters of the neural network using GD. It computes gradients using JAX's automatic differentiation feature (`jax.grad`) as follows:

```
@jax.jit
def update_network(
  params: NetworkParams,
  x: Array,
  y: Array,
  learning_rate: float,
) -> NetworkParams:
  grads = jax.grad(loss)(params, x, y)
  return tuple(
    (w - learning_rate * dw, b - learning_rate * db)
```

```
        for (w, b), (dw, db) in zip(params, grads)
    )
```

`learning_rate` is set to `0.001`, which determines the step size at each iteration of GD. This function is decorated with `@jax.jit` to compile it for faster execution. `jax.grad(loss)(params, x, y)` computes the gradients of the loss function with respect to the parameters. This step uses automatic differentiation to calculate the partial derivatives. The updated parameters are computed by subtracting the product of the learning rate and the corresponding gradient from each parameter (`w` for weights and `b` for biases).

We use **root mean square error** (**RMSE**) to evaluate the accuracy of the network:

```
def rmse(y_true, y_pred) -> Array:
    return jnp.sqrt(jnp.mean((y_pred-y_true)**2))
```

Finally, training the network can be implemented by iteratively adjusting its parameters to minimize the loss of the training data:

```
x_train, y_train = jnp.asarray(x), jnp.asarray(y)
for epoch in range(50_000):
    if epoch % 5_000 == 0:
        y_pred = neural_network(params, x_train)
        accuracy = rmse(y_train, y_pred)
        print(f"{epoch=:<6d} {accuracy=:<0.8f}")
    params = update_network(
        params, x_train, y_train, learning_rate=0.001
    )
```

The training loop runs for 50,000 epochs. The parameters of the neural network are updated using the `update_network` function with the current parameters, training inputs (`x_train`), and training targets (`y_train`).

The following figure shows the predicted current produced by the trained neural network:

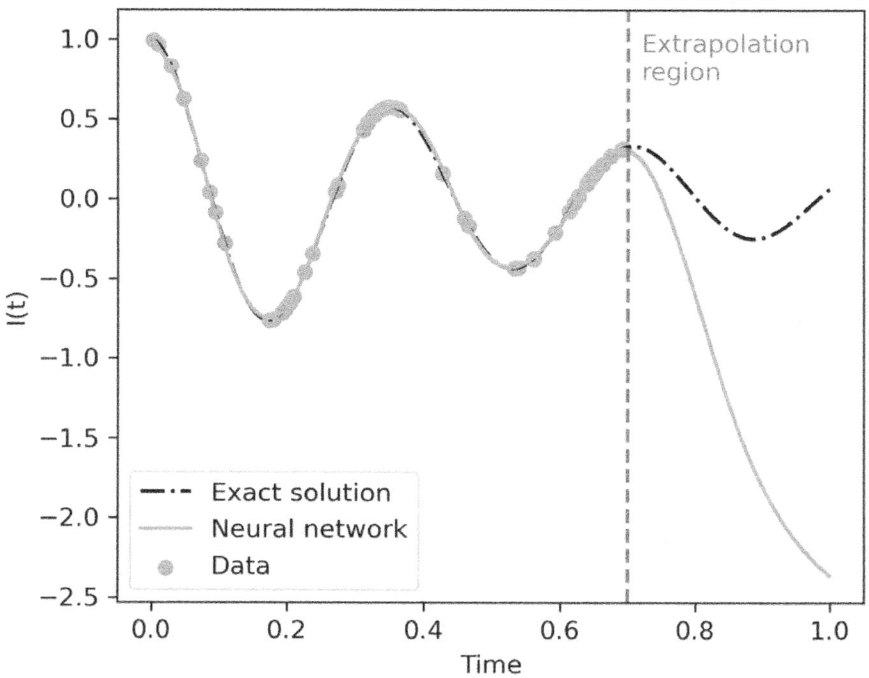

Figure 10.7 – Neural network predictions of the RLC circuit damped oscillation

Our neural network performs remarkably well in predicting the behavior of the RLC circuit within the range of the training data. However, it struggles to make accurate predictions outside this range. This limitation is common for neural networks that are trained exclusively on data; they excel at interpolation but often exhibit poor performance during extrapolation.

In the next section, we delve deeper and explore how to perform physics-informed training of our neural network to address this issue.

Training a physics-informed neural network

Conventional neural networks rely heavily on large amounts of labeled data to generalize effectively. In scenarios where only sparse data points are available, training can lead to overfitting or poor performance. **Physics-informed neural networks** (**PINNs**) are a powerful paradigm for integrating domain knowledge directly into the training process of neural networks. Unlike conventional neural networks, the key power of a PINN lies in its novel definition of the loss function, where known physical laws are embedded directly into the training process, which reduces the need for extensive labeled data. Standard neural networks interpolate well within the range of the training data but often fail to extrapolate to unseen conditions. PINNs, on the other hand, generalize better because the model includes known information about the governing laws, which remain valid regardless of the data's range. Even with noisy or incomplete data, the physics-informed loss acts as a regularizer, guiding the model toward physically plausible solutions.

The loss function used to train the PINN is formulated as a single objective that combines data fidelity and physical consistency. One component of the loss quantifies how closely the neural network predictions match the observed training data, for example, through the MSE. The second component enforces adherence to the governing physical laws by penalizing violations of the underlying equations, achieved by minimizing the residuals of the corresponding differential equation. In this way, the model is not only trained to fit the available data but is also constrained to produce solutions that are consistent with the RLC circuit differential equations. The relative contribution of each loss term to the total loss is typically controlled through weighting factors, allowing a balance between accurate data fitting and strict enforcement of the physical constraints.

To begin with, let us explore how to calculate gradients of currents with respect to time, which is necessary for solving the RLC equation. The following code illustrates the use of JAX's automatic differentiation capabilities to derive required first and second-order gradients:

```
helper_function = lambda p, x: neural_network_single(p, x)[0]
grad_y_single = jax.grad(helper_function, argnums=1)
grad_y = jax.vmap(grad_y_single, in_axes=(None, 0))
```

Here, `helper_function` takes two inputs (parameters and input), computes the output of the neural network for a single input, and returns the first element, which is assumed to be a scalar value. `jax.grad` requires the function's output to be scalar, while the output of `neural_network_single` is an array. `argnums=1` in `jax.grad` specifies that the gradient of `helper_function` should be computed with respect to the second argument (`time`). The default value is the first input argument, which is the network parameters for our case. `jax.vmap` vectorizes `grad_y_single` to apply it across a batch of inputs. By setting `in_axes=(None, 0)`, the first argument remains unchanged, and the second argument is batched along the first dimension.

Up to this point, we have implemented the `grad_y` function that takes the same inputs as the neural network and calculates the first-order gradients of the current with respect to time. We now proceed and calculate second-order gradients:

```
helper_function2 = lambda p, x: grad_y_single(p, x)[0]
grad2_y_single = jax.grad(helper_function2, argnums=1)
grad2_y = jax.vmap(grad2_y_single, in_axes=(None, 0))
```

Similarly, we define helper_function2, which takes the output of grad_y_single to extract the scalar value for a single input. Then, jax.grad computes its gradient with respect to the second parameter and uses jax.vmap to vectorize grad2_y_single across a batch of inputs. The grad2_y function calculates the second-order gradients.

We can now describe the governing physical law in terms of an RLC partial differential equation, using the new *physics-informed* loss function. This loss function integrates both data and physical constraints into the training process:

```
def physics_informed_loss(
        params: NetworkParams,
        x: Array,
        y: Array,
        x_physics: Array,
) -> Array:
    residual = (
        grad2_y(params, x_physics)
        + (R / L) * grad_y(params, x_physics) +
        (1 / (C*L)) * neural_network(params, x_physics)
    )
    loss_physics = 1.0e-4 * jnp.mean(residual**2)
    return loss(params, x, y) + loss_physics
```

This function takes one additional input argument, x_physics, which is used for enforcing physics-based constraints on a wider range of the training data. In addition to the data contribution to the loss, the physical constraint is enforced by computing it as a residual. jnp.mean(residual**2) calculates the MSE of the residual term, scaled by a small constant (1.0e-4). The introduction of these constants serves as a regularization component, ensuring that the physical constraint imposed by the physics-based model is weighted appropriately against the data-driven loss function.

We define the update_pinn function, which executes a single iteration of GD, allowing us to refine the model's parameters using the newly formulated physics-informed loss function:

```
@jax.jit
def update_pinn(
  params: NetworkParams,
  x: Array,
  y: Array,
  x_physics: Array,
  learning_rate: float,
```

```
) -> NetworkParams:
  grads = jax.grad(
      physics_informed_loss
  )(params, x, y, x_physics)
  return tuple(
      (w - learning_rate * dw, b - learning_rate * db)
      for (w, b), (dw, db) in zip(params, grads)
  )
```

And finally, the physics-informed training loop is implemented as follows:

```
params = initialize_network(hidden_sizes, key=jax.random.key(0))
x_train, y_train = jnp.asarray(x), jnp.asarray(y)
x_physics = jnp.linspace(0, 1.0, 20).reshape(-1, 1)

for epoch in range(50_000):
    if epoch % 5_000 == 0:
        accuracy = rmse(y_train, y_pred=neural_network(params, x_train))
        print(f"{epoch=:<6d} {accuracy=:<0.8f}")
    params = update_pinn(
        params, x_train, y_train, x_physics, learning_rate=0.001
    )
```

The two main differences with our previous training approach are the following:

- We additionally defined `x_physics`, which covers the entire domain we are interested in, since we don't need to provide a target value for it.
- We use the physics-informed loss function instead of the regular loss to update model parameters.

The following figure shows the model predictions using PINN training:

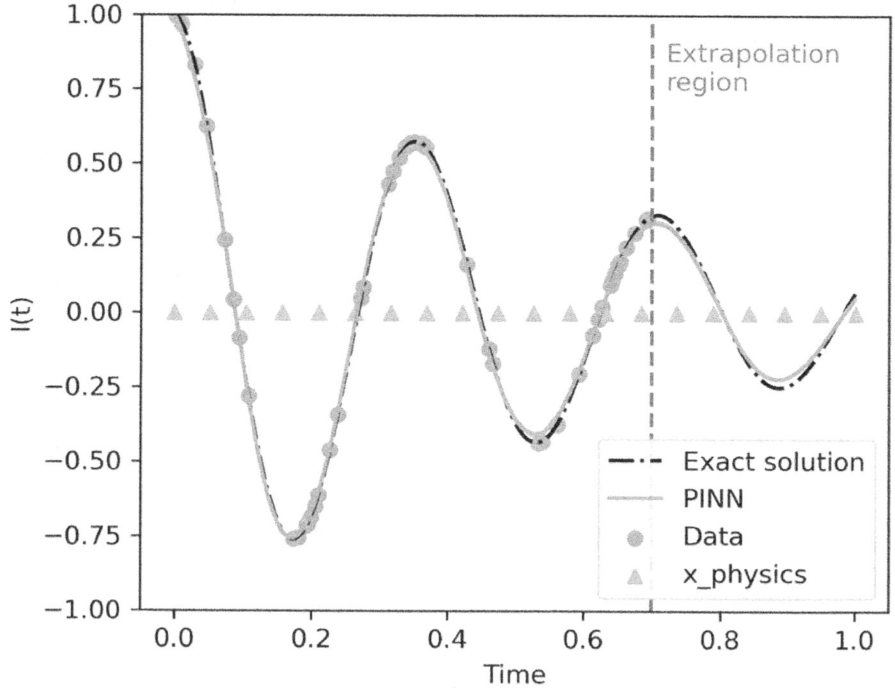

Figure 10.8 – PINN prediction for RLC circuit damped oscillation

It shows that PINN not only performs well for predicting RLC behavior in the region with data, but it also extrapolates better for the region without labeled data(measurements). PINNs combine the strengths of neural networks with physics-based constraints, enabling them to not only predict effectively within known data regions but also extend their capabilities to unknown areas, where traditional models may struggle. This advantage makes PINNs a valuable tool in scenarios where labeled data is limited and physically-informed predictions are necessary.

Even in the absence of data, neural networks can be used to approximate solutions to differential equations by using physics-informed learning. Initial conditions need to be enforced as constraints within the loss function to ensure that the learned solution satisfies both the differential equation and these initial values.

Summary

In this chapter, we explored the capabilities of the high-level JAX library to harness the power of GPU computing through various optimization examples. We began by demonstrating the impact of JIT compilation, achieving performance gains with its use. Next, we explored automatic differentiation, using JAX's autodiff features, which we combined with JIT. `vmap` allowed us to auto-vectorize our functions, further enhancing performance.

We then applied JAX to build a linear regression model and calculated electrical resistance. Next, we extended our approach by implementing a neural network from scratch. This neural network was used to describe the response of an RLC circuit.

To further improve our training process, we incorporated physical laws into the loss function, creating a physics-informed neural network. This enhancement enabled our model to extrapolate beyond its target training data, showcasing its superior advantages over the conventional neural network.

In the next chapter, we'll focus on solving heat equations on the GPU and showcasing a low-level implementation of a finite difference solver using Numba.

Questions

1. How does the accuracy of the PINN change when 10% random noise is added to the training data?
2. What effect does removing physics data from the extrapolation region have on the PINN model's performance?

Answers

1. PINN's accuracy remains relatively stable despite the addition of 10% random noise to the training data.
2. Eliminating physics data in the extrapolation region reduces our PINN's ability to generalize beyond the observed domain, as the model receives no physical constraints outside the observed data.

Get this book's PDF version and more

Scan the QR code (or go to `packtpub.com/unlock`). Search for this book by name, confirm the edition, and then follow the steps on the page.

UNLOCK NOW

Note: Keep your invoice handy. Purchases made directly from Packt don't require an invoice.

Part 4

Real-World Example Applications

This part puts theory into practice with hands-on GPU applications. You'll solve a partial differential equation using finite differences, implement image processing and object detection with convolutional filters and convolutional neural networks, and simulate molecular dynamics for atomic interactions. The final chapter covers building and training a transformer-based language model from scratch using JAX, Flax, and Optax. Each example demonstrates end-to-end GPU acceleration for real-world problems.

This part of the book includes the following chapters:

- *Chapter 11, Solving the Heat Equation on the GPU*
- *Chapter 12, Image Processing and Computer Vision on the GPU*
- *Chapter 13, Simulating Atomic Interactions on the GPU*
- *Chapter 14, Implementing Your Own Transformer-Based Language Model*

11

Solving the Heat Equation on the GPU

This chapter explores how to solve the heat equation, a fundamental **partial differential equation (PDE)** used in science and engineering, such as weather forecasting. We will apply previously introduced concepts, including parallel execution of CUDA kernels and utilization of memory layouts, to optimize the heat equation solver. Solving the heat equation as a **stencil** problem is well-suited for GPUs because each grid point is updated using only its nearest neighbors, meaning the same computation is applied independently, which can be mapped onto the thousands of threads available on a GPU. Additionally, stencil computations involve structured access to memory, which aligns well with GPU memory hierarchies such as caches and shared memory, enabling high throughput and efficient latency hiding. **Numba-CUDA** will be utilized to accelerate the computations, providing practical experience in solving time-dependent PDEs on the GPU. Note that while an understanding of the physical model and the mathematics behind it is beneficial, it's not strictly necessary for following along.

In this chapter, we will cover the following main topics:

- Understanding the basics of the heat equation and the numerical methods for solving it
- Implementing a 2D heat equation simulation
- Parallelizing the solver using CUDA for efficient parallel execution
- Utilizing shared memory for further optimization
- Profiling CUDA kernels and understanding the best practices for performance analysis

Technical requirements

We require a system equipped with a CUDA-enabled NVIDIA GPU that has 1 GB of VRAM. The necessary packages, including *Numba* and the *Nsight Compute CLI* tool, will be used in this chapter. We use Pixi as a dependency management tool that installs these packages. To set up the environment, simply run `pixi install` in the root directory of the book's GitHub repository. This will ensure that all dependencies are installed. Once the installation is complete, you can activate the environment using `pixi shell`.

Run the following command in the terminal to install Pixi.

```
pixi run jupyter-lab
```

This will start JupyterLab, a browser-based environment to run Jupyter notebooks.

The chapter's code is available on GitHub and can be accessed via this link: `https://github.com/PacktPublishing/GPU-Accelerated-Computing-with-Python-3-and-CUDA`. Please check the `README` file for more details and setup instructions.

The heat equation

The heat equation is a time-dependent PDE that describes how temperature evolves over time due to heat conduction in a spatial domain. The heat equation can be expressed as follows:

$$\frac{\partial u}{\partial t} = \alpha \nabla^2 u$$

In this equation, u is the temperature, which is a function of space and time, t. α is the *thermal diffusivity* coefficient, which describes how easily heat can flow through the material. $\nabla^2 u$ represents the **Laplacian** of u, which is a measure of the rate at which the temperature changes along spatial coordinates. In a two-dimensional Cartesian system with x and y as our spatial coordinates, it is given by the following:

$$\nabla^2 u = \frac{\partial^2 u}{\partial x^2} + \frac{\partial^2 u}{\partial y^2}$$

The solution to the 2D heat equation is the $u(x,y,t)$ function, which satisfies the differential equation and appropriate *initial* and *boundary* conditions. The initial condition is the temperature distribution at time $t=0$. The boundary conditions are the conditions that must be satisfied at all t at the boundary of our region of interest. There are some toy examples for which the heat equation can be solved analytically using complex mathematical machinery. However, in most cases, we must rely on numerical approaches, under **linearization** and **discretization** assumptions.

Discretizing the equation

Numerically solving the 2D heat equation involves discretizing both space and time. This means we must split the spatial domain into a grid of points and divide the time into discrete time steps. There are several numerical methods to solve the heat equation, including implicit and explicit methods, each with its own advantages and applications. Here, we will use the explicit **finite difference method** (**FDM**) because it is simple to implement and understand, and it can be used both for structured and unstructured grids. FDMs are part of a broader class of numerical algorithms known as **stencils**, which specify the local region used to approximate values at grid points. This is achieved by applying a small neighborhood around each grid point and using a method to calculate the value at the central point within that neighborhood. Note that numerical techniques always give only an approximate solution. Depending on how we discretize, the error can be made arbitrarily small.

Finite difference method

Let's consider a bounded domain with a uniform grid of points with spacing h in both the x and y directions (see *Figure 11.1*):

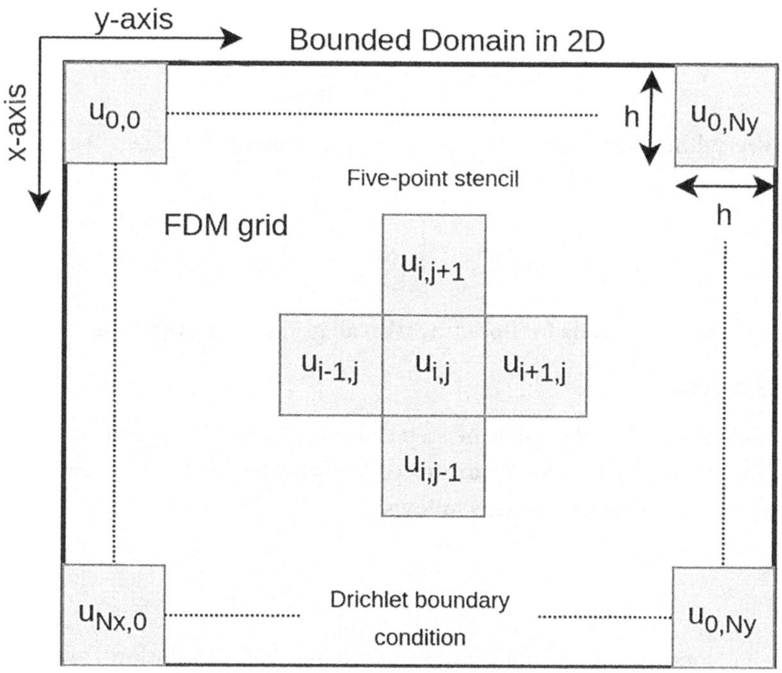

Figure 11.1 – Finite difference grid of points in 2D

$u_{i,jn}$ is the temperature at the grid point (x_i, y_j) at discrete time $t_n = n\delta t$, where n is an integer and δt is the time step. We can now use a finite difference approximation to replace the partial derivatives in the heat equation, essentially by comparing values at nearby points. The second spatial derivative $\partial^2 u/\partial x^2$ at a point (i, j) can be approximated as follows:

$$\frac{\partial^2 u}{\partial x^2}\Big|_{(i,j)} \approx \frac{u^n_{i+1,j} - 2u^n_{i,j} + u^n_{i-1,j}}{h^2}$$

Similarly, the second spatial derivative $\partial^2 u/\partial y^2$ can be approximated as follows:

$$\frac{\partial^2 u}{\partial y^2}\Big|_{(i,j)} \approx \frac{u^n_{i,j+1} - 2u^n_{i,j} + u^n_{i,j-1}}{h^2}$$

Substituting these approximations into the heat equation, we obtain the following:

$$\nabla^2 u\big|_{(i,j)} \approx \frac{u^n_{i+1,j} - 2u^n_{i,j} + u^n_{i-1,j}}{h^2} + \frac{u^n_{i,j+1} - 2u^n_{i,j} + u^n_{i,j-1}}{h^2}$$

For the time derivative, we use forward differentiation:

$$\frac{\partial u}{\partial t}\Big|_{(i,j)} \approx \frac{u^{n+1}_{i,j} - u^n_{i,j}}{\delta t}$$

Substituting everything into the heat equation and solving for *ui,jn*, we get the following equation:

$$u^{n+1}_{i,j} = u^n_{i,j} + \frac{\alpha \delta t}{h^2}\left(u^n_{i+1,j} + u^n_{i-1,j} + u^n_{i,j+1} + u^n_{i,j-1} - 4u^n_{i,j}\right)$$

This gives us an iterative formula for updating u on all grid points over time.

CFL condition

Choosing a small spacing h and small time step δt is crucial for obtaining accurate solutions with FDM. We need to make sure the **Courant–Friedrichs–Lewy** (**CFL**) condition is met. This condition is mathematically expressed as follows:

$$\frac{2\alpha \delta t}{h^2} \leq 1$$

Think of the CFL condition as a rule that keeps our numerical solution stable and accurate. It limits how big our time steps δt can be based on how small our spatial steps h are. If we choose a time step that's too large, the numerical solution can become unstable, leading to unpredictable results.

Initial condition

The initial condition *f(x, y)* at *t=0* is used to initialize the temperature at all grid points:

$$u_{i,j}^{0} = f(x_i, y_j)$$

For our specific example, we will initialize the temperature with a specific distribution centered in the simulation box.

Boundary conditions

We apply **Dirichlet** boundary conditions, which prescribe fixed temperature values at the boundary:

$$u_{0,j}^{n} = u_{N_x,j}^{n} = \text{prescribed value}$$

$$u_{i,0}^{n} = u_{i,N_y}^{n} = \text{prescribed value}$$

Here, N_x and N_y represent the number of points along each direction.

So far, we have all the required numerical formulas for solving our heat equation. The next step is to figure out how to implement them efficiently.

Solving the equation

To begin, let's first import the necessary modules and define aliases:

```
import math
import numpy as np
from numba import njit, cuda
from numpy.typing import NDArray

FLOAT = np.float32
Array = NDArray[FLOAT]
```

`FLOAT` allows us to specify the desired floating-point precision, and the `Array` type annotation alias helps to improve our code readability. Keep in mind that GPU performance can differ between `float32` and `float64` based on hardware support. Most modern consumer GPUs have specialized hardware that can process single-precision data very efficiently, while only data center GPUs (e.g., NVIDIA A100) provide strong double-precision support. We'll use `float32` precision for our simulations.

Initializations

We set all the required parameters, including the system mesh sizes (nx, ny), diffusion coefficient (alpha), spatial step (h), and time step (dt):

```
nx, ny = 1024, 1024
alpha = 0.1
h = 0.01
dt = 0.5 * (h**2 / (2 * alpha))
assert (2*alpha*dt/h**2) <= 1.0
nu = FLOAT(alpha * dt / h**2)
```

We set the time step to be half of the CFL requirement to ensure the numerical stability of the solution. The assertion statement further checks whether the calculated time step satisfies the CFL condition. If the condition is not met, this will raise an error. We also define the nu coefficient based on other parameters and explicitly cast it to FLOAT, as it will be used later in our JIT-compiled solver function.

Next, we implement the initialize_system function to set up the initial temperature distribution and boundary conditions for the given spacing:

```
def initialize_system((
    mesh: tuple[int, int],
    spacing: float,
) -> Array:
    nx, ny = mesh
    x, y = np.meshgrid(
        np.arange(nx, dtype=FLOAT) * spacing,
        np.arange(ny, dtype=FLOAT) * spacing,
    )
    # Set initial temperature distribution
    u = np.exp(
        -1.0 * ((x - x.mean()) ** 2 + (y - y.mean()) ** 2
    )
    # Apply boundary conditions
    u[0, :] = u[:, 0] = 0.0
    u[-1, :] = u[:, -1] = 0.0
    return u
```

The np.meshgrid function creates a grid of points for the x and y coordinates. We also initialize the temperature array using a *Gaussian distribution* centered at the middle of the grid points. As boundary conditions, we set all points on the edges of the mesh (first and last rows and columns) to `0.0`.

We can initialize the system as follows:

```
u = initialize_system(mesh=(nx, ny), spacing=h)
```

The following figure shows the initial temperature distribution of the system that has been set up:

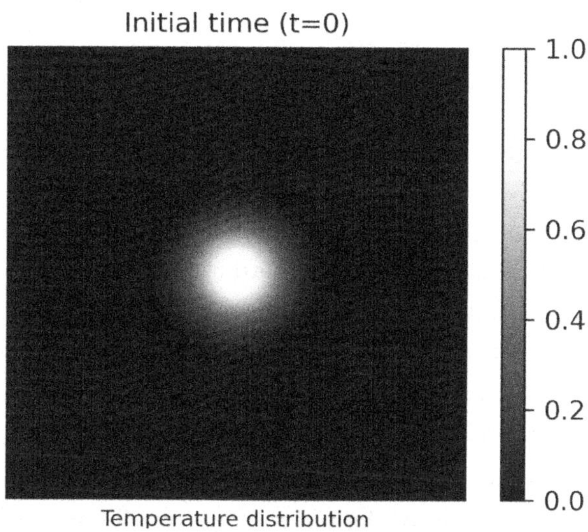

Figure 11.2 – Initial temperature distribution

The initial temperature is highest at the central point and decreases in intensity toward the edges in the form of a 2D bell shape. On the right side, the color bar shows how temperature values are mapped to colors. It may not be visible, but dark boundary lines exist at the edges of the plot in line with our boundary conditions.

Now, we will proceed to implement the solver that calculates the system evolution over time.

CPU implementation

Before delving into the GPU implementation, let's explore how to implement the solver on the CPU. Here's an example of how we might implement it using a function compiled with Numba JIT:

```
@njit
def solve_heat_equation(
    u: Array,
```

```
    u_new: Array,
    nu: FLOAT,
) -> None:
    for i in range(1, u.shape[0] - 1):
        for j in range(1, u.shape[1] - 1):
            uij = u[i, j]
            laplacian = (
                u[i + 1, j] + u[i - 1, j]
                + u[i, j + 1] + u[i, j - 1]
                - 4 * uij
            )
            u_new[i, j] = uij + nu * laplacian
```

The preceding implementation is straightforward, following the FDM formula we've already discussed. We use two nested loops over the `i` and `j` indices to iterate over all the points in the mesh. Note that we exclude the boundary, so our boundary conditions remain valid. The updated temperature distribution is stored in the `u_new` output array, which is passed as an argument. Numba JIT compilation, enabled through the `numba.njit` decorator, aims simply to get acceptable performance. We also ensure efficient data access by iterating over `j` as the inner loop. This minimizes cache misses as the default arrangement of data on the memory location is row major. This will be discussed further in the GPU memory layout section.

Next, we call this solver iteratively to find the temperature distribution for a specified number of steps. This simulates the evolution of the temperature distribution, starting with a centered Gaussian temperature distribution and Dirichlet boundary conditions:

```
%%time
u_new = u.copy()
for step in range(10_000):
    if step % 1_000 == 0:
        print(f"Step -> {step:<6d} u_max: {u.max():<0.8f}")
    solve_heat_equation(u, u_new, nu)
    u, u_new = u_new, u
```

The `u_new` is the temperature distribution at the next step. It is initialized as a copy of `u` to ensure that the boundary conditions remain valid. The `for` loop runs 10,000 time steps. Each iteration represents a small time increment in the simulation. To monitor the computation, every 1,000 steps, we print the time step and the maximum temperature. Here are the timing results:

```
CPU times: user 5.13 s, sys: 0 ns, total: 5.13 s
Wall time: 5.13 s
```

The heart of this simulation, the `solve_heat_equation` function, updates the temperature distribution from the current time, `u`, to the next step, `u_new`. After each step, we use a useful trick of swapping `u` and `u_new` to prepare for the next time step with `u, u_new = u_new, u`. In Python, this is a zero-copy operation that just swaps the `u` and `u_new` pointers, meaning that `u` for the next time step points to the data of `u_new` of the previous step, and `u_new` for the next time step points to `u` from the previous time step, which is data that can safely be overwritten. This allows us to run the simulation without constantly having to allocate new memory.

The following figure displays the final temperature distribution after 10,000 time steps. The initial temperature at the center has dissipated due to heat transfer to the edges, where the temperature is lower:

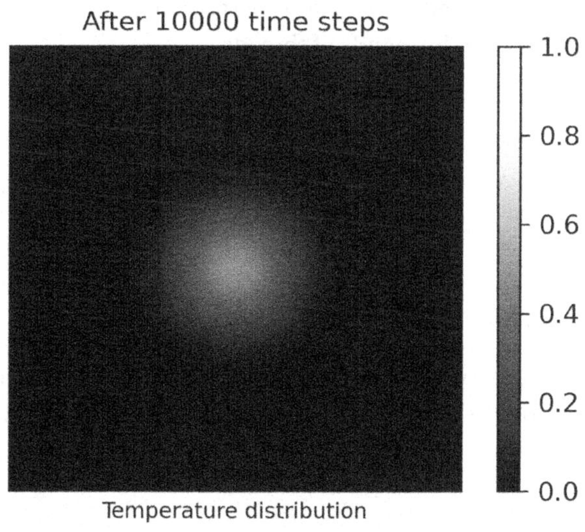

Figure 11.3 – Final temperature distribution

We have also used the straightforward Numba's automatic parallelization capabilities. A multithreaded implementation of this solver using `njit(parallel=True)` and `prange` increases performance up to 2–3× when using 8 CPU cores, depending on CPU specifications. While it's certainly possible to delve deeper and further optimize the code using multiple threads, this goes beyond the scope of this book. Therefore, let's proceed with the GPU implementation instead.

The similar time results for the multithreaded version (note the total and wall time differences due to the parallelization):

```
CPU times: user 29 s, sys: 1.86 s, total: 30.9 s
Wall time: 2.34 s
```

GPU implementation

A GPU implementation of the heat equation solver can potentially improve performance due to the GPU's parallelism and superior memory bandwidth. In the next two sections, we'll focus on implementing the GPU solver and delve deeper into memory layouts afterward.

Parallelizing tasks across threads

The value of each grid point at the next time step *un+1* depends solely on its neighboring points at the current time step *un*. This inherent parallelism means that each grid point can be updated independently in a single GPU thread. By creating a 2D grid of threads on the GPU, we can concurrently update all grid points without needing the `for` loops that we previously used in the CPU implementation. This can lead to improved performance as GPUs excel at handling large-scale parallel computations with thousands of threads.

We first configure the dimensions of CUDA threads and blocks as follows:

```
threads = 32, 32
blocks = tuple(math.ceil(n / t) for n, t in zip((nx, ny), threads))
print("Threads: ", threads)
print("Blocks: ", blocks)
print("Grid:", tuple(t * b for t, b in zip(threads, blocks)))
```

We set the number of threads in each block to 32 by 32, resulting in a total of 1,024 threads. The number of blocks in the grid is then calculated based on the grid size and the number of threads per block for each dimension.

> **Note**
>
> We need to differentiate between the FDM grid and the CUDA grid. The FDM grid defines the **spatial discretization** of the physical system, whereas the CUDA grid handles **parallel execution**. The mapping between these grids can vary depending on the algorithm used and specific optimizations for the GPU.

The `solve_heat_equation_gpu` CUDA kernel implements the heat equation solver in a very straightforward way:

```
@cuda.jit
def solve_heat_equation_gpu(
    u: Array,
    u_new: Array,
    nu: FLOAT,
) -> None:
    nx, ny = cuda.gridsize(2)
    i, j = cuda.grid(2)

    if 0 <  i < nx - 1 and 0 < j < ny - 1:
        uij = u[i, j]
        laplacian = (
            u[i + 1, j] + u[i - 1, j]
            + u[i, j + 1] + u[i, j - 1]
            - 4 * uij
        )
        u_new[i, j] = uij + nu * laplacian
```

The `cuda.jit` decorator converts the decorated function into a CUDA kernel. Like the CPU implementation, it takes the same three parameters: the current temperature distribution, `u`, an array to store the updated temperature distribution, `u_new`, and the diffusion-related coefficient, `nu`. `cuda.gridsize(2)` retrieves the total number of threads in each dimension (x and y), and `cuda.grid(2)` obtains the global thread ID within its block for both dimensions.

The `if` condition ensures that we only update interior grid points and avoid accessing out-of-bounds indices. Note that we skipped using stride loops over the `i` and `j` for simplicity, which limits our CUDA kernel to operate within the maximum supported grid size defined by the underlying GPU hardware. The Laplacian is calculated using central differences for the interior points. At each point `(i,j)`, the updated temperature is now stored in `u_new` without using any loops, unlike in our previous CPU implementation.

We're ready now to initialize the system by creating device arrays on the GPU:

```
u = initialize_system((nx, ny), h)
u_device = cuda.device_array(u.shape, dtype=FLOAT, order="F")
cuda.to_device(u, to=u_device)
```

```
u_new_device = cuda.device_array_like(u_device)
cuda.to_device(u_device, to=u_new_device)
```

Using a **device array** instead of a direct NumPy array in the Numba JIT function is much more efficient because it avoids the slow host-to-device and device-to-host data transfers.

To achieve the best performance, data should be accessed sequentially in global memory to take advantage of the cache lines, including L2 and L1 caches. Additionally, threads within each warp should access **contiguous** data to achieve **coalesced** memory access, which improves performance by maximizing parallel throughput. Given our kernel implementation and the way in which we access data in arrays, we set the order of the device array for both `u` and `u_new` to column-major (`"F"`). This means that all the elements of the first column are stored contiguously, followed by all the elements of the second column, and so on. This ensures that sequential threads within each warp, which are indexed based on `threadIdx.x`, can efficiently access consecutive data, which minimizes cache misses. It is very important to carefully arrange our data access patterns because memory access often becomes a bottleneck in either CPU or GPU computations.

We execute the GPU-accelerated heat equation solver for 10,000 steps as follows:

```
%%time
kernel = solve_heat_equation_gpu[blocks, threads]
for step in range(10_000):
    if step % 1000 == 0:
        print(
            f"Step -> {step:<6d} "
            f"u_max: {u_device.copy_to_host().max():<0.8f}")
    kernel(u_device, u_new_device, nu)
    u_device, u_new_device = u_new_device, u_device

cuda.synchronize()
```

After each kernel iteration, the input, `u`, and output, `u_new`, device arrays are swapped to prepare for the next iteration. The `cuda.synchronize()` ensures that all asynchronous device operations have completed *before stop* before the host proceeds.

The timing result indicates that running the simulation on the GPU takes much less time compared to the CPU implementation. By making minimal adjustments, we successfully optimized our heat equation solver, achieving a speedup of 13× on an A100 GPU. These are the timing results for the GPU implementation:

```
CPU times: user 381 ms, sys: 3.94 ms, total: 385 ms
Wall time: 382 ms
```

Further details can be extracted by profiling the kernel execution and collecting computing and memory access metrics:

```
Device "NVIDIA GeForce MX130"
Kernel: solve_heat_equation_on_gpu
       Metric Name                        Metric Description          Avg
               ipc                              Executed IPC     2.137461
achieved_occupancy                        Achieved Occupancy     0.820373
    gld_throughput                    Global Load Throughput   35.689GB/s
    gld_efficiency             Global Memory Load Efficiency       90.99%
    gst_throughput                   Global Store Throughput   6.5074GB/s
    gst_efficiency            Global Memory Store Efficiency       99.80%
```

The warp occupancy metric of `0.82` indicates that the kernel is utilizing approximately 82% of the available warps on the GPU, which is a reasonable level of utilization. Also, the kernel executes an average of `2.14` **instructions per clock** (**IPC**) cycle, showing a high efficiency in instruction execution. The results show efficient use of global memory in our kernel by achieving a load efficiency metric of `90.99%` and a store efficiency metric of `99.80%`. These values indicate whether our kernel performs well on coalesced reading and writing operations. Additionally, the high global memory throughput of `35.68 GB/s` (peak performance of MX130 GPU is `40.08 GB/s`) indicates that we are making good use of the available memory bandwidth.

> **Note**
>
> CUDA profiling results can be different depending on the specific GPU model being utilized. Factors such as peak memory bandwidth, the number of warps supported, and compute capability can influence the profiling outcomes. To make it clear in the text, we always specify the type of GPU used when profiling.

The following figure shows the speedup achieved by a GPU implementation of the heat equation solver compared to a CPU implementation for multiple system sizes. The y axis represents the runtime on a logarithmic scale, while the x axis shows the size of the system in terms of the number of threads used for the computation:

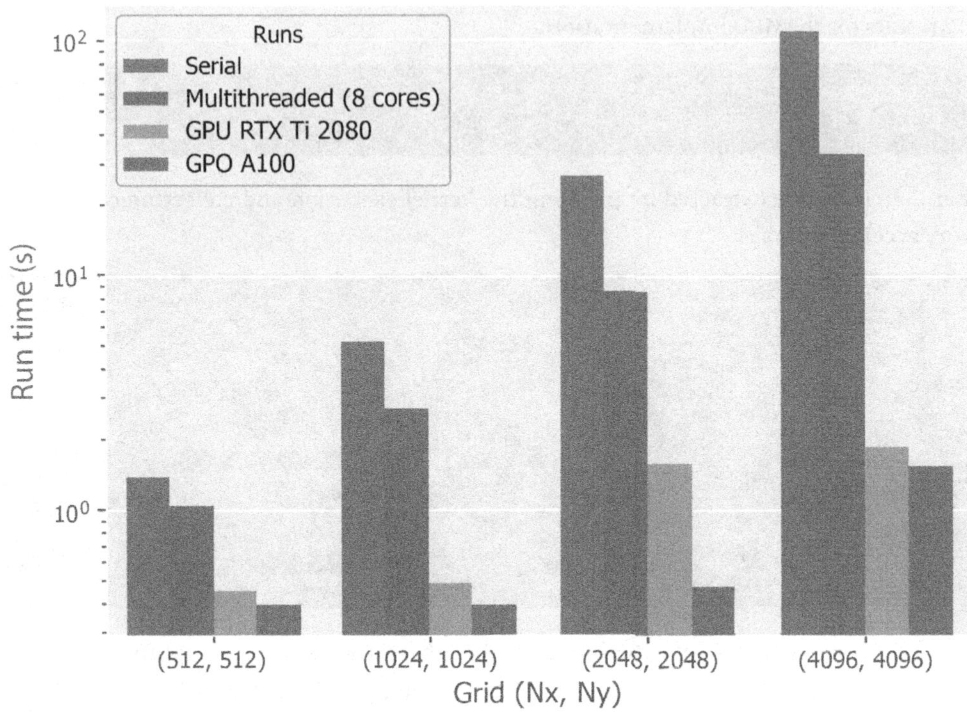

Figure 11.4 – Heat equation solver runtime comparison

It shows that the speedup improves as the system size increases, which is attributed to GPUs' ability to efficiently handle many threads. The *RTX 2080* consumer-grade GPU provides a speedup of up to 58 times, whereas an *A100* data center GPU offers a remarkable speedup of up to 70 times for a large system of *(4096, 4096)*. This performance improvement on the GPU in the heat equation solver indicates that utilizing a GPU for this task provides a significant speedup compared to using a CPU.

In the next section, we will explore how to use shared memory in this problem.

Efficient use of memory layouts

Here, we will use shared memory, which is a powerful feature for CUDA kernels that can help reduce the number of global memory accesses needed per thread. In our specific case, the heat equation solver requires reading data from the current element $u_{i,j}$, along with its four neighboring elements, $u_{i-1,j}$, $u_{i+1,j}$, $u_{i,j-1}$, and $u_{i,j+1}$ (two neighbors along each direction, x and y). Directly accessing these data from global memory can be slow, but most importantly, most elements need to be accessed five times independently by five threads. To address this, we can cache a subset of the data in the form of a **tile** array in shared memory. This reduces the latency required for threads to access the data and can improve the performance for memory-bound operations. However, shared memory per block has limited capacity (e.g., 16 to 48 KB), so not all needed data can be loaded into shared memory at once. To ease kernel implementation, we've ensured that the grid size is perfectly aligned with the block size.

Let us reimplement our heat equation solver using shared memory. We first need to determine the shared memory array size based on the number of threads per block and include additional space (for the left and right halo regions) in both the x and y directions. This is known as the **halo** region. A halo region is an additional layer of data surrounding the main grid that includes the elements required for stencil operations but are outside the immediate local neighborhood of a thread's current position.

By including this extra layer in shared memory, threads can access their required data more efficiently without needing to load the same data multiple times from global memory:

```
THREADS_PER_BLOCK = 32, 32
TILE_SHAPE = THREADS_PER_BLOCK[0] +2, THREADS_PER_BLOCK[1] + 2
TILE_SIZE = math.prod(TILE_SHAPE)

threads = THREADS_PER_BLOCK
blocks = tuple(n // t for n, t in zip(u.shape, threads))
grid = tuple(t * b for t, b in zip(threads, blocks))
```

We will utilize a 1D array for shared memory, but then we will access it column-wise as a 2D tile. The index mapping is done using the inline device function (`get_index`) as follows:

```
@cuda.jit(device=True, inline=True)
Def get_index(sx: int, sy: int) -> int:
    return sx + TILE_SHAPE[0] * sy # column-major
```

This ensures that accessing the shared memory array happens column-wise, matching our `u` and `u_new` arrays, and makes the implementation more straightforward. It also helps avoid bank conflicts.

An alternative approach is keeping everything row-wise, but this would require transpose mapping between the FDM grid and the CUDA grid, along with swapping the row and column indices.

The following `solve_heat_equation_gpu_shared` implementation solves the 2D heat equation on the GPU while utilizing shared memory:

```
@cuda.jit
def solve_heat_equation_gpu_shared(
    u: Array,
    u_new: Array,
    nu: FLOAT,
) -> None:

    tile = cuda.shared.array(TILE_SIZE, dtype=FLOAT)
    # Global indices
    x, y = cuda.grid(2)
    nx, ny = cuda.gridsize(2)
    # Thread indices
    tx, ty = cuda.threadIdx.x, cuda.threadIdx.y
    bw, bh = cuda.blockDim.x, cuda.blockDim.y
    # Local shared memory indices
    sx, sy = tx + 1, ty + 1

    # Load values into shared memory
    if x < nx and y < ny:
        # Internal region
        tile[get_index(sx, sy)] = u[x, y]
        # Halo regions
        if tx == 0 and x > 0:
            tile[get_index(sx - 1, sy)] = u[x - 1, y]
        if tx == bw - 1 and x < nx - 1:
            tile[get_index(sx + 1, sy)] = u[x + 1, y]
        if ty == 0 and y > 0:
            tile[get_index(sx, sy - 1)] = u[x, y - 1]
        if ty == bh - 1 and y < ny - 1:
            tile[get_index(sx, sy + 1)] = u[x, y + 1]
    cuda.syncthreads()

    if 0 < x < nx - 1 and 0 < y < ny - 1:
        tile_xy = tile[get_index(sx, sy)]
        laplacian = (
              tile[get_index(sx - 1, sy)] + tile[get_index(sx + 1, sy)]
            + tile[get_index(sx, sy - 1)] + tile[get_index(sx, sy + 1)]
            - 4 * tile_xy
```

```
    )
    u_new[x, y] = tile_xy + nu * laplacian
```

A static shared memory array named `tile` is allocated using `cuda.shared.array` inside the kernel function with a size of `TILE_SIZE`. Each element is of the `FLOAT` type, which is the same as two temperature arrays in the global memory. Similarly, the grid and block dimensions are set using `cuda.gridsize` and `cuda.grid`, and `nx` and `ny` represent the number of blocks in each dimension. The local thread indices `tx` and `ty` are determined using `cuda.threadIdx`. The block dimensions, `bw` and `bh`, are obtained via `cuda.blockDim`. The `sx` and `sy` indices for accessing elements in the shared memory array are adjusted to ensure that each thread has a valid position within the tile, shifted by one element to accommodate the halo regions.

The following figure represents how we map the block shared memory with halo regions for solving the heat equation in two dimensions:

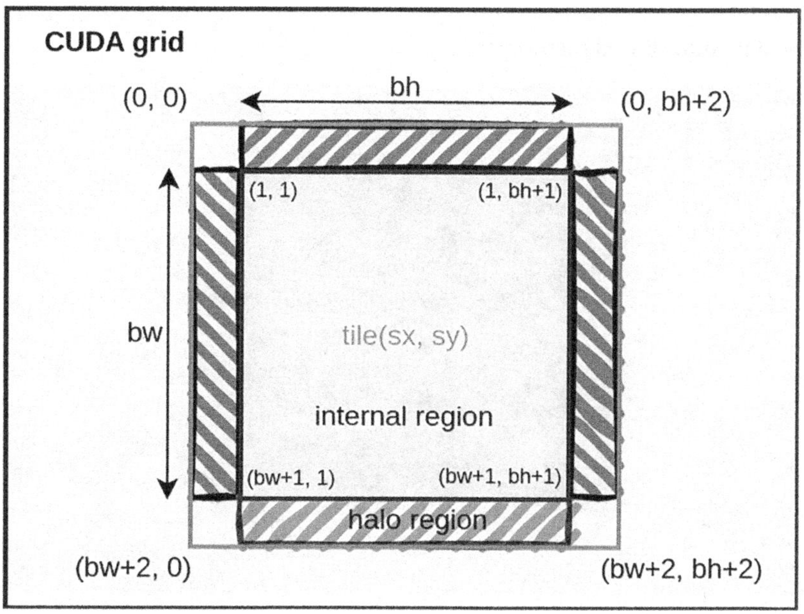

Figure 11.5 – Shared memory internal and halo regions in each CUDA block

Next, we load values from global memory into shared memory. This includes two steps: the internal region and the halo regions. For the internal region, each thread copies the value at its position from the input array, `u[x, y]` (global indices), into the shared memory array, `tile[sx, sy]` (local indices). For the halo regions, boundary threads including top, `tx == 0`, and bottom, `tx == bw-1`, left, `ty == 0`, and right, `ty == bh-1`, copy values from neighboring elements in the global array into the halo regions on the shared memory. After this, we use the synchronization barrier `cuda.syncthreads()` to ensure that all threads have completed loading their respective values into shared memory in each block before proceeding.

Finally, threads within each block can utilize cached values from shared memory rather than accessing global memory directly. The updated temperature distribution is then stored in the output array, `u_new`.

> **Note**
>
> For stencil calculations, we don't particularly need halo regions at the corners; otherwise, those values must also be copied from global memory by using additional `if` statements.

The profiling results this time show improved computing metrics; IPC increases to `3.28` and achieved warp occupancy of `0.94`, almost at its limit. The global load throughput is reduced as we're caching data into shared memory:

```
Device "NVIDIA GeForce MX130"
Kernel: solve_heat_equation_kernel
          Metric Name                         Metric Description          Avg
---------------------------------------------------------------------------------
                  ipc                               Executed IPC     3.279804
   achieved_occupancy                         Achieved Occupancy     0.944062
       gld_throughput                     Global Load Throughput   9.2621GB/s
       gld_efficiency              Global Memory Load Efficiency       75.54%
       gst_throughput                    Global Store Throughput   5.3359GB/s
       gst_efficiency             Global Memory Store Efficiency       99.80%
---------------------------------------------------------------------------------
shared_load_transactions_per_request   Shared Memory Load Ratio     1.000000
shared_load_throughput              Shared Memory Load Throughput  26.679GB/s
     shared_efficiency                    Shared Memory Efficiency       76.92%
```

We can gain more insights by focusing on additional shared memory-related metrics, such as load transactions per request, shared memory throughput, and efficiency. Bank conflicts in shared memory can lead to reduced memory access performance because multiple threads accessing elements within the same cache line (bank) cause contention. An average value of `1.0` suggests that each request involves exactly one transaction, indicating efficient use of shared memory. If each request results in the accessing of multiple elements that fall into the same cache line due to bank conflicts, the kernel might need to perform multiple transactions per request to resolve the conflicts. Therefore, the average value of this metric would be greater than `1.0` in such a case.

We have already learned how to use shared memory, including challenges such as handling halo regions and avoiding bank conflicts. Despite our efforts to utilize fast shared memory instead of global memory, we did not achieve much of a performance improvement. Why is that? In the next section, we will attempt to answer these questions.

Performance analysis

For this specific example, we see high computing metrics relative to memory throughput and efficiency metrics. This indicates that our performance is likely limited by **compute** capability rather than **memory access**. To verify this, we can calculate the value of `nu` explicitly inside the kernel using *αt/h2* instead of passing it as a constant:

```
u_new[x, y] = tile_xy + (dt * alpha / (h * )) * laplacian
```

Performing this dummy additional calculation, especially the division operation, increases the runtime by 6%, which is an indication of a compute-bound problem. If the performance were memory-bound, this computation is expected to have minimal impact on the performance.

Accordingly, we can improve the kernel by reducing the use of conditional statements while loading the halo regions into shared memory. This is because branching can be computationally expensive as it introduces additional latency and warp synchronization. The following code shows the same implementation with fewer branches:

```
# Loading halo regions into the shared memory
if tx == 0:
    tile[get_index(tx, sy)] = u[x - 1, y]
    tile[get_index(sx + bw, sy)] = u[x + bw, y]
if ty == 0:
    tile[get_index(sx, ty)] = u[x, y - 1]
    tile[get_index(sx, sy + bh)] = u[x, y + bh]
```

This results in an improved IPC metric of `3.52` and leads to a 12% reduction in runtime.

The key point here is that we must always identify the precise location of the performance bottleneck and focus our efforts there. Measuring metrics such as IPC, achieved warp occupancy, memory efficiency, and throughput are crucial for determining whether our problem is compute-bound or memory-bound and where to direct optimization efforts. For compute-bound problems, the focus should be on optimizing kernel performance by simplifying logic, choosing efficient data structures, and increasing thread count. For memory-bound problems, it should be directed at optimizing memory access patterns to ensure coalesced accesses, using shared memory for prefetching while avoiding bank conflicts, and minimizing global memory reads and writes.

Additionally, incorporating shared memory into a GPU kernel leads to unwanted complications. One of the main drawbacks is that it often requires additional branching logic, making each thread's task more complex. As a result, the GPU scheduler faces difficulties in optimizing the execution of threads and memory transactions concurrently. This complexity can outweigh any potential benefits from using shared memory, ultimately leading to equal or even less performant implementations compared to not using shared memory at all. However, if the cached data in shared memory is used frequently enough, it can compensate for the added complexity and actually lead to improved performance by reducing slow global memory access. In other words, the benefits of using shared memory become more apparent when its contents are highly utilized within the kernel.

Summary

In this chapter, we explored the practical implementation of solving the heat equation on a GPU. We began by reviewing the fundamentals of the heat transfer equation and its solution using the finite difference methods through spatial and temporal discretization. Then, we demonstrated how to initialize a 2D system and implemented a CPU-based solver to simulate its evolution over multiple time steps.

We then transitioned to GPU computing by implementing the solver with Numba CUDA, first naively and then using shared memory to minimize global memory accesses and to leverage cached data within each block. Finally, we profiled our GPU kernels and discussed strategies for identifying bottlenecks and ways to alleviate them.

In the next chapter, we will shift our attention to a different practical application of GPU computing: image processing.

Questions

1. How would using row-major arrays affect the global memory efficiency metrics for load and store operations?
2. If we switch from `float32` to `float64` precision, how would it impact the bank onflict metric, and what is the reason behind this change?
3. Do you think that using shared memory is always the best initial step for further optimizing a CUDA kernel? What profiling metrics can help guide this decision?

Answers

1. Row-major (`order="C"`) and column-major (`order="F"`) layouts determine how data in the grid is stored in memory, which directly affects data contiguity. If the access pattern matches the memory layout, threads read neighboring memory locations, enabling coalesced memory access and more efficient load/store operations. When the layout and access pattern are misaligned, memory access becomes strided and less efficient, reducing overall performance.
2. Switching from `float32` (4 bytes) to `float64` (8 bytes) typically increases the bank conflict metric on many GPUs. The reason is that shared memory is organized into fixed-size banks (commonly 4 bytes wide). A `float32` value maps neatly to a single bank, but a `float64` value spans two consecutive banks. As a result, when multiple threads in a warp access double-precision values with certain stride patterns, they are more likely to contend for the same banks, leading to more frequent bank conflicts and reduced shared memory efficiency.
3. No, shared memory is not always the best first optimization. It is most useful for large problems where threads within a block repeatedly access the same global memory data, as copying a tile into shared memory reduces expensive global memory transactions. However, it increases code complexity and may not help if the kernel is not memory-bound, so profiling first is recommended.

Get this book's PDF version and more

12

Image Processing and Computer Vision on the GPU

This chapter applies the GPU programming topics covered in *Chapters 1* to *10* of this book to real-world image processing and computer vision tasks. Traditionally, the GPU is used in games and graphical software to **render** images on the screen. This chapter is concerned with the **inverse problem**: processing an image to measure or identify objects in the image, or to learn something about the process that generated the image. Not in scope is processing images or photographs for aesthetic purposes, though many of the techniques that are discussed (e.g., filters) are also employed in image processing software such as Photoshop. This chapter will also introduce the **cuCIM** library, which is part of the RAPIDS ecosystem and provides a large collection of tools for easily processing images on the GPU.

The learning outcomes of this chapter are as follows:

- Having a basic understanding of how a computer represents an image
- Understanding how images can be manipulated as N-D arrays using a GPU
- Implementing an image filter from scratch with a CUDA kernel
- Using high-level libraries such as cuCIM to extract useful information from images
- Using JAX to build and train a convolutional neural network for image classification

Technical requirements

To run the code in this chapter, an installation of Python 3 with a number of packages is needed, as well as the CUDA Toolkit. It's recommended to create a `pixi` environment based on the `pixi.lock` file in the GitHub repository associated with this book:

https://github.com/PacktPublishing/GPU-Accelerated-Computing-with-Python-3-and-CUDA

The details are explained in *Chapter 2* and README.md.

How a computer represents images

There are two main types of images: **grayscale** and **red-green-blue (RGB)**.

To represent a grayscale image, a computer stores one intensity value per pixel. This is represented in memory as a 2D array, with each element representing the intensity of a pixel. These intensity values can be mapped to shades of gray of pixels on the screen.

To illustrate, let's examine a grayscale sample image from the scikit-image library:

```
from skimage import data

camera_image = data.camera()
```

This is a 2D NumPy array of shape (512, 512), and a uint8 data type (i.e., one byte meaning the values range from 0-255). Matplotlib can visualize the image as follows:

```
import matplotlib.pyplot as plt

plt.imshow(camera_image, cmap="gray")
```

Figure 12.1 – The "camera" sample grayscale image from the scikit-image library

The `cmap` argument stands for `colormap`. It maps intensity values in the array to colors on the screen. The `gray` colormap maps low intensity to black and high intensity to white. All the available color maps are listed in the official documentation: `https://matplotlib.org/stable/gallery/color/colormap_reference.html`.

> Note
>
> **Data types for pixel intensities**
>
> To conserve memory and disk space, most images use the `uint8` data type. This means that intensities are discretized to 256 levels. For the human eye, this is fine; humans can hardly distinguish between grays that are very closely spaced. However, for performing numerical operations on images, pixels are preferably represented using the `float32` or `float64` data types; this is more convenient and avoids excessive error accumulation.

RGB images represent a pixel using three values: an intensity value for red, green, and blue. Therefore, an RGB image is represented in memory as a 3D array, with the color values of one pixel aligned along the **channel** axis. The image pixel intensities map to the intensity of tiny red, green, and blue LEDs that are contained within each pixel of a computer screen. The human eye contains three different types of receptors, which are each sensitive to either red, green, or blue light. By mixing different intensities of red, green, and blue light, the brain perceives different colors. For example, "yellow" is perceived when red and green light are mixed, "white" is perceived when all colors are equally mixed, and no intensity is interpreted as "black."

`scikit-image` also contains RGB sample images, for example:

```
astronaut_image = data.astronaut()
```

The `astronaut_image` image has shape `(512, 512, 3)` and a dtype of `uint8`. Matplotlib can plot the image as follows:

```
plt.imshow(astronaut_image)
```

Figure 12.2 – The "astronaut" sample RGB image from the scikit-image library

Note the `cmap` argument is no longer used, since the image pixel already encodes the screen pixel color.

> Note
>
> **Seeing colors**
>
> In the print version of this book, the colors of the images may be absent. Seeing the colors is not essential for understanding this chapter, but the accompanying GitHub repository with full code examples can be used to see all images in color.

Matplotlib automatically detects that the image is an RGB image because it has three dimensions, and the last axis has length 3. Most libraries in the scientific Python ecosystem, like Matplotlib, use the convention that the channel axis is last. However, some deep learning libraries, such as PyTorch, use the channel-first convention.

Besides RGB, there are other ways to parametrize colors. For example, a common and useful representation for color is **hue, saturation, and value (HSV)**. The hue represents the color (e.g., blue), the saturation represents the *color purity* (i.e., how much it differs from gray), and the value represents the brightness (i.e., how much it differs from black). For some image processing tasks, it is convenient to convert RGB colors to a different color space.

Finally, while grayscale or RGB images are the most common types of images, images can be generalized. **Multi-spectral** images, for example, from satellites, may contain more than three channels. In addition, images can be **N-dimensional**. For example, a CT scan produces a 3D image. The focus of this chapter is restricted to 2D images.

So far, images have been represented using NumPy arrays on the host because this is easy for visualization. They can be represented on the GPU using CuPy arrays (see *Chapter 8*). The astronaut can be transferred to the GPU as follows:

```
import cupy as cp

astronaut_gpu = cp.asarray(astronaut_image)
```

Now that images and their representation in memory have been introduced, the next section covers the basics of how to process them.

The basics of image processing

An image is represented in memory as an N-dimensional array. Therefore, all operations discussed in *Chapter 8* apply and can, in principle, be considered image processing.

However, let's be more precise. Images are a special subclass of N-dimensional arrays in which some axes have a **spatial** meaning. This implies that neighboring pixel values tend to be correlated, and that correlated regions of pixels often correspond to features or real-world objects of interest.

In image processing, the goal is often to extract **structure** and, ultimately, some form of **interpretation** from an image. This may involve transforming the image so that the signal of interest is enhanced for a human observer. Alternatively, the goal may be for the computer to interpret the image automatically. Common tasks include **segmenting** an image (i.e., partitioning pixels into meaningful regions), identifying or **classifying** objects, or extracting quantitative information such as area, perimeter, or bounding boxes. The latter is typically referred to as **computer vision**.

To achieve these aims, several types of operations need to be combined. The most common classes of operations include the following:

- **Point-wise operations** apply a function independently to each pixel. This is comparable to the **ufuncs** introduced in *Chapter 8*, although point-wise operations may combine information across the channel axis. Examples include adjusting contrast and brightness (i.e., **exposure**), transforming colors, or **thresholding** an image to segment it based on pixel intensity.

- **Filters** enhance or suppress specific components of the image signal. Typical applications include blurring, smoothing, denoising, and edge or blob enhancement.
- **Geometric transformations**, such as rotation, rescaling, or warping an image, rely on **interpolation** between pixel values.
- **Segmentation** or **clustering** of pixels into regions includes simple approaches such as intensity-based thresholding, while more advanced methods may employ machine-learning algorithms such as k-means.
- **Morphological operations** manipulate the shapes of regions, most commonly in binary (black-and-white) images. Examples include removing small objects or filling holes.
- **Feature detection** aims to identify edges, corners, or other distinctive regions of interest. This often combines filtering with some form of thresholding or segmentation.
- **Registration** involves matching features across multiple images, for example, to estimate motion or align image sequences.
- **Measurement** is typically performed on segmented images to extract quantitative descriptors.

The art of image processing lies in knowing which types of operations to apply, and in which order, to achieve a desired result. The case study later in this chapter provide hands-on experience with all these operation classes.

High-level image-processing libraries such as `scikit-image` and cuCIM organize their functionality in modules that roughly mirror these categories. Once the goal and a path to the solution are clear, this structure makes it straightforward to locate appropriate tools in the documentation.

> Note
>
> **OpenCV**
>
> While this chapter focuses on cuCIM and `scikit-image` for their simple API and interoperability with the rest of the scientific Python ecosystem, serious computer vision practitioners should also consider **OpenCV**, which offers a broader range of algorithms and hardware compatibility. OpenCV has been around for a long time and is a standard in the industry. OpenCV also has optional support for GPU acceleration via CUDA.

Before diving into these high-level libraries, the next section takes a closer look at **convolutional filters** and how to implement them from scratch on both the CPU and GPU. This will provide a deeper understanding of one of the most fundamental operations in image processing and help build intuition for when and why such filters are useful.

Implementing a convolutional filter from scratch

In this section, a spatial-domain convolutional filter for 2D grayscale images is implemented. The convolution operation is very common in signal and image processing. It will be used to blur an image and to enhance edges.

In a spatial-domain convolution, a small (e.g., 3×3 or 5×5) array, also called a **kernel** (not to be confused with a CUDA kernel), is slid across the image. The kernel weights and the corresponding image pixel values are multiplied, and the corresponding products are summed up. The sum is stored in the output pixel that corresponds to the kernel position.

> Note
>
> **Spatial domain versus frequency domain convolution**
>
> Mathematically, the convolution is equivalent to a multiplication in Fourier (frequency) space. Therefore, convolutions can also be calculated by multiplying the 2D Fourier transforms of the inputs and taking the inverse Fourier transform of the product. For images of comparable size, convolution in Fourier space is more efficient. However, for small kernels, spatial-domain convolution is more efficient. Frequency-domain convolution comes up later in this chapter.

Let's implement a naive CPU version of the 2D convolution in the spatial domain, using Numba as follows:

```
from numba import njit

@njit
def convolve_2d_cpu(
    img: NDArray,
    kernel: NDArray,
    output: NDArray,
) -> None:
    c_x = kernel.shape[1] // 2
    c_y = kernel.shape[0] // 2

    for y in range(output.shape[0]):
        for x in range(output.shape[1]):
            output[y, x] = sum_of_products(
```

```
            img, kernel, y - c_y, x - c_x
        )
```

First, the center pixel of the kernel (c_x, c_y) is calculated to center the kernel over the position of interest when the sum of products is calculated. Two nested loops iterate over all pixels in the output image, which represent positions of the sliding kernel. At each position, the sum of pixel products with the kernel weights is calculated using the yet to be defined `sum_of_products` function.

The `sum_of_products` function requires as input the image, the kernel, and the coordinates of the pixel in the image that corresponds to weight `(0, 0)` in the kernel. It is implemented as follows:

```
from numba import float64

@njit(inline="always")
def sum_of_products(
    img: NDArray,
    kernel: NDArray,
    y_start: int,
    x_start: int,
) -> float:
    result = float64(0.0)

    for y_k in range(kernel.shape[0]):
        for x_k in range(kernel.shape[1]):
            coord_y = y_start + y_k
            coord_x = x_start + x_k

            if (
                coord_y >= 0 and
                coord_y < img.shape[0] and
                coord_x >= 0 and
                coord_x < img.shape[1]
            ):
                result += img[coord_y, coord_x] * kernel[y_k, x_k]

    return result
```

Two nested loops iterate over all the elements in the kernel to calculate the product of the weight and the corresponding image pixel; this is added to `result`. The most complex part of this code is the bounds check that must be performed to ensure image pixel coordinates are valid. When the kernel operates on the edges of the image, the absence of a bounds check could result in invalid memory being accessed.

Because convolutional filters combine information from neighboring pixels through a kernel, this simple idea can be used for many different purposes depending on the weights of the kernel. For example, the following kernel can be used to blur an image:

```
blur_size = 15
blur_kernel = np.ones((blur_size, blur_size), dtype="float64")
```

The blurring effect of this kernel is illustrated on the "camera" image as follows:

```
camera_float = camera_image.astype("float64")
out_blur = np.empty_like(camera_float)
convolve_2d_cpu(camera_float, blur_kernel, out_blur)
```

Before `convolve_2d_cpu` is called, the image is first converted to `float64`. The result, `out_blur`, looks as follows:

Figure 12.3 – The "camera" image blurred with a convolution

Convolving images with this kernel blends the intensities of pixels from a large area, which results in a blurring effect. In practice, blurring or smoothing is usually performed using a **2D Gaussian** kernel (i.e., the weights in the kernel correspond to the height of a 2D bell-curve).

Gaussian smoothing is better at preserving edge structure; the uniform kernel used here introduces artifacts near regions of sharp contrast transitions, for example, near the camera tripod.

Detecting features such as edges is a common preprocessing step for measurement or object detection applications. Edges are strong discontinuities in intensity and can be detected using edge-enhancing filters such as **Sobel** filters. Sobel filters have the following characteristic kernels:

```
kernel_x = np.array([
    [-1, 0, 1],
    [-2, 0, 2],
    [-1, 0, 1],
], dtype="float64")

kernel_y = np.array([
    [-1, -2, -1],
    [0, 0, 0],
    [1, 2, 1],
], dtype="float64")
```

These effectively calculate the x and y components of the intensity gradient, so pixels near edges where intensity rapidly changes will have a large positive or negative value. Convolutions with both kernels are calculated separately, with the results stored in out_x and out_y, respectively. The magnitude of the intensity gradient is calculated using the Pythagorean theorem:

```
magnitude = np.sqrt(out_x ** 2 + out_y ** 2)
```

The result contains a few very bright pixels, which makes the overall image look dim when plotted. One way to alleviate this is by using a **gamma correction**, which corresponds to raising the pixel values to a power smaller than 1. For example, `magnitude ** 0.3` looks as follows:

```
fig, ax = plt.subplots(figsize=(6, 6))
ax.imshow(magnitude ** 0.3, "gray")
fig.savefig("images/camera_edges.png")
```

Figure 12.4 – The magnitude of the intensity gradient of the "camera" image calculated using Sobel filters

The edges are strongly enhanced.

Let's now create a GPU implementation of spatial-domain convolution using Numba-CUDA. A very natural approach is to adapt the `sum_of_products` function and convert it to a naive CUDA kernel as follows:

```
from numba import cuda, float64

@cuda.jit
def convolve_2d_gpu(
    img: NDArray,
    kernel: NDArray,
    out: NDArray,
) -> None:
    x, y = cuda.grid(2)
    if x >= out.shape[1] or y >= out.shape[0]:
        return

    c_x = kernel.shape[1] // 2
    c_y = kernel.shape[0] // 2
    y_start = y - c_y
```

```
    x_start = x - c_x

    result = float64(0.0)

    for y_k in range(kernel.shape[0]):
        for x_k in range(kernel.shape[1]):
            coord_y = y_start + y_k
            coord_x = x_start + x_k

            if (
                coord_y >= 0 and
                coord_y < img.shape[0] and
                coord_x >= 0 and
                coord_x < img.shape[1]
            ):
                result += img[coord_y, coord_x] * kernel[y_k, x_k]

    out[y, x] = result
```

The blurring operation can be executed on the GPU as follows:

```
blur_kernel_gpu = cp.ones((blur_size, blur_size), dtype="float64")
camera_gpu = cp.asarray(camera_image, dtype="float64")
out_gpu = cp.empty_like(camera_gpu)

TPB = (16, 16)
BPG = (
    (out_gpu.shape[1] + TPB[1] - 1) // TPB[1],
    (out_gpu.shape[0] + TPB[0] - 1) // TPB[0],
)
convolve_2d_gpu[BPG, TPB](camera_gpu, blur_kernel_gpu, out_gpu)
```

It can easily be verified that this produces the same output as before. However, the GPU version is more than 80 times faster on an A100 GPU compared to the CPU (1 ms compared to 80 ms).

Notice that this implementation is very naive and far from optimized. How does it hold up to optimized implementations? Where are the bottlenecks, and how could the kernel be improved?

One potential concern that jumps out immediately by inspecting the kernel is pressure on global memory. Many threads repeatedly load the same image data from global memory. In fact, most image elements are loaded *N* times, where *N* is the number of weights in the convolution kernel. This suggests that shared memory tiling could significantly improve performance, especially as the kernel size increases. Additionally, the convolution kernel itself is read-only and shared by all threads, making it a good candidate for storing it in **constant memory**.

Another concern is the boundary check nested deep inside the convolution loops, which could lead to thread divergence. A more refined implementation might separate the "image interior" and "image edge" cases into different kernels. Alternatively, the input image could be padded with a border of zeros to eliminate the conditional entirely.

These hypotheses can be investigated using the Nsight Compute (`ncu`) profiling tool:

```
ncu --set "full" python kernel_profiling_script.py
```

`kernel_profiling_script.py` contains the full implementation and can be found in the associated GitHub repository. For a general introduction to Nsight Compute and interpretation of its output, see *Chapter 4* and *Chapter 5*.

Running the kernel on a large 10,000×10,000 image (to ensure the measurements reflect kernel inefficiencies rather than small input size effects), produces the following results on an NVIDIA A100 GPU:

- The `Source Counters` section shows `Branch Efficiency` of 99.9%. This indicates that thread divergence is largely irrelevant. For large images, this is expected: most warps operate entirely within the image interior and therefore follow identical control paths. Only the warps near the image boundaries exhibit divergent behavior. This is only a small fraction of all the warps.
- In the `GPU Speed Of Light Throughput` section, `Compute (SM) Throughput` is approximately 86%, with an average of 3.43 issued instructions per cycle. Achieved occupancy is also high, at around 88%. This shows that the SMs are busy most of the time, and that instruction and memory latencies are well hidden through warp scheduling.
- However, the `GPU Speed Of Light Roofline Chart` section reports that the kernel achieves only about 3% of the device's peak FP32 performance. This indicates that while many instructions are being executed, relatively few of them are floating-point operations. Indeed, the `Compute Workload Analysis` section reports that the ALU pipeline is the most heavily utilized, dominated by integer and logic operations. Therefore, the kernel spends most of its time performing loop control, index arithmetic, and address calculations rather than useful numerical computation.
- Despite the large number of global memory loads, memory bandwidth utilization is low, at around 14–15%, with L1 and L2 cache hit rates exceeding 75%. This mostly reflects the

strong spatial locality of the access pattern: neighboring threads repeatedly load the same cache lines. Nsight Compute also reports uncoalesced global accesses, indicating that memory transactions are not used efficiently.

Taken together, these results show that the kernel is not limited by memory bandwidth or floating-point throughput. Instead, it is limited by the large number of integer, logic, and address-calculation instructions, as well as redundant global memory loads. Using shared memory tiling would reduce both the number of global memory transactions and the associated address and cache-management instructions, increasing FP32 instruction intensity and improving performance. Further gains could be achieved by improving memory access patterns through more appropriate block shapes and indexing strategies. Exploring these strategies is left as an exercise for the readers.

Using convolutional filters from high-level libraries

Spatial domain convolution is so common that an optimized implementation is provided in `scipy.ndimage` for the CPU and in `cupyx.scipy.ndimage` for the GPU. The following achieves the same blurring effect as in the previous section:

```
from cupyx.scipy.ndimage import convolve as gconvolve

gconvolve(camera_gpu, blur_kernel_gpu, out_gpu, mode="constant")
```

This only takes 600 µs on the A100, an improvement of 40% over the naive CUDA kernel implemented in the previous section. Additionally, `convolve` provides options such as `mode` to change the behavior at the boundary of the image. With `mode="constant"`, the behavior is the same as before: 0 is used for out-of-bounds elements.

For specific kernels such as Sobel or Gaussian, specialized and optimized filter functions are available through `scikit-image` and `scipy.ndimage` for the CPU and through `cuCIM` and `cupyx.scipy.ndimage` for the GPU:

```
from skimage.filters import gaussian, sobel
from scipy.ndimage import gaussian_filter as scipy_gaussian, sobel as scipy_sobel
from cucim.skimage.filters import gaussian as ggaussian, sobel as gsobel
from cupyx.scipy.ndimage import gaussian_filter as gscipy_gaussian, sobel as
gscipy_sobel
```

With an equivalent kernel size, `ggausian` is two times faster than `gconvolve` (roughly 300 µs on the A100) and `gscipy_gaussian` is more than 2.5× faster (220 µs on the A100).

Now that one of the most fundamental image processing techniques has been covered, let's explore a realistic image processing case study.

Case study: detecting and classifying objects in a noisy image

In this section, the problem of extracting and identifying objects in images is explored. Realistic images have noise, which presents an additional challenge for this task.

Exploring the problem

Consider the following image, which contains several objects on a mostly uniform background:

Figure 12.5 – An RGB image containing several randomly oriented, sized, and colored objects on a uniform background

The objects in this image are pieces of clothing sampled from the famous **MNIST Fashion dataset** (`https://github.com/zalandoresearch/fashion-mnist`), a dataset of 70,000 grayscale images of 28x28 pixels, which is commonly used for testing computer vision algorithms. The objects are randomly oriented, sized, and colorized, then randomly positioned on a white canvas. Then, **Gaussian pixel noise** was added to the image, which means that pixel colors are randomly shifted with values drawn from a Gaussian distribution. The code for generating this image can be found in the accompanying GitHub repository.

The goal in this case study is to find the positions of all the objects and identify (classify) them using various techniques. The **object detection** problem is very common when dealing with images. This may come up in a factory, where objects that pass by on a conveyor belt need to be identified and sorted at high speeds. In a lab, a biologist may be looking at microscopy images of bacterial colonies and want to automatically count, size, and identify the bacteria.

In general, object detection follows two steps. First, the image must be **segmented**, such that pixels corresponding to individual objects are grouped. Secondly, the segments are measured and/or **classified**.

Object detection and classification can also be performed in a single step using specialized **neural network** models. Notable examples of object detection models include YOLO (`https://docs.ultralytics.com/tasks/detect/`) and detectron2 (`https://ai.meta.com/tools/detectron2/`). These models are very performant, even enabling real-time object detection in video feeds, and are state-of-the-art when it comes to accuracy. For real object detection problems, using one of these models is probably the best starting point.

However, training one of these models requires a very large amount of labeled data and computing resources, so building one from scratch is not feasible for most people. Using a pre-trained black-box model is of limited educational value. Therefore, the primary focus here is on classical image processing techniques, which do not require any data.

The segmentation and classification strategy depends on the structure of the data and will be different for every problem. Therefore, the first step is to get a good *feeling* for the data to decide on the best strategy.

First, let's have a look at the shape and dtype of the image:

```
print(img.shape)
print(img.dtype)
```

The image shape is `(1000, 1000, 3)` and the dtype is `uint8`. Therefore, this is a typical RGB image.

Next, let's visualize the distributions of pixel intensities using a **histogram**, which shows how many pixels have a particular intensity. Since there are three channels (RGB), three histograms could be plotted. However, this is not very informative since the spatial correlation between the different channels is lost. More interesting is the histogram of the mean over the channel axis, which is calculated as follows:

```
mean_pixel_values = img.mean(axis=-1).ravel()
```

The following graph shows the histogram of `mean_pixel_values` on two scales:

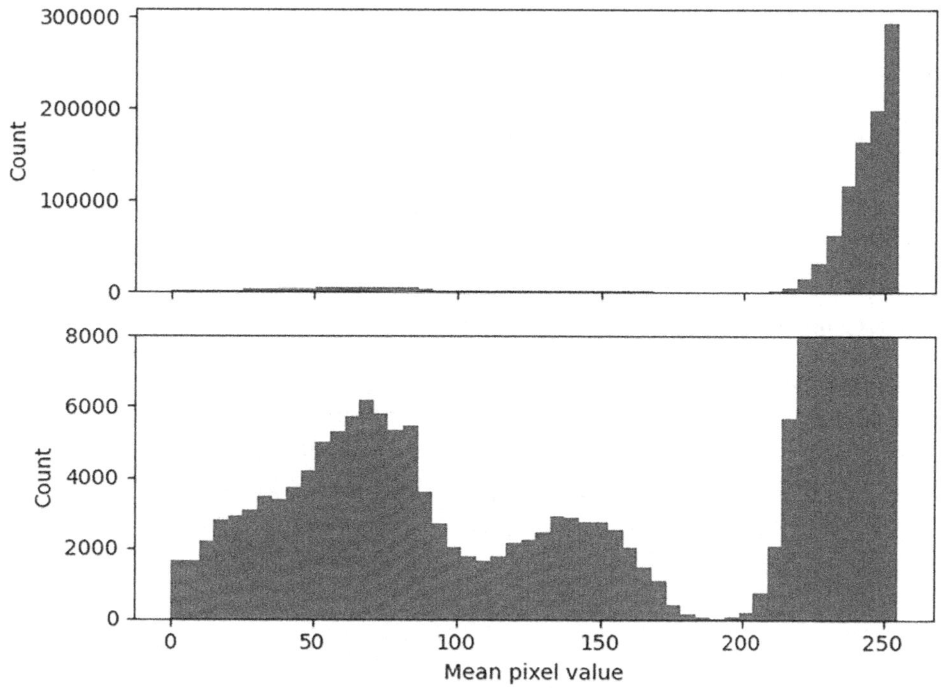

Figure 12.6 – Histogram of the mean pixel value, shown for different scales of the y axis

The two graphs show the same data, but in the second image, the *y* axis is magnified to reveal two additional small peaks. There is a very large peak near 255, which corresponds to the nearly white pixels that compose the background. White in RGB representation is `[255, 255, 255]`, so the average is 255. There are two additional peaks near 75 and 150, slightly below 1/3 and 2/3 of 255. The first peak corresponds to the objects colorized with red (`[255, 0, 0]`), green (`[0, 255, 0]`) or blue (`[0, 0, 255]`). The second peak corresponds to yellow (`[255, 255, 0]`), magenta (`[255, 0, 255]`), or cyan (`[0, 255, 255]`) objects. This suggests segmentation can be based on pixel color differences.

Segmenting the image

From here on out, processing of the image takes place on the GPU. The image is transferred to the device as follows:

```
img_gpu = cp.asarray(img)
```

The objects in the image do not overlap. This is convenient because it means that individual objects can be easily identified by computing a **mask** for the background. A mask is a binary image (pixels are either `True` or `False`), which can be interpreted as a type of segmentation. The first goal is to create a mask the same size as the image, in which the pixels corresponding to objects are `True`, and the pixels corresponding to the background are `False`. In this mask, contiguous regions of `True` pixels correspond to individual objects.

Color differences between the objects and the background can be used as a starting point for creating a mask. The background is mostly white, and all the objects range from black to a solid color. In RGB color space, establishing a criterion that separates the background from the foreground (the objects) is difficult. However, it becomes trivial in HSV color space, which was mentioned earlier in the chapter. The image is converted to HSV as follows:

```
from cucim.skimage.color import rgb2hsv

im_hsv = rgb2hsv(img_gpu)
```

Recall that the saturation, the *S* channel in HSV, indicates how intense the color is. This means that objects are expected to have a high saturation, whereas the background is expected to have a low saturation. Plotting `saturation = img_hsv[:,:,1]` as a grayscale image shows the objects light up against the background:

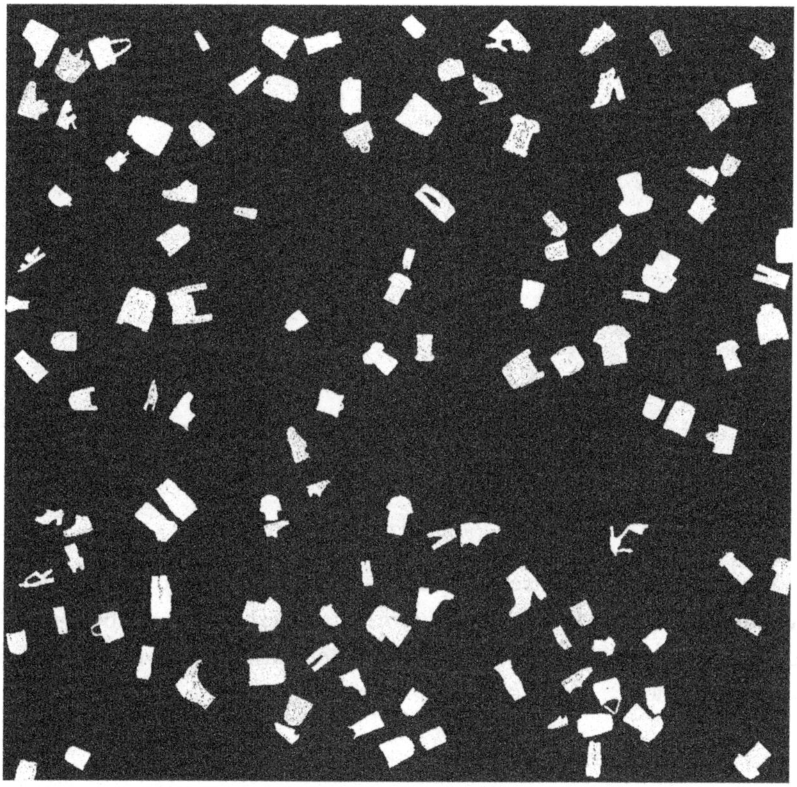

Figure 12.7 – Pixel saturation of the image

The histogram of the saturation shows the stark difference between the background (saturation near 0) and the foreground (saturation near 1):

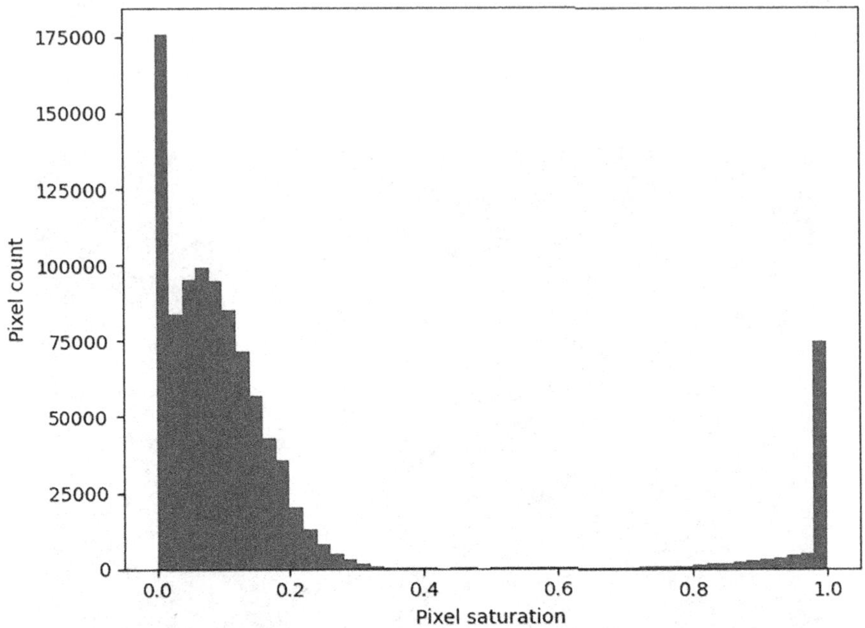

Figure 12.8 – Histogram of the pixel saturation

Using the saturation channel, the background pixels can be separated from the foreground pixels using a **threshold** value. Based on the histogram, this threshold should be somewhere between 0.4 and 0.6. There are methods to automatically determine an optimal thresholding value, for example, the **Otsu** method:

```
from cucim.skimage.filters import threshold_otsu

threshold = threshold_otsu(saturation)
```

The Otsu method suggests an optimal threshold value around 0.52.

Note

Applicability of the Otsu method

The Otsu method assumes a bimodal distribution of pixel intensities, where the optimal threshold separates the two modes by maximizing between-class variance. While it will always compute a threshold, the result may be unreliable if the intensity distribution is not bimodal (e.g., unimodal or multimodal), as the threshold may not correspond to a natural separation in the data.

The mask is created from the threshold as follows:

```
mask = saturation > threshold
```

The mask can be visualized as the following black-and-white image:

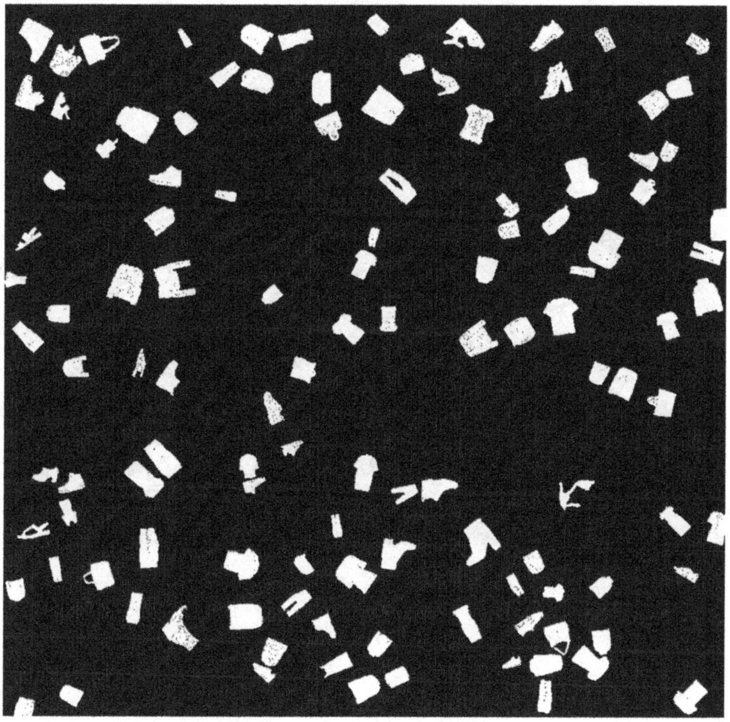

Figure 12.9 – Initial mask based on thresholding the saturation image

This is already pretty good. One remaining issue is that some pixels inside the object are black because of noise. There may also be a few lone bright pixels in the background. These artifacts can be cleaned from the mask using **morphology** operations – in this case, `remove_small_holes` and `remove_small_objects`, as follows:

```
from cucim.skimage.morphology import remove_small_holes, remove_small_objects

clean_mask = remove_small_objects(remove_small_holes(mask))
```

The result looks as follows:

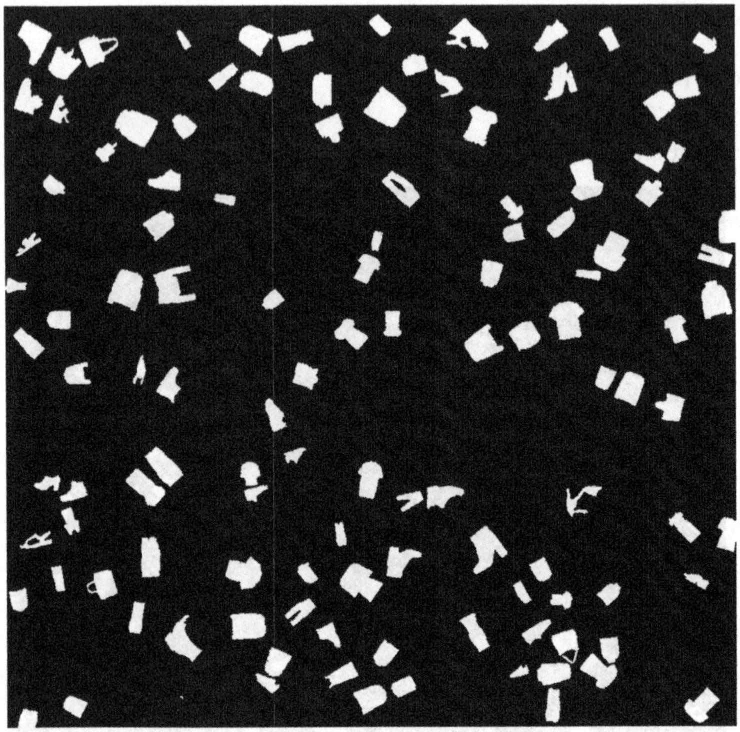

Figure 12.10 – Cleaned mask after removing small artifacts

The next step is to find contiguous regions of white pixels and group them into objects. Fortunately, cuCIM already has a built-in `label` function that does exactly this:

```
from cucim.skimage.measure import label

segmented = label(clean_mask)
```

The `label` function fills each contiguous region with consecutive integers. The background pixels get the label `0`, the first object `1`, and so on. The largest label corresponds to the number of detected objects, so the total number of objects detected is calculated as follows:

```
segmented.max()
```

This returns 120, which indeed corresponds to the number of objects in the image.

The `label` function returns an image with all the pixels labeled. To measure these labeled regions and extract them from the larger image, cuCIM has the `regionprops` function:

```
from cucim.skimage.measure import regionprops

properties = regionprops(segmented, intensity_image=img_gpu)
```

By passing the original image to `regionprops`, masked cut-outs are made of the original objects. The returned `properties` is a list of `RegionProperties`, which are cuCIM objects containing lots of measurements about each region. Properties include the centroid and the coordinates of the bounding box, which can be accessed as follows:

```
prop_obj_1 = properties[1]
print(prop_obj_1.centroid)
print(prop_obj_1.bbox)
```

The following figure shows all the bounding boxes and the labels of the objects superimposed on the original image:

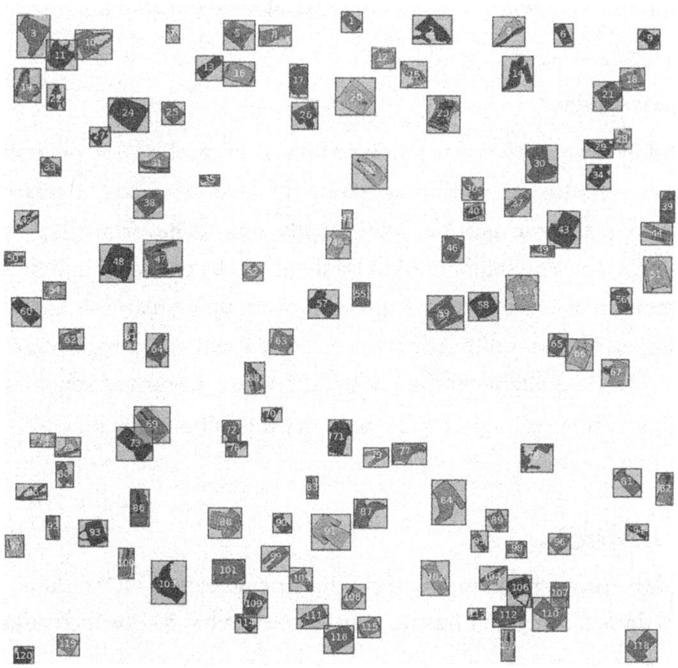

Figure 12.11 – Image showing object bounding boxes obtained through segmentation and labeling

This demonstrates that the segmentation and labeling were successful: all individual objects were separated from the background. The masked cut-out of each object is accessed as follows:

```
obj_extracted = prop_obj_1.image_intensity
```

This is a small CuPy array of shape `(43, 58, 3)`, an RGB image of the blue shoe (object 2, at the top, slightly right of the middle):

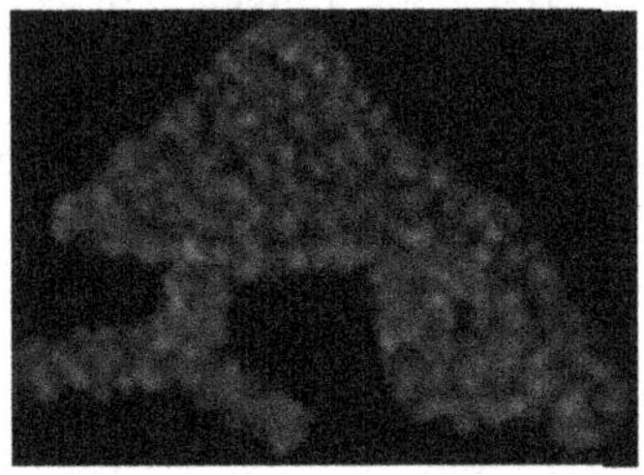

Figure 12.12 – Image showing object 2 extracted from the large image, a blue woman's shoe

Hence, the first part of the problem, segmentation, is solved. Pixels associated with objects have been correctly extracted from a large, noisy image. In the next part, the goal is to extract meaning and interpretation (i.e., to answer the question of what each object is).

> Note
>
> **Segmentation strategies**
>
> The segmentation strategy that was followed for this example is not generally applicable to most images. The fact that objects have bright colors made it relatively easy to separate them from the background. Additionally, objects never overlap, which greatly simplifies the problem. The segmentation strategy will be entirely different for grayscale images or complex real-world RGB images with overlapping features. Each problem and dataset is different, and a lot of time may need to be spent exploring different strategies. Have a look at what is available in the `cucim.skimage.segmentation` module for more advanced segmentation strategies, and when they might be applicable.

Classifying objects

The second part of the problem is finding out what the objects are. Of course, without additional context or external data, a computer has no way to know what a shoe looks like.

In this case, the objects in the image were taken from a well-known labeled image dataset. This means that there is data available to compare the segmented objects to. In addition, since the image was generated, the correct label (the **ground truth**) is known. This makes it possible to evaluate the performance of classification techniques. This section explores how well two classical approaches and a machine-learning-based approach can recover the object types.

Comparing objects based on shape descriptors

For this problem, there exists a library of labeled images containing all the objects that are expected to be found in the image. Unfortunately, it is not possible to perform a pixel-for-pixel comparison of an object with all the objects in the library. The objects that were extracted from the large image are rotated, scaled, colorized, and noisy; the images in the library are grayscale, a fixed size, and have one fixed orientation. Therefore, a method for comparing similarity is needed that is scale- and rotation-invariant.

One such method is to use **Hu moments** as descriptors. Hu moments are 7 numbers that describe the shape of an object. These values are nearly invariant to scale and rotation, so segmented objects can be classified by comparing their Hu moments to those of the objects in the library and selecting the closest matches. Hu moments are **shape descriptors**; they should be calculated on a binary mask to ensure values are comparable.

For the segmented objects, the Hu moments were already calculated on the mask by `regionprops`. They can be accessed as follows:

```
prop_obj_1.moments_hu
```

In this case, the result is a 1D CuPy array:

```
array([ 2.3578712e-01,  8.7864967e-03,  4.3456061e-03,  3.0608239e-04,
       -1.9235887e-07, -5.3977628e-06,  2.9599269e-07], dtype=float32)
```

To collect the Hu moments for all the segmented objects in a 2D CuPy array, `cupy.stack` is used as follows:

```
moments_hu_objects = cp.stack([prop.moments_hu for prop in properties])
```

Now the Hu moments need to be calculated for the objects in the library. The library data can be downloaded and prepared as raw data as follows:

```
from sklearn.datasets import fetch_openml
mnist = fetch_openml("Fashion-MNIST", version=1, as_frame=False)
images = mnist.data.reshape(-1, 28, 28).astype("uint8")
labels = mnist.target.astype(int)
```

The images array is of shape (70000, 28, 28) and the labels contain integers that each map to a class of objects. The labels map onto an index in the following list of class names:

```
class_names = [
    "T-shirt/top", "Trouser", "Pullover", "Dress", "Coat",
    "Sandal", "Shirt", "Sneaker", "Bag", "Ankle boot",
]
```

The images and labels are transferred to the GPU as follows:

```
images_gpu = cp.asarray(images)
labels_gpu = cp.asarray(labels)
```

To calculate the Hu moments, the images first have to be converted into binary images. After some experimentation, the following function, consisting of a thresholding and a sequence of morphology operations, was found to give a good result:

```
from cucim.skimage.morphology import (
    binary_dilation, remove_small_holes,
    remove_small_objects, binary_erosion,
)

def extract_foreground_mask(img: NDArray) -> NDArray:
    mask = img > 20
    pad = 2
    padded_mask = cp.pad(mask, pad)
    cleaned_mask = (
        binary_erosion(
        remove_small_objects(
        remove_small_holes(
        binary_dilation(padded_mask)
    ))))
    return cleaned_mask[pad:-pad, pad:-pad]
```

The reason two pixels of padding are added on all sides and removed at the end is to ensure the morphology operations don't create artifacts between the object and the boundary of the image.

Manually checking a few random objects and their masks side by side shows that the function produces a decent result. An example of a shoe is shown in the following figure:

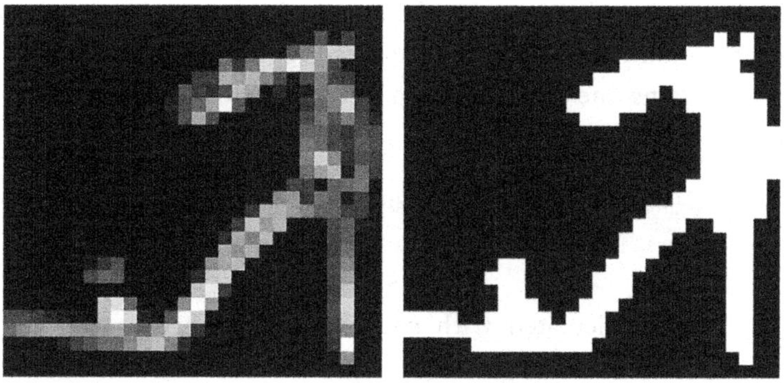

Figure 12.13 – Image of a random library object (a shoe) and its mask

This function works on individual library objects. However, calculating the masks for all objects in the library with this function is too slow. This would require a Python loop over the first axis of the array to process each tiny image sequentially on the GPU. The performance is much worse than performing the same operation on the CPU.

Instead, the operation can be performed on all the images simultaneously by padding the image cube and reshaping it into a 2D image as follows:

```
pad = ((0, 0),(2, 2),(2, 2))
concat_img = cp.pad(images_gpu, pad).reshape(-1, 32)
```

All the images are padded on all sides, then the first two axes are combined. The result is an image of shape `(2240000, 32)` with all the images stacked along the height. The thresholding and morphology operations can be performed directly on this single image:

```
concat_img_thresh = concat_img > 20
cleaned_masks = (
    binary_erosion(
    remove_small_objects(
    remove_small_holes(
    binary_dilation(concat_img_thresh)
))))
```

Now, the reshaping and padding can be reversed to get a stack of binary images:

```
mask_library = cleaned_masks.reshape(-1, 32, 32)[:, 2:-2, 2:-2]
```

To calculate Hu moments of these masks, the same approach as was used for the segmented objects can be used. Finding and labeling connected regions is unnecessary; since each binary image in the stack contains one object, objects can be labeled by multiplying the stack by a 1D array of labels (using broadcasting):

```
mask_labels = cp.arange(1, mask_library.shape[0] + 1, dtype="int32")
labeled_library = mask_library * mask_labels[:, None, None]
```

Region properties can be calculated with `regionprops`, as before, using the same trick of unrolling the first axis to process a single large image:

```
mask_library_props = regionprops(labeled_library.reshape(-1, 28))
```

The `mask_library_props` list only contains 69,998 regions, which means that two objects are missing. This can only be explained by two masks containing zero `True` pixels. Collapsing each image to a single Boolean using the any method over the x and y axes produces a 1D Boolean array that indicates whether there are any `True` pixels in the mask:

```
contains_mask = mask_library.any(axis=(-1, -2))
```

`cupy.where` can be used to find the indices where `contains_mask` is `False`:

```
no_mask_idx = cp.where(~contains_mask)[0]
```

This returns the indices of the following two items in the library:

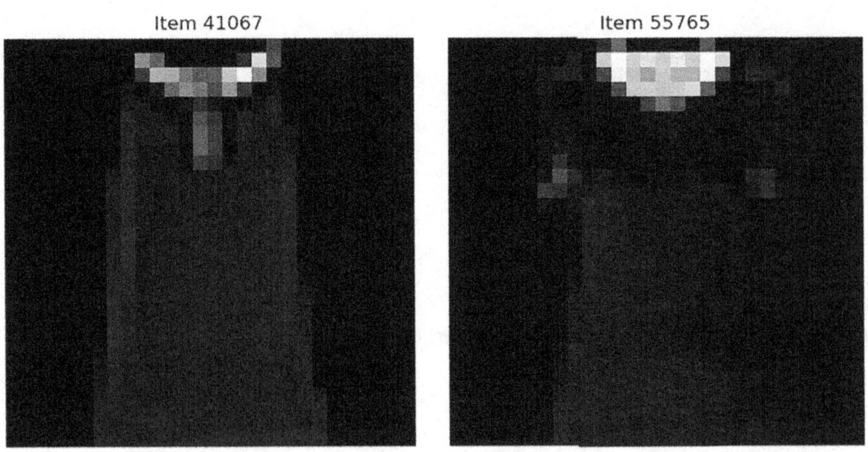

Figure 12.14 – Image of items in the library that were incorrectly masked

The reason for the masking failure is that these clothing items are darker than the selected threshold. Only the collar shows some intensity, but these pixels are probably removed by the morphological operations.

The masking procedure can be further tuned, but for now, these two items will be removed from the library. The Hu moments for all remaining library objects are collected in a CuPy array as follows:

```
moments_hu_library = cp.array([prop.moments_hu for prop in mask_library_props])
```

This takes a few seconds because it must run through a Python loop. Fortunately, this only has to be done once for the entire library.

To be able to compare Hu moments, two additional steps must be taken. First, since Hu moments span multiple orders of magnitude, they are scaled with the signed logarithm using a function, as follows:

```
def scale_hu_moments(moments: NDArray) -> NDArray:
    eps = 1e-30
    return -cp.sign(moments)*np.log10(cp.abs(moments) + eps)
```

The reason a very small positive number is added to the moments is that some moments can be exactly 0, which cannot be passed into the logarithm.

Secondly, to assess similarity, a metric of *closeness* is required. As a first test, **Euclidean distance** can be used. However, Euclidean distance only makes sense if the data in all seven dimensions follow a similar distribution. This can be ensured using `StandardScaler` from cuML.

Hence, the Hu moments from the extracted objects and the Hu moments from the library objects are preprocessed as follows:

```
from cuml.preprocessing import StandardScaler
scaler = StandardScaler()
X_library = scaler.fit_transform(scale_hu_moments(moments_hu_library))
X_observed = scaler.transform(scale_hu_moments(moments_hu_objects))
```

To label `X_observed`, the labels of the closest points in `X_library` are assumed to be the class label. The closest points can be found using a distance matrix or a **KDTree** from `cupyx.scipy.spatial`. Then, these points need to be mapped back to library objects and labels. However, more convenient and compact is to use `KNeighborsClassifier` from cuML as follows:

```
from cuml.neighbors import KNeighborsClassifier
neighbor_classifier = KNeighborsClassifier(n_neighbors=100)
```

The classifier will find the 100 nearest neighbors for each point, then label the point according to the label of the majority. To *fit* the model, `X_library` and the corresponding labels are passed to the `fit` method as follows:

```
filtered_labels = labels_gpu[contains_mask]
neighbor_classifier.fit(X_library, filtered_labels)
```

The labels for `X_observed` can be predicted as follows:

```
y_pred = neighbor_classifier.predict(X_observed)
```

The original image was generated, so the ground truth labels (`y_true`) are known. This can be used to assess the accuracy of this method as follows:

```
from cuml.metrics import accuracy_score
acc = accuracy_score(y_true, y_pred)
```

The accuracy score is 66.7%, meaning two-thirds of the objects in the image were correctly classified. Not too bad considering just 7 numbers are used to describe the shape of the objects!

To identify which objects the method works well for and for which objects it does not, the **confusion matrix** is a very helpful tool. It is shown in *Figure 12.15*:

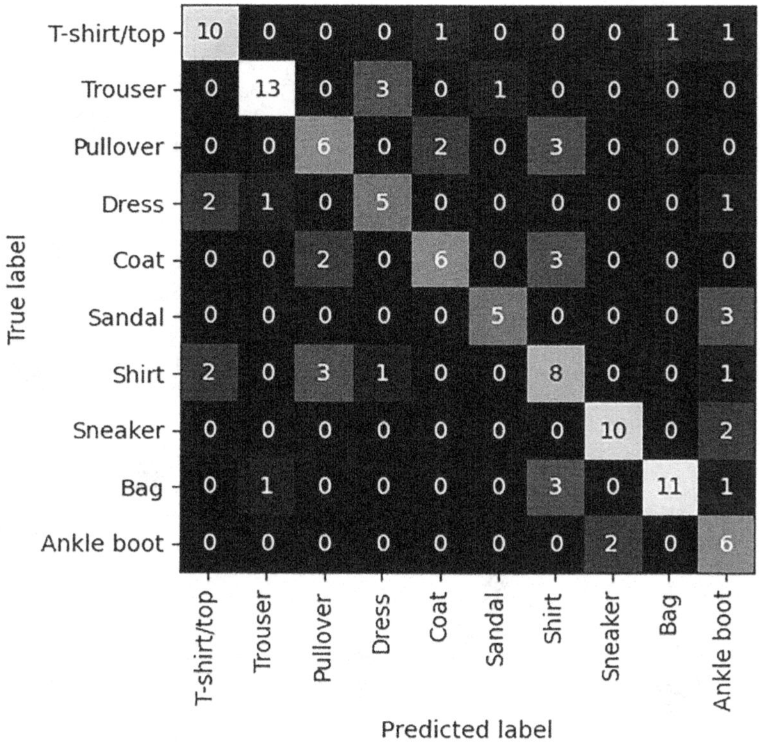

Figure 12.15 – Confusion matrix of the true versus predicted label using the Hu moment method

The values in the confusion matrix show the counts of true labels versus predicted labels. The diagonal shows the number of correct predictions for each class. Off-diagonal elements are incorrect predictions. This reveals which classes are problematic for the method.

The method performs quite well for t-shirts, trousers, sneakers, bags, and ankle boots. The method performs worse on objects that have very similar shapes: pullovers, coats, and shirts. Objects that have a lot of shape variation, such as dresses and sandals, also perform relatively worse. *Figure 12.16* shows the original image, including predicted class labels. Objects with incorrect labels have a box around them:

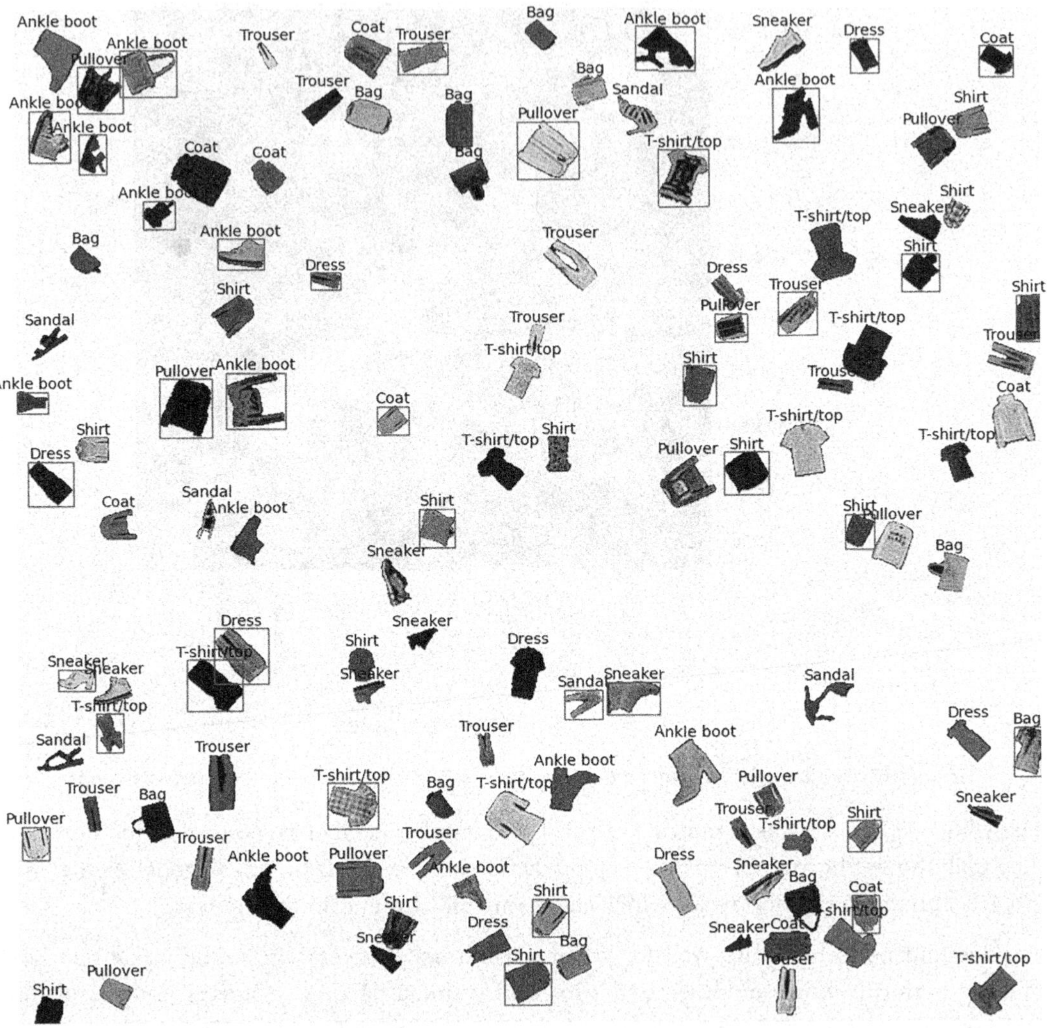

Figure 12.16 – Image showing objects with labels predicted by the Hu method

A classification method that is only 66% accurate is probably not satisfactory. It suggests that for these objects, the Hu moments retain insufficient information to fully describe the object details and retrieve the object class. However, it is a quick, simple, explainable, and scale- and rotation-invariant method to match shapes to templates.

Note

Other feature descriptors

There exist other techniques to automatically extract numerical features from images, including Zernike coefficients, HOG descriptors, ORB descriptors, and more. These can then be matched with another image or a library of images. Each of these methods has specific use cases, advantages, and limitations. For details, have a look at the documentation of the various methods in `cucim.skimage.feature`.

Next, let's look at an alternative method: directly comparing images with template matching.

Direct image comparison: template matching

Instead of comparing objects based on simplified descriptors, template matching compares images pixel-per-pixel to a library of labeled examples. In the guiding example of this section, this is difficult to do directly because objects are rotated and scaled. Rotating each object through all possible rotations and scales and comparing it to each object in the library results in a dauntingly large search space.

There is a more efficient way to do the same thing by leveraging **polar-coordinate** transformations and Fourier transforms. The principle will be illustrated here with the object with label 2 stored in `prop_obj_1`.

The first step is to ensure the segmented objects and library templates are properly centered; if the centers are misaligned, this method will not work. Segmented objects are also first converted to grayscale. The easiest way to do this is to use the "value" channel after converting the colors to HSV space as follows:

```
obj_1_gray = rgb2hsv(prop_obj_1.image_intensity)[:, :, 2]
```

An image can be centered with subpixel precision using the following function:

```
from cupyx.scipy.ndimage import shift, center_of_mass

def center_image(img):
    pad = max(img.shape) // 2
    img_padded = cp.pad(img, pad)

    cy, cx = center_of_mass(img_padded)
    h, w = img_padded.shape
```

```
    shift_y = h / 2 - cy
    shift_x = w / 2 - cx

    shifted = shift(
        img_padded,
        shift=(shift_y, shift_x),
        order=1,
        mode='constant',
        cval=0.0
    )
    return shifted
```

First, the image is padded on all sides with half the maximum image dimension to ensure all the object features are preserved when the object is shifted. Then the image is shifted such that the center of mass (cx, cy) aligns with the image center. It is applied to the grayscale image as follows:

```
centered_obj_1_gray = center_image(obj_1_gray)
```

The library object to which this object corresponds is centered in the same way. The resulting images are shown side by side in *Figure 12.17*:

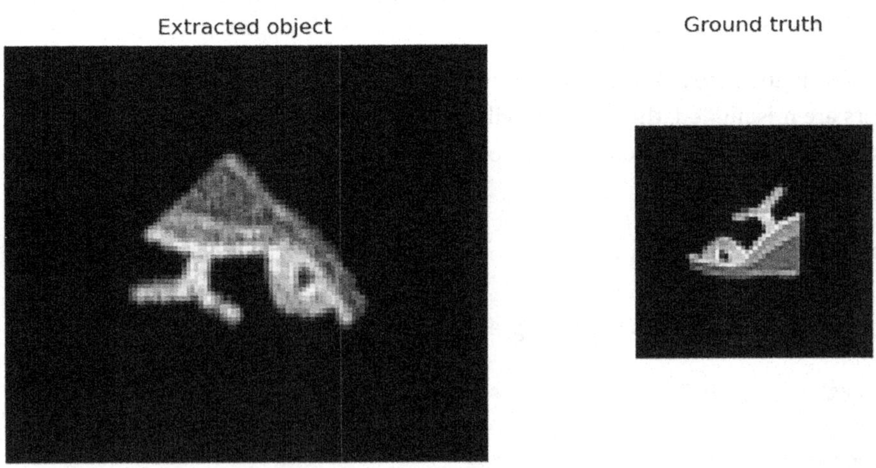

Figure 12.17 – Side-by-side comparison of the centered extracted object and the corresponding library object

Once the images are properly centered, they can be transformed to the **log-polar** domain, as follows:

```
from cucim.skimage.transform import warp_polar

radius = 60
n_rotations = 100
polar_extracted = warp_polar(
    centered_obj_1_gray, radius=radius, scaling='log',
    output_shape=(n_rotations, radius),
)
```

The results are shown side by side here:

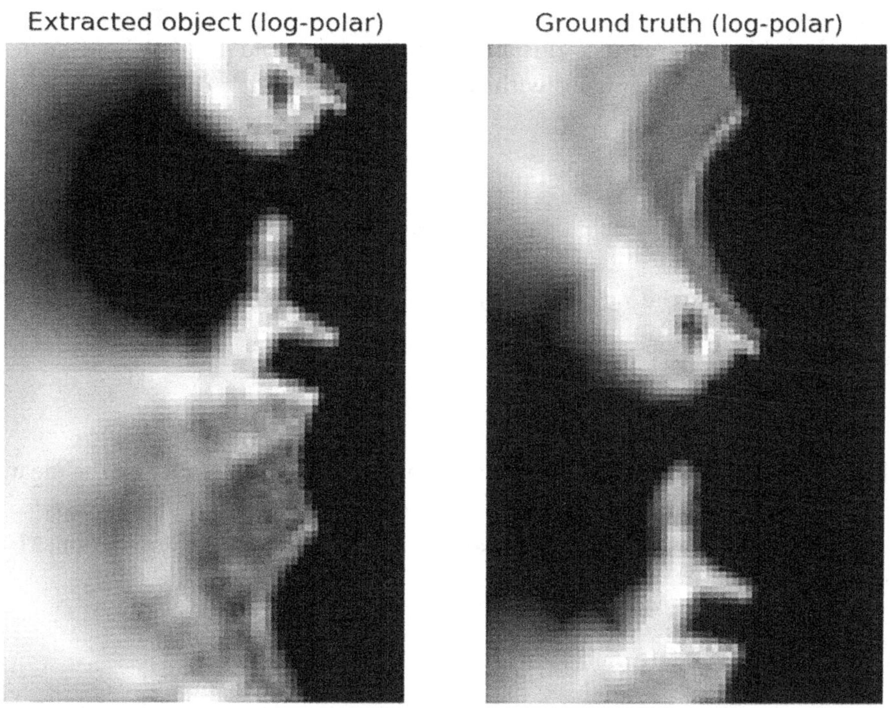

Figure 12.18 – Side-by-side comparison of the extracted object and the corresponding library object in log-polar coordinates

In the polar transform, the y axis of the image represents the angular dimension, and the x axis represents the radial dimension. The radial axis starts at the center of the original image. The radial dimension samples the image logarithmically: there are many closely spaced sampling points near the origin and fewer points further away. In log-polar space, a rotation corresponds to a shift in the y-direction (with wrap-around), and a rescaling corresponds to a shift in the x-direction.

The similarity between features in the two images is apparent. The images could be aligned using a translation, which corresponds to a rotation and rescaling in the original images. The relative translation between the log-polar images can be found using the **cross-correlation** between the images, an operation closely related to convolution. The cross-correlation between two similarly sized images is most efficiently calculated using the Fourier transform.

Before calculating the cross-correlation, two additional steps of preprocessing are needed.

Firstly, the log-polar transform oversamples the center of the object, meaning that the intensity of the central pixels contributes disproportionately to the cross-correlation. The first columns on the left side of the log-polar image represent a very smeared-out view of a few pixels near the center of the original image, even though these contain very little information on the scale or rotation of the object. To correct this bias, the pixels should be weighted such that the contribution increases exponentially with increasing radius. This can be achieved using the following `weights` array:

```
weights = cp.exp(cp.linspace(0, 1, radius)) - 1
weights /= weights.max()
```

The weights are applied to the log-polar-transformed images as follows:

```
weighted_polar_extracted = polar_extracted * weights
weighted_polar_truth = polar_truth * weights
```

Secondly, the mean pixel intensity is subtracted from each image. Subtracting the mean removes the constant-brightness component from the images, ensuring that the cross-correlation measures similarity in spatial intensity variations rather than overall illumination. The mean is subtracted as follows:

```
weighted_polar_extracted -= weighted_polar_extracted.mean()
weighted_polar_truth -= weighted_polar_truth.mean()
```

The first step in calculating the cross-correlation is calculating the **fast Fourier transform** (**FFT**) of both preprocessed log-polar-transformed images as follows:

```
from cupyx.scipy.fft import rfft2, irfft2
```

```
fft_polar_extracted = rfft2(weighted_polar_extracted)
fft_polar_truth = rfft2(weighted_polar_truth)
```

The cross-correlation is the magnitude of the **inverse fast Fourier transform (iFFT)** of the product of one FFT with the conjugate of the second:

```
cross_correlation = np.abs(
    irfft2(fft_polar_extracted * fft_polar_truth.conj())
)
```

The result is also a real-valued 2D image, which looks as follows:

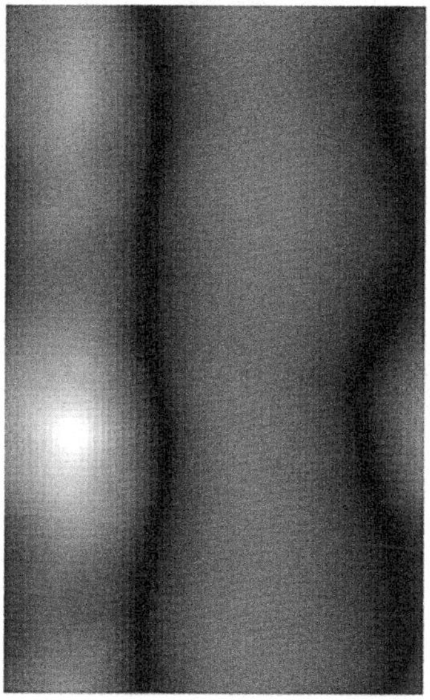

Figure 12.19 – Cross-correlation between the log-polar transforms of the extracted and ground truth images

The bright spot in the image corresponds to the shift that best aligns the log-polar images. The coordinates of this maximum are calculated as follows:

```
y_peak, x_peak = cp.unravel_index(cp.argmax(cross_correlation),
cross_correlation.shape)
```

These values correspond to relative scale and rotation (in degrees) differences between the two images. The rotation and scale differences are calculated as follows:

```
rotation = float(y_peak * (360 / n_rotations))
scale = float(1 / (cp.exp(x_peak * cp.log(radius) / radius)))
```

The result is a relative rotation of 223 degrees and a scaling factor of 0.54 to match the extracted object with the object from the library. This is extremely close to the ground truth: a rotation of 225 degrees and a scaling factor of 0.53.

The extracted object can be rotated and scaled down to confirm the match as follows:

```
from cucim.skimage.transform import rotate, rescale
matched = rescale(rotate(obj_1_gray, rotation, resize=True), scale)
```

The result is shown side by side with the ground truth in the following figure:

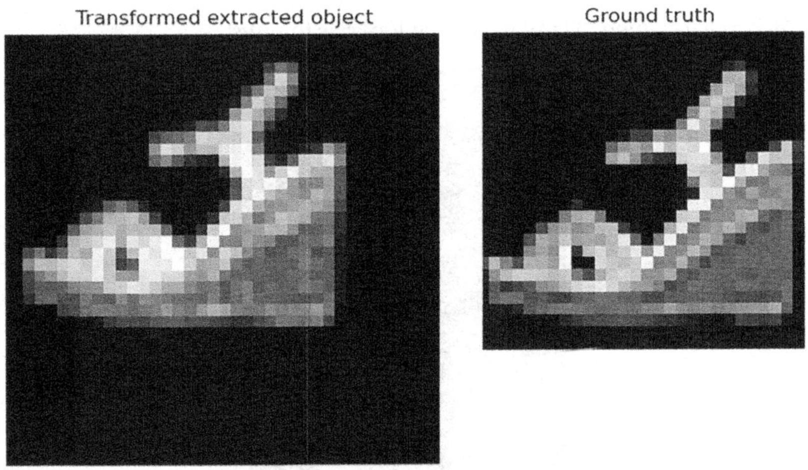

Figure 12.20 – Comparison of the transformed extracted object after template matching with the original object

The template-matching technique is hereby illustrated.

So far, a single object has been compared to the matching original object. In reality, each extracted object needs to be compared to every template. The template for which the peak correlation is highest is selected as the match. In principle, this is one of the few techniques that can recover exact matches. In practice, the technique is very sensitive to finding the correct center, pixel noise, and outliers, and it is computationally very expensive. For brevity, the full template-matching implementation to compare each object with each image in the library will not be worked out here, but if motivated to, the readers are encouraged to take it up as an exercise. An implementation can be found in the associated GitHub repository.

To compare with the Hu-moments-based analysis, the results are shared here. The classification accuracy of the template-matching approach is around 80%; 97 out of 120 objects extracted from the image were correctly classified. For 54 out of 120 objects, just over 45%, an exact match with the original library object was found. *Figure 12.21* shows the confusion matrix:

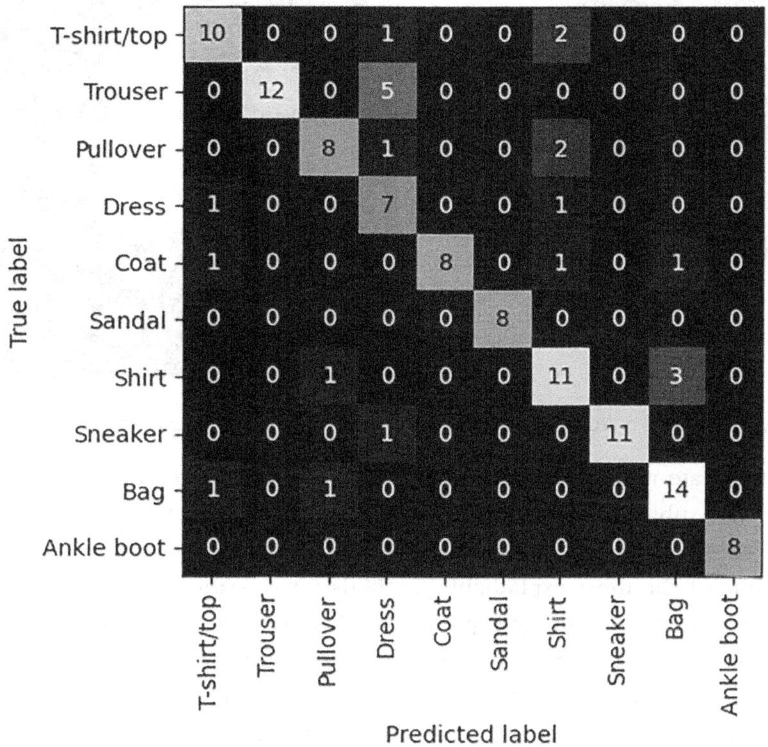

Figure 12.21 – Confusion matrix for template-matching classification

Trousers are often confused with dresses. By comparing an incorrectly classified example, it becomes clear how the algorithm can get confused between these classes:

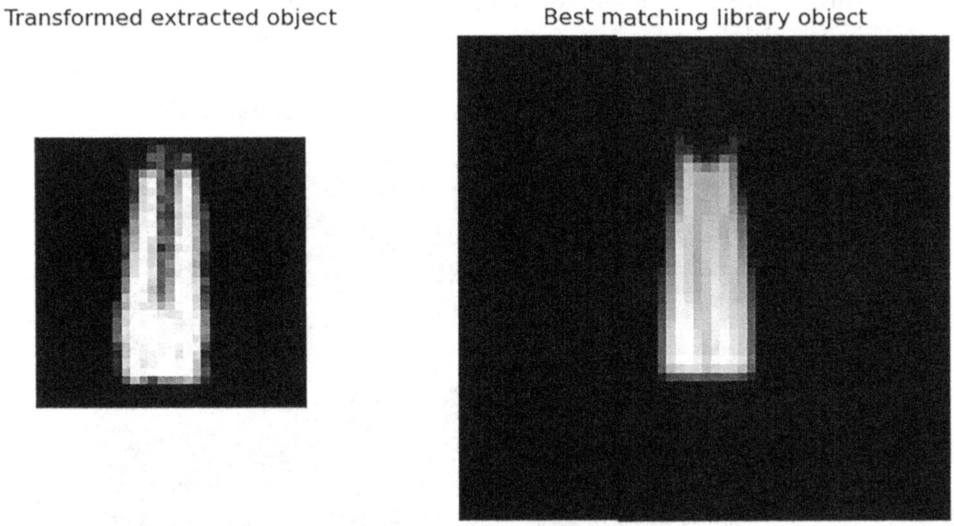

Figure 12.22 – Example of trousers getting confused with a dress by the template-matching procedure

Overall, the template-matching approach is more accurate than the Hu-moment approach. However, it is also substantially slower. The Hu-moment approach takes a few milliseconds to classify all the objects in the image, whereas the template-matching approach takes longer than a minute. It is one of the most explainable methods for classifying objects, but the results are sensitive to noise and the quality of centering. In this example, the template library consists of many very similarly shaped objects in low-resolution images. Given that the extracted objects contain quite a lot of pixel noise, 80% accuracy and perfect matching of 45% of objects is pretty good. Using additional preprocessing steps, such as filters, can further refine the method for improved accuracy.

The last section explores one final approach for image classification, which has become a de facto standard in the industry: **convolutional neural networks** (**CNNs**).

Classifying objects with a CNN

The previous methods all relied on smart image processing and some knowledge about the structure of the data to classify objects. The benefit is that these methods are all explainable. The drawback is that setting up a classification pipeline is time-consuming because it requires a lot of experimentation. In addition, the pipeline is likely to be very brittle; small tweaks to these procedures have a large influence on the classification result.

An alternative approach is to use a CNN. CNNs are a type of neural network that has **convolutional** layers that perform 2D convolutions on their inputs. The difference between convolutional layers and the 2D convolution function implemented earlier in this chapter is that the weights of the kernels in these layers are **learnable parameters**. Based on lots of labeled examples, the network is **trained** to find optimal weights to transform inputs to the desired outputs, much like a function is fit to data. The convolutional layers serve to automatically extract distinguishing features from images. These features are fed to **dense** layers to get classification results. The convolutional neural network allows any image classification task to be approached using a formulaic approach that usually achieves good results.

Let's illustrate this procedure for the classification problem at hand. The Flax framework, which builds on JAX, will be used to build a CNN. A very simple CNN is constructed as follows:

```
from flax import linen as nn

class SimpleCNN(nn.Module):
    num_classes: int

    @nn.compact
    def __call__(self, x, train=False):
        x = nn.Conv(features=32, kernel_size=(3, 3))(x)
        x = nn.relu(x)
        x = nn.avg_pool(x, window_shape=(2, 2), strides=(2, 2))

        x = nn.Conv(features=64, kernel_size=(3, 3))(x)
        x = nn.relu(x)
        x = nn.avg_pool(x, window_shape=(2, 2), strides=(2, 2))

        x = x.reshape((x.shape[0], -1))
        x = nn.Dense(128)(x)
        x = nn.relu(x)
        x = nn.Dense(self.num_classes)(x)
        return x
```

This is a **feed-forward** network composed of multiple **layers**, each serving a different purpose. The input is passed to the first layer, the output from the first layer is handed to the next layer, and so on, until the output is returned from the last layer. There are four essential layer types in this network:

- `Conv` (convolutional layer): This layer learns convolutional kernels that extract local features from the input. Convolution is what allows the network to capture spatial relationships in images. The `features` argument specifies the number of kernels to learn, while `kernel_size` specifies their spatial size. For example, in the first `Conv` layer, the network learns 32 kernels of size 3×3. Since the input has one channel, this results in 3×3×1×32 = 288 trainable weights. By default, a bias term is added for each feature map, resulting in an additional 32 trainable parameters. The outputs of these convolutions are stored along the channel (last) dimension.

- **Rectified linear unit (ReLU)**: ReLU is an elementwise operation defined as `max(0, x)`. Negative values are set to zero, while positive values are left unchanged. ReLU is a popular activation function used to introduce nonlinearity into the network. This is essential for fitting nonlinear relationships. Dense and convolutional layers are typically followed by an activation layer. Activation layers have no trainable parameters.
- `avg_pool`: Average pooling reduces the spatial dimensions of its input by aggregating nearby values, in this case by taking their average. The `window_shape` parameter specifies the size of the region to aggregate, while `strides` determines how the window is moved across the input. In `SimpleCNN`, the pooling layer averages non-overlapping 2×2 regions. Pooling reduces spatial resolution, making the representation more compact and helping the network become less sensitive to small spatial shifts. Pooling layers have no trainable parameters.
- `Dense`: A dense layer computes weighted sums of input values, with the weights being learned parameters. Dense layers serve to combine the features learned by the convolutional layers to produce a final classification. Mathematically, a dense layer performs a matrix multiplication on its input, with the matrix elements being learnable parameters.

Note

The nn.compact decorator

The `nn.compact` decorator makes it possible to define the network with all its layers directly in the `__call__` method without re-initializing layers.

The model is essentially a function that turns a stack of images into an array of labels. It is composed of a number of sequential layers, some of which need many tunable parameters. To illustrate how the model is used, let's instantiate the model and its parameters. The model is instantiated by providing the number of classes (10 types of clothing):

```
model = SimpleCNN(num_classes=10)
```

Contrary to other deep learning frameworks, Flax models do not store their parameters as internal state. Random model parameters can be initialized by making a call to the model's `init` method as follows:

```
import jax
import jax.numpy as jnp

dummy_input = jnp.ones((1, 28, 28, 1))
rng = jax.random.PRNGKey(0)
variables = model.init(rng, dummy_input)
```

The method requires a key for generating random numbers, which ensures the starting state is reproducible, and some dummy input data for deriving the shapes of parameter arrays. Stored in `variables` is a Python dictionary, with names of layers as keys and JAX arrays as values.

Take note of the shape of `dummy_input`. Flax `Conv` layers expect input arrays following the convention `(batch_size, height, width, channel)`. In the clothing example, images are 28 by 28 and grayscale (channel = 1). For performance, inference and training happen on multiple images simultaneously in a **batch**, which is why a 4D array is passed. Batch size does not influence the shapes of parameter arrays, so a batch size of 1 can be chosen for initialization. For training and inference, a different batch size can be used.

The model and the parameters can be used for inference on a batch of 100 images as follows:

```
X_test = jnp.ones((100, 28, 28, 1))
scores = model.apply(variables, X_test)
```

The shape of the output is `(batch_size, num_classes)` (i.e., a row of 10 numbers for each image). These numbers correspond to a "score" that the image is of a particular class.

To assign an image to a class, a decision rule needs to be chosen. The simplest decision rule is to assign an image to the class with the highest corresponding score. This amounts to finding the index of the maximum along the columns:

```
class_index = jnp.argmax(scores, axis=-1)
```

So far, the model can only make completely useless predictions because the parameters are random. Parameters need to be found that allow the model to make useful predictions. This is done by training the model with labeled data.

The first step in optimizing the parameters is to create a `TrainState`. This is a helper object that bundles parameters, the model, and an optimizer. A `TrainState` is created as follows:

```
from flax.training import train_state
import optax

learning_rate = 1e-3
tx = optax.adam(learning_rate)
state = train_state.TrainState.create(
    apply_fn=model.apply,
    params=variables["params"],
    tx=tx,
)
```

The optimizer determines how parameters are updated during training. The `adam` optimizer is a popular choice in neural network training.

The training procedure is defined as follows:

```
def train(state,
          X_train, y_train,
          X_val, y_val,
          batch_size,
          epochs):

    num_train = X_train.shape[0]
    n_batches = num_train // batch_size

    for epoch in range(epochs):
        perm = np.random.permutation(num_train)

        train_loss = 0.0
        train_acc  = 0.0

        for i in range(0, num_train, batch_size):
            idx = perm[i:i+batch_size]
            batch = (X_train[idx], y_train[idx])
            batch = augment(batch)
            state, loss, acc = train_step(state, batch)
            train_loss += loss
            train_acc  += acc
```

```
        train_loss /= n_batches
        train_acc  /= n_batches

        val_loss, val_acc = eval_step(
            state, augment((X_val, y_val))
        )

        print(
            f"Epoch {epoch+1}: "
            f"train acc={train_acc:.4f}, "
            f"val acc={val_acc:.4f}"
        )

    return state
```

At first glance, this looks long and complicated, but the essence is quite simple. The model is trained over multiple **epochs**, where each epoch corresponds to a complete pass over the training dataset and results in incremental updates to the model parameters. In each epoch, the training data is shuffled using `np.random.permutation` to generate a random permutation of indices. The inner loop iterates over batches of the training dataset. First, the batch is **augmented** to ensure the model generalizes across different effects, such as object rotation. Then, the augmented batches and the training state are passed to a `train_step` function that has yet to be defined. The `train_step` function should return an updated `state`, as well as the **loss** and accuracy for the batch. The loss is a number that measures a "distance" between the predictions and the true values. The goal of training a network is to minimize the loss. To calculate the loss, a loss function needs to be defined. At the end of the inner loop, the loss and accuracy are averaged over the batches. The loss and accuracy are also calculated on a validation dataset to check whether the model generalizes across data that is not used in the optimization. If the validation loss increases and the validation accuracy decreases, it suggests that the model is overfitting.

The `train_step` function is defined as follows:

```
@jax.jit
def train_step(state, batch):
    imgs, true_labels = batch

    def loss_fn(params):
        scores_pred = state.apply_fn({'params': params}, imgs)
        scores_true = jax.nn.one_hot(true_labels,
```

```
                                    scores_pred.shape[-1])
        loss = optax.softmax_cross_entropy(scores_pred,
                                           scores_true,
                                          ).mean()
        return loss, scores_pred

    (loss, scores_pred), grads = jax.value_and_grad(
        loss_fn, has_aux=True)(state.params)

    state = state.apply_gradients(grads=grads)

    pred_labels = jnp.argmax(scores_pred, axis=-1)
    acc = jnp.mean(pred_labels == true_labels)
    return state, loss, acc
```

This requires some unpacking. The main goal of `train_step` is to update the model parameters in a way to minimize the loss.

The nested `loss_fn` function computes the loss by comparing model predictions with true labels. First, the predicted scores are computed using the `state.apply_fn` method, which takes the parameters and images as input. The ground truth labels are converted into one-hot vectors, which represent the correct class as a probability distribution. These one-hot labels are compared to the predicted class scores using Optax's `softmax_cross_entropy` function, which measures how well the predictions match the true labels. The loss for the batch is then defined as the mean cross-entropy across all images, resulting in one scalar value.

Using JAX's automatic differentiation capabilities, the gradients of this loss function with respect to the model parameters are calculated with `jax.value_and_grad`. The `has_aux=True` flag allows the loss function to return auxiliary outputs (in this case, the predicted scores) without differentiating through them.

The parameters stored in `state` are updated using the gradients via the optimizer stored inside `state`. This produces an updated `TrainState`.

The predicted scores are also used to compute the predicted class labels and evaluate accuracy on the batch. Accuracy is simply the fraction of predictions that match the true labels.

Finally, the function returns the updated state, the batch loss, and the batch accuracy. The `train_step` function is decorated with `@jax.jit` to JIT-compile it, which maximizes performance.

The next piece of the training puzzle is to define the evaluation step, `eval_step`. This function is very similar to `train_step`, but simpler since only loss and accuracy need to be evaluated without updating the state. The function can be implemented as follows:

```
@jax.jit
def eval_step(state, batch):
    imgs, true_labels = batch
    scores_pred = state.apply_fn({'params': state.params}, imgs)
    scores_true = jax.nn.one_hot(true_labels,
                                 scores_pred.shape[-1])
    loss = optax.softmax_cross_entropy(scores_pred,
                                       scores_true).mean()

    pred_labels = jnp.argmax(scores_pred, axis=-1)
    acc = jnp.mean(pred_labels == true_labels)
    return loss, acc
```

Note

Code deduplication

Since the loss and accuracy calculations are duplicated in multiple places, the logic could be moved into dedicated functions. Thanks to the `jax.jit` decorator on the outer functions, this will not negatively impact performance.

The final piece that needs to be implemented is the data augmentation procedure (i.e., the `augment` function). Since the model should be roughly invariant to translation by design, the main effect the model should generalize across is object rotation. Therefore, the model needs to see examples of rotated objects. Rotating the images in a batch by a random angle can be done as follows:

```
from scipy.ndimage import rotate

def augment(batch):
    imgs, true_labels = batch
    angle = np.random.uniform(0, 360)
    rotated = rotate(
        imgs,
        angle,
        axes=(1, 2),
```

```
        reshape=False,
        mode='nearest',
    )
    return (rotated, true_labels)
```

The augmentation is performed on the host, since benchmarks showed this was not a bottleneck. All images in a batch are rotated by the same random angle to get acceptable performance.

Artificial noise could also be added to the data as part of the augmentation procedure to make the network more robust. However, before complicating things, the performance of the model will be evaluated without explicitly adding noise to the training data.

The last step is to split the data into a training and validation set, which is done as follows:

```
n_images = images.shape[0]
idx = np.random.permutation(n_images)

n_train = int(0.8 * n_images)

train_idx = idx[:n_train]
val_idx   = idx[n_train:]

X = (images.astype(np.float32) / 255.)[..., None]
y = labels
X_train = X[train_idx]
y_train = y[train_idx]
X_val = X[val_idx]
y_val = y[val_idx]
```

80% of the library is used for training, and 20% is used for validation. In a real-world case, an additional `test` set would be created that is only used at the end of training to evaluate the model. In the example case, the test set consists of the objects extracted from the noisy image.

Notice also that the images are converted to `float32`. The pixel values are rescaled to a range from 0 to 1, and an extra channel axis is added at the end of the array using `[..., None]`.

The model is trained as follows:

```
state = train(state, X_train, y_train, X_val, y_val, batch_size=200, epochs=50)
```

After 50 epochs, a training and validation accuracy of around 88% is achieved. Since data is augmented in a randomized fashion, convergence is likely very slow. The model may improve further with longer training. The state can be saved to disk, and training can be resumed later.

For now, this is good enough. Let's evaluate the model on the extracted objects. As in the template-matching approach, the `value` channel from the images is used. Objects also need to be downscaled and padded to get an array with the shape expected by the model. This can be done as follows:

```
X_test = np.zeros((len(extracted_images_value), 28, 28, 1),
                  dtype=np.float32)
for i, extracted_image in enumerate(extracted_images_value):
    largest_dimension = max(extracted_image.shape)
    zoom_factor = 28 / largest_dimension
    scaled_image = zoom(extracted_image, zoom_factor)
    y_min = 14 - scaled_image.shape[0] // 2
    y_max = y_min + scaled_image.shape[0]
    x_min = 14 - scaled_image.shape[1] // 2
    x_max = x_min + scaled_image.shape[1]
    X_test[i, y_min:y_max, x_min:x_max, 0] = scaled_image
```

The labels for the extracted objects are predicted as follows:

```
scores_pred = state.apply_fn({'params': state.params}, X_test)
pred_labels = jnp.argmax(scores_pred, axis=-1)
```

As before, these labels can be compared to the ground truth using the accuracy score and the confusion matrix. The accuracy is 60%, which is somewhat disappointing. This indicates that pixel noise strongly influences the performance of the model. *Figure 12.23* shows the confusion matrix:

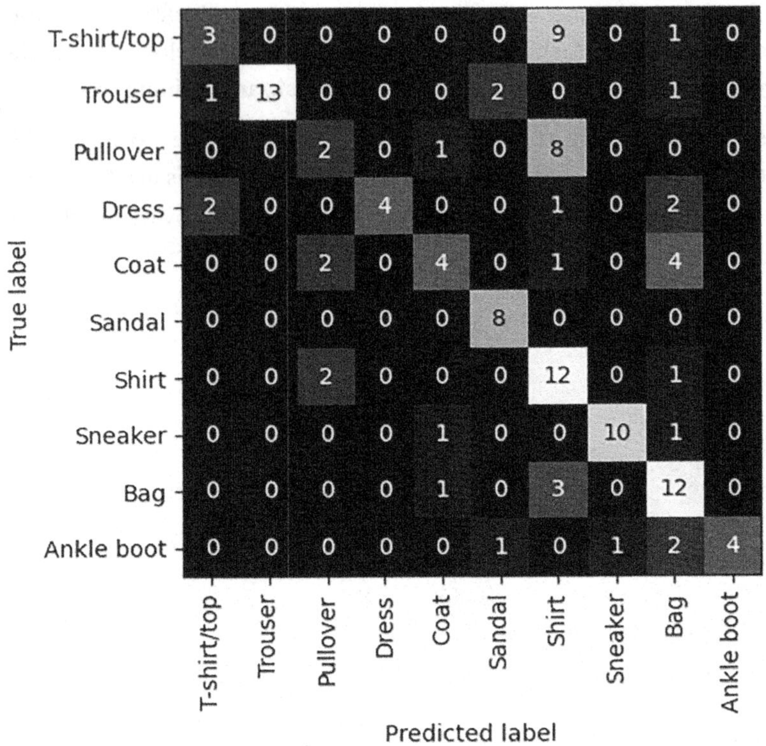

Figure 12.23 – Confusion matrix for CNN-model-based classification

The model performs well on objects with a distinctive shape, such as shoes and bags. Unlike the other approaches, the model does pretty well for trousers. For most upper-body clothing items, the model tends to favor the "shirt" classification, indicating either that the model has not yet learned to properly distinguish between these classes and more training is needed, or that the noise makes the class ambiguous.

To improve the model, much longer training (more epochs) could be considered. However, since training and validation accuracy are similar, the real problem is that the noisy extracted objects are out of distribution. Therefore, additional augmentation strategies need to be explored to improve the generalizability of the model. Alternatively, instead of creating a model from scratch, a very deep pre-trained neural net such as ResNet-18 (`https://huggingface.co/microsoft/resnet-18`) can be used as a base for a specialized model. Tweaking the last layers of a pre-trained model, by re-training it on a small and specific dataset, is called **transfer learning**, and it is a highly popular and effective approach.

Summary

In this chapter, GPU programming techniques and specialized libraries were applied to practical image processing and computer vision tasks. The chapter covered how images are represented in memory, how they can be manipulated as N-dimensional arrays, and how color is modeled in different color spaces. A 2D convolutional filter was implemented from scratch with a CUDA kernel. This implementation was profiled and compared to optimized implementations in high-level libraries such as cuCIM and `cupyx.scipy.ndimage`.

The bulk of the chapter was spent on a practical computer vision task: detecting and classifying objects in a large image. Objects were segmented from a noisy background using classical image processing methods and classified using three different approaches: shape descriptors (Hu moments), template matching, and a convolutional neural network. This case study illustrated the key building blocks of an image processing pipeline.

The next chapter explores a scientific application of GPU programming: simulating atomic interactions with molecular dynamics.

Questions

1. How are grayscale and RGB images represented in memory?
2. Why are images often stored as `uint8`, and why are floating-point types preferred for processing?
3. What is a spatial-domain convolution and how is it used in image processing?
4. Why was HSV color space useful for image segmentation in the case study?
5. What role do morphological operations play after thresholding?
6. Why does Hu-moment-based classification struggle with some object classes?
7. What are the main drawbacks of template matching?
8. Why are convolutional neural networks well-suited for image classification?
9. What is the purpose of data augmentation during CNN training?
10. When might classical image processing be preferred over deep learning?

Answers

1. A grayscale image is represented as a 2D array where each element corresponds to pixel intensity. An RGB image is represented as a 3D array with shape (height, width, 3), where the last axis stores red, green, and blue channel intensities.

2. `uint8` conserves memory and disk space and provides sufficient precision for visual display. Floating-point types (`float32` or `float64`) are preferred during processing because they reduce numerical errors and simplify arithmetic operations during filtering and transformations.
3. Spatial-domain convolution slides a small kernel over an image and computes a weighted sum of neighboring pixels for each output pixel. It is commonly used for blurring, smoothing, edge detection, and feature enhancement.
4. The saturation channel in HSV clearly separates colored objects from a nearly white background, making threshold-based segmentation straightforward and robust to intensity variations.
5. Morphological operations remove small holes and spurious objects, clean noise, and improve the connectivity of segmented regions, resulting in a more accurate binary mask.
6. Objects with similar silhouettes produce similar Hu moments, making it difficult to distinguish between classes such as shirts, coats, and pullovers.
7. It is computationally expensive, sensitive to noise and centering errors, and scales poorly when comparing many objects against large template libraries.
8. CNNs automatically learn hierarchical features through convolutional layers, require less manual feature engineering, and typically achieve higher accuracy across diverse datasets.
9. Data augmentation exposes the network to transformed versions of the data (e.g., rotations), improving generalization and robustness to variations not explicitly present in the training set.
10. Classical methods are preferable when interpretability, limited data, strict performance constraints, or deterministic behavior are required, or when the problem structure is well understood.

Get this book's PDF version and more

Scan the QR code (or go to `packtpub.com/unlock`). Search for this book by name, confirm the edition, and then follow the steps on the page.

UNLOCK NOW

Note: Keep your invoice handy. Purchases made directly from Packt don't require an invoice.

13

Simulating Atomic Interactions on the GPU

In this chapter, we will demonstrate how to use GPUs to efficiently model atomic interactions. We will implement a GPU-accelerated **molecular dynamics** (**MD**) simulator. MD is a technique often used for predicting the behavior of materials at the atomic scale. We will simulate a simple atomic system of an ideal gas, such as helium, in two dimensions, to minimize complex technical details that may require specialized expertise. *Numba CUDA* will be used to accelerate the computationally demanding kernels, including the particle-particle interactions and time integration. This approach will help reinforce the fundamental concepts and principles we have discussed in previous chapters, showing how to implement computationally intensive kernels in CUDA to solve real-world scientific problems.

In this chapter, we'll cover the following main topics:

- Knowing a brief theoretical background of MD simulations
- Learning step-by-step implementations of different components of an MD simulator
- Performance comparison of a GPU-accelerated simulator with serial and multithreaded CPU versions
- Utilizing kernel execution and memory access profiling insights for further optimization

Technical requirements

We require a system equipped with an Nvidia GPU that has at least 10 GB of memory. The necessary packages *Numba* and *NVIDIA Nsight Compute* will be used in this chapter. We'll use `Pixi` as a dependency management tool that installs these packages. To set up the environment, simply run `pixi install` in the root directory of the book's GitHub repository. This will ensure that all dependencies are installed. Once the installation is complete, you can activate the environment using `pixi shell`.

Then run the following:

```
jupyter-pixi run jupyter-lab
```

This will start JupyterLab, a browser-based environment to run Jupyter notebooks.

The chapter's code is available on GitHub and can be accessed via this link: `https://github.com/PacktPublishing/GPU-Accelerated-Computing-with-Python-3-and-CUDA`. We recommend cloning the repository and following the instructions in the README file to get started building the environment.

How MD simulations work

MD simulations are utilized in many scientific fields, offering a computational microscope for understanding the behavior of atoms and molecules that are challenging to observe experimentally.

An MD simulation can be broken into four main steps:

1. **System initialization**: The first step is initializing the state of our collection of particles and choosing simulation settings.
2. **Atomic interactions**: The next step is calculating the interactions between our particles, which determine how the particles move in response to forces. These interactions are typically governed by potential energy functions that describe how the potential energy of the system changes with respect to the positions of the particles.
3. **Time integration**: Once the forces between atoms are calculated, the next step is to determine how the atoms move over time. This is done by solving Newton's equations of motion for each particle using time integration.
4. **Data collection**: While a simulation runs, a subset of information must be periodically extracted for later analysis.

The following flowchart illustrates how these various steps of an MD simulation are executed.

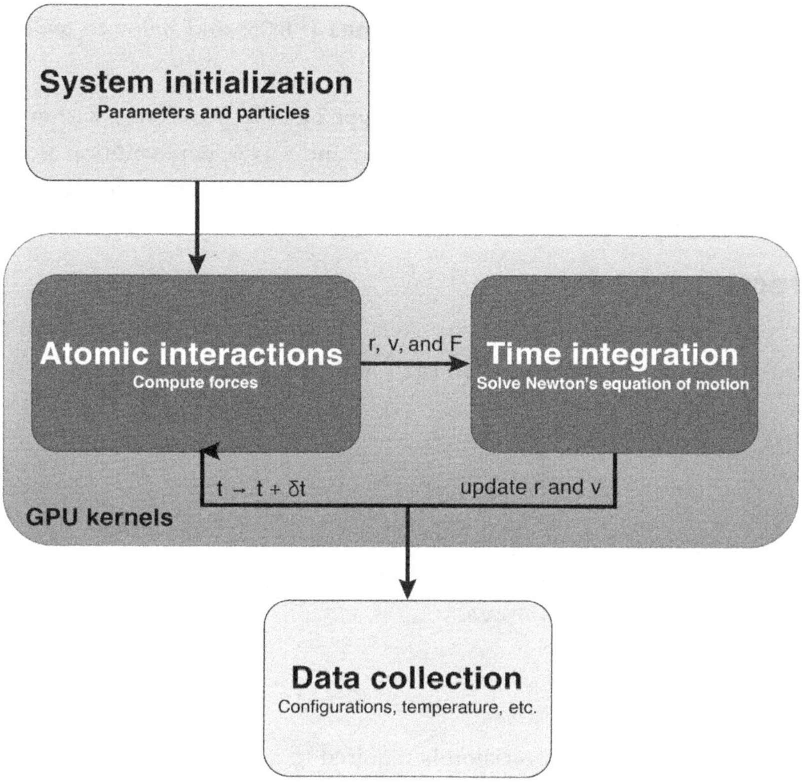

Figure 13.1 – Key steps in molecular dynamics (MD) simulation

Time is discretized into small intervals called time steps (δt). For each time step, there is an iterative process between force calculations and time integration. This process is repeated ($t \to t + \delta t$) to obtain the trajectories of the atoms over time.

In the remainder of this chapter, we will elaborate on each step and provide implementations as we progress.

System initialization

The system we want to model is a collection of particles. **Particles** are initialized with starting positions and velocities, based on experimental data and physical conditions such as desired temperature and pressure.

In an MD simulation, particles are constrained to a finite region of space called a *simulation box*. To mimic an infinite system, which is a good approximation for gases, liquids, and bulk materials, the boundaries of this box are usually defined to be periodic. This means when an atom moves outside one boundary, it reappears on the opposite side, mimicking a continuous space. This concept is known as **periodic boundary conditions** (**PBCs**) and helps to avoid edge effects, which would happen if boundaries were rigid.

Here, we consider a system composed of a single type of atom positioned within a 2D box. This setup restricts the particles to movement along the x and y axes, while motion along the z axis is prohibited. This configuration is ideal for our demonstration example, as it can be easily extended to three dimensions.

Parameters

To begin, we need to import `numpy` and `numba.cuda`. We also import some types (`NDArray`), define some aliases for type annotations (`TypeAlias`), and file-like objects (`TextIO`), which help to improve code readability.

```
import math
import numpy as np
from numba import cuda
from numpy.typing import NDArray
from typing import NamedTuple, TypeAlias, TextIO
FLOAT: TypeAlias = np.float64
Array: TypeAlias = NDArray[FLOAT]
```

In scientific simulations, `float64` precision is required to avoid numerical instability. However, there are reasons to prefer `float32` precision. Most GPUs are heavily optimized for `float32` operations; `float64` operations are typically slower unless data center GPUs are used. Less precise, `float32` (about 7 decimal digits) uses less memory as compared to the more precise `float64` (15 decimal digits). However, in scientific simulations, `float64` precision is often used to avoid small rounding errors from accumulating, leading to incorrect or unstable results. To be flexible, we defined an alias, `FLOAT`, which we can set to either `float32` or `float64`. The default precision is set to `float64`. Additionally, we defined the `Array` alias for multidimensional arrays that can hold elements of the type specified by `FLOAT`.

Next, we define system parameters using a *named tuple*, which allows us to create an immutable data structure with named fields. This is like a *C structure* and very useful when passing related data into Python functions with a single argument. Numba CUDA *JIT*-compiled functions accept tuples and named tuples as input arguments, which makes it quite convenient. We implement `SimulationParameters` as follows:

```
class SimulationParameters(NamedTuple):
    num_atoms: int
```

```
    time_step: float
    box_length: float
    atom_spacing: float
    velocity_std: float
```

In our simulation, we will set the number of atoms, `num_atoms=100`, and initial atom spacing, `atom_spacing=2.5`. The `time_step` represents the interval between simulation updates and is set to `0.0001`. The simulation box size length, `box_length`, is calculated based on the number of atoms and their spacing. Finally, the velocity standard deviation, `velocity_std`, is set to `10.0`.

```
num_atoms = 100
atom_spacing = 2.5

params = SimulationParameters(
    num_atoms=num_atoms,
    time_step=0.0001,
    box_length=math.sqrt(num_atoms) * atom_spacing,
    atom_spacing=atom_spacing,
    velocity_std=10.0,
)
```

In our demo system, these values don't have physical meaning since we use dimensionless units. In real-world simulations, these parameters would need to be determined based on experimental data or theoretical calculations.

> **Note**
>
> To set the box length, we considered both the number of atoms and the spacing between nearest neighbors. In general, atoms can be distributed evenly within a box using the formula $N^{1/dim} \times atom\ spacing$, where N is the number of atoms and dim represents the dimension of the box. In our case, since the dimension is 2, we use the square root.

Particles

We define an additional named tuple as `Particles`, which will store positions, velocities, and forces of all particles in the form of arrays with a shape of `(num_atoms, dim)`. Since we are simulating a 2D system, we use `dim=2`. Our example could be easily extended to a 3D system.

```
class Particles(NamedTuple):
    position: Array
```

```
    velocity: Array
    force: Array
```

We define two functions to set up the initial conditions: one for positions and one for the velocities. We will use these functions later to initialize position and velocity arrays.

The `initialize_position` function evenly distributes atoms in the 2D box, so that each atom is equidistant to its nearest neighbors. The position of atoms is determined based on the size of the box and the spacing between them.

```
def initialize_position(
    params: SimulationParameters,
) -> Array:
    atom_spacing = params.atom_spacing
    num_atoms_per_row = math.ceil(math.sqrt(params.num_atoms))
    position = np.empty(shape=(params.num_atoms, 2), dtype=FLOAT)
    atom_index = 0
    for index_j in range(num_atoms_per_row):
        for index_i in range(num_atoms_per_row):
            if atom_index < position.shape[0]:
                position[atom_index, 0] = (index_i + 0.5) * atom_spacing
                position[atom_index, 1] = (index_j + 0.5) * atom_spacing
            atom_index += 1
    return position
```

We also displace all the atoms by half of the spacing constant to center them in the simulation box. Note that the initial positioning does not reflect a realistic physical arrangement. It is simply a way to distribute atoms without causing overlap. The following figure shows the initial arrangement of our 100-atom box.

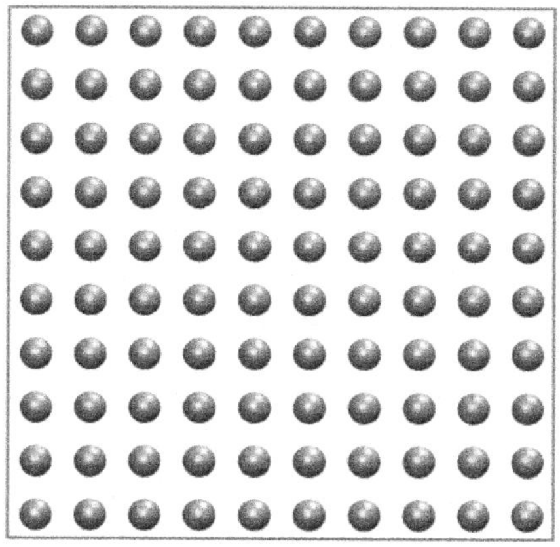

Figure 13.2: The initial configuration of 100 atoms in the simulation box

This visualizes atoms positioned at the predefined distance `atom_spacing`, with boundary lines indicating the PBC box.

Second, `initialize_velocity` assigns random initial velocities to all atoms using a random generator (`rng`). This creates a local RNG instance inside the function, which is safer and more predictable than the global state `np.random.seed` approach. The velocities are sampled from a 2D standard normal deviation, which is scaled by the `velocity_std` parameter. Randomizing the velocities ensures that the atoms start with a range of initial kinetic energies, such as thermal motion in the system. The velocities are adjusted by subtracting the mean velocity in each x and y direction (`axis=0`), centering the velocity distribution around zero, to ensure that the system's center of mass remains constant.

```
def initialize_velocity(
    params: SimulationParameters,
    rng: np.random.Generator,
) -> Array:
    velocity = rng.normal(size=(params.num_atoms, 2)).astype(FLOAT)
    velocity *= params.velocity_std
    velocity -= velocity.mean(axis=0)
    return velocity
```

With these two initialization functions in place, we can now proceed to create `Particles` as shown:

```
position = initialize_position(params)
position_dev = cuda.device_array(position.shape, dtype=FLOAT, order="F")
cuda.to_device(position, to=position_dev)

rng = np.random.default_rng(1234)
velocity = initialize_velocity(params, rng)
velocity_dev = cuda.device_array(velocity.shape, dtype=FLOAT, order="F")
cuda.to_device(velocity, to=velocity_dev)

force_dev = cuda.device_array(shape=(num_atoms, 2), dtype=FLOAT, order="F")
particles = Particles(position_dev, velocity_dev, force_dev)
```

We initialize the position and velocity on the host and copy them to the device. The `force` array does not need initial values, as it will be computed later based on the atom positions. This array is simply allocated on the device.

For the device arrays, we select *column major* (`"F"`) rather than the default *row major* (`"C"`). For the CUDA kernels that we will define later, this alignment minimizes global memory accesses because threads in the same warp access continuous memory addresses. This *coalesced* data arrangement will improve the performance on the GPU.

In the next section, we'll discuss parallelization strategies and the steps needed to calculate particle-particle interactions.

Atomic interactions

Potential energy determines how particles interact in any physical system. Like water that flows downhill, a system tends to evolve to a state of minimal potential. Forces experienced by particles can be derived from the *negative gradient* of the potential with respect to their positions. Forces give rise to the motion of the particles, and this will be a direction that reduces the potential.

To calculate the potential energy between atoms, we use a set of mathematical functions and parameters. It captures the effects of bonded and non-bonded interactions between atoms as a function of their separation distance. The parameters for potential are obtained from either experimental data or quantum mechanical calculations. In what follows, we will discuss an example of the Lennard-Jones potential, corresponding forces, and how to parallelize the force calculations.

The Lennard-Jones potential

Here, we consider the **Lennard-Jones (LJ)** potential, which is a simplified model used to describe the interaction between non-bonded atoms – for example, a system of ideal gases. The LJ potential energy assumes that two atoms repel each other when they are too close to each other, but attract when they are far apart. This model is given by the following equation:

$$V(r) = 4\epsilon\left[\left(\frac{\sigma}{r}\right)^{12} - \left(\frac{\sigma}{r}\right)^{6}\right]$$

The parameters ϵ and σ are chosen based on experimental or computational data, and they depend on the types of atoms that are involved. $V(r)$ is the potential energy as a function of the distance r between two particles. The ϵ parameter is the depth of the potential well, indicating the strength of the attraction (see the following figure). The σ parameter is the finite distance at which the inter-particle potential is zero, representing the effective diameter of the atoms.

The following figure shows the variation of the LJ potential and force between a pair of atoms.

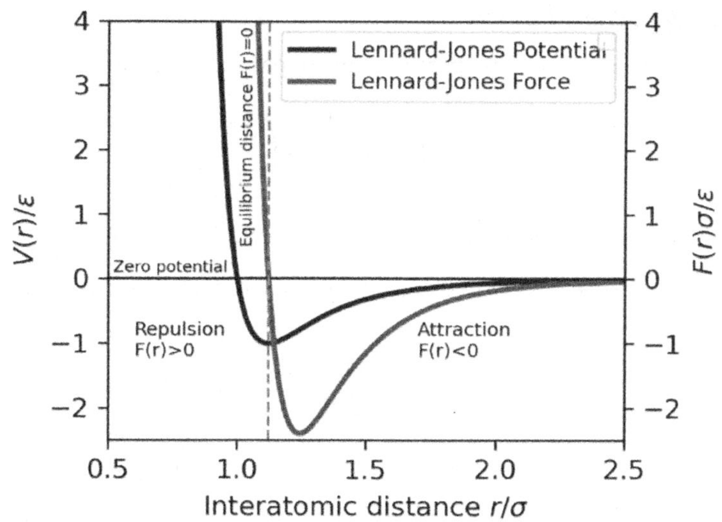

Figure 13.3: The Lennard-Jones potential and force between two atoms

This shows the equilibrium distance where the force experienced by atoms is zero. At closer distances, there is repulsion, and at greater distances, there is attraction. For atoms in a gas phase, the well depth is small, and due to thermal fluctuations, atoms tend to freely move at larger distances where attractions are minimal.

Note

For computational efficiency, a *cutoff radius* is typically applied to restrict the range of interactions. Interactions between particles beyond this cutoff are assumed to be zero, so calculations are only performed for particles within the specified range.

For a system of N atoms, the total potential energy U is the sum of pairwise interactions over all atom pairs as follows:

$$U = \sum_{i=1}^{N} \sum_{j>i}^{N} V\left(r_{ij}\right)$$

Where, r_{ij} is the distance between atom i and atom j. We must ensure each pair of particles is considered only once ($j > i$) and self-interactions must be excluded ($i \neq j$).

The Lennard-Jones force

The **Lennard-Jones force** vector $\vec{F}_{ij}$ on particle i due to particle j is given by:

$$\vec{F}_{ij} = 24\epsilon \left[2\left(\frac{\sigma}{r_{ij}}\right)^{12} - \left(\frac{\sigma}{r_{ij}}\right)^{6} \right] \frac{\vec{r}_{ij}}{r_{ij}^2}$$

Where $\vec{r}_{ij} = \vec{r}_i - \vec{r}_j$ represents the vector pointing from particle j to particle i.

For the total force on particle i, we sum the contributions from all other particles j:

$$\vec{F}_i = \sum_{j=1, i \neq j}^{N} \vec{F}_{ij}$$

This will give us the net force acting on particle i due to all other particles in the system while excluding the self-interaction.

Until now, we've derived the formulas needed to calculate the forces acting on each atom. Next, we'll explore how we can leverage the heterogeneous parallel processing capabilities of the GPU to perform these calculations in parallel with CUDA.

Parallelizing force calculations

We write a CUDA kernel to calculate forces for each particle in parallel by mapping each calculation onto a separate thread. This is feasible because force calculations for individual atoms do not depend on one another and can be easily executed as **embarrassingly parallel** tasks. Each thread reads all the atom positions from global memory and updates its own forces. Since each element in the `force` array is written to only once by one thread, this is a safe operation to perform in parallel, as it is free of *race conditions.* In the CUDA computation model, threads are grouped into warps of 32, which execute instructions in lockstep. Multiple warps in thread blocks can be active on a streaming multiprocessor simultaneously, allowing particle interactions to be computed in parallel while hiding memory latency. This parallelism eliminates the need for explicit loops over atom indices, as threads in the grid can perform these calculations concurrently.

The following implementation demonstrates how to distribute force calculation tasks across multiple GPU threads:

```
@cuda.jit
def compute_force(
    particles: Particles,
    params: SimulationParameters,
) -> None:
    force = cuda.local.array(shape=(2,), dtype=FLOAT)
    start, stride = cuda.grid(1), cuda.gridsize(1)
    for index_i in range(start, params.num_atoms, stride):
        ri = particles.position[index_i]
        fi = particles.force[index_i]
        # calculate per atom force
        force[0], force[1] = 0.0, 0.0
        for index_j in range(params.num_atoms):
            if index_i != index_j:
                rj = particles.position[index_j]
                pair_interaction(ri, rj, params.box_length, force)
        fi[0], fi[1] = force[0], force[1]
```

We first allocated an array force with `shape (2,)` in the GPU's *local* memory. This serves as a fast, temporary scratch space to store the x and y components of the computed net force on each atom.

Each thread computes the net force acting on one or multiple atoms based on `index_i`.

The loop over `index_i` ensures that each thread receives the correct index within the grid, even if the number of atoms exceeds the grid size. This can occur in very large systems containing many atoms. When `params.num_atoms > stride`, one thread may handle multiple atoms sequentially.

The inner loop over `index_j` iterates over all neighbor atoms, excluding the atom itself (`index_i != index_j`). For each pair of atoms, the `pair_interaction` device function is called to compute the force specifically between atom *i* (`ri`) and atom *j* (`rj`), and the results are written to the `particles.force` array in global memory.

The `pair_interaction` function calculates the force exerted between two atoms *i* and *j* based on their positions. It implements the force derived from the Lennard-Jones potential. We decorate this function with `cuda.jit(device=True)`, meaning it can be called as a *device* function within the `compute_force` CUDA kernel. Splitting out device functions helps us make kernels more modular and readable.

```
@cuda.jit(device=True)
def pair_interaction(
    position_i: Array,
    position_j: Array,
    box_length: FLOAT,
    force: Array,
) -> None:
    rij_x = apply_pbc(position_i[0] - position_j[0], box_length)
    rij_y = apply_pbc(position_i[1] - position_j[1], box_length)
    r2 = rij_x * rij_x + rij_y * rij_y
    r2i = 1.0 / r2
    r6i = r2i * r2i * r2i
    coef = 24.0 * r6i * (2.0 * r6i - 1.0)
    force[0] += rij_x * r2i * coef
    force[1] += rij_y * r2i * coef
```

Here, `rij_x` and `rij_y` help us to calculate the distance between two particles in symmetric 2D space. We use the `apply_pbc` function for each dimension to ensure periodic boundary conditions along the box length. This corrects the distance calculation so that atoms on opposite edges of the simulation box still interact correctly.

For optimization reasons, we use `r2` instead of `r` to avoid calling the computationally expensive square root (`sqrt`) function, which is one of the slowest math operations. While a multiplication typically takes only 1–3 CPU cycles, `sqrt` can take 20–50 cycles depending on the required precision. When this calculation is performed millions of times inside the main simulation loop, avoiding `sqrt` leads to a speedup. Similarly, since division (10-20 cycles) is generally more time-consuming than multiplication, we also use a temporary variable `r2i` to store the inverse of `r2`.

```
@cuda.jit(device=True, inline=True)
def apply_pbc(
    rij: FLOAT,
```

```
    box_length: FLOAT,
) -> FLOAT:
    L = box_length
    if rij >= 0.5 * L:
        rij -= L
    elif rij <= -0.5 * L:
        rij += L
    return rij
```

We add, in this case, `inline=True` to the function's decorator to specify that it should also be *inlined*. When a function is marked as inline, the compiler inserts the function's code directly into the calling code, avoiding a separate function call. This can optimize performance by reducing function call overhead and is always recommended for very small functions.

The conditional block adjusts the value of r_{ij} by applying periodic boundary conditions, wrapping it around to the negative or positive side when necessary. Finally, the function returns the modified value of r_{ij}.

At this point, we have a ready-to-use kernel that calculates forces for all the atoms in the simulation box, all in parallel. In the next section, we will learn how to update atomic positions and velocities for the next time step.

Time integration

The time integrator updates the positions and velocities of atoms as time in the simulation progresses. In principle, it numerically solves Newton's equations of motion for each atom in the system.

The **Verlet algorithm** is one of the simplest and most used time integrators in MD simulations, regarding its simplicity, computational efficiency, and numerical stability. In the Verlet integration, the new position $r(t + \delta t)$ of a particle is computed as follows:

$$\vec{r}(t + \delta t) = \vec{r}(t) + \vec{v}(t)\delta t + \frac{1}{2}\vec{a}(t)\delta t^2$$

Where, $\vec{r}(t)$, $\vec{v}(t)$, and $\vec{a}(t)$ are position, velocity, and the acceleration of the atom at the current time, and δt is the time step. Acceleration $\vec{a}$ relates to Newton's law via $\vec{F} = m\vec{a}$, where $\vec{F}$is the force and m is the mass. For our particles, we will take $m = 1$, which makes $\vec{F} = \vec{a}$.

The equation for the new velocity $\vec{v}(t + \delta t)$ is given by:

$$\vec{v}(t + \delta t) = \vec{v}(t) + \frac{1}{2}[\vec{a}(t) + \vec{a}(t + \delta t)]\delta t$$

The new positions and velocities for all atoms are updated, and the algorithm proceeds to the next time step $t \rightarrow t + \delta t$. This process repeats, with forces recalculated at each step to gradually build the trajectory of the particles.

Parallelizing the Verlet time integrator

We will follow the same approach to speed up the time integration: we parallelize over all the atoms.

The following CUDA kernel updates the position of atoms:

```
@cuda.jit
def verlet_integration_position(
    particles: Particles,
    params: SimulationParameters,
) -> None:
    r, v, f = particles
    dt, L = params.time_step, params.box_length
    start, stride = cuda.grid(1), cuda.gridsize(1)
    for index in range(start, params.num_atoms, stride):
        for dim in range(2):
            r[index, dim] = (
                r[index, dim] \
                + dt * (v[index, dim] + 0.5 * dt * f[index, dim])
            ) % L
            v[index, dim] += 0.5 * dt * f[index, dim]
```

The new position `r[idx, dim]` is obtained using the current velocity and force values according to the equation of the Verlet position.

The term `% L` ensures that the atom positions remain within the bounds of the simulation box `[0, L)` after updating if they go outside the simulation box. This step is crucial because without it, new positions could potentially **go out of range**, which can lead to issues when applying the periodic boundary conditions.

Notice that the velocity `v[idx, dim]` is already partially updated at this step. It will be updated a second time, once the new forces are calculated in the next integration step. We iterate over all the atom indices using the start and stride, allowing each thread to update multiple atoms if the grid size is smaller than the number of atoms.

We do the same thing for the final update to the velocity. The following kernel is invoked once the forces are updated with the new positions:

```
@cuda.jit
def verlet_integration_velocity(
    particles: Particles,
    params: SimulationParameters,
) -> None:
    v, f = particles.velocity, particles.force
    dt = params.time_step
    start, stride = cuda.grid(1), cuda.gridsize(1)
    for index in range(start, params.num_atoms, stride):
        for dim in range(2):
            v[index, dim] += 0.5 * dt * f[index, dim]
```

Next, we will iteratively apply these force and time integration kernels within a `for` loop, enabling us to run the MD simulation.

Data collection

A large amount of data is generated from an MD system, including atomic positions, velocities, and forces. This information can be used to track atomic motions, identify interactions, and calculate physical properties such as energies, temperature, and pressure. However, so far, we don't have any way to save the output of our simulation.

To allow us to post-process and visualize our data, we define a `save` function, which dumps the atomic position data into a file in the *XYZ* format. This is a standard way to represent molecular structures, making it compatible with molecular visualization tools:

```
def save(position: Array, file: TextIO) -> None:
    num_atoms = position.shape[0]
    file.write(f"{num_atoms}\n\n")
    for i in range(num_atoms):
        file.write(f"{'He'}\t{position[i, 0]} {position[i, 1]} {0}\n")
    file.flush()
```

The line with `file.flush()` ensures that all data is immediately written to the file.

Additionally, we calculate temperature (T), which is directly related to the average kinetic energy of the atoms within the system.

$$T \propto \frac{1}{N}\sum_{i=1}^{N}\frac{1}{2}m\vec{v}_i^2$$

This equation calculates the average kinetic energy of atoms in a system. $\vec{v}_i$ represents the velocity of atom number i, and m is the mass. To simplify the calculation, we assume all atoms have the mass of 1.0.

This allows us to calculate the temperature of the system with the `get_temperature` function as follows:

```
def get_temperature(velocity: Array) -> FLOAT:
    return 0.5 * (velocity**2).sum() / velocity.shape[0]
```

Up to this point, we have all the key MD components set up. We will next conduct an MD simulation for different time steps.

Running the simulation

We perform a GPU-accelerated MD simulation of the atoms using the `simulate` function as follows.

```
def simulate(
    params: SimulationParameters,
    particles: Particles,
    steps: int = 1,
    log_frequency: int = 100,
    filename: str = "configurations.xyz",
) -> None:
    print("GPU-accelerated Molecular Dynamics Simulation")
    print("Lennard-Jones Particles in a 2D Periodic Box")
    print(f"Number of atoms: {params.num_atoms}")
    print("Step    Time          Temperature")
    print("--------------------------------")
    threads = 32
    blocks = math.ceil(params.num_atoms / threads)
    compute_force[blocks, threads](particles, params)
    with open(filename, "w") as file:
        # Simulate
        for step in range(steps):
            if step % log_frequency == 0:
```

```
                temperature= get_temperature(particles.velocity.copy_to_host())
                print(
                    f"{step:<7d}"
                    f" {step * params.time_step:<12.8f}"
                    f" { temperature:<.8f}"
                )
                save(particles.position.copy_to_host(), file)
            # Next time step (update r, v, and F)
            verlet_integration_position[blocks, threads](particles, params)
            compute_force[blocks, threads](particles, params)
            verlet_integration_velocity[blocks, threads](particles, params)
    print("Done.")
```

This function simulates the system for a predefined number of time steps, allowing the particles to evolve according to the Lennard-Jones potential. Over time, the system may reach an equilibrium state where properties (i.e., temperature) stabilize. We also collect properties such as the position of atoms and temperature during the simulation.

We simulate the system for the next 1,000 time steps and collect the current temperature and save the atom positions every 100 steps.

```
simulate(params, particles, steps=1000)
```

The output of the `simulate` function prints the current step, time, and calculated temperature as the simulation progresses.

```
GPU-accelerated Molecular Dynamics Simulation
Lennard-Jones Particles in a 2D Periodic Box
Number of atoms: 100
Step    Time         Temperature
--------------------------------
0       0.00000000   95.76379342
100     0.01000000   95.76576249
200     0.02000000   95.77276531
...
900     0.09000000   95.79469347
Done.
```

Performance analysis

Here, we assess the performance of our implemented simulator and provide insights into its performance along with suggestions for further improvement.

Benchmarks

To illustrate the runtime performance of our GPU implementation of an MD simulator, we ran it for different system sizes – 100, 1,000, and 10,000 atoms – and compared it to two CPU implementations:

- A serial version of the same code optimized with Numba's JIT compilation
- A parallelized version on an 8-core CPU using Numba's JIT along with `prange` for multithreading

The GPU version was run on *A100*, a data center GPU, and additionally *RTX* Ti 2080, a consumer GPU. The following figure shows the elapsed runtime. Note that the y axis is logarithmically scaled, and precision is in `float64`.

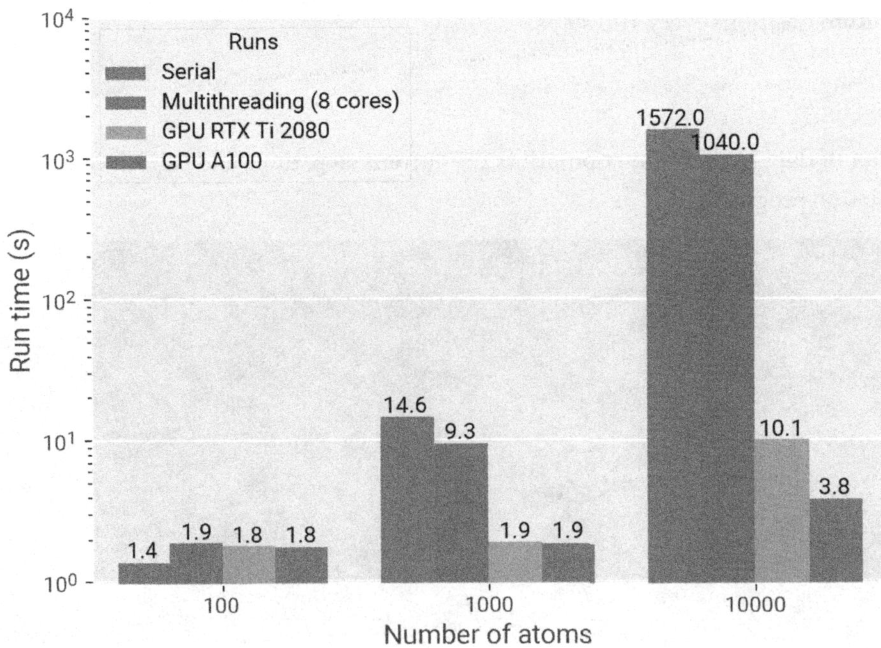

Figure 13.4: Our MD simulation benchmark runs on a different system for 1,000 time steps

For small systems, GPU computing offers few benefits due to its overhead and GPU underutilization. For large systems, the performance gains with the GPU are significant. The RTX GPU achieved up to 150x faster than the serial code, and the A100 GPU was nearly 400x faster. The significant difference in performance between the two GPU types is due to the higher computing capacity and the hardware support for floating-point operations in the data center GPU.

Profiling

Are there additional gains to be made in performance? Let's find out by profiling our MD simulator for 10,000 atoms using the *NVIDIA Nsight* CLI tool to gain a deeper understanding of kernel execution time and memory utilization. We first profile the GPU using the `nsys` command (see *Chapter 4* for more details on profiling):

```
$ nsys profile python molecular_dynamics.py
```

The GPU activity timeline shows that the GPU is busy executing kernels for more than 99.9% of the total runtime. Kernel execution time is overwhelmingly dominated by the `compute_force` kernel. Only H2D and D2H transfers are observed, corresponding to loading the initial system configuration and periodically saving atom trajectories. These data transfers account for a negligible fraction of the overall runtime and do not impact performance.

Next, we focus on profiling the compute performance of the force calculation kernel using the `ncu` command to quantify how well our MD simulator runs:

```
$ ncu --kernel-name compute_force \
  --section ComputeWorkloadAnalysis \
  python molecular_dynamics.py

    Section: Compute Workload Analysis
    ------------------- ----------- ------------
    Metric Name         Metric Unit Metric Value
    ------------------- ----------- ------------
    Executed Ipc Active  inst/cycle         1.91
    Executed Ipc Elapsed inst/cycle         1.89
    Issue Slots Busy              %        47.76
    Issued Ipc Active    inst/cycle         1.91
    SM Busy                       %        67.58
    ------------------- ----------- ------------
```

`SM Busy` (~68%) means that about two-thirds of the time, SMs are doing something useful. Combined with the IPC numbers (1.9), this points to a kernel that is **reasonably efficient** and fundamentally limited by how much parallel work it exposes per SM, not by raw instruction throughput.

Finally, we focus on global memory workload:

```
$ ncu --kernel-name compute_force \
  --section MemoryWorkloadAnalysis \
  python molecular_dynamics.py

Section: Memory Workload Analysis
    --------------------------- ----------- ------------
    Metric Name                 Metric Unit Metric Value
    --------------------------- ----------- ------------
    Memory Throughput               Mbyte/s        15.76
    Mem Busy                              %        20.55
    Max Bandwidth                         %        20.55
    L1/TEX Hit Rate                       %        99.21
    L2 Compression Success Rate           %            0
    L2 Compression Ratio                                0
    L2 Compression Input Sectors     sector            0
    L2 Hit Rate                           %        99.87
    Mem Pipes Busy                        %        10.27
    --------------------------- ----------- ------------
```

However, the throughput is tiny for an A100, memory pipes are barely busy, and both L1 and L2 hit rates are ~99%. That means almost all loads are being satisfied from the cache with very low latency. Because of that, `Mem Busy` and `Max Bandwidth` at ~20% are not limiting factors at all. The kernel simply doesn't ask for much memory bandwidth, and when it does, the accesses are extremely cache-friendly. Therefore, we conclude that this kernel is FP64 **compute-bound** with limited warp-level parallelism. Further improvement can be achieved by increasing active warps per SM, breaking dependency chains, and unrolling or restructuring math to expose more instruction-level parallelism.

At the **algorithmic level**, we have used a basic approach to identify neighboring atoms by looping over all atoms, resulting in a computational complexity of $O(N^2)$, where N is the number of atoms. Advanced methods, such as neighbor lists, domain decomposition, and linked-cell algorithms, can reduce this complexity to $O(N)$, enabling MD simulations to efficiently handle larger systems with millions of atoms. Interested readers can find further details in this repository: `https://github.com/hghcomphys/linear-md`.

Summary

In this chapter, we explored the practical aspects of implementing GPU-accelerated molecular dynamics simulations. We began by understanding the basics of MD simulations. We then implemented a system of particles, specifically utilizing Numba-CUDA to parallelize force calculation and time integration.

Additionally, we discussed how to effectively use device functions and when to inline them for optimal performance. This allowed us to develop an MD simulator capable of simulating thousands of atoms.

Next, we compared our implementation to both a serial and multithreaded version, demonstrating simulation speeds up to two orders of magnitude faster. We covered essential profiling techniques to measure kernel execution and global memory access, identifying a compute-bound problem as the bottleneck in our simulation. Finally, we provided a few hints on how to address this issue.

Having successfully applied our knowledge of CUDA to parallelize a real-world MD simulation, we will now proceed to the next chapter: implementing a custom large language model from scratch.

Questions

1. How does the runtime of the MD simulation on the GPU change when using `float32` precision instead of `float64`? What about memory access efficiency?
2. What would be the impact of using `C` ordering instead of `F` in `Particles` on memory load and store efficiency?
3. Do you think that using CUDA *streams* could help improve performance?

Answers

1. Data center GPUs provide strong performance for `float64` computations, with throughput closer to that of `float32`. In contrast, consumer GPUs have significantly fewer FP64 execution units; therefore, reducing precision from `float64` to `float32` can lead to a noticeable performance improvement.
2. This behavior is directly related to coalesced memory access and data alignment, as discussed in previous chapters. Poor alignment reduces load/store efficiency, meaning

that the raw memory throughput may remain unchanged, but a smaller fraction of it is effectively utilized by active threads, with the remainder wasted as unused bandwidth.

3. For this simple example, the Nsight Systems GPU activity analysis shows that execution time is dominated by `compute_kernel`. As a result, introducing multiple streams to overlap kernel execution or device-host data transfers does not lead to noticeable performance improvement.

Get this book's PDF version and more

Scan the QR code (or go to `packtpub.com/unlock`). Search for this book by name, confirm the edition, and then follow the steps on the page.

UNLOCK NOW

Note: Keep your invoice handy. Purchases made directly from Packt don't require an invoice.

14

Implementing Your Own Transformer-Based Language Model

In the previous chapter, we demonstrated how GPU-accelerated computing can be used for molecular simulations. Now, let's shift our focus to a more tangible topic: generating human-like text using a **Large Language Model (LLM)**. In this chapter, we will build our own language model using JAX to explore how this technology works. We will make a small **Generative Pretrained Transformer (GPT)** model for text generation tasks and train it on a lightweight example dataset. Along the way, we will cover topics such as attention mechanisms, transformer architecture, embeddings, tokenization, and autoregressive text generation step by step. The principles and techniques learned through these exercises can be applied to larger and more complex models. To keep this chapter manageable, we'll use two additional libraries, **Flax** and **Optax**, built on top of **JAX**, to facilitate creating neural network layers and using more advanced optimization algorithms. However, foundational concepts such as neural network implementation and gradient descent optimization have already been discussed in *Chapter 10*.

By the end of this chapter, you will have acquired a solid grasp of the following topics:

- Understanding attention mechanisms in language models
- Implementing a self-attention transformer layer
- Constructing a small GPT encoder
- Understanding token and positional embeddings
- Learning the basics of the tokenization of text data
- Training a text generation language model

Technical requirements

To be able to run the example code provided in this chapter, you will need a system equipped with an NVIDIA GPU that has at least 10 GB of memory. We use Pixi as a dependency management tool that installs all of the required packages, including JAX and dependent libraries. To set up the environment, simply run `pixi install` in the root directory of the book's GitHub repository. This will ensure that all dependencies are installed. Once the installation is complete, you can activate the environment using `pixi shell`.

Then, run the following:

```
pixi run jupyter-lab
```

The chapter's code is available on GitHub and can be accessed via this link: https://github.com/PacktPublishing/GPU-Accelerated-Computing-with-Python-3-and-CUDA. We recommend cloning the repository and following the instructions in the `README` file to get started with building the environment.

Introduction to language models

A language model is a type of natural language processing algorithm specifically designed to predict and generate human language. These models, often referred to as LLMs, have become increasingly common nowadays in numerous applications, including chatbots, machine translation, coding assistants, and text summarization. However, at their core, these advanced models are essentially sequence-to-sequence models. This means that they take a sequence of input data, such as words or sentences, and produce another sequence of output data. The current success of LLMs relies on two key factors: access to vast amounts of training data and the availability of powerful GPUs. This particularly highlights the importance of GPU computing in advancing modern AI technology, as it enables efficient training and inference of LLMs. Without such accelerated computational capabilities, LLMs would not be feasible for practical applications.

LLMs particularly differ from traditional approaches such as **Recurrent Neural Networks (RNNs)** in their ability to leverage **attention mechanisms**, which enable **transformers**, a kind of neural network architecture introduced in 2017 by Vaswani et al., to focus on different parts of the input sequence. This capability allows LLMs to capture *context* within text, making their outputs more coherent and contextually relevant. Before we dive into the technical details, let's see a high-level overview of a typical language model.

Overview of transformer-based LLM architecture

An LLM, such as a GPT or similar architecture, consists of several key components that work together to process input texts. These components can generally be categorized into the following:

- **Tokenization**: Maps raw text into a sequence of tokens and unique integer **token IDs**.
- **Embeddings**: Convert input token IDs into dense floating-point vector representations that can be processed by the model. Additionally, positional embeddings are always used to preserve the order of each token in the input sequence.
- **Attention mechanism**: The attention mechanism allows the model to focus on different parts of the input sequence simultaneously and weigh their importance. This is achieved through attention heads, which compute attention weights based on the input sequence. We'll dive deeper into attention mechanisms later when discussing the attention kernel.
- **Transformer layer**: Processes the sequence of embeddings using self-attention and feed-forward networks to produce contextualized representations.
- **Classification head**: The classification head is used for specific tasks, such as language modeling and text classification. It takes the output of the transformer layer and generates a probability distribution over possible classes (e.g., the next word in the sequence).

The following figure shows a schematic representation of these components and how they are connected in text generation language mode:

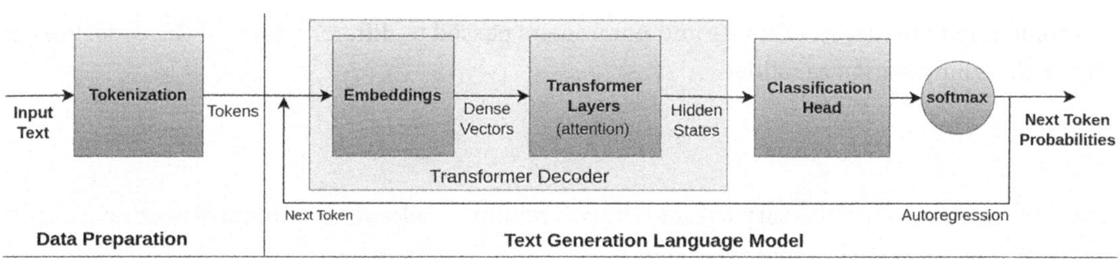

Figure 14.1 – An overview of key components in a text generation language model

In this diagram, the input text data is first tokenized, then the sequence of tokens is embedded in dense vector representations. The transformer layers apply attention on multiple levels to the input embeddings, and after that, a classification head with the `softmax` activation function gives us the next token probabilities. The predicted token is eventually appended to the input tokens, and this process repeats autoregressively to generate text.

Next, we will discuss the attention mechanism. We will then construct a transformer layer, which will serve as the foundation for building a text generation model. Finally, we will elaborate on data preparation, tokenization, and model training toward the end of this chapter.

Initializing constant parameters

We will use a configuration `dataclass` throughout this chapter. Instead of passing a long list of parameters to each function or class, we'll define them once in a `Config` object and reference them wherever needed:

```
from dataclasses import dataclass

@dataclass
class Config:
    epochs: int = 5
    batch_size: int = 16
    embedding_dim: int = 256
    num_attention_heads: int = 4
    intermediate_dim: int = 128
    dropout_probability: float = 0.1
    vocab_size: int = 50257
    max_seq_length: int = 512
    num_hidden_layers: int = 3
```

We will use these parameters when implementing different LLM components. This is a clean and Pythonic way to manage constants and parameters passed to different parts of the code. We can define the configuration as follows:

```
cfg = Config()
```

Here, `cfg` provides the necessary parameter with minimal boilerplate, while still making it easy to override specific settings when necessary.

Understanding the attention mechanism

The attention mechanism is the heart of transformers and functions like a spotlight, enabling the model to selectively focus on relevant parts of the input sequence when generating an output. When reading a sentence, you naturally emphasize certain words, such as names or verbs, that are necessary for understanding the sentence's meaning. Similarly, the attention mechanism allows the transformer model to weigh the importance of each token in relation to others, rather than treating them all equally. Also, attention allows the model to dynamically focus on different parts of the input when processing each token. This is especially powerful in capturing **long-range dependencies**, in cases where the meaning of a word depends on another word far away in the sequence (the context).

Consider the input sequence `This is an example`:

```
Tokens: ["This", "is", "an", "example"]
Token IDs: [1212, 318, 281, 1036]
```

Each token, a basic unit of text such as a word or symbol, in this sequence is converted into a high-dimensional **embedding vector**, typically of fixed size *M*. The token IDs come from a prebuilt vocabulary dictionary of the tokenizer that internally maps every possible token to a unique integer ID. Embeddings turn each token into a dense vector of numbers (e.g., `[0.12, -0.47, 0.85, ...]`).

For a sequence of *T* tokens, we get a set of vectors:

$$v_1, v_2, \ldots, v_T \in \mathbb{R}^M$$

In the attention mechanism, each of these vector representations is updated by taking a **weighted sum** of all embedding vectors in the sequence:

$$\tilde{v}i = \sum_j w_{ij} v_j$$

Here, the result is the new embedding vector for token `i`, and w_{ij} is the attention weight indicating how much token `i` attends to token `j`. These weights help the model focus more on relevant words and less on unrelated ones.

We can rewrite this entire process using matrix multiplication. We can stack all the embeddings as rows in a matrix, *V*:

$$V = \begin{bmatrix} \mathbf{v}_1 \\ \mathbf{v}_2 \\ \vdots \\ \mathbf{v}_T \end{bmatrix} \in \mathbb{R}^{T \times M}$$

We can define the attention weight matrix, *W*, and then the new embeddings for the entire sequence can be written as follows:

$$\tilde{V} = WV, \qquad W \in \mathbb{R}^{T \times T}$$

Each row is a new representation for a token, based on the attention it gives to others. When processing multiple sequences in batches, the embedding is represented as a 3D array of shape *(B, T, M)*, where *B* is the batch size. This means that all the matrix operations must be vectorized along the batch dimension (the first index), which makes a perfect case for a powerful framework such as JAX with its automatic vectorization. We will now focus on calculating the attention weights via the **scaled dot product** kernel.

Scaled dot product attention kernel

The scaled dot product is the most widely used attention kernel, especially in transformer architectures such as GPT. To compute the weights, we use three different projections of each token's embedding as separate vectors: the **query** (`Q`), **key** (`K`), and **value** (`V`). The query captures what a token is looking for, the key represents what each token offers, and the value holds the actual content aggregate. The attention weights are obtained based on the *similarity* between the query and key vectors. To quantify it, we use the dot product. The dot product gives us raw scores, which we need to scale and normalize using the `softmax` function:

$$\tilde{V} = softmax\left(\frac{QK^T}{\sqrt{d_k}}\right)V$$

Here, d_k represents the projected dimensionality of the query and key vectors, and not necessarily the full embedding dimension, *M*. This scaling factor gives a probability distribution over values, and `softmax` particularly prevents large values, which improves numerical stability. The resulting output is a weighted sum of the value vectors, enabling each token to collect relevant information from the entire sequence. Note that the *shape of the embedding array remains unchanged* before and after applying the attention mechanism. Although the values within the embeddings are now transformed, typically, to incorporate contextual information from other tokens, the overall tensor shape stays the same. For example, if the input to the attention layer has the shape *(B, T, M)*, the output will also have the same shape. This consistency in shape is crucial for stacking multiple layers and preserving the structure needed for downstream components.

In the following code, we implement a function for computing the scaled dot product attention. This attention kernel will be used later to build our transformer layer. We start with importing the necessary modules, including `jax`, `jax.numpy`, and `flax.linen`:

```
import jax
import jax.numpy as jnp
import flax.linen as nn
```

`flax.linen` is a module from Flax, a Python library that provides convenient abstractions on top of JAX for defining neural network layers and models, to build and train deep learning architectures. We also define type hints such as Array, KeyArray, and Optional to improve readability:

```
from numpy.typing import NDArray as Array
from typing import Optional
KeyArray = jax._src.prng.PRNGKeyArray
```

The scaled_dot_product_attention function takes three inputs, query, key, and value, for computing the attention. An optional input mask provides a way to selectively apply the attention mechanism based on certain conditions. If not provided, it defaults to None, and no masking will be applied:

```
def scaled_dot_product_attention(
    query: Array,
    key: Array,
    value: Array,
    mask: Optional[Array] = None,
) -> Array:
    scores = jax.lax.batch_matmul(
        query,                              # Q
        jnp.transpose(key, axes=(0, 2, 1)), # K^T
    ) / jnp.sqrt(query.shape[-1])           # (QK^T) / sqrt(d_k)
    weights = nn.softmax(scores, axis=-1, where=mask)
    attention = jax.lax.batch_matmul(weights, value)
    return attention
```

jax.lax.batch_matmul performs a **batched matrix multiplication** between the query and key tensors. This is a JAX low-level vectorized matrix multiplication along the first dimension; however, we could use jax.vmap for this task as well. The key array is transposed using jnp.transpose(key, axes=(0, 2, 1)), which swaps its last two dimensions, but the first dimension for batches remains unchanged. The result of the matrix multiplication is then divided by the square root of the last dimension of the query tensor (jnp.sqrt(query.shape[-1])).

nn.softmax applies the softmax activation function to the score tensor along its last dimension (axis=-1). This gives a probability distribution (weights) along with an embedding index for each token. Additionally, the optional input mask restricts attention to valid positions, such as preventing a token from attending to future tokens in attention (causal mask), ignoring padded tokens in sequences of different lengths (padding mask). We will come back to this when implementing the transformer encoder. The final step performs the second batched matrix multiplication between the `weights` and `value` tensors using the `jax.lax.batch_matmul` function, resulting in the `attention` array, which is in fact a weighted sum of the `value` vectors.

Here's an example of how you might use this function:

```
input_embeddings = jax.random.uniform(
    jax.random.key(2025),
    shape=(
        cfg.batch_size,      # B
        cfg.max_seq_length, # T
        cfg.embedding_dim    # M
    ),
)
query = key = value = input_embeddings
attention = scaled_dot_product_attention(query, key, value)
assert attention.shape == input_embeddings.shape
```

The preceding example calculates the scaled dot product attention output for the given query, key, and value arrays initialized with random values.

Implementing the transformer block

Now that we have the attention kernel in place, we proceed with creating the transformer layer. The transformer layer is a fundamental building block of the more complicated transformer architecture, including decoders. For example, we can stack multiple such layers to build deeper models (e.g., 6 or 12 layers) and refine the sequence of representations.

Each transformer layer consists of two main components:

- Multi-head self-attention
- Feed-forward network

We will discuss and implement these two components in detail in the two following sections.

Multi-head self-attention

Multi-head self-attention is an attention block that runs multiple attention operations in parallel and then concatenates their outputs. This allows the model to capture different aspects of the input sequence at once, rather than just one type of relationship. The word *self-attention* means that a token in a sequence attends to other tokens in the same sequence. We primarily need to implement one attention head, which is essentially a single instance of performing scaled-dot product attention, as we discussed earlier.

Note

Cross-attention

In more complex architectures, such as encoder-decoder transformers used in tasks such as machine translation, the key and value vectors in the attention mechanism don't always come from the same input as the query. Instead, they can originate from a different component of the model (typically the encoder), while the query comes from the decoder. This setup is known as cross-attention:

```
class AttentionHead(nn.Module):
attention_dim: int

def setup(self) -> None:
self.query=nn.Dense(self.attention_dim)
self.key=nn.Dense(self.attention_dim)
self.value=nn.Dense(self.attention_dim)


def __call__(
self,
inputs: Array,
mask: Optional[Array] = None,
) -> Array:
return scaled_dot_product_attention(
self.query(inputs),
self.key(inputs),
self.value(inputs),
mask=mask,
)
```

The preceding `AttentionHead` class defines a single attention head as a neural network layer using the Flax library (`nn.Module`). Note that each head has its own set of learnable parameters for linear projecting query, key, and value inputs.

We define the `setup()` method to initialize three dense layers. Each of these later learns to extract different types of features from the input into query (*Q*), key (*K*), or value (*V*) vectors during the model training. The constant `attention_dim` attribute is the size of projected vectors (d_k) used for queries, keys, and values. The `__call__()` method is the forward pass of the attention head. `inputs` is first passed separately through the query, key, and value linear layers. Then, these transformed vectors are used to compute the scaled dot product attention kernel. The optional mask can be used to prevent attention to certain positions (e.g., causal mask).

Next, we define the `MultiHeadAttention` class to use multiple attention heads in parallel. It involves splitting the input into multiple heads, applying scaled dot product attention on each head, concatenating, and, finally, linearly transforming the results. This allows the attention block to attend to different aspects of the sequence simultaneously and combine their information:

```
class MultiHeadAttention(nn.Module):
    cfg: Config

    def setup(self) -> None:
        cfg = self.cfg
        assert cfg.embedding_dim % cfg.num_attention_heads == 0
        attention_dim = cfg.embedding_dim // cfg.num_attention_heads
        self.attention_heads = [
            AttentionHead(attention_dim)
            for _ in range(cfg.num_attention_heads)
        ]
        self.output_layer = nn.Dense(cfg.embedding_dim)

    def __call__(
        self,
        inputs: Array,
        mask: Optional[Array] = None,
    ) -> Array:
        x = jnp.concatenate(
            [head(inputs, mask=mask) for head in self.attention_heads],
            axis=-1,
        )
        return self.output_layer(x)
```

`MultiHeadAttention` takes a configuration object that contains configuration parameters for the model, including the embedding dimensionality (`cfg.embedding_dim`) and number of attention heads (`cfg.num_attention_heads`).

In the `setup()` method, we must ensure that the total embedding dimension can be evenly split among all attention heads, and `cfg.attention_dim` is the internal size for each individual head. We create a list of `AttentionHead` modules, one for each head. After attention outputs are combined, this linear layer projects them back to the original embedding size. The `__call__()` method similarly takes two arguments: `inputs` and `mask`. It applies each attention head to the input array. Also, the mask is passed to each attention head if provided. The outputs are concatenated along the last dimension (`axis=-1`) using `jax.concatenate`. The concatenated output is then passed through `output_layer` (a dense neural network layer) to produce the final output.

Feed-forward network

The feed-forward network is a dense neural network that transforms the output of the self-attention mechanism. It is made of two linear layers, often with a **ReLU** activation function in between. Often, a **dropout layer** is added to prevent the model from relying heavily on any one feature and help the model generalize better. A dropout layer is a regularization technique that randomly "drops out" (i.e., sets to zero) a fraction of the neurons during training.

In the following code block, we implement the `FeedForward` module, which is initialized from the input configuration object:

```
class FeedForward(nn.Module):
    cfg: Config

    def setup(self) -> None:
        cfg = self.cfg
        self.linear_1 = nn.Dense(cfg.intermediate_dim)
        self.linear_2 = nn.Dense(cfg.embedding_dim)
        self.dropout = nn.Dropout(cfg.dropout_probability)

    def __call__(
        self,
        inputs: Array,
        deterministic: bool = True,
        rng: Optional[KeyArray] = None,
    ) -> Array:
        x = self.linear_1(inputs)
```

```
        x = nn.relu(x)
        x = self.linear_2(x)
        outputs = self.dropout(
            x, deterministic=deterministic, rng=rng
        )
        return outputs
```

In the `setup()` method, we create two dense neural network layers. The `linear_1` layer, with an output dimensionality of `cfg.intermediate_dim`, is used to transform the input array into a lower-dimensional space. Another layer, `linear_2`, with an output dimensionality of `cfg.embedding_dim`, is used to transform the output from the previous layer back into the original embedding space. We also initialize a dropout layer (`nn.Dropout`) with a probability of `cfg.dropout_probability`, helping prevent overfitting.

The `__call__()` method takes three inputs. The `inputs` array is the output from the attention block. But more interesting is `deterministic` as a Boolean flag indicating whether the dropout layer should operate or not. This control flag is needed to activate dropouts during training but not when predicting. The dropout layer introduces randomness to our model. That's why we also need a random seed, `rng`, that is used to generate random numbers for the dropout layer if needed. The **ReLU** activation function (`nn.relu`) is used in this implementation because it is a common choice for hidden layers in neural networks. It maps all negative values to zero and all positive values to their original value, helping to introduce non-linearity into the model.

The transformer layer

With these two multi-head self-attention and feed-forward network components, we are finally ready to build the transformer layer. We connected them in a specific sequence with a **residual connection** and a **normalization layer** applied at each step to stabilize training and improve gradient flow. The following figure shows a schematic diagram of the transformer layer:

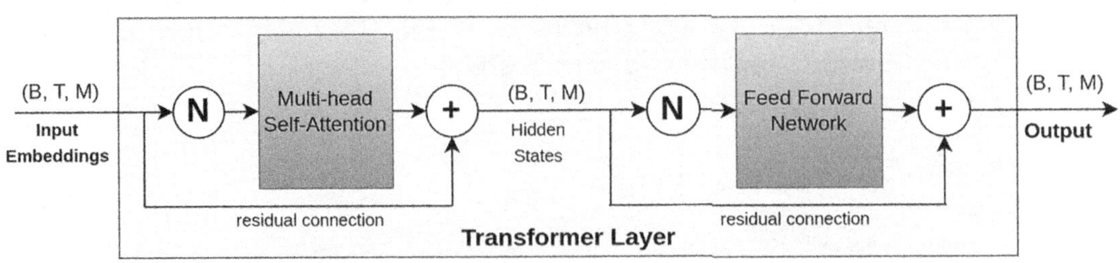

Figure 14.2 – Internal components and connections of the transformer layer

The residual connection (+) means that the original input is added separately to the output of each attention and feed-forward block. This helps in training deeper networks by mitigating issues such as **vanishing gradients**. The normalization layer (**N**) is used to normalize the activations of each layer, which helps with training stability.

Here is the implementation of the transformer layer:

```
class TransformerLayer(nn.Module):
    cfg: Config

    def setup(self) -> None:
        cfg = self.cfg
        self.norm_layer_1 = nn.LayerNorm()
        self.norm_layer_2 = nn.LayerNorm()
        self.attention = MultiHeadAttention(cfg)
        self.feed_forward = FeedForward(cfg)

    def __call__(
        self,
        inputs: Array,
        mask: Optional[Array] = None,
        deterministic: bool = True,
        rng: Optional[KeyArray] = None,
    ) -> Array:
        x = inputs
        x = x + self.attention(
                    self.norm_layer_1(x),
                    mask=mask,
               )
        x = x + self.feed_forward(
                    self.norm_layer_2(x),
                    deterministic=deterministic,
                    rng=rng,
               )
        return x
```

There are two residual connections in the `__call__()` method. `x + self.attention(self.norm_layer_1(x), ...)` adds the original input array to the output from the attention mechanism. And, for the second time, `x + self.feed_forward(self.norm_layer_2(x), ...)` adds the output from the previous step to the output from the feed-forward network. These two normalization layers are applied to normalize the input data before applying the attention mechanism and feed-forward network, which helps stabilize the training process. `TransformerLayer` is always stacked multiple times to form a deep network. Each layer processes the output from the previous layer, allowing the model to learn complex representations of the input data.

In the next section, we will discuss how a transformer layer, together with embeddings, can be used to build a transformer encoder and then eventually a language model.

Building the language model

So far, we've successfully implemented the **transformer layer** (see *Figure 14.1*), which serves as the core building block of our language model. The next step is to prepare the inputs in a form that the model can understand. This begins with converting token IDs into vector representations through a process known as **embedding**. These embeddings allow the model to work in a continuous vector space rather than directly with discrete tokens. Once the embeddings are in place, we'll proceed to construct the **transformer decoder**, which is the architecture responsible for modeling dependencies in the input sequence. Finally, we will integrate these components to build our full **language model**. This will be a model capable of predicting the next token ID given a sequence of previous tokens, forming the foundation for tasks such as text generation.

Embeddings

Embeddings are a way to represent discrete tokens as continuous vectors of real numbers. Instead of using simple one-hot encodings, which are sparse and don't capture meaning, embeddings allow the model to work with rich, learnable representations of text. In transformer-based language models, the input text is converted into embeddings before being processed.

These embeddings consist of two parts:

- **Token embedding**: Each token is first converted into a vector using a token embedding matrix. These vectors are learned during training so the model can represent semantic relationships between words.
- **Positional embedding**: Transformers do not process tokens sequentially like RNNs, but they handle all tokens in parallel. This means they don't inherently know the order of tokens in a sentence. To address this, we must add positional embeddings to each token embedding. This tells the model where each token appears in the sequence. These positional vectors can be learned or fixed.

The following figure shows how these embedding types are combined:

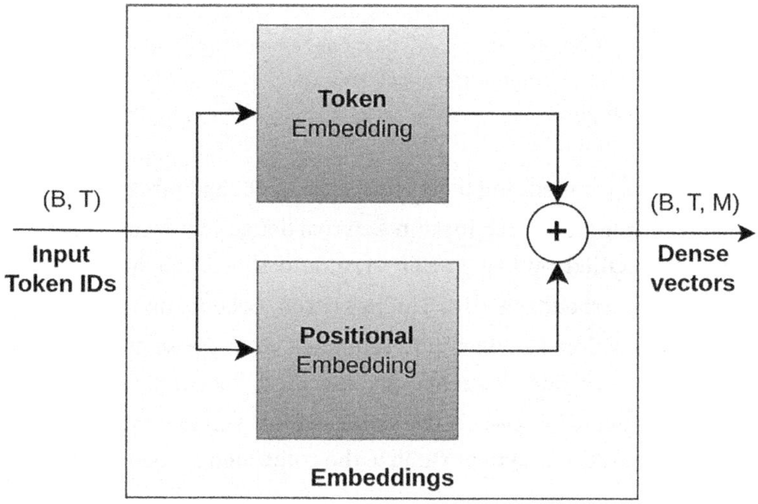

Figure 14.3 – Token and positional embeddings

It shows that token and positional embeddings are the same size and are added directly to result in a vector that carries both semantic meaning and position.

We can implement both token and positional embeddings in a single `Embeddings` class, as follows:

```
class Embeddings(nn.Module):
    cfg: Config

    def setup(self) -> None:
        self.token_embedding = nn.Embed(
            cfg.vocab_size, cfg.embedding_dim
        )
        self.position_embedding = nn.Embed(
            cfg.max_seq_length, cfg.embedding_dim
        )
        self.layer_norm = nn.LayerNorm()

    def __call__(self, input_ids: Array) -> Array:
        seq_length = input_ids.shape[1]
        position_ids = jnp.expand_dims(
            jnp.arange(seq_length), axis=0
        )
        token_embedding = self.token_embedding(input_ids)
```

```
        position_embedding = self.position_embedding(position_ids)
        embeddings = token_embedding + position_embedding
        embeddings = self.layer_norm(embeddings)
        return embeddings
```

This module initializes two embedding layers using the `nn.Embed` function. `token_embedding` is a token embedding layer that maps each input token to a dense vector representation. The number of possible tokens is specified by `cfg.vocab_size`, and the dimensionality of the embedding space is specified by `cfg.embedding_dim`. The `position_embedding` is our position embedding layer that maps each position in the input sequence to a dense vector representation. The maximum length of the input sequence is specified by `cfg.max_seq_length`, and the dimensionality of the embedding space is the same as for token embeddings. We also use a layer normalization layer (`nn.LayerNorm`) to normalize the combined embeddings.

The `__call__()` method takes token IDs (`input_ids`), which are a 2D array containing the input token IDs, with shape *(B, T)*. We create a 2D `position_ids` array with shape *(1, T)* of integers from 0 to `seq_length` – 1. Here, the position IDs are generated using a simple range-based approach. In some models, more complex position encoding schemes may be used, such as sinusoidal. Next, we apply the token and positional embeddings to the input IDs and position IDs, respectively, in order to get a learnable vector representation of each. The `embeddings` output at the end is the element-wise addition of the token and position embeddings. Note that a positional embedding with a shape of *(1, T, M)* is broadcast along the batch (first dimension) when added to the token embedding *(B, T, M)*.

Transformer decoder

For the text generation task, a **decoder-only** transformer model following the GPT-2 design is well suited. A decoder transformer basically consists of embeddings and a stack of identical transformer layers that use *causally masked* multi-head self-attention (see *Figure 14.2*). This masking ensures that each token can only attend to itself and the tokens that came before it (not future tokens).

We are ready to define the `TransformerDecoder` module, as follows:

```
class TransformerDecoder(nn.Module):
    cfg: Config

    def setup(self) -> None:
        self.embeddings = Embeddings(cfg)
        self.dropout = nn.Dropout(cfg.dropout_probability)
        self.transformer_layers = [
```

```
            TransformerLayer(cfg)
            for _ in range(cfg.num_hidden_layers)
        ]

    def __call__(
        self,
        input_ids: Array,
        deterministic: bool = True,
        rng: Optional[KeyArray] = None,
    ) -> Array:
        seq_length = input_ids.shape[1]
        causal_mask = jnp.tril(
            jnp.ones(shape=(seq_length, seq_length))
        )
        x = self.embeddings(input_ids)
        x = self.dropout(x, deterministic=deterministic, rng=rng)
        for layer in self.transformer_layers:
            x = layer(x, causal_mask, deterministic, rng)
        return x
```

In the `setup()` method, we initialize an instance of `Embeddings` that is responsible for generating token embeddings and position embeddings for the input sequence. We also initialize a dropout layer (`nn.Dropout`) with a dropout probability specified by `cfg.dropout_probability`. More importantly, we add `transformer_layers`, which contains a list of `TransformerLayer` instances. The number of layers is determined by `cfg.num_hidden_layers`.

In the forward-pass `__call__()` method, first we generate a causal mask matrix (`causal_mask`) using the `jnp.tril` function (short for "triangle lower"). The resulting `causal_mask` matrix has 1s below the diagonal and 0s above. This mask is used in the scaled dot product attention (basically in `nn.softmax(..., where=mask)`), which ignores all attention weights above the diagonal, effectively preventing the model from attending to future tokens. This is because the `softmax` function only considers the unmasked elements when computing the normalized attention weights.

After passing the input IDs through the embedding and dropout layers, we iterate through the list of transformer layers, applying each layer to the output of the previous layer. Each layer additionally takes the `causal_mask`, `deterministic`, and `rng` inputs.

The language model

The transformer decoder can be used on its own to build different types of models, depending on the task, such as text generation, dialogue systems, and code completion. Each of these models uses the same core mechanism: a stack of decoder layers with masked self-attention to ensure that the model can only attend to past tokens, not future ones. We will specifically focus on using the decoder architecture to build a text generation model. Our goal is to generate human-like text by predicting one token at a time in an *autoregressive* manner. This means that, at each step, the model takes the current sequence of tokens as input and predicts the next token. This predicted token is then appended to the input sequence, and the updated sequence is fed back into the model to generate the next token. This process continues iteratively until a desired length is reached, or a special end-of-sequence token is generated.

Let's implement our own language model that predicts the next token ID based on the input sequence:

```
class LanguageModel(nn.Module):
    cfg: Config

    def setup(self) -> None:
        cfg = self.cfg
        self.decoder = TransformerDecoder(cfg)
        self.dropout = nn.Dropout(cfg.dropout_probability)
        self.classifier = nn.Dense(cfg.vocab_size)

    def __call__(
        self,
        inputs_ids: Array,
        deterministic: bool = True,
        rng: Optional[KeyArray] = None,
    ) -> Array:
        x = self.decoder(inputs_ids)
        x = self.dropout(x, deterministic=deterministic, rng=rng)
        logits = self.classifier(x)
        return logits

    @classmethod
    def predict_next_id(
        cls,
        logits: Array,
        rng: KeyArray,
```

```
        top: int = 50,
    ) -> list[list[int]]:
        probs = nn.softmax(logits[:, -1, :], axis=-1)
        probs, ids = jax.lax.top_k(probs, top)
        predicted_ids = []
        for i in range(probs.shape[0]):
            rng, _ = jax.random.split(rng)
            selected_id = jax.random.choice(
                rng,
                ids[i],
                p=probs[i],
                axis=-1,
            )
            predicted_ids.append([int(selected_id)])
        return predicted_ids
```

The `setup()` method initializes model components, including a transformer decoder, a dropout layer, and a classification head. The `__call__()` method takes three arguments: `input_ids`, `deterministic`, and `rng`, like our previous implementations. The classifier outputs `logits` for each possible next token in the vocabulary dictionary of the tokenizer (`cfg.vocab_size`).

We add a `classmethod` `predict_next_id()`, which generates token ID predictions based on the model's output logits. We could simply select the most likely token as the next token. However, it often samples from a distribution of top tokens to make the generated text more human and less robotic. The `top` argument in the function is the number of top predictions to consider (default set to `50`). This method computes the `softmax` probabilities for each possible next token based on the last token's logits (`logits[:, -1, :]`). It selects the top-k predicted tokens and their corresponding probabilities using `jax.lax.top_k`. For each input sequence, it randomly selects a predicted token with a different seed from the top-k list based on the computed probabilities.

To generate text, we additionally define the `generate_text` function, which takes input example IDs and generates text for a specific number of tokens:

```
def generate_text(
    example_ids,
    params,
    model,
    tokenizer,
    repeat=100,
    rng=jax.random.PRNGKey(0),
```

```
    show_input_text=True,
):
    if show_input_text:
        input_tokens = tokenizer.convert_ids_to_tokens(example_ids[0])
        input_text = tokenizer.convert_tokens_to_string(input_tokens)
        print(input_text, "[GENERATED TEXT]", end='')
    for _ in range(repeat):
        rng, _ = jax.random.split(rng)
        logits = model.apply(params, example_ids)
        predicted_ids = model.predict_next_id(logits, rng=rng)
        example_ids = jnp.concatenate(
            [example_ids, jnp.array(predicted_ids)], axis=1
        )[..., 1:]
        tokens = tokenizer.convert_ids_to_tokens(example_ids[0, -1:])
        text = tokenizer.convert_tokens_to_string(tokens)
        print(text, end='')
```

This function takes an input of token IDs (with shape *(1, T)*), runs it through the model to predict the next token repeatedly, and prints the generated text as it evolves. `model.apply(params, example_ids)` runs a forward pass through the model, producing output logits (predicted scores for the next token). `predict_next_id()` is the defined custom method that samples the next token from the logits using the top-k approach. We update the sequence by appending the new token to the current input sequence and removing the first token so that the sequence length remains constant. We also convert the prediction to text and print it without a new line (`end=''`) so that the output appears as continuous generated text. This loop runs `repeat` times to generate new tokens one at a time.

Now that we have successfully built the language model, the next step is to prepare and tokenize our training data. In the next section, we'll process raw text into tokenized input suitable for feeding into the model, which will ultimately enable us to train it to generate coherent and meaningful text.

Loading data and tokenization

This section explains how to obtain the example text dataset and prepare it by tokenizing the individual samples.

Getting the dataset

To build our own language model, we need a text dataset that covers a wide range of general topics. Since training on a very large dataset typically requires a considerable amount of GPU computations, which may not be suitable for the educational scope of this chapter, we will work with a smaller, more manageable dataset. We will use **Hugging Face** (**HG**), an open source platform for working with LLMs and datasets, to download large movie reviews and a prebuilt tokenizer. It contains a total of 100,000 movie reviews that fit well for our text generation task. We can simply download this dataset from the HG data hub using just a few lines:

```
from datasets import load_dataset
dataset = load_dataset("stanfordnlp/imdb")
```

The `load_dataset` function allows us to easily download and load a wide variety of text datasets. `stanfordnlp/imdb` specifies the data provider. The function returns a `DatasetDict` object containing `train/test/unsupervised` splits:

```
DatasetDict({
train: Dataset({
features: ['text', 'label'],
num_rows: 25000
})
test: Dataset({
features: ['text', 'label'],
num_rows: 25000
})
unsupervised: Dataset({
features: ['text', 'label'],
num_rows: 50000
})
})
```

Here, `DatasetDict` is a special data structure provided by the HG datasets library that holds multiple subsets of a dataset and also supports features such as shuffling, batching, and filtering.

Next, we select a random sample from the training data and extract just their raw text into a list:

```
samples = dataset['train'].shuffle(1234).select([10])
samples_text = samples["text"]
```

The result is a list of text strings from the dataset:

```
Superb movie. Very good photography of 1969/70 Bolton, which seems now to be a
different world. Thoughtful and an excellent dramatization and production...
```

If we successfully train our model on the movie reviews dataset, the resulting language model will specialize in generating text that resembles movie reviews. While this may not be the most comprehensive or general-purpose use case, it would still allow us to explore and understand the core technical concepts involved in building and training a custom language model from scratch.

Tokenization

The raw text data cannot be given to language models as they only work with numbers. Therefore, input text is required to be split into smaller pieces, and afterward, each is converted into a unique integer, called a token ID. Each tokenizer has a vocabulary size, which is in fact the total number of unique tokens that a tokenizer can recognize. It defines the range of token IDs and corresponds to the number of entries in the tokenizer's vocabulary, and has a direct effect on memory usage and model performance. There is also a maximum length that refers to the maximum number of tokens that the tokenizer will accept in a single input sequence. Any input longer than this must be either truncated or split into smaller chunks. Longer sequences mean slower training and waste padding for smaller sequences.

We can load a read-to-use tokenizer from the HG Hub as follows:

```
from transformers import AutoTokenizer
tokenizer = AutoTokenizer.from_pretrained("gpt2")
```

`AutoTokenizer` is a flexible interface that automatically loads the correct tokenizer for a given model (such as BERT, GPT-2, etc.). In this case, we download the pretrained tokenizer associated with GPT-2, but you can load any tokenizer as we're training our own custom model. Once loaded, you can use the tokenizer to convert raw text into tokens (or token IDs) and also decode tokens back into readable text. GPT-2's tokenizer has a vocabulary size of 50,257. So, valid token IDs range from 0 to 50,256. The maximum length of any input sequence for GPT-2 is 1,024.

Let's try to tokenize an example text to numerical IDs and convert it back to the original text using a previously loaded tokenizer:

```
text = ["This is an example text."]
encoded_input = tokenizer(text)
```

`tokenizer` expects a batch input, such as a list of text. It processes the text by splitting it into tokens (subwords) and mapping tokens to their corresponding IDs. As output, it returns a dictionary typically containing the list of IDs, `input_ids`, and the corresponding binary mask of real (1) and padding (0) tokens, referred to as `attention_mask`.

The following is an example output:

```
{'input_ids': [[1212, 318, 281, 1672, 2420, 13]], 'attention_mask': [[1, 1, 1, 1, 1, 1]]}
```

We can always access the tokens or convert them back to the original string:

```
tokens = tokenizer.convert_ids_to_tokens(encoded_input["input_ids"][0])
text = tokenizer.convert_tokens_to_string(tokens)
```

The `convert_ids_to_tokens` method converts the list of token IDs back into their token (text) representations:

```
tokens = ['This', 'Ġis', 'Ġan', 'Ġexample', 'Ġtext', '.']
```

Please note that the GPT-style tokenizer often uses Ġ to indicate a space before the word. Also, the `convert_tokens_to_string()` method merges the tokens back to a single string:

```
'This is an example text.'
```

Let's tokenize all the training and validation samples using the supported `map` function for the loaded `DataSet` object, as follows:

```
from transformers.tokenization_utils_base import BatchEncoding

cols = dataset["train"].column_names

def tokenize(dataset) -> BatchEncoding:
    return tokenizer(dataset['text'])

tokenized_train_dataset = dataset["train"]\
    .shuffle(seed=1234)\
    .map(tokenize, batched=True, remove_columns=cols)

tokenized_test_dataset = dataset["test"]\
    .shuffle(seed=1234)\
    .select(range(2000))\
    .map(tokenize, batched=True, remove_columns=cols)
```

The tokenize function takes a batch of the dataset and applies the tokenizer to the text field. The map method applies the tokenize function to the batches of data, batched=True groups examples into batches for efficient processing, and remove_columns removes original columns such as text, keeping only the tokenized outputs.

Preprocessing

We must preprocess the input data before training the language model for text generation. Our custom model expects input sequences of a fixed length and does not support padding. This means all sequences must be the same size when fed into the model. We also need to provide the corresponding labels for training. These labels are simply the next token IDs that the model should learn to predict at each position in the input sequence. In more advanced setups, it's possible to use padding along with attention masks to support variable-length inputs. Attention masks help the model ignore padded positions during computation, offering more flexibility. However, for simplicity, our current implementation will stick to fixed-length sequences without padding.

The following preprocess function takes in a batch of tokenized datasets and joins, splits them into fixed-length chunks, and, finally, returns a grouped dataset of input IDs and labels:

```
def preprocess(examples):
    concatenated_examples = {k: sum(examples[k], []) for k in examples.keys()}
    total_length = len(concatenated_examples[list(examples.keys())[0]])
    total_length = (total_length // cfg.max_seq_length) * cfg.max_seq_length
    result = {
        k: [t[i : i + cfg.max_seq_length] for i in range(0, total_length,
cfg.max_seq_length)]
        for k, t in concatenated_examples.items()
    }
    result["label"] = result["input_ids"].copy()
    return result
```

We accordingly apply the preprocess function to the entire training and test datasets to generate preprocessed datasets that are ready for use during training:

```
preprocessed_train_dataset = tokenized_train_dataset.map(preprocess,
batched=True, num_proc=1)
preprocessed_test_dataset = tokenized_test_dataset.map(preprocess, batched=True,
num_proc=1)
```

Dataloader

As our final component for data preparation, we implement a basic **dataloader** to be able to create batches of data from a given dataset. This will be used as an iterator for feeding input data into the model chunk-wise during training or inference:

```
import random
from tqdm import tqdm
from typing import Iterator

def create_batches(
    dataset: list[dict],
    batch_size: int,
    shuffle: bool = True,
) -> Iterator[dict]:
    data_size = len(dataset)
    indices = list(range(data_size))
    if shuffle:
       random.shuffle(indices)
    num_batches = data_size // batch_size
    for index in range(num_batches):
        start = index * batch_size
        end = (index + 1) * batch_size
        batch = dataset[indices[start:end]]
        yield {
            "input_ids": jnp.asarray(batch["input_ids"]),
            "label": jnp.asarray(batch["label"]),
        }
```

The `create_batches` function takes `dataset`, splits it into chunks of size `batch_size`, and yields each batch as a dictionary containing `input_ids` and `label` arrays converted to JAX-compatible arrays using `jnp.asarray`.

After building our custom model and preparing the input data, the final step in our journey to create a language model from scratch is, of course, *training the model.*

Training the language model

To train `LanguageModel`, we use **Optax**, a gradient processing and optimization library for JAX, to define and initialize an optimizer. We also create Flax's **training state**. This training state conveniently bundles together the model parameters, the optimizer state, and any additional information needed to perform updates during training. Since our model is intended to be trained to predict the next token ID, it behaves like a multi-class classifier at each position in the sequence. Therefore, we use the **softmax cross-entropy loss**, where the target (i.e., the correct next token) is represented using **one-hot encoding**. The rest of the training process follows the typical pattern we've used in *Chapter 10*.

We define a training step that includes the following:

1. Performing a forward pass through the model to compute the predicted logits.
2. Calculating the loss function by comparing these logits with the target token IDs.
3. Computing the gradient of the loss with respect to the model parameters.
4. Finally, updating the parameters using the optimizer.

This training step is repeated for each batch of data, allowing the model to gradually improve its ability to predict the next token in a sequence. It would be interesting to check model predictions before any training. For this, we get the first batch of data, initialize the model with random weights, and then use the `generate_text` function to predict the next words, as follows:

```
batches = create_batches(preprocessed_train_dataset, batch_size=cfg.batch_size)
batch = next(batches)
example_ids = batch["input_ids"][0].reshape(1, -1)
```

The `create_batches` function generates batches from the preprocessed training (or test) dataset. We use `next(batches)` to retrieve the first batch from this iterator. From this batch, we extract the first sample's input IDs using `batch["input_ids"][0]`, and reshape it into a 2D array of shape *(1, -1)*. Here, `-1` tells the array to infer the appropriate sequence of length from the original data. This reshaping is necessary because the model expects input token IDs with shape *(B, T)*.

Next, we instantiate the `LanguageModel` class using the configuration object (`cfg`). We then call the model's `init()` method to initialize its parameters. This method requires two arguments: a random number generator (`rng`) and `example_ids`. The input example is used to infer the model's internal parameter shapes:

```
model = LanguageModel(cfg)

rng=jax.random.PRNGKey(1234)
params = model.init(rng, example_ids)
```

Finally, we call the generate_text function, which uses the initialized model and tokenizer to generate new text starting from the given input token IDs:

```
generate_text(
    example_ids,
    params,
    model,
    tokenizer,
    repeat=50,
    show_input_text=False,
)
```

An example of the generated output might look as follows:

```
[GENERATED TEXT]
fixmemillion vanillaDO Nation Rei insecure hazards Micheleulse drainedImages
franchisestairsQuantity masked revealing deserving resorts crust Werner
BenefitPhoneagos blasting orallyconcert FaulFINEbread BolsheAPDQuantity 56
ADVsoundingonis SourcesSolar Conqueruserc Alter virtual Gohanwithout insurg Score
connect action Guan
```

As expected, the generated text appears nonsensical. This is because the model's weights are still untrained, and thus the output token IDs are essentially random. Let's proceed with training the model. We start by importing the necessary modules, including optax and flax:

```
import optax
from flax.training import train_state
from flax.training.common_utils import onehot
```

flax.training.train_state is a module from the Flax library that provides a TrainState class for managing the training state of a model. flax.training.common_utils.onehot is for one-hot encoding the target token IDs and will be used later in the loss function.

We initialize the AdamW optimizer from Optax and a fixed learning rate:

```
optimizer = optax.adamw(learning_rate=0.001, weight_decay=0.00001)

state = train_state.TrainState.create(
    apply_fn=model.apply,
    params=params["params"],
```

```
    tx=optimizer,
)
```

AdamW is a variant of the popular Adam optimizer that includes weight decay, which helps prevent overfitting by adding **L2 regularization** to the model's weights. Also, TrainState is created from the Flax train_state module. This object manages the training state of the model, including its parameters, optimizer, and other relevant information. About the passed arguments, apply_fn=model.apply is a reference to the apply method of the model, which defines how the model's parameters are used to make predictions. params=params["params"] is the initial parameters of the model and tx=optimizer specifies the optimizer (AdamW in this case) that will be used to update the model's parameters during training.

We need to define the loss function. We break it into two functions, compute_loss and loss_fn. The compute_loss function calculates the **cross-entropy loss** between the model's output (logits) and the true token IDs (targets):

```
def compute_loss(
    logits: Array,
    targets: Array
) -> Array:
    return optax.softmax_cross_entropy(
        logits[..., :-1, :],
        onehot(targets[..., 1:], logits.shape[-1]),
    ).mean()
```

We must match each input token with the correct target (the next token) for training. To do this, we slightly shift the inputs and targets. logits[..., :-1, :] slices the logits array to *exclude the last prediction*. This is because we don't have a "next token" label for the last input token—there's nothing after it to predict. Also, onehot(targets[..., 1:], logits.shape[-1]) shifts the targets array *one position to the left*, excluding the first token and converting the rest into one-hot-encoded vectors. This gives us the actual target tokens that each input token should predict. The optax.softmax_cross_entropy function applies the softmax activation function to the logits input and then computes the cross-entropy loss between the resulting softmax output and the true labels. The .mean() method at the end computes the mean loss across all elements in the resulting array.

The `loss_fn` function defines the loss computation function for a given input model's parameters and a single batch of data:

```
def loss_fn(
    params: Array,
    state: train_state.TrainState,
    batch: dict[str, Array],
    deterministic: bool,
    rng: KeyArray,
) -> Array:
    logits = state.apply_fn(
        {'params': params}, batch['input_ids'], deterministic, rng
    )
    loss = compute_loss(logits, batch['label'])
    return loss
```

The model's output (`logits`) is computed by applying the model's `apply_fn` method to the input batch data using the provided parameters (`params`) and training state (`state`). The loss is computed by calling the `compute_loss` function with the predicted logits and target labels from the batch.

Now that we have succeeded in defining the loss function, the training step can be made by gradient of the loss function and updating the parameters using the optimizer. The following is the implementation of the `train_step` function:

```
@jax.jit
def train_step(
    state: train_state.TrainState,
    batch: dict[str, Array],
    rng: KeyArray,
) -> tuple[train_state.TrainState, dict]:
    grad_fn = jax.value_and_grad(loss_fn)
    loss, grads= grad_fn(
        state.params, state, batch, False, rng
    )
    state = state.apply_gradients(grads=grads)
    metrics = {'loss': loss}
    return state, metrics
```

jax.value_and_grad(loss_fn) defines a gradient function, grad_fn, by wrapping loss_fn using jax.value_and_grad. The grad_fn is then called with the current model parameters (state.params), training state (state), batch data (batch), and random number generator key (rng). The deterministic=False argument specifies that dropout layers must be used during gradient computation. state = state.apply_gradients(grads=grads) updates the training state by applying the computed gradients using the optimizer's apply_gradients method. This step performs a gradient descent update, adjusting the model parameters based on the computed gradients. The jax.jit decorator is used to compile the train_step function **Just in Time (JIT)** using JAX's XLA compiler. This compilation step significantly improves the performance of the function. The result is a tuple containing the loss value computed by loss_fn and the gradients of the loss with respect to the model parameters.

We can similarly implement the validation_step function. Two main differences between train_step and validation_step in this case are that no dropout is applied during validation and model parameters are not updated, as the purpose is solely to evaluate the model on unseen data, not to optimize its weights:

```
@jax.jit
def validation_step(
    state: train_state.TrainState,
    batch: dict[str, Array],
) -> tuple[train_state.TrainState, dict]:
    loss = loss_fn(
        state.params, state, batch, True, None
    )
    metrics = {'loss': loss}
    return state, metrics
```

Putting all these components together, the **training loop** for each epoch can then be implemented as follows:

```
for epoch in range(cfg.epochs):
    epoch_loss = 0.0
    training_batches = create_batches(
        preprocessed_train_dataset,
        batch_size=cfg.batch_size,
    )
    for batch_count, batch in tqdm(enumerate(training_batches, start=1)):
            rng, _ = jax.random.split(rng)
            state, metrics = train_step(state, batch, rng)
```

```
            epoch_loss += metrics["loss"]
    print(
        f"epoch: {epoch + 1}/{cfg.epochs}"
        f", loss: {epoch_loss / batch_count:.4f}"
    )
    # --- Validation ---
    epoch_loss_val = 0.0
    val_batches = create_batches(
        preprocessed_test_dataset,
        shuffle=False,
        batch_size=cfg.batch_size,
    )
    for batch_count, batch in enumerate(val_batches, start=1):
        _, metrics = validation_step(state, batch)
        epoch_loss_val += metrics["loss"]
    print(
        f"epoch: {epoch + 1}/{cfg.epochs}"
        f", val_loss: {epoch_loss_val / batch_count:.4f}"
    )
```

This code block trains the model for a specified number of epochs (`cfg.epochs`), with each epoch consisting of two phases: training and validation. During training, the model processes batches of data in a loop, updating its state and accumulating loss values using the `train_step` function. After training, the model's performance is evaluated on a validation set using the `validation_step` function. The losses are averaged over the number of batches processed, providing a measure of the model's performance during training and validation. `rng, _ = jax.random.split(rng)` gives a new random key each time the model makes a prediction during training.

Running the first loop takes longer due to the overhead time of the JIT compilation. After that, training proceeds as expected at least one order of magnitude faster. The following figure shows the process and memory utilization timeline of the model during training epochs of the model on the GPU:

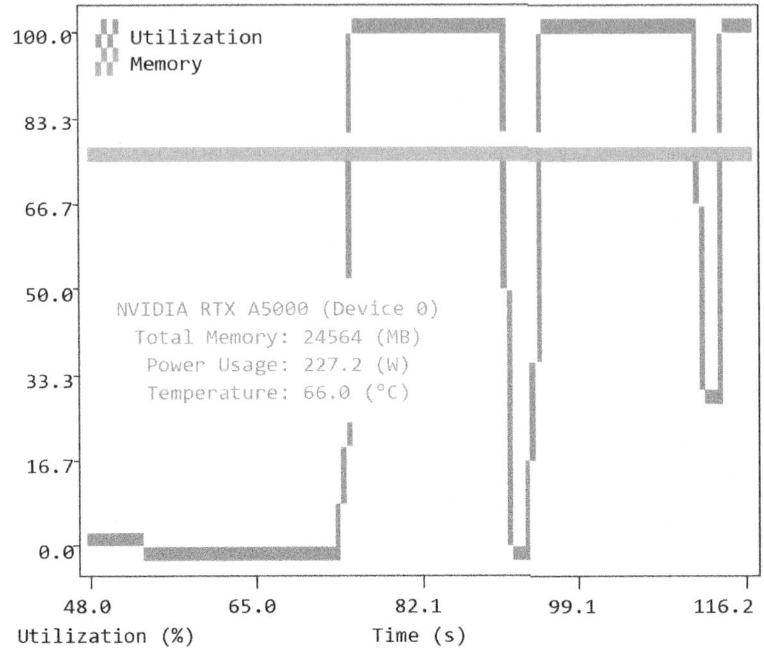

Figure 14.4 – GPU utilization when training the language model

After training the model for a few epochs, the generated text looks as follows:

```
[GENERATED TEXT]
it comes a little more about this, especially though every episode would be the
BBC, though Billy Hartley was the rest of the most popular magic, if they had, it
had been a lot better cast through the awesome lines...
```

The model predictions have noticeably improved, and our tiny language model is beginning to speak! While the generated sentences may still lack coherence, this is expected at this stage. With a larger dataset and number of learnable parameters in the model, better hyperparameter tuning, and further training, the model's performance can significantly improve. We've successfully built a language model from scratch in JAX that can generate text. For curious readers, there are still plenty of directions to explore, such as adding padding support, incorporating an end-of-sentence token to let the model determine when to stop, and refining the architecture.

Summary

We built a transformer-based language model using JAX, demonstrating the basics of how modern LLMs function under the hood. Our goal was to implement a small, GPT-style generative model capable of producing human-like text. We began by understanding the necessary components of transformer models, such as the attention mechanism, multi-head self-attention, and feed-forward networks. These formed the foundation for constructing a full transformer layer.

We also explored the concept of embeddings, covering both token and positional embeddings, to represent text in a format suitable for neural networks. With these pieces in place, we assembled a decoder-only transformer model following the GPT-2 architecture. We tokenized input text using HG's GPT-2 tokenizer and created fixed-length sequences of input for training.

Finally, we defined the loss function, optimizer, and training state. We implemented and ran a training loop to train our model. Though our initial model was small and trained on a lightweight dataset, the generated outputs began to reflect recognizable language patterns, an encouraging step toward more sophisticated language generation. We're now equipped with the technical foundations to explore and scale modern language models for more complex applications.

Questions

1. How do padding and attention masks enable the model to process variable-length input?
2. What changes are necessary to adapt a transformer architecture for classification tasks, such as predicting sentiment labels in movie reviews?
3. How can we include an **End-of-Sequence** (**EOS**) token to allow the model to determine when to stop generating text in the `generate_text` function?

Answers

1. Padding makes all sequences the same length so they can be processed in batches, while attention masks tell the model which positions correspond to real tokens and which are just padding. By masking out the padded positions, the attention mechanism ignores these unwanted parts of the vector representation, ensuring the model only attends to meaningful input tokens even when sequences have different original lengths.
2. To adapt a transformer for classification tasks such as sentiment prediction on movie reviews, the main change is adding a task-specific classification head (e.g., multi-layer perceptron with last `softmax` activation function) on top of the transformer encoder.
3. An EOS token must first be included in the tokenization. This teaches the model during training where sequences terminate, since the EOS token becomes part of the learned prediction targets. During text generation, as the model predicts tokens iteratively, we monitor the predicted token ID at each step. When the model outputs the EOS token, we

stop the generation loop. This allows the model to explicitly signal when the sequence should end instead of relying only on a fixed maximum length.

Get this book's PDF version and more

Scan the QR code (or go to `packtpub.com/unlock`). Search for this book by name, confirm the edition, and then follow the steps on the page.

UNLOCK NOW

Note: Keep your invoice handy. Purchases made directly from Packt don't require an invoice.

Part 5

Beyond This Book

This final part looks ahead, offering pathways to deepen your GPU programming expertise. We've added references and guidance on advanced topics and specialized applications so that you can continue expanding your skills beyond the foundations covered in this book.

This part of the book includes the following chapters:

15

Expanding and Deepening Your GPU Programming Knowledge

The aim of this book has been to build a solid foundation of GPU computing with Python. The book started by covering low-level CUDA primitives, such as kernels and streams, built up to high-level libraries, and finished with several case studies. This chapter will look at some advanced topics that may become relevant later in your GPU programming journey.

Technical requirements

To run the code in this chapter, an NVIDIA GPU with compute capability 7.5 or more is required. The CUDA Toolkit, Python 3, and a number of Python packages must also be installed. As explained in *Chapter 2*, it is recommended to create a `pixi` environment based on the `pixi.lock` file in the GitHub repository associated with this book:

`https://github.com/PacktPublishing/GPU-Accelerated-Computing-with-Python-3-and-CUDA`

The setup details are explained in the `README.md` file. To run the code snippets in this chapter, an A100 GPU was used; timing results will differ depending on the specific device that is used to run the examples.

Advanced low-level features

This section briefly introduces advanced low-level features that warrant further exploration for high-performance CUDA programming in Python.

Detailed breakdown of the different types of memory

The examples in this book have primarily relied on **global memory**, **shared memory**, **registers**, and hardware-managed **caches** (L1 and L2). These form the core memory hierarchy that most CUDA programs rely on.

Other types of memory have been mentioned only in passing. These additional memory spaces can be useful in specific situations, particularly when optimizing memory access patterns or interfacing with specialized hardware features. Therefore, this section provides a guide to the more niche types of memory in CUDA, both on the device and on the host.

The first memory space to mention is **local memory**. Local memory made a number of appearances in other chapters. Conceptually, local memory stores data that is private to each thread. Scalar values stored in variables inside a kernel are also private to threads. Usually, these are stored in the registers. Local memory offers the flexibility to store data private to threads that may not fit in the registers, such as arrays.

Local memory can be useful for passing data to device functions by reference instead of by value. To illustrate, consider the following Numba-CUDA example:

```
from numba import cuda

@cuda.jit(device=True)
def add_10(arr) -> None:
    arr[0] += 10

@cuda.jit
def kernel_with_local_memory(out) -> None:
    x = cuda.grid(1)
    if x > out.shape[0]:
        return
    local_arr = cuda.local.array(shape=(1,), dtype="int64")
    local_arr[0] = x
    add_10(local_arr)
    out[x] = local_arr[0]
```

In `kernel_with_local_memory`, each thread creates a local array that can store one element. This array can be passed to the `add_10` device function, which acts on the data in the array, mutating it in place without returning anything. The result is an array where each element contains the corresponding absolute thread ID plus 10. This would not work by directly passing a scalar variable to `add_10`, since these are passed by value, not by reference.

As an optimization, scalars and small arrays declared in local memory may be stored in registers if space allows. Otherwise, local memory spills over into VRAM, which has the same latency characteristics as global memory. The only way to know where the data resides is to inspect the PTX assembly or profile the kernel. Kernels that use more registers than are available spill this data automatically into local memory, with a negative impact on performance. Therefore, in practice, programmers often use local memory accidentally rather than explicitly.

Another memory space is **constant memory**. Constant memory is a small, **read-only** memory region that is cached and optimized for the case where *many threads access the same value* at the same time. It is well suited for storing constants, such as lookup tables, configuration parameters, or small coefficient arrays, that are read frequently but never modified by kernels. With Numba-CUDA, constant memory can be used in a kernel as follows:

```
CONST = np.array([1.0, 2.0], dtype="float32")

@cuda.jit
def line(x):
    coeffs = cuda.const.array_like(CONST)
    i = cuda.grid(1)
    if i >= x.size:
        return
    x[i] = coeffs[0] * x[i] + coeffs[1]
```

This kernel computes the y value in a linear relationship, where the coefficients are the slope and y-intercept, which are stored in constant memory. The coefficients are first declared outside the kernel as a NumPy array. Inside the kernel, the constant array is declared using `cuda.const.array_like`. Somewhat confusingly, the official documentation states that constant memory "is host allocated"; however, `cuda.const.array_like` must be called inside a kernel. The `CONST` values will be fetched at compile time, meaning when the kernel is first called.

Note

Using values defined outside the kernel

Data defined outside a kernel but referenced inside a kernel (without passing it in as an argument) exhibits some strange behavior. When data outside the kernel is modified after the first compilation, the kernel continues to use the old value. If the kernel is compiled again by calling it with different input data types, the modified value will be used. This is because the value is baked into the kernel during compilation, which only happens the first time a kernel is called for some input data types.

CUDA also provides **texture memory**, which is a read-only memory space with a dedicated cache optimized for **spatial locality**. Texture memory was originally designed for graphics workloads, but it can also be useful in general-purpose computing for some access patterns. However, at the time of writing, texture memory is not accessible through Numba-CUDA, and its use cases are generally quite niche.

In addition to device memory spaces, CUDA supports several **host memory** types that affect data transfer behavior. **Pinned** (or page-locked) host memory prevents the operating system from paging the memory to disk, enabling faster and more predictable transfers between the host and device. Pinned memory is particularly important for high-throughput or asynchronous data transfers, as discussed in *Chapter 6*. A pinned array can be created with Numba-CUDA as follows:

```
pinned_array = cuda.pinned_array(
    shape=(64,),
    dtype="int64",
)
```

The data in a pinned array can be set like a NumPy array with slice indexing:

```
pinned_array[:] = 0
```

Data in a pinned array can be copied to the device just like any host array, for example, a NumPy array:

```
dev_arr = cuda.device_array_like(pinned_array)
dev_arr.copy_to_device(pinned_array)
```

Data from the device can be written to a pinned array on the host as follows:

```
dev_arr.copy_to_host(pinned_array)
```

CUDA also supports unified memory, which provides a single address space accessible from both the CPU and GPU. Unified memory simplifies programming by automatically migrating data between the host and device, though this convenience comes at the cost of reduced control over data movement and, in some cases, lower performance. As discussed in *Chapter 9*, tools such as `cudf.pandas` leverage unified memory internally.

In Python-based CUDA workflows (e.g., with Numba-CUDA), the benefits of unified memory may not be immediately obvious. For example, when passing a host-resident NumPy array to a Numba-CUDA kernel, the data is automatically copied to the device—sometimes with a warning about implicit transfers. The advantage of unified memory over implicit copies is that the GPU can dynamically manage data movement, transferring only what is needed and when it is needed.

Numba-CUDA provides the `managed_array` primitive to explicitly use unified memory. A managed array can be created as follows:

```
managed_array = cuda.managed_array(
    shape=(64,),
    dtype="int64",
)
```

It can be passed directly into a kernel that expects a device array, and it can also be accessed on the host.

Finally, CUDA has **mapped memory**, which allows kernels to directly access data on the host without first copying the data to the device. This is some of the slowest memory available and is only relevant when global memory is insufficient for the problem. An array can be allocated in mapped memory with Numba-CUDA as follows:

```
mapped_array = cuda.mapped_array(
    shape=(64,),
    dtype="int64",
)
```

It can be passed directly to a kernel that expects a device array.

In practice, many CUDA programs rely primarily on global memory, shared memory, and registers. The additional memory spaces discussed here become relevant when pushing performance further, reducing memory traffic, or simplifying data movement in complex applications. Understanding that these memory types exist and what problems they are designed to solve is often sufficient until more specialized optimization is required.

Refining the cache behavior of memory operations

Data locality is essential to the performance of most CUDA kernels. To hide latency and make data transfers as efficient as possible, the GPU uses multiple layers of cache. Throughout the book, caches were assumed to be controlled by the driver.

However, the GPU's caching behavior can be *guided* by explicitly using different loading and storing operations. Normally, these exist at the PTX level, but Numba-CUDA also exposes them directly. For example, when performing a load operation (e.g., reading a value from an array in global memory), this can be done via the `ldca` or `ldcg` instruction. Different load and store operations have different use cases, but discussing them in detail here is beyond the scope of the book. Have a look at the official documentation here: `https://nvidia.github.io/numba-cuda/reference/cache_hints.html`.

> Note
>
> **Default load and store behavior**
>
> The default load and store operations are `ldca` and `stwb`, respectively.

On modern architectures such as Ampere, the performance impact of using specific load and store instructions is minimal for most kernels.

Using Tensor Cores

Throughout the book, arithmetic was primarily performed using **CUDA cores**. This is mostly a marketing term that refers to the ALUs that perform floating-point and integer calculations inside the streaming multiprocessors. However, modern GPUs are also equipped with a specific type of computing capability, known as **Tensor Cores**. Tensor Cores are specialized matrix-multiply-accumulate hardware units introduced by NVIDIA and present in modern architectures such as Volta, Turing, Ampere, and Hopper. These cores are designed to accelerate dense linear algebra operations, particularly matrix multiplications, which are the backbone of deep learning and scientific computing.

Tensor Cores operate on small matrix tiles, for example, 4×4, 8×8, or 16×16, depending on the GPU generation and on **reduced-precision** data types. They achieve their speedups by using lower-precision arithmetic with high-precision accumulation. Tensor Cores can perform mixed-precision computations, for example, FP16 × FP16 → FP32 accumulation, or BF16 × BF16 → FP32. **FP16 and FP32** stand for **16-bit and 32-bit floating-point precision**, respectively. **BF16** stands for **brain floating point, 16-bit**. It has the same range as FP32 but lower precision (2–3 decimal digits instead of 6–7), making it well suited for machine learning where numbers need to span large orders of magnitude but don't need to be very precise.

The following table summarizes the most common data types supported by the NVIDIA Tensor Cores, along with their approximate numerical precision and typical use cases. It provides a quick reference for understanding which precisions are available on different hardware generations and how they are commonly used in deep learning and high-performance computing workloads.

Data Type	Name	Approx. Decimal Digits	Typical Use Case
FP16	Half Precision	~3–4	Deep learning training and inference
BF16	Bfloat16	~2–3	Training with improved numerical stability
TF32	TensorFloat-32	~6–7	Accelerating FP32 training and HPC workloads
FP32	Single Precision	~7	General-purpose training and inference
FP64	Double Precision	~15–16	Scientific computing and high-performance computing
INT8	8-bit Integer	Exact	Quantized inference
INT4	4-bit Integer	Exact	Ultra-low precision inference

Table 15.1 – Common data types supported by the NVIDIA Tensor Cores

Note that the FP64 data type (double precision) is only supported on the Tensor Cores of most recent GPUs, such as A100 and H100.

Tensor Cores are accessible through low-level CUDA libraries, which wrap specific PTX assembly instructions. In practice, they are invoked when matrix or tensor operations are expressed using supported data types, including FP16, BF16, or INT8, and executed via these libraries. NVIDIA libraries such as **cuBLAS** and **cuDNN** automatically dispatch compatible matrix multiplications and convolutions to Tensor Cores when data types meet the required conditions. At a higher abstraction level, frameworks such as Numba-CUDA, JAX, PyTorch, and TensorFlow rely on these CUDA libraries and therefore use Tensor Cores whenever possible. As a result, operations such as matrix multiplication and convolutions can use Tensor Cores, which leads to improved performance and reduced energy consumption.

The following example illustrates how JAX automatically utilizes Tensor Cores when the precision is reduced to FP16:

```
import jax.numpy as jnp

def use_tensor_cores(n: int = 1024) -> None:
    x = jnp.ones((n, n), dtype=jnp.float16)
    y = jnp.dot(x, x)
    return y

use_tensor_cores()
```

The `nsys` command runs NVIDIA Nsight Systems to profile the example Python script. It collects detailed GPU metrics, including Tensor Core usage. Note that the GPU must support Tensor Cores to measure Tensor Core activity:

```
nsys profile --gpu-metrics-devices=all python tensor_core_example.py
```

The following figure shows an Nsight Systems profile on an A100 GPU:

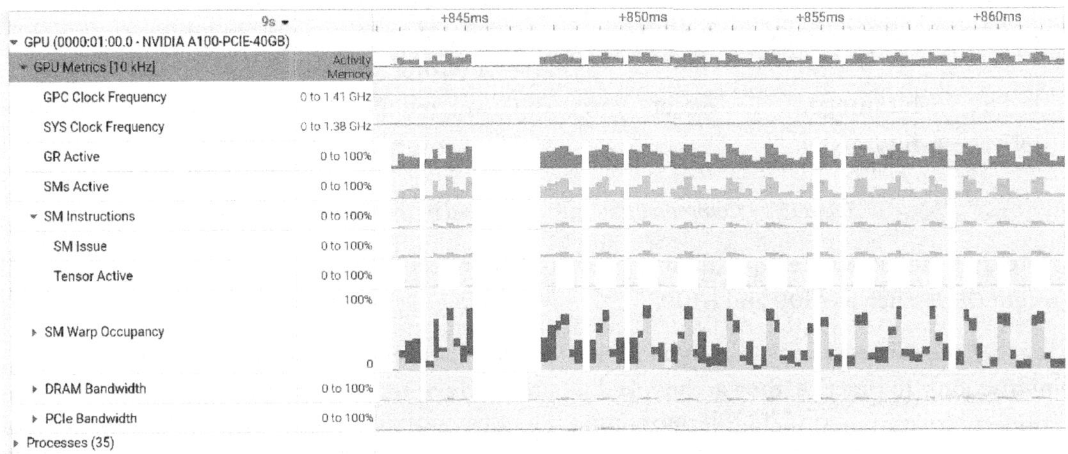

Figure 15.1 – Tensor Cores utilization profiled using NVIDIA Nsight Systems

The **Tensor Active** row in the figure indicates a low level of Tensor Core utilization. Running the same example with a larger matrix results in higher Tensor Core usage. The A100 GPU PCIe 40 GB, which features NVIDIA's Ampere architecture, has 432 third-generation Tensor Cores integrated into the chip. These accelerate matrix multiplications, convolutions, and other tensor operations using mixed-precision formats.

The next section will discuss how to access CUDA-X libraries from Python.

Using optimized NVIDIA libraries in CUDA kernels with nvmath-python

`nvmath-python` is a relatively new and open source library that bridges the gap between the scientific Python ecosystem and the optimized NVIDIA math libraries. The library wraps the low-level NVIDIA library functionality and exposes it through intuitive Python APIs.

The following example demonstrates basic matrix multiplication of CuPy arrays using the generic API available in `nvmath-python`:

```
import cupy as cp
import nvmath

m, n, k = 1024, 1024, 1024
a = cp.random.rand(m, k)
b = cp.random.rand(k, n)

result = nvmath.linalg.matmul(a, b)
cp.cuda.get_current_stream().synchronize()
```

The example uses CuPy to create random matrices directly on the GPU and then performs a GPU-accelerated matrix multiplication using `nvmath-python`'s linear algebra interface. `nvmath-python` integrates well with existing Python tensor frameworks, such as NumPy, CuPy, and PyTorch. The result of the matrix multiplication is a CuPy tensor, the same framework that was used to pass the inputs. `nvmath-python` additionally supports Numba-CUDA kernels and enables calling cuBLAS routines (e.g., `nvmat.device.MatMul`) from within those kernels. This makes it possible to mix custom GPU kernels with optimized NVIDIA math libraries. Refer to the `nvmath-python` example repository for detailed usage examples.

`nvmath-python` also supports **epilogs**. Epilog is a concept inherited from the cuBLAS library. It refers to a post-processing stage that runs immediately after a core math operation without launching a separate kernel. Common epilog operations include bias addition, element-wise scaling, activation functions (e.g., ReLU), matrix accumulation, and type quantization.

Epilogs execute extra computations after an operation in a single fused kernel. Instead of computing `A @ B`, writing the result to memory, and then launching another kernel to modify the result, an epilog applies extra logic before the result is written to memory. This avoids unnecessary kernel launches and reduces global memory traffic.

The following example demonstrates the usage of a bias epilog after matrix multiplication:

```
bias = cp.random.rand(m, 1)

epilog = nvmath.linalg.advanced.MatmulEpilog.BIAS
result = nvmath.linalg.advanced.matmul(a, b, epilog=epilog,
epilog_inputs={"bias": bias})

cp.cuda.get_current_stream().synchronize()
```

`nvmath-python` offers a range of advanced features that may be of interest to readers seeking finer control and higher performance. These include support for **stateful** operations (such as persistent matrix multiplication configurations), the ability to perform general **tensor contractions**, and mechanisms for executing operations on non-default **CUDA streams**, enabling better overlap of computation and data movement and more flexible integration into complex GPU workflows.

> Note
>
> **nvmath-python (beta)**
>
> The `nvmath-python` library is currently in beta and actively under development. This means its APIs are evolving rapidly, and working with it may require frequent changes as the library evolves.

The next section explores how to call a CUDA-C function inside a Numba-CUDA kernel.

Using CUDA C from Numba-CUDA kernels

Numba-CUDA provides support for **foreign function interfaces (FFIs)**, allowing Python code to interoperate directly with compiled CUDA C code, external GPU libraries, and low-level CUDA APIs. This makes it possible to combine the productivity of Python with the performance of optimized GPU kernels written in languages such as C.

Consider the following example written in CUDA C. The following device function multiplies two numbers and stores the result in a pointer that is provided as input:

```
extern "C" __device__ int
mul_f32_f32(
    float* return_value,
    float x,
    float y
)
{
    // Compute result and store in caller-provided slot
    *return_value = x * y;

    // Signal that no Python exception occurred
    return 0;
}
```

Suppose this device function is written to a file, `ffi/functions.cu`. Now, this device function will be used from a Numba-CUDA kernel.

To do so, the function must first be declared in Python as follows:

```
mul = cuda.declare_device("mul_f32_f32", "float32(float32, float32)")
```

This does not specify the implementation of the function; it only tells Numba the name and signature of the function so that it can be called from within a CUDA kernel. The actual implementation is expected to exist in the CUDA source code and to be compiled and linked into the kernel.

The `mul` device function can be used in a Numba-CUDA kernel by linking to the `functions.cu` file as follows:

```
functions_cu = os.path.abspath("ffi/functions.cu")

@cuda.jit(link=[functions_cu])
def multiply_vectors(r, x, y) -> None:
    i = cuda.grid(1)
    if i < len(r):
        r[i] = mul(x[i], y[i])
```

Instead of expressing all GPU logic in Python, this links an external `.cu` file at compile time and invokes the device function defined previously. To make this possible, the device function needs to live in the specified path so that Numba can find it. The name of the device function in the file needs to match the name in the function declaration in Python.

The `multiply_vectors` kernel is defined with `@cuda.jit(link=[functions_cu])`. The `link` argument is what connects the Python kernel to the external CUDA source. When Numba compiles this kernel, it also compiles and links the contents of `functions.cu`, making the foreign device function available.

Inside the kernel, each thread computes a global index and, if that index is within bounds, multiplies corresponding elements of the input arrays by calling `mul`. From the point of view of the kernel, this looks like a normal function call, even though the implementation lives in separate CUDA C code. This example demonstrated a basic use of a C-defined device function within a Numba-CUDA kernel. However, far more complex implementations are possible. For more details, check the official documentation at `https://nvidia.github.io/numba-cuda/user/cuda_ffi.html`.

Finally, the kernel can be tested as follows:

```
N = 32
cp.random.seed(1)
x = cp.random.rand(N).astype("float32")
y = cp.random.rand(N).astype("float32")
r = cp.zeros_like(x)

# Run the kernel
multiply_vectors[1, N](r, x, y)
```

The next section explores how random numbers can be generated directly on the GPU.

Pseudo-random number generation inside CUDA kernels

Up until now, random input arrays were generated either using NumPy on the host or directly on the device using CuPy. In some cases, such as in Monte Carlo simulations, random numbers need to be generated directly on the GPU inside CUDA kernels, both for performance reasons and to avoid host-device transfers.

Random number generation is directly supported in Numba-CUDA for fast, parallel, and per-thread randomness. Numba provides CUDA-compatible RNG algorithms that work inside `@cuda.jit` kernels without host intervention.

As an example, the following kernel implements a GPU-based Monte Carlo simulation to estimate the value of π using Numba-CUDA:

```
from numba.cuda.random import (
    create_xoroshiro128p_states,
    xoroshiro128p_uniform_float32,
)

@cuda.jit
def compute_pi(rng_states, iterations, out):
    thread_id = cuda.grid(1)

    count_inside = 0
    for _ in range(iterations):
        x = xoroshiro128p_uniform_float32(rng_states, thread_id)
        y = xoroshiro128p_uniform_float32(rng_states, thread_id)
        if x * x + y * y <= 1.0:
            count_inside += 1
```

```
    out[thread_id] = 4.0 * count_inside / iterations
```

This example comes from the official documentation: https://nvidia.github.io/numba-cuda/user/random.html.

The kernel may look cryptic, so let's break it down. Each thread runs multiple iterations of generating a random x value and a random y value, both between 0 and 1, using xoroshiro128p_uniform_float32. This function takes both rng_states and thread_id as arguments; basically, each thread needs to use a different random state. The kernel then checks whether the point (x, y) falls inside a unit circle (radius = 1) centered on the origin (0, 0); if so, a counter is incremented. The probability that the point lies inside the circle is equal to the area of the quarter unit circle (=$\pi/4$) divided by the area of the unit square in which points can be generated (=1). By choosing random points, this probability is estimated empirically and calculated as count_inside / iterations. Therefore, to estimate π, these probabilities are set to be equal and solved for π.

The kernel is run as follows:

```
threads_per_block = 512
blocks = 128
rng_states = create_xoroshiro128p_states(threads_per_block * blocks, seed=123)
out_dev = cuda.device_array(threads_per_block * blocks, dtype=np.float32)

compute_pi[blocks, threads_per_block](rng_states, 100_000, out_dev)
```

This example runs many GPU threads in parallel, with each thread independently performing many random trials. To make this possible, random number generation cannot rely on a single global generator as it would on the CPU (e.g., NumPy). Instead, the code explicitly creates a separate **random number generator (RNG)** state for *each* thread using create_xoroshiro128p_states. These RNG states are stored in GPU memory and initialized with a fixed seed so that the computation is reproducible, while still ensuring that each thread produces an independent sequence of random numbers.

The final result is *N* independent estimates of π, with *N* being the total number of threads. To get a single number, the mean is calculated:

```
print(f"Estimate π: {out_dev.copy_to_host().mean():0.8f}")
```

The output is a very good estimate of π:

```
Estimate π: 3.14160228
```

Note

Numba-CUDA random number generation algorithms

Numba's GPU RNG is not based on cuRAND, an optimized library for random number generation. Instead, Numba's GPU RNG is an implementation of the **xoroshiro128+** algorithm. This algorithm has a period of 2**128 – 1, which is shorter than the period of the **XORWOW** algorithm used by default in cuRAND, but **xoroshiro128+** still passes the BigCrush tests of RNG quality.

Other CUDA Python libraries

CUDA Python is a new, rapidly evolving collection of libraries designed to make CUDA programming more accessible from Python. Numba-CUDA, which was used extensively throughout this book, and `nvmath-python`, which was mentioned earlier in this chapter, are both part of CUDA Python.

However, CUDA Python offers a much broader toolkit for those looking to dive deeper or optimize performance further. The libraries can be grouped into three main categories:

- **Core CUDA access**: Tools such as `cuda.core` and `cuda.bindings` provide Python-friendly interfaces to CUDA's runtime and low-level APIs, making it easier to interact with the GPU without writing C/C++.
- **Performance and algorithms**: Libraries such as `cuda.coop` (for cooperative thread primitives), `cuda.compute` (for optimized parallel algorithms such as sort/reduce), and `cuda.tile` (for writing NumPy-like kernel code) help optimize and simplify complex computations.
- **Profiling and system integration**: Tools such as Nsight Python and CUPTI Python enable kernel profiling and performance analysis, while `nvshmem4py` enables multi-GPU communication.

CUDA Python will be the modern entry point to CUDA programming with Python. Explore the documentation here: `https://nvidia.github.io/cuda-python/latest/index.html`.

Specialized applications

This book has explored several applications of GPGPU, including structured data processing with cuDF, image processing, language models, array computation, and scientific computing. Covering all application areas of GPGPU in a single book is impossible. This section dives a bit deeper into applications that were skimmed over and introduces additional applications that may be of interest to the readers of this book.

Deep learning

Deep learning, the training of neural networks for all kinds of tasks in language, computer vision, and scientific applications, is probably *the* application of GPGPU that has generated the most excitement in recent years. It is a field on its own, so much so that many practitioners often do not know anything about the underlying CUDA infrastructure. Instead, they use high-level **deep learning frameworks** that offer high-level abstractions for designing, training, and deploying neural networks, while benefiting from hardware accelerators such as GPUs and TPUs. These frameworks enable rapid AI experimentation and development, and they underpin most modern AI systems.

Here, the three most popular deep learning frameworks will be briefly discussed: JAX, PyTorch, and TensorFlow.

JAX

JAX was already used extensively throughout previous chapters. Originally developed by Google, JAX is a high-performance numerical computing library for Python, designed for array operations, automatic differentiation, and hardware acceleration. Together with libraries such as **Flax**, which provides additional abstractions for easily defining neural network architectures, and **Optax**, which offers a collection of optimization algorithms and gradient-processing utilities, JAX becomes a very flexible machine learning framework. As demonstrated in previous chapters, JAX can be used to implement simple models such as linear regression (*Chapter 10*), complex but standard architectures such as convolutional neural networks (*Chapter 12*), and complex custom architectures such as large language models (*Chapter 14*). In addition, it's easy to customize the loss function, which can be used for physics-aware training of deep learning models.

JAX is particularly well suited for highly customizable research scenarios where experimenting with new models and training methods is essential. For this reason, this book has focused on JAX.

PyTorch

PyTorch is one of the most widely used deep learning frameworks, originally developed by Meta (Facebook), and valued for its intuitive interface and dynamic computation graphs. It simplifies the implementation of standard neural network architectures, such as convolutional, recurrent, and fully connected networks, with minimal boilerplate. PyTorch leverages GPU acceleration via CUDA, enabling efficient training on modern hardware.

Like JAX, PyTorch supports performance optimization through **just-in-time (JIT)** compilation with `torch.jit`. However, PyTorch's JIT is less flexible, particularly for dynamic control flow or arbitrary Python code. In contrast, JAX explicitly exposes compilation and transformation semantics (e.g., `jax.jit`, `jax.vmap`, and `jax.grad`) and provides fine-grained control over hardware acceleration, functional purity, and automatic differentiation.

Despite these differences, PyTorch's balance of simplicity and performance and a rich ecosystem has made it the framework of choice for much of the deep learning community.

To illustrate PyTorch, a small feed-forward neural network with one hidden layer is implemented as follows:

```
import torch
import torch.nn as nn

class SimpleModel(nn.Module):
    def __init__(self):
        super(SimpleModel, self).__init__()

        self.fc1 = nn.Linear(10, 5)
        self.relu = nn.ReLU()
        self.fc2 = nn.Linear(5, 1)

    def forward(self, x):
        x = self.fc1(x)
        x = self.relu(x)
        x = self.fc2(x)
        return x
```

This model is a simple fully connected neural network designed for regression tasks, consisting of an input layer with 10 features, one hidden layer with 5 neurons and a ReLU activation, and a single-neuron output layer that produces one continuous value.

The neural network can be created by instantiating the `SimpleModel` class:

```
model = SimpleModel()
```

This sets up the network's layers and initializes its learnable weights.

To make predictions, input data is passed to the model similar to how a Python function is called. Here, `inputs` is a batch of 8 samples, each with 10 features:

```
inputs = torch.randn(8, 10)
predictions = model(inputs)
```

The model applies the first linear layer, a ReLU activation, and then the second linear layer to produce the output.

The model's predictions can be compared to the true target value using a loss function as follows:

```
targets = torch.randn(8, 1)
criterion = nn.MSELoss()
loss = criterion(predictions, targets)
```

To improve the model performance, the weights need to be updated using an optimizer, which relies on gradients computed via **backpropagation**. In PyTorch, this is done as follows:

```
optimizer = torch.optim.SGD(model.parameters(), lr=0.01)

optimizer.zero_grad()   # Clear old gradients
loss.backward()         # Compute gradients
optimizer.step()        # Update parameters
```

To train the network on data, these steps need to be performed multiple times as part of a training loop. The training loop typically consists of an inner loop that iterates over batches of the training data, and an outer loop of epochs that repeats the training over the entire dataset.

TensorFlow

TensorFlow is another widely used deep learning framework, originally developed by the Google Brain team. It is slightly older than PyTorch and is losing popularity in research contexts, though it is still very common in enterprise and production contexts thanks to tools such as TensorFlow Serving, TensorFlow Lite, and TFX. Like PyTorch, it supports GPU acceleration. Like JAX, it also has strong support for TPU execution through the **Accelerated Linear Algebra** (**XLA**) compiler, which optimizes vectorized computations across devices. However, the TensorFlow framework is more rigid than JAX in research-oriented workflows.

TensorFlow provides high-level APIs such as **Keras** for quickly building standard neural networks. The same network as the PyTorch example is implemented in TensorFlow as follows:

```
import tensorflow as tf
from tensorflow.keras import layers, models

model = models.Sequential([
    layers.Dense(5, activation='relu', input_shape=(10,)),
    layers.Dense(1)
])
```

The model is used to make predictions as follows:

```
import numpy as np

inputs = np.random.randn(8, 10).astype(np.float32)
predictions = model(inputs)
```

Before training, a loss function and optimizer need to be specified:

```
model.compile(
    optimizer=tf.keras.optimizers.SGD(learning_rate=0.01),
    loss='mse',
)
```

Keras provides a simple `fit` method for training:

```
targets = np.random.randn(8, 1).astype(np.float32)
model.fit(inputs, targets, epochs=100, batch_size=8)
```

Keras will automatically handle the forward pass, loss computation, backward pass, and weight updates.

Blockchain

A blockchain is a **distributed data structure** in which records, or "blocks," are linked together using cryptographic techniques and replicated across many independent participants. Rather than relying on a central authority, blockchain systems use **consensus mechanisms** to agree on the current state of the data. One of the earliest and most widely known consensus mechanisms is **proof of work**, in which participants compete to solve computationally expensive cryptographic puzzles to add new blocks to the chain.

Proof-of-work algorithms are designed to be easy to verify but difficult to compute, often requiring repeated evaluation of **cryptographic hash functions**. These workloads exhibit a high degree of data parallelism, making them well suited to GPU architectures. As a result, GPUs were widely used for so-called **mining** during the early growth of cryptocurrencies such as Bitcoin and Ethereum.

In recent years, the role of GPUs in blockchain systems has diminished, as many platforms have either moved away from proof of work or toward specialized hardware. Today, blockchain primarily serves as an illustrative example of GPU-accelerated cryptographic computation rather than a major driver of modern GPGPU development.

Big data and distributed computing

Beyond single-node acceleration, GPUs are increasingly used within **distributed data processing systems** consisting of multiple communicating nodes. Engines such as Apache Spark (`https://spark.apache.org/`) are widely used in industry for distributed analytics, machine learning, and data processing at petabyte scale, while Dask (`https://docs.dask.org/en/stable/index.html`) is commonly used in Python-centric environments. Both engines can be extended with plugins that allow them to make use of GPUs via CUDA. Rather than acting as standalone compute devices, GPUs typically serve as accelerators for specific parts of a distributed processing pipeline.

For Spark, NVIDIA provides **spark-rapids** (`https://nvidia.github.io/spark-rapids/`), which uses cuDF under the hood to accelerate Spark DataFrame workloads in a distributed environment. For Dask, cuDF includes **dask-cudf**, which accelerates Dask DataFrames. For non-DataFrame workloads, Dask can be extended with **dask-cuda** (`https://github.com/rapidsai/dask-cuda`), which exposes GPU devices to the Dask scheduler as workers.

A major bottleneck in distributed systems is the overhead of data transfer between nodes. When GPUs are introduced, there is additional overhead associated with transferring data between host and device memory. High-bandwidth interconnects such as **NVLink** play an important role in reducing communication overhead within a node, particularly between GPUs, and can significantly improve the performance of multi-GPU workloads.

Embeddings and vector-based similarity search

Many modern machine learning systems represent data as high-dimensional vectors, often referred to as **embeddings**. Embeddings arise in applications such as image retrieval, natural language processing, recommendation systems, and semantic search. A core operation in such systems is **similarity search**: finding the nearest neighbors of a query vector within a very large collection of vectors.

Similarity search is computationally expensive and memory-intensive. GPUs are well suited to this workload because they can evaluate many distance computations in parallel. RAPIDS **cuVS** (`https://rapids.ai/cuvs/`) provides GPU-accelerated implementations of nearest-neighbor search and various clustering algorithms.

Graph analytics

Many real-world datasets are most naturally represented as **graphs**, where entities are connected by relationships rather than arranged in regular arrays or tables. Examples include social networks, communication graphs, biological interaction networks, and logistics chains. Graph algorithms such as **breadth-first search**, **shortest paths**, and **community detection** aim to extract information from these data structures.

While graph workloads do not map as directly to GPUs as dense numerical computations, modern GPU architectures can provide significant speedups when graph algorithms are carefully designed to exploit parallelism. The RAPIDS ecosystem includes **cuGraph** (`https://github.com/rapidsai/cugraph`), which implements a range of graph algorithms on the GPU and enables accelerated graph analytics.

Data visualization and interactive exploration

This book has mainly relied on Matplotlib for data visualization. This is fine for small datasets that need to be visualized in static images, and there are no latency requirements. As dataset sizes grow and latency requirements become more stringent, for example, in real-time or interactive visualization, GPUs become attractive for producing visual output.

With GPUs, data visualization can be integrated with live data processing, including filtering and aggregation. The RAPIDS ecosystem includes **cuxfilter**, a GPU-accelerated framework for building interactive dashboards that operate on cuDF DataFrames. Many of the official examples can be explored directly in a Jupyter notebook.

Other GPU programming platforms

This book focused on CUDA and the tooling in the Python ecosystem built on top of CUDA. CUDA is currently the dominant platform for GPU programming, particularly in machine learning and HPC, largely due to its mature ecosystem and tooling. However, other general-purpose GPU computing frameworks and platforms exist, for example, for non-NVIDIA graphics cards. This section explores the two main competing heterogeneous computing platforms.

ROCM

There are two big manufacturers of GPU devices for gaming and data centers: NVIDIA and AMD. CUDA is supported on NVIDIA devices, which makes NVIDIA dominant in the GPGPU space. ROCm is AMD's open source GPU computing software stack, analogous to NVIDIA's CUDA platform, providing compilers, runtimes, libraries, and programming models for AMD GPUs. Unlike CUDA, ROCm does not support all AMD GPUs; official support is largely limited to certain data center and workstation-class devices, which has hindered broader adoption.

While ROCm is far less popular than CUDA overall, it plays an important role in HPC and is supported by major machine learning frameworks such as PyTorch and TensorFlow. The Numba HIP (`https://github.com/ROCm/numba-hip`) project provides an experimental ROCm backend for Numba, but it currently has limited feature coverage and is not yet widely used in production environments. **Heterogeneous-computing Interface for Portability** (**HIP**) is a programming model within ROCm that enables source-level portability between AMD GPUs and NVIDIA CUDA-enabled GPUs, though not all CUDA features or performance characteristics translate directly. The API aims to closely mimic CUDA. The following example from the Numba-HIP documentation shows a kernel adding two arrays elementwise:

```
from numba import hip

@hip.jit
def f(a, b, c):
    tid = hip.grid(1)
    size = len(c)

    if tid < size:
        c[tid] = a[tid] + b[tid]
```

OpenCL

Besides NVIDIA and AMD, there are other manufacturers that make or design chips for graphics or computation, including Intel and ARM (and historically Apple, which has since deprecated OpenCL in favor of its own **Metal** framework). All these companies are members of the **Khronos Group**, an organization that maintains open standards. One of the standards maintained by the Khronos Group is **OpenCL**, a framework for heterogeneous computing. The idea is that OpenCL applications could be executed across many different types of devices: CPUs, GPUs, FPGAs, and more. Both NVIDIA and AMD GPUs can run OpenCL applications, although OpenCL support on NVIDIA hardware is generally less optimized and less actively developed than CUDA.

The OpenCL standard primarily specifies the OpenCL C kernel language, along with SPIR-V as an intermediate representation; higher-level language support is provided through external libraries rather than the standard itself. Support for writing OpenCL applications in Python is limited. The library with the best support is PyOpenCL (`https://github.com/inducer/pyopencl`). However, writing OpenCL kernels with PyOpenCL requires a user to write in-line OpenCL C code in Python strings. Consider the following example to add two arrays, which can be found in the documentation:

```
import pyopencl as cl

ctx = cl.create_some_context()

prg = cl.Program(ctx, """
__kernel void sum(
    __global const float *a_g, __global const float *b_g, __global float *c_g)
{
  int gid = get_global_id(0);
  c_g[gid] = a_g[gid] + b_g[gid];
}
""").build()
```

Unfortunately, this is quite a bit less ergonomic than Numba-CUDA. There used to be an experimental OpenCL backend for Numba here: `https://github.com/SPIRV/NUMBA`. Unfortunately, it seems to be no longer maintained.

Graphics APIs

So far, this book has focused on GPUs as general-purpose compute devices, primarily through CUDA. Historically, however, GPUs were designed for graphics rendering, and many of the APIs that shaped GPU hardware were created for that purpose. Even today, graphics APIs remain highly relevant, both for visualization, games, and certain classes of high-performance computation.

This section briefly introduces the most important graphics APIs and how they can be approached using Python. In general, graphics programming is usually done entirely in a high-performance language such as C or C++. One advantage of using Graphics APIs is that they are cross-platform and run on non-CUDA graphics cards.

OpenGL

OpenGL (which stands for **Open Graphics Library**) is a long-standing, cross-platform API for rendering 2D and 3D graphics. It is maintained by the Khronos Group, which also maintains OpenCL, and has been one of the dominant graphics APIs for decades. Going into detail on how graphics APIs and shaders work would be beyond the scope of this book. For experimentation with OpenGL-based rendering in Python, either the older PyOpenGL (`https://`

`pyopengl.sourceforge.net/`) or the newer ModernGL (`https://github.com/moderngl/moderngl`) can be used.

Vulkan

Vulkan is a modern, low-level graphics and compute API, also maintained by the Khronos Group. It was designed as a successor to OpenGL, with an explicit focus on performance and predictable behavior on modern GPU hardware. Unlike OpenGL, Vulkan exposes much more control over the hardware, which makes it significantly more verbose but also more efficient for performance-critical applications. Due to its low-level nature and complexity, Vulkan is almost exclusively used from C or C++, and while Python bindings exist, they are typically limited to experimentation or tooling rather than production rendering code. Interested readers can experiment with the `vulkan` (`https://github.com/realitix/vulkan`) library.

Other graphics APIs

Besides OpenGL and Vulkan, Microsoft provides **DirectX**, a Windows-only graphics API, and Apple provides **Metal**, a macOS/iOS-only graphics API; neither has official Python support. Also noteworthy are **WebGL** (legacy) and **WebGPU** (cutting edge), which are OpenGL- and Vulkan-inspired graphics API standards implemented in browsers, allowing direct rendering of graphics in HTML canvases.

Summary

This final chapter broadened the book's perspective on GPU programming, moving beyond the core concepts introduced earlier. It explored advanced low-level features, delved into diverse GPGPU applications, and examined alternative GPU programming paradigms. The goal was to provide you with a solid foundation for further exploration based on your interests.

Questions

1. Why is pinned memory used?
2. How could GPGPU be performed on an Intel CPU with integrated graphics?
3. How can Tensor Cores be utilized?
4. Why can't a single random seed be passed to a kernel for generating random numbers?
5. Why is CuPy not a deep learning framework?

Answers

1. Pinned memory prevents the operating system from paging the data. It enables faster and more predictable host–device data transfers; it is necessary for asynchronous data exchange.
2. OpenCL can be used to run compute kernels on Intel-integrated GPUs, which do not support CUDA. Alternatively, the problem could be reformulated as a graphics task and solved using Vulkan or OpenGL—an approach that predates CUDA. However, performance may be worse than CPU-based computation. Frameworks such as Intel's OpenVINO (`https://docs.openvino.ai/2025/index.html`) can leverage integrated GPUs for specific tasks, such as AI model inference, but general-purpose GPGPU typically relies on OpenCL.
3. Tensor Cores are used automatically by libraries and frameworks such as JAX and PyTorch when performing matrix operations with supported reduced-precision data types, such as FP16 or BF16. Alternatively, low-level CUDA libraries that explicitly target Tensor Cores can be used through `nvmath-python`.
4. A single random seed cannot be shared because each GPU thread needs an independent random number stream to avoid identical or correlated results.
5. CuPy is an array library that lacks automatic differentiation, neural network layers, or training abstractions, which are key building blocks in a deep learning framework. While it is possible to implement these features manually using custom CUDA kernels, CuPy itself does not provide them out of the box.

Get this book's PDF version and more

Scan the QR code (or go to `packtpub.com/unlock`). Search for this book by name, confirm the edition, and then follow the steps on the page.

UNLOCK NOW

Note: Keep your invoice handy. Purchases made directly from Packt don't require an invoice.

16

Unlock Your Exclusive Benefits

Your copy of this book includes the following exclusive benefits:

DRM-Free PDF Version

Download DRM-free PDF and ePub copies of this book.

7-Day Packt Library Access

Get 7-day unlimited access to 8,000+ books and videos. No credit card required.

Available for first-time Packt+ trial users only.

Next-Gen Reader Access

Read this book on Packt Reader with progress sync, dark mode and note-taking.

Follow the guide below to unlock them. The process takes only a few minutes and needs to be completed once.

Unlock this Book's Free Benefits in 3 Easy Steps

Step 1

Keep your purchase invoice ready for *Step 3*. If you have a physical copy, scan it using your phone and save it as a PDF, JPG, or PNG.

For more help on finding your invoice, visit `https://www.packtpub.com/en-us/unlock?step=1`.

> Note
>
> **Note**: If you bought this book directly from Packt, no invoice is required. After *Step 2*, you can access your exclusive content right away.

Step 2

Scan the QR code or go to `packtpub.com/unlock`.

On the page that opens (similar to *Figure 16.1* on desktop), search for this book by name and select the correct edition.

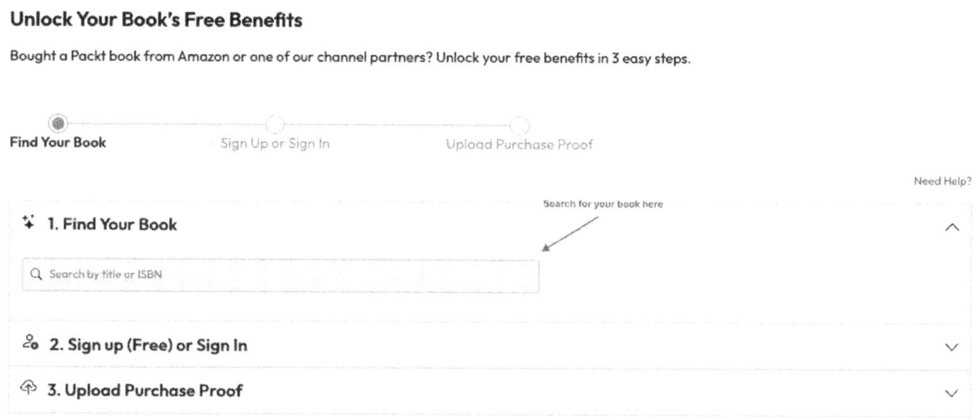

Figure 16.1 – Packt unlock landing page on desktop

Step 3

After selecting your book, sign in to your Packt account or create one for free. Then upload your invoice (PDF, PNG, or JPG, up to 10 MB). Follow the on-screen instructions to finish the process.

Need Help

If you get stuck and need help, visit `https://www.packtpub.com/unlock-benefits/help` for a detailed FAQ on how to find your invoices and more. This QR code will take you to the help page.

Note

Note: If you are still facing issues, reach out to `customercare@packt.com`.

Other Books You May Enjoy

If you enjoyed this book, you may be interested in these other books by Packt:

GPU Programming with C++ and CUDA

Paulo Motta

ISBN: 9781805124542

- Manage GPU devices and accelerate your applications
- Apply parallelism effectively using CUDA and C++
- Choose between existing libraries and custom GPU solutions
- Package GPU code into libraries for use with Python
- Explore advanced topics such as CUDA streams
- Implement optimization strategies for resource-efficient execution

Hands-On Software Engineering with Python

Brian Allbee

ISBN: 9781835888018

- Distinguish software engineering from general programming
- Break down and apply each phase of the SDLC to Python systems
- Create system models to plan architecture before writing code
- Apply Agile, Scrum, and other modern development methodologies
- Use dataclasses, pydantic, and schemas for robust data modeling
- Set up CI/CD pipelines with GitHub Actions and cloud build tools
- Write and structure unit, integration, and end-to-end tests
- Evaluate and integrate tools like Poetry, pytest, and Docker

Packt is searching for authors like you

If you're interested in becoming an author for Packt, please visit `authors.packt.com` and apply today. We have worked with thousands of developers and tech professionals, just like you, to help them share their insight with the global tech community. You can make a general application, apply for a specific hot topic that we are recruiting an author for, or submit your own idea.

Subscribe to Deep Engineering

Join thousands of developers and architects who want to understand how software is changing, deepen their expertise, and build systems that last.

Deep Engineering is a weekly expert-led newsletter for experienced practitioners, featuring original analysis, technical interviews, and curated insights on architecture, system design, and modern programming practice.

Scan the QR or visit the link to subscribe for free.

`https://packt.link/deep-engineering-newsletter`

Share your thoughts

Now you've finished *Practical Systems Programming in Go*, we'd love to hear your thoughts! Scan the QR code below to go straight to the Amazon review page for this book and share your feedback or leave a review on the site that you purchased it from.

https://packt.link/r/1806112191

Your review is important to us and the tech community and will help us make sure we're delivering excellent quality content.

Index

Symbols

A

B

C

H

I

J

P

R

Made in the USA
Monee, IL
18 October 2026

66036208R10293